FROM ANCIENT TABLETS TO MODERN TRANSLATIONS

FROM ANCIENT TABLETS TO MODERN TRANSLATIONS

A GENERAL INTRODUCTION TO THE BIBLE

DAVID EWERT

Academie Books Grand Rapids, Michigan
Zondervan Publishing House

FROM ANCIENT TABLETS TO MODERN TRANSLATIONS:
A GENERAL INTRODUCTION TO THE BIBLE
Copyright © 1983 by The Zondervan Corporation
Grand Rapids, Michigan

ACADEMIE BOOKS is an imprint of Zondervan
Publishing House, 1415 Lake Drive, S.E.,
Grand Rapids, Michigan 49506

Library of Congress Cataloging in Publication Data

Ewert, David, 1922–
    From ancient tablets to modern translations.

    Bibliography: p.
    Includes index.
    1. Bible—Introductions.   2. Bible—Versions.
I. Title.
BS475.2.E93   1983   220.4   82-17473
ISBN 0-310-45730-0

Edited by Mark Hunt
Designed by Stanley N. Gundrey

Printed in the United States of America

86 87 88 89 90 91 92 93 94 / 14 13 12 11 10 9 8 7 6 5 4 3

To David and Margaret Ewert, my parents, who first taught me by word and deed the truths of the sacred Scriptures.

CONTENTS

LIST OF CHARTS, MAPS, AND CREDITS

>   Taken from Textual Commentary on the Greek New Testament by Bruce M. Metzger,
>   copyright 1971 by the United Bible Societies. Used with the author's permission.

>   Weymouth: From Weymouth's New Testament in Modern Speech by Richard Francis
>   Weymouth. By special arrangement with James Clarke & Company Ltd. Reprinted by
>   permission of Harper & Row, Publishers, Inc.
>   Moffat: From The Bible: A New Translation by James Moffat. Copyright 1935 by Harper
>   & Row, Publishers, Inc. Reprinted by permission.
>   Knox: From The New Testament of Our Lord and Savior Jesus Christ: A New Transla-
>   tion by Ronald A. Knox. Copyright 1944.
>   Revised Standard Version: From the Revised Standard Version of the Bible, copyrighted
>   1946, 1952 © 1971, 1973.
>   Jerusalem Bible: From The Jerusalem Bible, copyright © 1966 by Darton, Longman &
>   Todd Ltd. and Doubleday & Company, Inc. Used by permission of the publisher.
>   Good News Bible: From the Good News Bible, the Bible in Today's English Version.
>   Copyright © American Bible Society, 1976.
>   New English Bible: From The New English Bible. © The Delegates of the Oxford Univer-
>   sity Press and The Syndics of the Cambridge University Press 1961, 1970. Reprinted by
>   permission.
>   New American Standard Bible: From the New American Standard Bible. © The
>   Lockman Foundation 1960, 1962, 1963, 1971, 1972, 1973, 1975, 1977.
>   Living Bible: From The Living Bible, copyright 1971 by Tyndale House Publishers,
>   Wheaton, Ill. Used by permission.
>   New International Version: Taken from the Holy Bible: New International Version ©
>   1978 by the New York International Bible Society. Used by permission of Zondervan
>   Bible Publishers.
>   The New King James Version: From The New King James Version. Copyright © 1979,
>   1980, 1982, Thomas Nelson, Inc., Publishers.

PICTURES AND CREDITS

PREFACE

The story of how the Bible came to us has been told many times, as one can readily see from the bibliography at the back of this book. And just as English-speaking Bible readers must have asked repeatedly in the past few decades, "Why another version?" so one might legitimately ask, "Why another book on the history of the Bible?"

One answer is that this story can be told in such an infinite number of ways that the temptation to tell it in yet another form is hard to resist. The Evangelist Luke recognized that many others had undertaken to write gospels, but this did not deter him from writing another, ordering the material in his own unique way. While we cannot claim to stand in the tradition of the biblical writers, it was our conviction that there was room for another volume on this fascinating subject. Some of the books on the history of the Bible are too technical for the ordinary reader to appreciate; the more popular volumes tend to avoid the difficult and problematic areas of the Bible's history. This volume seeks to strike a happy medium.

Several years ago the writer published a series of articles in a denominational paper on the text and canon of Scripture. The response to this series was so favorable that the editor had the articles published in pamphlet form. Since then the need for a somewhat more substantial volume on this topic has been expressed repeatedly. It appears that Bible institutes and colleges often look for a suitable textbook on this subject. Moreover, the many versions of the Scriptures now available ask for a guide in choosing a Bible. Also, the attacks and counterattacks that every new version seems to be subjected to call for more light on the subject of translation.

The first fourteen chapters of this book survey the history of the Bible from the time when the biblical books were written to the end of the first millennium of the Christian era. With chapter fifteen we leave the transmission of the sacred Scriptures behind and trace the thousand-year story of the English Bible—beginning with the attempts to render portions of the Bible into Anglo-Saxon, prior to the days of Wycliffe, and ending with the more recent English versions. The final chapter seeks to answer such questions as, Why are there so many versions? How might one go about choosing a version? How can one develop meaningful ways of reading the Scriptures?

The writer wishes to thank the administration of the seminary where he taught for freeing him from classroom responsibilities for one quarter of the academic year to prepare this volume for publication. The manuscript was completed in the Advent season, and one could not help but recall the witness of the Fourth Evangelist, "The Word became flesh and dwelt among us" (John 1:14). Just as the Living Word took on human nature, so the written Word has come to us in a very earthly form. It is hoped that the glory of God's revelation to man will not be hidden from our eyes as we read this account of the history of the written Word of God.

DAVID EWERT
Advent, 1981

INTRODUCTION

One significant difference between the God of the Bible and the gods of the nations is that the God of Abraham, Isaac, and Jacob, the Father of our Lord Jesus Christ, chose to make himself known. Not only are his footprints visible in the realms of nature and human history, but he revealed himself to ancient Israel and, finally, in Jesus Christ.

That the God who created heaven and earth, and who sustains the universe, should be willing to make known his saving purposes to man, is an expression of his love and grace. Had people not been created in the image of God, they would not have been in the position to receive a revelation from God. But even a sinful, fallen person, when enlightened by God's Spirit, has the apparatus for receiving messages from the heavenly world. Human life on earth would have been one long night of darkness and despair, had God chosen to hide himself from mankind. But in his infinite mercy he chose to make himself known, and by his gracious self-disclosure he has brought light into our darkness.

God did this by choosing human agents, who were authorized to receive his revelation and to make it known to their contemporaries. Mention could be made of the patriarchs, of Moses and the prophets. God's final revelation in human history came through Jesus Christ—a revelation that the apostles witnessed. All these divinely inspired agents of God's revelation spoke in the languages of the societies in which they lived. Although they were deeply conscious of the fact that their messages came from God, they proclaimed them in human words.

Had tape recorders or record players been available in antiquity, the oral messages of prophets and apostles might have been transmitted by such instruments. As it happened, however, God's revelation was put in writing. Fortunately written alphabetic languages were available to record divine revelation. Also, the writing materials on which to record the messages of God's servants, and the instruments for doing this, had already been developed. God's revelation, therefore, has been preserved for us in written form.

Although the books of the Bible look like other ancient writings, they are "inbreathed" *(theopneustos)* by God (2 Tim. 3:16), and this sets them apart from all other writings which came, as Peter puts it, "by the will of man" (2 Peter 1:21).

God's Word to humanity, as recorded in the biblical books, has had an amazing power through many centuries to grip the human soul. The Bible, in part or in whole, has been the most published book of the world. After laboriously producing handwritten copies for several millennia, the Bible streams today from presses in millions of copies. Relatively few of this world's books are translated into other languages, but the Bible has been translated and retranslated in hundreds of languages. All over the world today translators are at work, making the Bible, or at least part of it, available in every human tongue.

When compared with ancient books of comparable age, no book has survived in so many copies as the Bible. The Bible has resisted not only the ravages of time but also repeated attempts of the enemies of God to obliterate it. Neither have the literary attacks on the Bible, often made with great sophistication and learning, been able to silence the message of the Scriptures. Unfortunately, such destructive criticism has done untold damage to the faith of Bible readers, but the Bible's message is still received gladly by millions of God's people.

And while the message of the Scriptures has often been resisted, the influence of these writings on human culture has been profound. Where the Bible was read it left its stamp on the literature, the laws, the philosophies, the politics, and the arts of a people. Moreover, the literature that has been and still is inspired by the Bible is simply phenomenal, as all Christian book publishers today know. It is read in humble cottages and stately cathedrals; it is studied in Sunday schools and in the classrooms of secular universities; its message is heard in the steaming jungles and frozen wastelands of this world. Perennially it has the power to grip the human heart.

Is there anything in classical literature that can match the majesty and depth of the creation account? Which writer has delved so deeply into the problem of suffering as does Job? Where could one find a book of religious verse to match the Hebrew Psalter? Who in pre-Christian times ever rose to the spiritual heights of the prophets? And what can compare with the Beatitudes, the Lord's Prayer, the parables of Jesus? Who plumbed the depth of human sin and of divine grace as did Christ's servant Paul? Who has given us such a brilliant vision of the world to come as did the Seer on Patmos? The Bible commences at the ultimate point of beginnings and ends with the final consummation of human history and the dawn of the age to come.[1]

Since the church holds that the Bible is its final authority in all matters of life and doctrine, it is only to be expected that all Bible readers would want to know as much as possible

---

[1]For an elaboration of these and other aspects of the Bible's phenomenology, see Bernard Ramm, *Protestant Christian Evidences* (Chicago: Moody Press, 1953), pp. 224–52.

about the formation, transmission, and translation of the Scriptures. Information about the Bible obviously is no substitute for a grasp of its message; but our appreciation for the Scriptures is bound to increase with a better understanding of its history. Although we confess that the Bible is God's gift to humanity, it did not fall from heaven as a leather-bound volume. The sixty-six books that comprise the sacred Scriptures, were written, transcribed, and collected over a long period of time. It will be our task in this book to tell the fascinating story of how our Bible came to us.

Chapter 1

The Book Called "The Bible"

I. THE MEANING OF "BIBLE"

A. The Name of a Plant

When we call the Holy Scriptures "the Bible" we are actually using a word that in ancient times designated the papyrus plant. This reed plant, which grew on the banks of rivers, was particularly abundant in antiquity along the marshes of the Nile and in Syria.

There are several references to this plant in the Old Testament (Exod. 2:3; Job 8:11; Isa. 18:2; 35:7), but Greek and Latin authors have more to say about it.[1] The Hebrew word for the marsh plant is *gōme*—a word that is translated into Greek as *papuros* (the Latin spelling is *papyrus*).[2] Clearly our English word "paper" (French *papier*, German *Papier*) is derived from papyrus, the writing material of the ancient world.

Another name given to this fibrous

Papyrus plants, from which early writing materials were made, growing in the Hulah reservoir in northern Israel.

---

[1]For Pliny's description of the preparation of papyrus, see C. K. Barrett, *The New Testament Background: Selected Documents* (New York: Harper and Row, 1961), pp. 23–26.

[2]*Suph* also describes waterplants and rushes. See L. Koehler and W. Baumgartner, *Lexicon in Veteris Testamenti Libros* (Grand Rapids: Eerdmans, 1953), s.v.

plant was *bublos* (the later spelling is *biblos*),[3] which has given us the Greek word for book, namely *biblion*. Since large quantities of papyrus were used and shipped from the Syrian port of Byblos it is surmised that the Greek word for book may have been derived from that place-name.[4]

Until the third century A.D., writing was commonly on papyrus. This was made from the pith of the papyrus plant, which could be as thick as a man's arm. It was cut in strips about a foot long, placed on a flat surface and glued together crosswise like ply-board. When dried the whitish surface was polished smooth with a stone or other implement.

On the front *(recto)* side the fibers ran horizontally, on the back *(verso)* side vertically. Since the front side was smoother than the back, one normally wrote only on that side. Only rarely was the back side, where the fibers ran vertically, used for writing. If it was, then the scroll was called an opistho-graph. The roll that John saw in the hands of the One seated upon the throne, had "writing on both sides" (Rev. 5:1), to indicate the fullness of God's plans and purposes.

Sheets of papyrus, and sometimes entire rolls, were called *chartes* (Latin *charta*—from which we get chart, charter, etc.). This word is translated as "paper" in 2 John 12—the only place it occurs in the New Testament. Papyrus, *biblos* (or *bublos*) and *chartes* all refer to writing material made from the reed plant.

B. The Name of a Roll

Although single sheets of papyrus served a variety of literary purposes, longer documents demanded that sheets of papyrus be spliced together to form rolls. Even though papyrus sheets were somewhat thicker than modern writing paper, they could be rolled quite easily. Rolls up to thirty feet in length were not at all uncom-mon. They were normally rolled around a stick, called the navel. The writing on these rolls of papyrus was done in columns.

This roll (or scroll) was then called a "book," a *biblion*—a word which was derived from *biblos*, the name of the rush plant. The New Testament word *biblion* (book) is really a diminutive of *biblos*. However, it lost its diminutive force, and another diminutive is used, namely, *biblaridion*. John the apostle was bidden by an angel to swallow such a "little scroll" (Rev. 10:9). The rolling up of a scroll provided this apostle with a vivid figure of speech, for in Revelation 6:14 the sky is de-scribed as vanishing "like a scroll *(biblion)*, rolling up."

Papyrus rolls were often wrapped with cloth or parchment and stored in some kind of container, which at times had the author's name and the title of the book on it.

A major literary production called for several scrolls to be used. A single roll of a multivolume work was called a *tomos* (our "tome") or *logos* ("word," as Luke calls his Gospel in Acts 1:1).[5]

---

[3]Jack Finegan, *Encountering New Testament Manuscripts* (Grand Rapids: Eerdmans, 1974), p. 20.

[4]P. R. Ackroyd and C. F. Evans, *The Cambridge History of the Bible* (Cambridge: Cambridge University Press, 1970), Vol. 1, p. 30.

[5]In Latin the word *volumen* (from the verb *volvere*, "to roll") means "a thing rolled up," hence "a roll-book."

The entire work might be called a *teuchos* (our word Pentateuch means "five books").

C. The Name of a Book

As we have just seen, the word *biblos*, from which our word *book* (Bible) is derived, at first designated the papyrus plant, and then the sheets or rolls produced from papyrus. Eventually, however, the word was used for the book or codex as we know it today.

The roll form of a book was in many ways inconvenient, and this led to the development of the codex. Four or more double-size sheets were laid on top of each other, folded in the middle and bound together, forming a codex. The Latin word *codex* originally meant the trunk of a tree, and then a block of wood split up into tablets or leaves. Such wooden tablets (perhaps coated with wax) were bound together to make a book. The same was done with leaves or sheets of papyrus. A codex, then, is a leaf book.

While rolls and codices existed side by side for some time, eventually the codex won out over the roll as the better book form. One advantage of the codex was that one could more easily write on both sides of the individual leaves, and so the codex was cheaper to produce. Also it was much easier to locate passages in a codex than in a scroll, which had to be rolled back to locate the appropriate place.

It is believed that Christians helped to accelerate the changeover from scroll to codex. For example, Luke's Gospel would demand an entire scroll. With a codex, however, all four Gospels could be brought together in a single codex book. Moreover, with the development of the codex, papyrus fell more and more into disuse and more durable material, namely parchment, began to take over.

So then, the Greek word *biblion* (book) was first the name of the papyrus plant, second the name of the papyrus scroll, third the name of a codex. Finally, the Greek plural, *biblia*, was used by Latin-speaking Christians as a singular to designate the collection of the books that comprise the Old and New Testaments, our Bible.

II. TWO BOOKS IN ONE

A. The Meaning of "Testament"

If someone unacquainted with the Bible were suddenly introduced to a copy of the Scriptures and this person looked through it rapidly, he would soon discover that it falls into two unequal parts, called "The Old Testament" and "The New Testament" respectively. What would not be immediately obvious to such a novice is the reason why these two parts are called "testament." As the word is used in English today it reminds one of someone's "last will and testament." But the names of the two divisions of the Bible have little to do with that meaning. In fact it is a bit unfortunate that the word "testament" was ever applied to these parts of the Bible, particularly since there is a more suitable word in English, namely "covenant."

The blame for the use of "testament" to designate the two collections of sacred writings in English Bibles rests with Latin Christianity. In the standard Latin version of the Bible the two collections of books are called respectively *Vetus Testamentum* and *Novum Testamentum*. The Latin word *testamentum* translates the Greek word *diatheke*. This word can have the meaning of "testament," as we use it in English today, but it can also mean "covenant."

Diatheke is the word the translators of the Old Testament used to render the Hebrew *berit* (covenant) into Greek. There was another Greek word (*syntheke* = covenant) that they might have used, but it has the connotation that a covenant is made between equals. *Diatheke* was better suited to the biblical idea of a covenant that God initiates by his saving grace and freely bestows on his people.[6]

When we speak of the Old Testament we mean the collection of those books that were produced by writers who were members of the covenant established by God with Israel. By New Testament we mean the writings of apostles who were members of the new covenant people, the church. "Old" is not a pejorative term; it simply refers to the books written prior to the time of Christ, who inaugurated the new covenant. From a chronological point of view the books of the New Testament are very old also.

In the Greek-speaking church the two parts of the Bible came to be called *palaia diatheke* (Old Covenant) and *nea diatheke* (New Covenant). Latin Christians bequeathed on us the translation *Vetus Testamentum* (Old Testament) and *Novum Testamentum* (New Testament), and we will have to live with those titles.

However, whether we speak of covenant or testament, a new reader of the Bible may still ask why these two collections should be so designated. And so we must inquire into the background of these titles.

B. Old and New Covenants

1. *The Historical Background.* The two pivotal points in redemption history that form the historical background for calling the two parts of the Bible "old" and "new" covenants are, if we may speak geographically, Sinai and the Upper Room. When Jesus in the high hour of his passion took the cup and said, "This cup is the new covenant in my blood" (Luke 22:20), he linked his death with the covenant made at Sinai in the days of Moses—a covenant ratified by blood. In that more distant past Moses was the mediator of a covenant; in the Upper Room Christ was the Mediator of a new covenant between God and humanity.

But why a new covenant? Why did not the old remain? Did God's promises to Israel fail? No, God was faithful; Israel broke the covenant. Did God not foresee that a sinful people would fail in its obedience to the demands of a holy God? Indeed he did, but he had made gracious provisions for his people to renew its covenant with Yahweh and to remain in fellowship with him. Israel, however, became apostate.

Nevertheless, in spite of Israel's waywardness, God did not give up on his gracious purposes toward his people. The prophet Jeremiah, among others, saw a day coming when God would make a new covenant with the house of Israel, "It will not be like the covenant which I made with their forefathers . . . because they broke my covenant" (Jer. 31:31–32). This hope of a new covenant was fulfilled in the

---

[6]F. F. Bruce, *The Books and the Parchments*, 3rd rev. ed. (Old Tappan: Revell, 1963), pp. 74f.

death of Christ. On the night of his betrayal, when Jesus took the cup and said, "This is my blood of the covenant, which is poured out for many for the forgiveness of sins" (Matt. 26:28), he inaugurated the new covenant.

Looking back over Israel's sacred history, the church eventually called those books that were written during the period prior to the coming of Christ, "old" covenant, and those books that witnessed to the Christ-event, "new" covenant.

2. *The Theological Problem.* At the outset the church had the same Bible as the Jewish synagogue. The Scriptures of the apostolic church were those books that later came to be called the Old Testament. The church, of course, read these Scriptures from a different vantage point than did the synagogue. The Jewish Scriptures belonged to the period of preparation and were interpreted in the light of the Cross and the exaltation of Jesus. Jesus was God's Messiah who had fulfilled the hopes of the Scriptures. In fact the early church claimed that the Jews who refused to accept Jesus as Messiah did not understand their own Scriptures; a veil hung over their eyes, and this veil could be removed only by turning to Christ (2 Cor. 3:15–16).

When the Scriptures, which the church had inherited from the synagogue, were expanded to include the Gospels, the Acts, the Epistles, and the Revelation, the two collections came to be divided into the Old and New Testament. In retrospect, the writer to the Hebrews could say, "In the past God spoke to our forefathers through the prophets at many times and in various ways, but in these last days he has spoken to us by his Son" (Heb. 1:1–2).

Although the church quite early broke with the synagogue, it did not reject the Jewish Scriptures. In fact the church insisted that these sacred writings properly belonged to the church. Without them one could not really understand what God had done in Christ. Moreover, they regarded them as the living voice of God, even though God had spoken his final word in Christ. And that set the stage for a theological problem that the church had to wrestle with from its inception: the problem of the unity of the Bible.

That there are differences between the books of the Old and New Covenants is obvious. Such differences are to be expected when one remembers that God's revelation was spread over a long period of human history and that it reached its climax in Jesus Christ. But what are Christians to make of those parts of the Old Testament that, as the writer to the Hebrews put it (8:5), belong to the shadow in contrast to the reality that has come in Christ? Even more complex is the question of how to deal with those aspects of Old Testament ethics that stand in contradistinction to those of the New Testament.

And yet the church has always felt that there is an organic unity between the two Testaments. How will this unity be explained?

III. THE UNITY OF THE TWO COVENANTS

A. Challenges to Their Unity

The first major challenge to the unity of the Bible came from a man by the name of Marcion. He was a native of Sinope, in Asia Minor, and came to Rome about A.D. 140, where he established a sect that flourished for many years. He held that the OT had been superseded so thoroughly by the NT that it was now obsolete. In his work called the *Antitheses* he put the two Testaments in opposition to each other. In fact he held that the God of the OT was not the God of the NT. The result was that he repudiated the OT and defined the Christian canon as consisting of one Gospel and ten epistles of Paul.[7]

In the end Marcionism was discredited by the church, but challenges to the unity of the Bible have persisted. As late as the twentieth century, scholars such as Adolf von Harnack of Berlin, have felt embarrassed by the church's insistence that the OT should still be viewed as God's Word to man.

The church, however, has never felt free to repudiate the OT, if for no other reason than that it was the Bible of our Lord, of the apostles, and of the early church. Jesus' high view of the Scriptures (i.e., the OT) makes it incumbent on us to look on the OT as a message inspired by God's Spirit that has permanent validity. But, having said that, how are we to establish the unity of the two Testaments?

B. Establishing Their Unity

1. *Unity by Allegory.* Marcion's repudiation of the OT was in part the consequence of his rejection of the allegorical method of interpreting the OT. Some Christians, in their attempt to make the OT a "Christian" book, imposed NT teachings on OT texts quite arbitrarily. An early representative of this kind of interpretation was a Christian teacher named **Barnabas.** About A.D. 130 he wrote a letter in which we are introduced to his method of allegorizing the OT. When, for example, Genesis mentions Abraham's 318 servants (14:14), Barnabas explains that they represent the crucified Christ. It so happens that the number eighteen is the sum of the two Greek letters *iota* and *eta*, the first two letters of Jesus' name. The number three hundred was represented by the Greek letter *tau*, or T, which he took to represent the cross. So, 318 servants really meant Christ on the cross.

In his attempt to make the OT relevant for Christians he also allegorized the food laws of Leviticus. What, for example, should the church do with the prohibition against the eating of pork? The answer of Barnabas is that Christians must not associate with people who behave like swine. Such an approach robs the OT texts of their historical significance. Nevertheless, this method of reading the OT became very popular in the church. Outstanding teachers of the Alexandrian Christian community, Clement and Origen, furthered the allegorical interpretation of the OT, and this practice of "Christianizing" the OT has not died out even to this day. The unity between the two Testaments that is established by this method of interpretation is really quite fanciful and, at best, superficial. Already in the third century an Egyptian bishop named Nepos wrote a *Refutation of the Allegorists*.[8] In fact an entire school of interpretation, with its center in Antioch, sought to counteract the Alexandrian allegorists.

---

[7]On Marcion, see E. C. Blackman, *Marcion and His Influence* (London: SPCK, 1948).

[8]R. M. Grant, *A Short History of the Interpretation of the Bible* (New York: Macmillan, 1972), p. 89.

2. *Unity by Typology.* Typology differs from allegory in that the historical meaning of the OT text is taken seriously (in allegory the literal meaning of the text is overlooked). In typology a person, thing, or event that had a real existence and significance of its own symbolizes, represents, or prefigures someone or something greater at a later time.[9] The typology method is validated by the Bible itself, particularly by the NT, where Christ is seen as the fulfillment of that which was typified in the OT. When, for example, Paul says that Christ, our Passover, has been slain (1 Cor. 5:7), he sees in Christ the antitype of the Jewish Passover. Or, to give another example, the Suffering Servant of Isaiah 53 was a type of the suffering Messiah (Acts 8:32ff.).

Typology, however, has its limitations. First, there is the danger of seeing types everywhere in the OT. We do violence to the OT when every reference to wood is made to symbolize the Cross; every reference to water, baptism; and every mention of the color red, the blood of Christ. Second, this kind of interpretation may mislead the Bible reader into thinking that only those OT passages that lend themselves to typology are significant. Third, if we restrict our use of the OT entirely to those portions that have some correspondence to the NT, we end up with a small canon within the larger canon of the OT, and we excise large sections of the OT that do not lend themselves to typology.[10] If these dangers are avoided, it is quite legitimate to illustrate the unity of the Bible by seeing correspondence between the Old and New Testaments.

3. *Unity as Promise and Fulfillment.* Since God is the Lord of history he knows the beginning from the end, and we should, then, expect his earlier revelations to anticipate the later. This is, of course, precisely what we find in the Bible. The OT is to the NT as bud is to flower. What is latent in the OT, becomes patent in the New. There are, for example, a great many prophecies in the OT that are fulfilled in the NT. The many OT strands of hope for a new day find their fulfillment in Christ.

And yet it is hard to fit all parts of the OT into this scheme. Much of what we find in the historical books, the Wisdom literature, and even in the Prophets can hardly be classified as promise. If one concentrates too narrowly on the so-called messianic passages of the OT, one overlooks a great deal of the OT. Moreover, one can hardly group all of the NT under "fulfillment," for it too holds great promise for an age yet to come. Therefore, while one can legitimately describe the relationship of Old and New Testaments in terms of promise and fulfillment in a general sense, it leaves many questions about the unity of the Bible unanswered.

4. *Thematic Unity.* The great truths of the Bible, such as sin, redemption, hope, and many others, take their rise in the OT and find their fuller development in the New. This is sometimes called "the-unity-of-ideas" approach to the Scriptures. As long as one does not hold such "ideas" to be simply the products of religious geniuses, but revealed truth, this approach greatly enriches our understanding of the Bible's message, as every good NT lexicon will demonstrate. (A. M. Hunter

---

[9]R. B. Laurin, "Typological Interpretation of the Old Testament," in *Hermeneutics*, ed. B. Ramm (Grand Rapids: Baker, 1967), p. 118.

[10]Laurin, "Typological Interpretation," p. 128.

makes bold to say that the OT "is the lexicon, or word-book, of the New.")[11] The thematic approach takes us even further and seeks to show the unity of the two Testaments by tracing their underlying themes.

There is in both Old and New Testaments the revelation of one and the same God. The God who created all things at the beginning of time is the God who is seen in the face of Jesus Christ. Both Old and New Testaments are one grand story of redemption, accomplished, to be sure, in stages. The God who delivered Israel out of Egyptian bondage offers salvation to the world through Jesus Christ. Also, there is a people of God in the OT, as there is in the NT. In fact, Abraham, Israel's founding father, is the prototype of all those believers in the NT who, like him, are justified by faith. Other themes could be mentioned but these three (God, salvation, the people of God) will suffice to show that the two parts of the Bible are tied together by great themes. A book such as F. F. Bruce's *The New Testament Development of Old Testament Themes*, shows how fruitful this approach can be.[12]

5. *Dramatic Unity.* The unity of the Bible cannot be established simply by finding as many similarities between the two Testaments as possible (sometimes called "homology"). One must also take into account that God's revelation was progressive. This has nothing to do with the evolution of religion, but is a way of saying that God did not make his salvatory purposes known fully at the beginning of sacred history. There are high points of revelation in the OT, to be sure, but the climax of

God's saving purposes was made manifest in Christ.

One cannot, therefore, treat the two Testaments as if they represented one flat plane. If one does, serious errors will be made. It can be argued, for example, that the Bible teaches a state church on the grounds that the Israel of the OT was a people of God within a national structure. Indeed, some gross violations of ethics have occurred in the history of the church when Christians took their models from the OT.

If, however, the Bible is viewed as a drama, one allows for the element of progression and newness, while at the same time affirming the unity of the Scriptures. A play can be studied in its individual parts. Acts, scenes, and ideas have some meaning, quite independent of the rest of the drama. At the same time one must allow subsequent acts in the play to supplement and even correct the meanings one has derived from the earlier parts of the story. However, all the acts and all the scenes are understood fully only after one has seen the last act of the drama. That is why some people may read the last chapter of a novel first, for then they know where the story will end (writers of novels will call that cheating, of course).

The two Testaments proclaim the drama of redemption. The earlier scenes of this drama have a lot of meaning in their own right, quite independent of what follows. Often, however, Bible readers are puzzled by the ways of God in the earlier stages of redemption history. When one reads the Book of Judges, for example, one seriously wonders at times where God

---

[11]A. M. Hunter, *Jesus, Lord and Savior* (Grand Rapids: Eerdmans, 1976), p. 5.

[12]F. F. Bruce, *The New Testament Development of Old Testament Themes* (Grand Rapids: Eerdmans, 1968).

is going; his ways seem so hidden. But his purposes become clearer as time goes on, and when we come to the last act of drama, the birth, life, death, and exaltation of Jesus Christ, the diverse pieces of the puzzle all fall into place; what was revealed in the earlier stages of the drama is now seen in a new light.

Emil Brunner compares the OT to the first part of a sentence, and the NT as its second and concluding part. This comparison is more forceful in Brunner's native German, in which sentences can be interminably long and where the sense of the whole is not understood until the verb is tacked on at the end. So God spoke the first part of his salvation-bringing sentence in the OT; his last word was spoken in his Son.[13]

After 1900 years, books on the unity of the Bible are still being published.[14] Such writings witness, on the one hand, to the fact that the relationship of the two Testaments is not easy to define. On the other hand, they also express the deep conviction that the church's Bible is comprised of both Old and New Testaments.

SUGGESTED READING

Barrett, C. K. **The New Testament Background: Selected Documents.** *New York: Harper and Row, 1961. See pages 22–47 for the preparation and use of papyrus.*

Bruce, F. F. **The New Testament Development of Old Testament Themes.** *Grand Rapids: Eerdmans, 1968. Bruce demonstrates the unity of the Bible by tracing several themes from the Old Testament through the New.*

———. **The Books and the Parchments,** *3rd rev. ed. Old Tappan: Revell, 1963. See chapter 6, "The Two Testaments."*

Gaebelein, F. R. *"The Unity of the Bible,"* **Revelation and the Bible,** *ed. C. F. H. Henry. Grand Rapids: Baker, 1958, pp. 387–401.*

Martens, E. A. **God's Design: A Focus on Old Testament Theology.** *Grand Rapids: Baker, 1981. See chapter 4 for a study of the "covenant" idea.*

Metzger, B. M. **Manuscripts of the Greek Bible: An Introduction to Greek Paleography.** *New York: Oxford University Press, 1981.*

Tasker, R. V. G. **The Old Testament in the New Testament.** *Philadelphia: Westminster, 1947.*

Wiseman, D. J. *"Books in the Ancient Near East and in the Old Testament,"* **Cambridge History of the Bible,** *3 vols. ed. P. R. Ackroyd and C. F. Evans. Cambridge: Cambridge University Press, 1970, Vol. 1, pp. 30–66.*

[13]Bruce, *Books and Parchments*, p. 87.

[14]For example, H. H. Rowley, *The Unity of the Bible* (Philadelphia: Westminster, 1955).

Chapter 2

The Books of the Bible

We have learned that the word "Bible" simply means "book." Also, we have observed that this book is divided into two somewhat unequal halves, called Old and New Testament, respectively. As we examine these two Testaments individually we notice they are, one might say, mini-libraries, with thirty-nine books in the OT and twenty-seven in the NT.

This collection of literature came into being over a period of some 1400 years. Although the writers were largely Jews, they were a rather heterogeneous lot. There were kings, legislators, statesmen, courtiers, as well as herdsmen and fishermen. Some were priests and prophets; one was a Greek physician; another a tent-making rabbi; still another, a former tax collector. A number of the biblical books are anonymous, and we do not really know who wrote them.

The writers of the various books lived not only in different periods of history, but also in different lands—Palestine, Italy, Greece, Asia Minor, and the Land of the Two Rivers. Moreover, the style of the different writers varies considerably, not to mention the different literary types which they produced. Some books are histories, others lawbooks, still others poetry. There are parables and allegories, diaries and letters, and distinctively biblical types of literature such as prophecies and gospels.

We will have to ask later how these books were formed into one volume that we now call the Bible. At the moment it is sufficient to say that the Bible is not simply an anthology, for the books of the Bible have a basic unity. Besides, an anthology demands an anthologist, but we know of no such person who compiled the books of the Bible.[1] Just from the standpoint of its growth and development (quite apart from its message) there is something about this book of sacred writings that makes it unique. Not only did God's Spirit inspire the writers of the

---

[1] F. F. Bruce, *The Book and the Parchments*, 3rd rev. ed. (Old Tappan: Revell, 1963), p. 88.

sixty-six books that comprise the Bible, but God also superintended the transmission of these writings and their collection.

We must now take a look at the shape and form of the Old and the New Testament collection of these sacred books that comprise the church's Bible. We begin with the books of the Old Testament.

I. THE BOOKS OF THE OLD TESTAMENT

A. Their Number

Our English OT, as we have it today, is divided into thirty-nine books. This division, however, is no older than the Protestant Reformation (Roman Catholic Bibles include the apocrypha). The Hebrew OT was divided as a rule into twenty-four books; not that there is less material in the Hebrew Bible than there is in the English, but books such as 1 and 2 Samuel, 1 and 2 Kings, 1 and 2 Chronicles were treated as single books in the Hebrew canon, reducing the number by three. Also, Ezra-Nehemiah were treated as a unity. Most importantly, our twelve Minor Prophets were known simply as the Book of the Twelve, reducing the number by eleven. Altogether there are fifteen fewer books in the Hebrew canon, although that is in name only, for these twenty-four are the equivalent of our thirty-nine.

According to Origen, there was also a twenty-two book reckoning among the Jews, in which Ruth was connected with Judges and Lamentations with Jeremiah. Origen and some other Fathers explained this number as corresponding to the twenty-two letters of the Hebrew alphabet. Jerome also speaks of a twenty-two book canon, and draws the same numerical parallel with the Hebrew alphabet.[2] Interestingly, he adds the five Hebrew consonants that are written in alternative forms, and correspondingly five books emerge, making a total of twenty-seven. To arrive at twenty-seven, five books (Samuel, Kings, Jeremiah-Lamentations, Chronicles, Ezra-Nehemiah) are counted as ten. But this is obviously a bit fanciful. Whether the Hebrew canon originally was divided into twenty-two or twenty-four books is difficult to determine.

B. Their Grouping

Some English Bibles group the books in four sections: (1) the Pentateuch (Genesis to Deuteronomy), (2) the historical books (Joshua to Esther), (3) five poetical books (Job to Song of Songs), (4) the Prophets (Isaiah to Malachi). In some editions of Luther's Bible there are only three sections: (1) historical books, (2) didactic books, (3) prophetic books. Some modern versions no longer group the books, but simply list them seriatim. The Hebrew Bible, however, has a threefold division, called "the Law," "the Prophets," and "the Writings."

1. *The Law.* The Law contains five books, Genesis, Exodus, Leviticus, Numbers, and Deuteronomy. In Hebrew these books are called the Torah (Law).[3]

---

[2] G. W. Anderson, "Canonical and Non-Canonical," *The Cambridge History of the Bible,* eds. P. R. Ackroyd and C. F. Evans (Cambridge: Cambridge University Press, 1970), Vol. 1, pp. 137f.

[3] *Torah* can refer to single laws or, *pars pro toto,* be used to designate the Pentateuch or the entire OT.

THE TWENTY-FOUR BOOK DIVISION OF THE HEBREW OLD TESTAMENT

I. THE LAW (Torah)

Genesis
Exodus
Leviticus
Numbers
Deuteronomy

II. THE PROPHETS (Nebiim)	III. THE WRITINGS (Ketubim)	
The Former Prophets	Poetical Books:	Psalms
Joshua	*(The Book of Truth)*	Proverbs
Judges		Job
Samuel	Five Scrolls:	Song of Songs
Kings	*(Megilloth)*	Ruth
The Latter Prophets		Lamentations
(Writing Prophets)		Ecclesiastes
		Esther
Isaiah	Historical Books:	Daniel
Jeremiah		Ezra-Nehemiah
Ezekiel		Chronicles
The Twelve		

Origen seems to have been the first writer to call the Torah "Pentateuch" (from the Greek words *pente* = five, and *teuchos* = scroll), but the term may have been used earlier by Alexandrian Jews. The term corresponds to the Talmudic description of the Torah as "five fifths of the Law."[4]

The division of the Torah into five parts was prompted, no doubt, by the nature of the subject matter as well as by the fact that there was a practical limit to the length of individual scrolls. However, we should view the Pentateuch as a single work in five volumes, rather than a collection of five books.

2. *The Prophets.* The second division of the Hebrew canon is known as the Prophets (Nebiim) in Hebrew (from *nabi*, prophet). This division was again subdivided into four Former Prophets and four Latter Prophets, making eight prophetic books.

The Former Prophets are Joshua, Judges, Samuel, and Kings. They are anonymous works that recount the history of Israel from the time of the entrance into the land up to the exile to Babylon. We may call them historical books, but in Israel these books were believed to have been written by prophets. Also, these books record the ministry of the great oral prophets, Elijah and Elisha. Moreover, these historical books were written not simply to record Israel's past, but were designed to guide future generations. They have a prophetic message and so are quite properly called Prophets.[5]

The Latter Prophets are Isaiah, Jeremiah, Ezekiel, and the Twelve (i.e.,

---

[4]R. K. Harrison, *Introduction to the Old Testament* (Grand Rapids: Eerdmans, 1969), p. 495.
[5]Harrison, *Introduction*, p. 664.

our Minor Prophets). The men for whom these books are named are generally acknowledged as having written their message, and so they are known as "Writing Prophets"; but this does not deny the fact that their messages were first given orally. The division of these books into "major" and "minor" prophets has to do with length and not with importance. Isaiah, Jeremiah, and Ezekiel are much longer than any one of the Minor Prophets, known as the Book of the Twelve.

3. *The Writings.* The third division of the Hebrew canon is called the Writings (Ketubim in Hebrew, from the word *katab*, "to write"). They are also known by the Greek word *hagiographa*, meaning "holy writings." Eleven books belonged to this division. These eleven were again subdivided, although not always in the same manner. Psalms, Proverbs, and Job were known as poetical books, and were given a mnemonic title, "The Book of Truth." (The word "truth" in Hebrew [*emet*] is composed of the initial letters of each of these three books—*aleph* for Job, *mem* for Proverbs, and *tau* for Psalms.)[6]

Another section in the Writings was called the Five Scrolls (*Megilloth* in Hebrew): Song of Songs, Ruth, Lamentations, Ecclesiastes, and Esther. Evidently they were singled out to be read on special occasions. Song of Songs was associated with Passover; Ruth with the Feast of Weeks, i.e., Pentecost; Lamentations was read at the anniversary of the destruction of Jerusalem; Ecclesiastes was read at the Feast of Tabernacles to remind a prosperous Israel not to forget God; Esther was read at Purim—a post-Exilic festival commemorating the deliverance of the Jews in Babylon from certain death.

Finally, there were three so-called historical books: Daniel, Ezra-Nehemiah, and Chronicles.

The Jews today often call their Bible (our OT) "Tanak," and this word reflects the threefold division of the Hebrew canon ("T" stands for Torah, "N" for Nebiim, and "K" for the Ketubim).

This tripartite division of the Hebrew Bible was known before the time of Christ, and Jesus himself witnessed to it when he spoke of the things written "in the Law of Moses, the Prophets and the Psalms" (Luke 24:44). Since the Psalms stood first in the Writings, the entire third section of the canon was at times simply called "the Psalms." What has always been a bit puzzling to Bible readers is the order in which the individual books appear in the Hebrew Bible, and why some of the books that we would have expected to be in the second division appear in the third.

C. Their Order

As is to be expected, the order of the books of the Pentateuch is fixed. This is true also of the Former Prophets (Joshua, Judges, Samuel, and Kings) in which we have a narrative in chronological sequence. In the Syriac version of the OT the Book of Job usually came between the Pentateuch and Joshua. This was due to the belief that Moses was the author of Job. Latter Prophets are not always in the same order in the manuscripts. In some instances Isaiah stands at the head of the list, in others Jeremiah. The arrangement of the Twelve is intended to be chronological, beginning with Hosea in the eighth

---

[6]Harrison, *Introduction*, p. 965.

century and ending with Malachi in the Persian period.

The Writings show greater fluidity in their order. Sometimes they were divided into the Former Writings (Psalms, Job, and Proverbs), the Latter Writings (Daniel, Ezra-Nehemiah, Chronicles), and the Five Megilloth. At times they were divided into the Major Writings (Psalms, Job, Proverbs), the Minor Writings (Song of Songs, Ecclesiastes, Lamentations), and the Latter Writings (Esther, Daniel, Ezra-Nehemiah, Chronicles).[7]

We can readily understand why the Torah should form the first division. It was always considered unique. According to a rabbinic saying, if Israel had not sinned she would not have received the Prophets and the Writings; the Torah alone would have sufficed. Indeed, it was thought that in the messianic age, when sin would be removed, only the Torah would remain.[8]

It is also to be expected that the Prophets should be grouped in a separate section. But when we come to the Writings we are puzzled, and what the underlying principle might have been by which the Prophets and the Writings were distinguished has often been asked.

Some have suggested that the tripartite division is based on degrees of inspiration, but there is no evidence for that. Others argue that the three divisions represent the stages in which the books were accepted as canonical, but that cannot be proved either. Another suggestion is that the content

or nature of the books determined the threefold division. There is some merit in that observation, but it does not explain why Daniel should be among the Writings or why Kings should be among the Prophets, when Chronicles is not.

There are scholars who argue that the eight books of the Prophets come from men who had both the prophetic calling and the prophetic gift but not the prophetic office. One objection to this view might be that Lamentations, the work of a prophet, is listed with the Writings. The fact is, Lamentations was at times joined with Jeremiah (as was Ruth with Judges) in a twenty-two book canon. It was probably included for liturgical purposes in the Megilloth.

A greater difficulty is that Daniel is found in the third division, when in our Bibles it is grouped with the Major Prophets. Daniel, however, is not called a prophet in the OT, but a seer and a wise man. The Talmud indicates clearly that Daniel was never placed among the major prophets.[9] Perhaps also because Daniel had to do with heathen kings rather than with the people of Israel, he was not classified with the other Hebrew prophets.[10] This is not to deny that he had a prophetic gift. The NT, in fact, speaks of him as a prophet (Matt. 24:15), perhaps somewhat in the sense that David is called a prophet (Acts 2:29–30).

It seems quite impossible to explain the threefold division of the OT books on the basis of one simple principle. A number of factors appear to have been involved. Chronology, status of writ-

---

[7]W. Barclay, *The Making of the Bible* (New York: Abingdon, 1961), pp. 31f.

[8]H. L. Strack and P. Billerbeck, *Kommentar zum Neuen Testament aus Talmud und Midrash* (Munich: Beck, 1922–1961), Vol. 4, p. 435.

[9]Harrison, *Introduction*, pp. 1106f.

[10]J. H. Raven, *Old Testament Introduction* (Old Tappan: Revell, 1910), p. 42.

ers, liturgy, and content may all have played their part. It is even possible that the desire for a happy ending helped to put Chronicles rather than Ezra-Nehemiah at the end of the Hebrew canon.

A question we still need to ask is, why is the order of the books in our English Bibles so different from that of the Hebrew? The blame for this rests, first of all, with the Septuagint—a Jewish translation of the OT into Greek prior to the time of Christ. Not only did the Septuagint put the books in a different order, but it also included the so-called Apocrypha.

In the Codex Sinaiticus (fourth century A.D.) and Codex Alexandrinus (fifth century A.D.) the prophets follow the narrative and precede the poetical books; but in the Codex Vaticanus (fourth century A.D.) the prophets come last. The order of Vaticanus is gener-

ally adopted in printed editions of the Septuagint. It is as follows (including the Apocrypha): Genesis, Exodus, Leviticus, Numbers, Deuteronomy, Joshua, Judges-Ruth, 1–4 Kingdoms (i.e., 1 and 2 Samuel, 1 and 2 Kings), 1 and 2 Chronicles, 1 Esdras, 2 Esdras (i.e., Ezra-Nehemiah), Psalms, Proverbs, Ecclesiastes, the Song of Songs, Job, the Wisdom of Solomon, Ecclesiasticus, Esther, Judith, Tobit, Hosea, Amos, Micah, Joel, Obadiah, Jonah, Nahum, Habakkuk, Zephaniah, Haggai, Zechariah, Malachi, Isaiah, Jeremiah, Baruch, Lamentations, the Epistle of Jeremy, Ezekiel, Daniel.

This, however, is not the only order of the books in manuscripts of the Septuagint. The Latin Vulgate leaned heavily on the Septuagint in the way it ordered the books, but made some adaptations. The order of the books in the English Bibles was determined

---

THE THIRTY-NINE BOOK DIVISION OF THE ENGLISH OLD TESTAMENT

I. The Law (Pentateuch)—5		III. Poetical Books—5	
Genesis		Job	
Exodus		Psalms	
Leviticus		Proverbs	
Numbers		Ecclesiastes	
Deuteronomy		Song of Songs	

II. Historical Books—12		IV. Prophets—17	
Joshua		A. Major	B. Minor
Judges		Isaiah	Hosea
Ruth		Jeremiah	Joel
1 Samuel		Lamentations	Amos
2 Samuel		Ezekiel	Obadiah
1 Kings		Daniel	Jonah
2 Kings			Micah
1 Chronicles			Nahum
2 Chronicles			Habakkuk
Ezra			Zephaniah
Nehemiah			Haggai
Esther			Zechariah
			Malachi

largely by the Vulgate, about which we will have more to say later.

II. THE BOOKS OF THE NEW TESTAMENT

We shall discuss the formation of the NT canon in a later chapter; at this point we are simply describing the contents of the NT. Just as the OT is a collection of a great many books of various literary genres, so is the NT. But there are many differences between these two collections. First of all, the OT books were originally written in Hebrew or the closely related Aramaic. Also, the thought patterns of the OT writers belong to the ancient East, while those of the NT lie on the borderline between the Semitic and the Hellenistic world. Moreover, the OT took shape over a period of more than a thousand years, whereas the NT was written in a few decades. Furthermore, the OT books were written in the context of the national history of Israel, but the NT books revolve basically around a single person, Jesus of Nazareth. And from the standpoint of length, the NT is less than a third as long as the OT. Let us then look at this collection of books that we call the New Testament.

A. Their Number

Our NT is comprised of twenty-seven books. Although the apostolic writers who produced them were conscious of divine inspiration, and the books bore the stamp of God on their faces, it took some time before these twenty-seven books were clearly set off from other Christian literature. In the middle of the second century, Marcion, whom we have already men-

tioned, accepted only one Gospel (the Gospel of Luke—after excising the genealogy of Christ) and ten letters of Paul (omitting the Pastorals). This truncated canon was, however, rejected by the church.

From the writings of the church fathers we know that there was considerable debate in the first few centuries of the Christian era as to the number of books that should be admitted to the NT canon. As late as the fifth century, manuscripts of the NT were published that vary in the number of the NT books. Codex Sinaiticus, for example, includes the Epistle of Barnabas and the Shepherd of Hermas, together with the twenty-seven books of the NT. Codex Alexandrinus has 1 and 2 Clement, besides the twenty-seven NT books. Eventually, however, only our twenty-seven books were accepted as canonical. The reasons for this will become clearer as we go along.

B. Their Divisons

The OT collection of sacred books has a rather clearly defined tripartite division. The NT books, if they are divided at all, are grouped according to their literary genre. On that principle one can divide the NT into three parts: (1) five narrative books, (2) twenty-one epistles, (3) one apocalypse.

That may be acceptable as a general classification. However, on more careful investigation, one discovers that the Gospels are really a unique literary type and one hardly does justice to them by simply calling them narrative books. And even though Acts is the second volume of a two-volume work by Luke, it is not a gospel in the same sense as the Gospel of Luke. Perhaps it

THE BOOKS OF THE NEW TESTAMENT

I. GOSPELS	II. ACTS
Matthew Mark Luke John	The Acts of the Apostles

III. EPISTLES

Pauline:		General:
Romans	1 Thessalonians	Hebrews
1 Corinthians	2 Thessalonians	James
2 Corinthians	1 Timothy	1 Peter
Galatians	2 Timothy	2 Peter
Ephesians	Titus	1 John
Philippians	Philemon	2 John
Colossians		3 John
		Jude

IV. APOCALYPSE

The Revelation

is better, then, if we allow for a fourfold division: Gospels, Acts, Epistles, Revelation.

There is nothing sacred about the order of the NT books, and yet there is a rationale for the traditional canonical arrangement. It is only natural that the Gospels should stand first, for without them the rest of the NT would hardly make sense. They introduce us to the person of Christ who fulfilled the hopes of the OT by his redeeming work. The Gospels, however, call for a sequel, and Acts provides that by its account of the beginning and the growth of the early church. On the other hand, without the Book of Acts, the letters that the apostles wrote to the churches would be without a historical setting. They are messages addressed largely to the churches whose founding is described by Luke in Acts.

It also stands to reason that the NT collection should close with the Book of Revelation. While the book may not be the last apostolic book to be written (although some would insist that it was), it certainly forms a uniquely fitting climax to the whole history of salvation, by giving us a glimpse of the glory that awaits the children of God in the age to come.

There has been little dispute about the sequence of the several groups of books in the NT (although Codex Sinaiticus has Paul's letters before Acts). The order of the individual books within these larger sections, however, varies considerably in the early lists of NT books. To this day the order of the epistles in Luther's Bible is different from that of our English Bibles (although earlier English Bibles also followed the Lutheran order). Luther pushed Hebrews, James, and Jude as far back as possible, just before Revelation.

If one looks at some of the early records one finds that, although the Gospels always head the lists, they are not always in the same order. There is, for example, the so-called "Western" order, in which the Gospels come in the following sequence: Matthew, John, Luke, Mark (found, for example, in the sixth-century Codex Bezae). It is to be expected that Matthew should head the list of Gospels since he provides a good link with the OT. However, in two rather important third-century Egyptian versions, the Bohairic and the Sahidic, John heads the list of the four Gospels, followed by Matthew, Mark, and Luke.

There is even greater fluidity in the order of the epistles. First of all, the General Epistles (also called "Catholic," meaning "universal"), sometimes precede the Paulines, contrary to the order of the epistles in our English NTs. Then within these two bodies of letters there is considerable variation. In Marcion's canon Galatians headed the list. In the Canon of Muratori (c. A.D. 180) the list begins with 1 Corinthians. The order of the Pauline letters in the modern NT was determined not by chronology but by length. Romans stands at the head of the list of those letters addressed to churches, and 2 Thessalonians ends the list. Then come the Pauline letters to individuals, beginning with 1 Timothy, the longest, and closing with Philemon, the shortest.

The General Epistles are not always in the same order either. In the Sinaiticus, Alexandrinus, and Vaticanus they appear in the order: James; 1 and 2 Peter; 1, 2, and 3 John; and Jude. In the canon list found in Codex Claromontanus the order is: 1 and 2 Peter; James; 1, 2, and 3 John; and Jude. The Epistle to the Hebrews does not have a fixed place in the order of NT books in the early centuries. Because it is an anonymous book, it is listed at times with the Paulines and then again, with the Catholic Epistles.

Before we leave our description of the shape of the two Testaments, perhaps we should make a few comments on the titles of the biblical books.

III. THE TITLES OF THE BIBLICAL BOOKS

By way of introduction it should be pointed out that a number of the biblical books are anonymous. Evidently, because the writers were convinced that they were proclaiming God's Word, they took no pride in authorship. It does not follow, of course, that those writers who did attach their names to these sacred books wanted to make a name for themselves. Not only do we have a number of anonymous OT books (such as Joshua, Judges, Samuel, and Kings), but NT books as well are anonymous (the Gospels, for example, the Epistle to the Hebrews, and 1 John).

This does not mean that we have no idea as to who wrote some of these books; but the authors do not mention their names as Paul does in his letters, for example.

Moreover, some of the titles that the books now have were added later and did not form part of the original text. It was a Hebrew custom to entitle books by the first word or phrase of the book. For instance, the Hebrew title for the first book of the Bible is *berēshīt*, meaning "in the beginning." The English title "Genesis" was derived from the Greek translation of Genesis 2:4a, where the Septuagint has "the *gene-*

seos of heaven and earth." The Book of Joshua was named after its principal character. The Books of Chronicles are entitled *diberē hayamīn* ("the words of the days" or "acts of the days" in Hebrew). In the Septuagint the title is "things omitted" (*paraleipomenon*, i.e., omitted from Samuel and Kings). Jerome, in his Latin translation, proposed the title that has given us the name Chronicles in English.

These few illustrations should suffice to show the origin of the names of the OT books in our English Bibles.

The names of the NT books also have an interesting history. The first line of Mark's Gospel reads: "the beginning of the gospel of Jesus Christ, the Son of God." Some scholars hold that this was meant to be the title of the Gospel. Then, when other Gospels were written, they had to be distinguished, so now we have the titles "According to Matthew," "According to Mark," and so forth.

The title "The Acts of the Apostles" does not appear until the latter part of the second century. From about the same time comes a canon list which gives it as "The Acts of All the Apostles." One enterprising editor added the adjective "holy" to Apostles.[11] No NT book, however, has had such a variety of names as the Revelation. To "The Revelation of John" was added "the divine" or "the evangelist" or "the apostle." A late manuscript takes the palm: "The Revelation of the all-glorious evangelist, bosom friend of Jesus, virgin, beloved to Christ, John the theologian, son of Salome and Zebedee, but adopted son of Mary the Mother of God, and Son of Thunder."[12]

Enough has been said, we believe, to make us aware of the fact that the titles of the biblical books as they now appear in our English Bibles, are not necessarily the original titles.

Our first chapter was an attempt to describe the Bible as a book with two Testaments. This chapter has sought to give the reader a general overview of the books that comprise the Bible. These books were written in alphabetic scripts (Hebrew, Aramaic, Greek), and we shall now have to say something about these written languages.

SUGGESTED READING

For books of the Old Testament see:

Archer, G. L. **A Survey of Old Testament Introduction.** *Rev. ed. Chicago: Moody, 1974.*

Harrison, R. K. **Introduction to the Old Testament.** *Grand Rapids: Eerdmans, 1969.*

Unger, M. F. **Introductory Guide to the Old Testament.** *2nd ed. Grand Rapids: Zondervan, 1956.*

Young, E. J. **An Introduction to the Old Testament.** *Grand Rapids: Eerdmans, 1953.*

For books of the New Testament see:

Gundry, R. H. **A Survey of the New Testament.** *2nd ed. Grand Rapids: Zondervan, 1982.*

Guthrie, D. **New Testament Introduction.** *Downers Grove: InterVarsity, 1976.*

Martin, R. P. **New Testament Foundations.** *2 vols. Grand Rapids: Eerdmans, 1975, 1979.*

Stott, J. R. W. **Basic Introduction to the New Testament.** *Grand Rapids: Eerdmans, 1964.*

[11]F. F. Bruce, *The Book of Acts* (Grand Rapids: Eerdmans, 1955), p. 17.

[12]B. M. Metzger, *The Text of the New Testament*, 2nd ed. (New York: Oxford University Press, 1968), p. 205.

Chapter 3

The Languages of the Bible

A language is a way of thinking, not simply a set of words or a unique way of structuring sentences. Language has been called "the speaking face of the heart." That is why biblical languages are so important; they represent ways of thinking, of seeing things.

The fact that the Bible was written in known spoken languages is an aspect of its humanity. Although the Hebrew, Aramaic, and Greek words are carriers of a divine message, they are, nevertheless, earthly not heavenly words. And the reason several languages were used by God to make his saving purposes known to man was that God's revelation was given over a long period of time. The earlier books of the Bible were written in Hebrew, since that was the language of Israel when she entered the Promised Land. As time went on, however, Israel adopted the lingua franca of the Fertile Crescent and so some portions of the OT were written in Aramaic. By the time the gospel came to be proclaimed in the Mediterranean world, Greek was the common language of communication, and so the books of the NT were written in Greek.

These ancient tongues should not be thought of as dead languages. Hebrew is today the official language of Israel, and even when Palestine was a British mandate, Hebrew was one of its three official languages. Aramaic is still spoken by a remnant of Christians in Syria, Iraq, and Iran, and Greek is the language of some seven or eight million Greeks today. In the long history of these languages changes naturally took place, as happens to all spoken tongues. Latin, by contrast, is a dead language in the sense that it is not the spoken language of any group of people today. It lives only in its derivatives, the Romance languages.

Let us now look briefly at the three languages in which larger or smaller portions of the Bible were written.

I. THE HEBREW LANGUAGE

A. Its Family

With the exception of several chapters of Daniel and Ezra, which are writ-

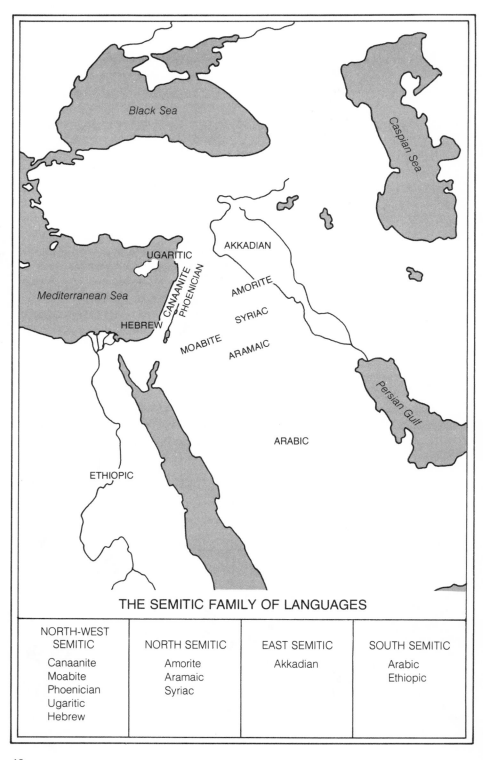

THE SEMITIC FAMILY OF LANGUAGES

NORTH-WEST SEMITIC	NORTH SEMITIC	EAST SEMITIC	SOUTH SEMITIC
Canaanite	Amorite	Akkadian	Arabic
Moabite	Aramaic		Ethiopic
Phoenician	Syriac		
Ugaritic			
Hebrew			

ten in Aramaic, the language of the OT is Hebrew. This language, however, is nowhere called "Hebrew" in the OT itself. Once it is called "the language of Canaan" (Isa. 19:18); usually it is spoken of as the "language of Judah" (Neh. 13:24). Some translations render these phrases as "Hebrew," but this is an interpretation of what actually appears in the Hebrew text and is intended to help the modern reader. In the NT, however, this language is called "Hebrew" (e.g., Rev. 9:11; 16:16), although in some passages where the word "Hebrew" occurs in the NT, Aramaic seems to be meant.

Hebrew was no isolated language in OT times; it was one of a number of Semitic tongues. The word "semitic" is derived from Shem, one of the sons of Noah. However, even Hamites might speak a Semitic tongue (e.g., the Canaanites). "Semitic," then, is rather a linguistic, not a racial term. The ancient habitat of the Semitic languages may be defined as Mesopotamia, Syria-Palestine, Arabia, and Ethiopia.[1]

To the southwest, languages such as Ethiopic and Arabic are related to Hebrew (Arabic is the most widely spoken Semitic tongue today, one that has gone far beyond its original home). In the northeast the Babylonians and Assyrians had inherited Akkadian, the oldest written Semitic language, which replaced the non-Semitic Sumerian in the second millennium B.C. In the Fertile Cresent, Aramaic and its twin, Syriac, were spoken. Aramaic represents a widespread linguistic group. In the eighth century B.C. it was the language of diplomacy in the Assyrian Empire. To the northwest we find Semitic languages such as Canaanite, Ugaritic, Moabite, Phoenician, and Hebrew.

When we speak of a family of languages (such as the Semitic) we mean that these languages developed from dialects of one original language.[2] What in an earlier stage were dialects that were mutually intelligible eventually became distinct languages. Since geography was an important factor in the development of these independent languages, their classification is determined largely by geography. However, the Semitic languages are all related and must not be sharply distinguished one from another by geography.

B. Its Origin

The earliest history of the Hebrew languages is shrouded in mystery. Like some other languages, it grew by interaction with other tongues. The ancestors of the Israelites apparently spoke Aramaic, (although Akkadian elements probably persisted). Aramaic was the language spoken in Paddan-Aram by the relatives whom the patriarchs left behind.

When Abraham and his clan settled in Canaan, they evidently picked up "the language of Canaan," with Aramaic and Akkadian elements persisting. As can be learned from the Jacob stories, the language of the patriarchs was not simply the Aramaic of the Fertile Crescent. After serving his father-in-law, Laban, for many years, he returned to Canaan. Laban pursued him, and when they finally parted company they made a heap of stones

[1] M. Black, "Language and Script," *Cambridge History of the Bible*, eds. P. R. Ackroyd and C. F. Evans (Cambridge: Cambridge University Press, 1970), Vol. 1, p. 2.

[2] F. F. Bruce, *The Books and the Parchments*, 3rd rev. ed. (Old Tappan: Revell, 1963), p. 34.

to witness to their agreement. Jacob called it "Galeed," but Laban "Jeger Sahadutha" (Gen. 31:47).

Jacob and his clan eventually moved to Egypt where for some 430 years Israel lived in relative isolation, providing the setting for the development of an independent language. It is not surprising that a dose of Egyptian words was added to the Hebrew vocabulary at this time. When the Israelites left Egypt and came back to Canaan, they spoke what we might now call the "Hebrew" tongue.

There has been some debate over the origin of the word "Hebrew." Some find the explanation in Genesis 10:21, where Shem is said to be "the ancestor of all the sons of Eber." The name in the form of *Habiru* is now known from sources as early as the second millennium B.C. Etymologically the word "Hebrew" may be derived from *'abar*, "to cross over" (i.e., over the River). Abraham, who came from across the Euphrates, is called "the Hebrew" (Gen. 14:13), and Joshua reminds Israel later, "I took your father Abraham from the land beyond the River and led him throughout Canaan" (Josh. 24:3). But there are other possible explanations of the etymology of Hebrew.

The application of the name "Hebrew" to the language of the Hebrews appears for the first time in the prologue to the Wisdom of Ben Sirach (second century B.C.) where the Greek adverb *hebraisti* describes the language of the Jews. The rabbis preferred to call it "the holy tongue."

Although the tribes of Israel spoke the same Hebrew language when they conquered Canaan after their long Egyptian sojourn, dialectical differences tended to emerge. For example, in a war between the Ephraimites west

of Jordan and the Gileadites east of Jordan, the latter took the fords of the river and made all who wanted to cross over say "Shibboleth." In this way they were able to detect the enemy, for the Ephraimites said "Sibboleth" (Judg. 12:6).

The Hebrew language was generally maintained up to the time of the exile of Israel and Judah, although Aramaic had by then made inroads on it. The exile accelerated the changeover from Hebrew to Aramaic, and while Hebrew continued to be the sacred language, Aramaic was spoken in Palestine at the time of Christ. However, Hebrew as a spoken language in everyday life did not die out.

C. Its Character

It may be helpful for those who have not had the opportunity to study Hebrew to have a few characteristics of this language explained. Hebrew and Aramaic are relatively simple and uncomplicated languages as far as syntax and grammar are concerned.

Semitic word stems are generally triliteral, meaning that they consist of three consonants. (Hebrew vowels were originally not represented in writing.) There are few words with four consonants, and Hebrew is not known for its polysyllabic words. There is, however, great word-variety. English may have ten times as many words, but Hebrew, it has been said, has ten times as many word-roots. Moreover, some words have a great variety of meanings, depending on the context in which they are used. *Mishpat*, for example, can mean judgment, verdict, justice, duty, or salvation.

As for its syntax, Hebrew (and

Aramaic) has a paratactic structure. English is hypotactic, meaning that it has principal and subordinate clauses; Hebrew basically has only principal clauses that are bound together by an overwhelmingly infinite number of "ands." Usually a great many of these "ands" are eliminated when the Hebrew Bible is translated into English, and the woman who undertook the wearisome task of counting all the "ands" in the English Bible no doubt missed a good many.

To a Westerner the Hebrew verb seems to function in a rather unique manner. There are only two tenses: perfect and imperfect. These tenses express modes of actions, as complete or describing a state or condition (perfect), or as incomplete and continuous (imperfect). Strictly speaking there are no moods in Hebrew, but the verbs are found in different stems, expressing varying degrees of intensity. These may be called "conjugations," of which there are seven in number.

The Hebrew of the OT is known for the vividness of its style. It is rich in imagery. A stubborn people is criticized for being "for backward, not forward"; divided loyalties are described in terms of "a heart and a heart"; God's anger may be described as shortness of breath or redness of the nostrils. Contrast is often expressed in extreme terms. "I loved Jacob, but Esau I have hated" (Mal. 1:2–3); "I desire mercy, not sacrifice" (Hos. 6:6).

The vividness of Hebrew style can be seen also in the use of nouns, where we might use adjectives. Instead of saying "a beautiful garden," the Hebrew prefers to speak of "a garden of beauty." Instead of "holy mountain" it is a "mountain of holiness." Naughty boys are "sons of Belial." This has definitely influenced the NT Greek, where expressions such as "the Father of glory," or "sons of disobedience," betray a Semitic background.

The psychology of the OT is concrete and very physical. Bodily organs stand for emotions. Fear and distress may be described by such expressions as: "my liver is poured out," or "my bones melted." The fulcrum of life (thought, emotion, will) is the heart. When God searches the deep recesses of a person's life he investigates the kidneys (the "reins" in KJV English).

The Hebrew of the OT is rich in metaphor and simile. Israel is described as a "wild heifer," "a crooked bow," "a cake unturned."

Although images of God in wood and stone are forbidden, the OT writers have no reservations about the use of word images. Anthropomorphisms (God's eye, his hand, his arms, his feet, etc.) and anthropopathisms (divine anger, sorrow, repentance, etc.) are found in abundance.

It is always precarious to make value judgments on any language, but perhaps we may be allowed to say that Hebrew is well-suited for narrative and verse but lacks the precision of Greek. What is important is that those who speak non-Semitic languages learn to enter into the thought-world of OT Hebrew, so that they grasp its message. A good translation of the OT into English will seek to obliterate the Semitic character of Hebrew, but it should not be forgotten that people who speak Hebrew and Aramaic express themselves quite differently from those who speak English. But let us now turn to Aramaic.

II. THE ARAMAIC LANGUAGE

A. Its Use in the Near East

Two considerable portions of the OT (Dan. 2:4b–7:28; Ezra 4:8–6:18; 7:12–26) are written not in Hebrew but in Aramaic. The first reference to Aramaic in the OT is in Genesis 31:47, where Laban gives the heap of stones that marked the place where he and Jacob had made a treaty, an Aramaic name. In OT times Aramaic was spoken to the north and northeast of the Hebrew and Canaanite-speaking area.[3]

It was the language of the kingdom of Syria, and was spoken also in the upper regions of the Euphrates Valley. Inscriptions from the tenth to the eighth century B.C. give evidence of the use of "Old Aramaic" in the Fertile Crescent, stretching from Syria (called "Aram" in Hebrew) to Assyria. Its successor was the so-called Imperial Aramaic, the official language of the Persian Empire and the international medium of cultural and commercial intercourse from the Euphrates to the Nile[4] from about the tenth to the fourth century B.C.[5]

An interesting example of the use of Aramaic in international diplomacy is found in 2 Kings 18:17–37. The king of Assyria (c. 701 B.C.) sent some of his officers to Jerusalem to demand the surrender of the city. King Hezekiah's delegation went out to confer with them outside the wall, and several of the citizens watched the proceedings from the top of the wall. The leader of the Assyrian delegation addressed Hezekiah's men so loudly in Hebrew that they became worried about the demoralizing effect this might have on the citizens on the wall, and asked the Assyrian to use Aramaic, which King Hezekiah's delegation could also understand. The Assyrian, however, made clear that he was using the Hebrew deliberately so that the inhabitants of Jerusalem might know the fate that awaited them if Judah refused to submit to Sennacherib. With that he addressed the people on the wall directly, in order to undermine their allegiance to Hezekiah.

This diplomatic use of Aramaic continued until Alexander the Great made an end of the Persian Empire in 331 B.C. It is interesting to observe that the Aramaic sections of Ezra contain a good deal of official correspondence belonging to the Persian kings. Some well-known Aramaic words in the book of Daniel, *mene, mene, tekel, uparsin,* are known to most readers of the English Bible.

With the conquests of Alexander the Great, Greek became the world language. Aramaic, however, continued to be spoken in certain areas. By the beginning of the Christian era, Aramaic had split into two branches, West and East Aramaic (the latter was to provide the Syriac Church with its medium of literary expression).

B. The Change From Hebrew to Aramaic

As the story from 2 Kings 18 indicates, Aramaic was not unknown in Judah in the sixth century B.C. With strong Aramaic-speaking states, such as Damascus, Israel's close neighbor, this should not surprise us. With the

---

[3]Bruce, *Books and Parchments*, p. 48.

[4]Black, "Language and Script," p. 6.

[5]R. K. Harrison, *Introduction to the Old Testament* (Grand Rapids: Eerdmans, 1969), p. 203.

end of the Northern Kingdom (722 B.C.) and of Judah (586 B.C.), and the exile of masses of Jews to the land of the Two Rivers, Hebrew as the language of daily communication suffered a severe setback and was displaced by Aramaic.

Under the Persians the use of Aramaic by the Jews was accelerated, and when they finally were allowed to return to their homeland, they spoke Aramaic. Those who had remained in Judea probably spoke Aramaic by now also, for many of them had intermarried with non-Jews, and Nehemiah was incensed when he discovered they could no longer understand Hebrew (Neh. 13:24).

This does not mean that Hebrew had died out completely, for the post-exilic prophets still gave their oracles in Hebrew. However, from the time of the exile onward Aramaic spread at the expense of the Hebrew, and Hebrew became restricted more and more to religious purposes. A well-known scene in Nehemiah 8 bears this out. At the Feast of Tabernacles (c. 445 B.C.) a vast congregation had gathered to hear Ezra and his assistants read the Book of the Law of Moses. Evidently they had difficulty in understanding the Hebrew, for we are informed that the readers read "giving the meaning" (v. 8), so that the people could understand. It seems as if the Law was read in Hebrew and an oral translation was given in Aramaic. By the time of Christ, Aramaic had already long been the everyday language of Palestinian Jews.

Not only in Palestine but also in Egypt, where a large colony of Jews was established at Elephantine, Aramaic was spoken during the Persian period, as can be seen from the Elephantine papyri.[6] This situation changed, no doubt, when Egypt revolted against Persia in 400 B.C.

C. Aramaic at the Time of Jesus

When Jesus was born, the language of the entire Mediterranean world was Greek. In Palestine, Syria, and some of its neighboring territories, however, Aramaic persisted until the time of the Arab conquests in the seventh century A.D.

Aramaic, then, was widely used at the time of Jesus and the apostles. There is good evidence for this from Qumran and Murabbaat, where Aramaic texts have been found in the caves beside the Dead Sea. But there is considerable evidence for this even in the Greek texts of the NT. A number of Aramaic words and phrases have been taken up into Greek and transliterated. The following sentences in Aramaic, which come from the lips of Jesus, are familiar to most Bible readers: *talitha koum* (Mark 5:41), *ephphatha* (Mark 7:34), *Eloi, Eloi, lama sabachthani* (Mark 15:34). (Mark's Gospel seems to have more Aramaisms than others.) Also, words such as *Abba, Marana tha, mamon,* and *Gabbatha* have a familiar ring to them.

Furthermore, the syntax of Greek seems to have been influenced considerably by the spoken Aramaic that lies behind the Greek of the NT. There is no evidence that our Gospels were originally written in Aramaic (there may have been summaries of Jesus' sayings in Aramaic), but the Greek of the gospels, at least at some points,

---

[6]I. M. Price, *The Ancestry of Our English Bible.* 3rd ed., revised by W. A. Irwin and Allen P. Wikgren (New York: Harper and Row, 1956), p. 322.

can be explained only if one takes into account its Aramaic background.

It appears as if the Aramaic spoken in Palestine at the time of Christ reflected at least two distinct dialects, a Judean and a Galilean. This can be detected, for example, in the story of Peter's denial, where a maid observed that Peter is a Galilean because his speech betrayed him (Matt. 26:73). It was said the Galileans swallowed their gutterals.

Eastern Christianity continued the Aramaic tradition by speaking Syriac, which is essentially Aramaic. The gospel that spread to the western part of the Roman Empire, however, appeared in Greek dress. All the books of the NT were written in a form of Greek known as Koine, meaning "common." We must say more about this language.

III. THE GREEK LANGUAGE

Although the revelation under the old covenant had been given to a people that spoke Hebrew, and later, Aramaic, the books that comprise the NT were written in Greek—the language spoken in all the lands surrounding the Mediterranean at the time of Christ. Latin was the language of government and of the military under the Romans, but Greek was spoken on the streets of Rome, Alexandria, Jerusalem, Antioch, and Ephesus, as well as Athens. In God's providence the gospel had no language barriers to overcome in the days of the apostles. Paul, for example, could preach in Greek wherever he went. We should then say a few words about the development of NT Greek.

A. The Indo-European Family of Languages

The Greek language is one of a number of languages that constitute the Indo-European family. About 3000 B.C. there was a vast movement of people from central Europe; one stream flowed to the west, into Europe, another to the east, into India. These migrations brought about the development of sister languages that found their roots in a common parent language. The oldest attested representative of this Indo-European family is Sanskrit, which lies at the base of most Indian languages. Greek written records go back almost as far as the Sanskrit records, making Greek the second-oldest attested member of this family.

The Indo-European languages can be grouped in different ways; one is to group them into ten languages or language clusters: (1) the Indian languages; (2) Iranian; (3) Slavonic (which embraces Russian, Ukranian, Polish, Czech, Slovak, Bulgarian, Serbian, and Croatian); (4) Baltic (Latvian and Lithuanian); (5) Germanic (with Icelandic, Danish, Norwegian, and Swedish to the north, and Dutch, Frisian, German, and English to the west); (6) Celtic; (7) Italic (represented earlier mainly by Latin and today by the Romance languages, such as Italian, Spanish, Portuguese, French, Sardinian, and Rummanian); (8) Illyrian (represented today by Albanian); (9) Thraco-Phrygian (represented today by Armenian); and (10) Greek. How did the Greek language, the language of the NT develop?

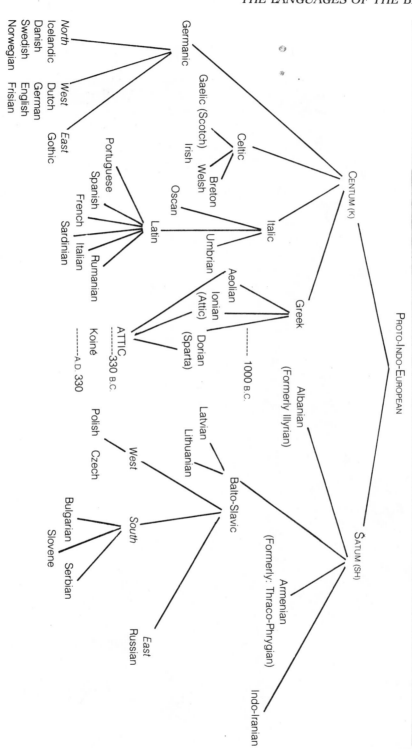

THE INDO-EUROPEAN FAMILY OF LANGUAGES:

B. The Development of the Greek Language

In pre-Homeric times (c. 1500–1000 B.C.) successive waves of immigrants entered the Balkan Peninsula from the north, known respectively as Ionians, Achaeans, and Dorians. The first settlers, the Ionians, were pushed beyond the Aegean into Asia Minor and elsewhere by the new waves of immigrants. Some, however, settled permanently in Attica. In this formative period (prior to 1000 B.C.) the various dialects of these immigrants interacted with one another, with several dialects in use during the classical period.

The dialects of the classical period (c. 1000–330 B.C.), have given the world great monuments of literature, such as the Homeric epics titled the *Iliad* and the *Odyssey*. Of this Greek period E. K. Simpson has said: "In its golden prime it presents an unrivalled combination of elegance and vigour, of variety of style and precision of statement."[7] By the end of the classical period Attic, through economic and political events, gained dominance over other dialects.

In 338 B.C. Philip of Macedon imposed a political unity on the Greek city states. His son, Alexander the Great, inherited his father's political ambitions and undertook the conquest of most of the then known world. Not only did he conquer the lands around the Mediterranean, but he spread Hellenistic culture, including the Greek language, wherever his conquests took him.

The Greek of Alexander's time gathered its elements from various dialects and spread throughout the empire. This new form of the language was a Greek *koine* (*he koine dialektos* would be the full name, meaning "the common dialect") and is known as Koine Greek today. Greek became the official language of all the lands conquered by Alexander. And when his domains were eventually taken over by the Romans, Greek continued to be spoken throughout the Roman Empire. If one uses round numbers, the period of Koine stretches from 330 B.C. to A.D. 330.

It was in this period, prior to the time of Christ, that the Alexandrian Jews undertook the translation of the Hebrew OT into Greek, since their children no longer understood the Hebrew but spoke Greek like the rest of the world. And when the books of the NT came to be written, they were written in Koine Greek. Paul wrote his letter to the Roman Christians living in the heart of the empire, not in Latin, but in Greek. Toward the end of the first Christian century, when Clement of Rome wrote a letter to the Corinthians, he had no difficulty writing in Greek.

The period from about A.D. 330 to 1453 is described as the Byzantine period, beginning with the demise of the Roman Empire and ending with the capture of Constantinople (the old Byzantium) by the Muslim Turks. The period from A.D. 1453 to the present is known as the Modern period.

The Greek language, then, has a known history of some three thousand years, and it preserves some of the greatest literary treasures of mankind.

---

[7]E. K. Simpson, *Words Worth Weighing in the Greek New Testament* (London: Tyndale, 1944), p. 5.

Language, however, like a river, may have many tributaries and also change its course from time to time; but it remains the same river. And this is certainly true of the Greek language. The American grammarian, A. T. Robertson, expressed this in these words: "It is one language whether we read the Epic Homer, the Doric Pindar, the Ionic Herodotus, the Attic Xenophon, the Aeolic Sappho, the Atticist Plutarch, Paul the exponent of Christ, an inscription in Pergamus, a papyrus letter in Egypt...."[8] One cannot, therefore, judge the quality of NT Greek by comparing it to classical literature; it is simply the Greek of a later period. As a body of literature, however, the language of the NT has some unique features.

C. The Greek of the New Testament

It must be stated, first of all, that the NT books were written in contemporary Greek. This was not the common view a hundred years ago. Some scholars thought the NT was written in a special "Holy Ghost" language. Others saw it differently. Bishop Lightfoot, of Cambridge, for example, ventured to suggest that if there were words in the NT not found in classical literature, it did not mean that these words were not known in everyday Greek. "If we could only recover letters that ordinary people wrote to each other," he said, "we should have the greatest possible help for the understanding of the language of the NT generally."[9] He was confirmed in this observation when several years later (beginning about 1880) papyrus writings whose language was that of the NT were discovered in the sands of Egypt. The Greek of the NT turned out to be the language of the common man. For example, the rare adjective *epiousios* ("daily") was not found in any known Greek literature until it was discovered in the papyri in a woman's shopping list. Those who had interpreted it to mean the Bread of life or the Lord's Supper now had to give up such "spiritual" interpretations. The language of the NT turned out to be the language of the common man. How else would people in the days of the apostles have understood the gospel, had it not been proclaimed in their mother tongue, Koine Greek?

These discoveries brought about a minor revolution in NT vocabulary studies. One could no longer simply read classical meanings into NT Greek words; one had to ask how a given word was used at the time of Paul. The change in word meaning over time can be illustrated, for example, by the word *arrabōn* that in Ephesians 1:14 means a "downpayment" or "deposit," but in Modern Greek means "engagement ring."[10]

To say that the books of the NT were written in contemporary Greek does not mean, of course, that all these books reflect the same literary style, or that the NT is written in an exalted style in comparison to secular documents. Writers such as Luke have a somewhat more sophisticated style than Paul, but Paul also reaches literary heights on occasion in his correspondence (think only of 1 Corinthians

---

[8]A. T. Robertson, *A Grammar of the Greek New Testament in the Light of Historical Research* (Sevenoaks, England: Hodder and Stoughton, 1919), p. 42.

[9]Quoted in F. F. Bruce, *Books and Parchments*, p. 63.

[10]F. F. Bruce, *The Epistle to the Ephesians* (Glasgow: Pickering and Inglis, 1961), p. 37.

13), and so to say that the writers of the NT write in contemporary Greek does not necessarily mean that they indulge in colloquialisms or fail to achieve literary excellence.

Although the books of the NT were written in contemporary Greek, they reflect a linguistic environment that has left its imprint on the Koine of the NT. The Greek of the NT was strongly influenced by the Hebrew of the OT. Both the syntax and the meaning of NT words are colored by their Semitic background. Take only, for example, the word "glory." In classical Greek *doxa* meant "opinion," then "reputation" or "honor." But when the NT uses the word "glory" it uses it in the OT sense of "glory" *(kabōd)*, where it stood for the manifested power, splendor, majesty, and holiness of God. The Hebrew *kabōd* had been translated by *doxa* in the Septuagint version, and so the Greek word was dyed with the Hebrew meaning—a meaning which, as Hunter puts it, "would have made a classical Greek stare and gasp."[11]

The syntax of the Greek NT has also been influenced by the style of Hebrew and Aramaic. Those who know German notice immediately when they read Coverdale's Germanized translation of 2 Corinthians 9:15, "Thanks be unto God for his unoutspeakable gift," that he was following Luther. Similarly, Semitic scholars can easily detect Hebraisms and Aramaisms in the NT. The tension between the Jewish biblical heritage and the Hellenistic world vitally affects the language of the NT.

Besides the Semitic environment in which the NT books were written, there is also a Latin influence. Not only do we find Latin idioms here and there in the NT, but the Greek NT has preserved a number of Latin words for us (transliterated into Greek, of course). Most of these transliterations are to be found in areas where we might have expected them: in the monetary, legal, and military spheres. *Denarion* (Latin, *denarius*), for example, is a common monetary term in the NT. *Kenturion* (Latin, *centurio*) is a military word. *Praitorion* (Latin, *praetorium*) could be translated as "government house," again, a Latin designation. One could easily find a dozen Latinisms in the NT without much effort.

It is quite impossible to characterize within a single formula the complex nature of the language of the NT. Although it represents the Hellenistic period of the Greek language that follows on the Classical, it has been strongly influenced by the Hebrew OT (especially in its Greek version, the Septuagint), the Aramaic, spoken in Jesus' day, and the Latin of the then ruling power. Therefore, in several respects at least, the language of the NT is unique.

---

[11]A. M. Hunter, *Probing the New Testament* (Richmond: Knox, 1971), p. 60.

Suggested Reading

Bruce, F. F. **The Books and the Parchments,** 3rd rev. ed. Old Tappan: Revell, 1963. See "The Hebrew Language," chapter 3; "The Aramaic Language," chapter 4; "The Greek Language," chapter 5.

Colwell, E. C. "The Greek Language," **Interpreter's Dictionary of the Bible,** 4 vols. ed. G. A. Buttrick. Nashville: Abingdon Press, 1938. Vol. 3, pp. 479–87.

Deissmann, A. **Light from the Ancient East,** trans. L. R. M. Strachen. New York: Doran, 1927.

Geisler, N. L. and Nix, W. E. **From God To Us.** Chicago: Moody, 1974. See "Languages and Materials of the Bible," pp. 126–38.

Hughes, P. E. "The Languages Spoken by Jesus," **New Dimensions in New Testament Study,** eds. R. N. Longenecker and M. C. Tenney, Grand Rapids: Zondervan, 1974, pp. 127–43.

Metzger, B. M. "The Language of the New Testament," **Interpreter's Bible,** 12 vols. ed. G. A. Buttrick. Nashville: Abingdon, 1951, Vol. 7, pp. 43–59.

Thomas, D. W. "The Language of the Old Testament," **Record and Revelation,** ed. H. Wheeler Robinson. Oxford: Clarendon, 1938, pp. 374–402.

Chapter 4

God's Word Written

God's revelation to man was communicated in many instances in oral form. The prophets, for example, proclaimed their messages to their audiences orally, and in the case of the writing prophets, these messages were written down later. Our Lord's teachings also were given in oral form, and within a generation after his glorification the Evangelists put them in written form. Oral tradition can be transmitted from generation to generation in a fairly accurate manner, but it always leaves the door open to innovations, additions, or deletions. We can, therefore, be very grateful that the revelation of God in history was put into writing.

This would not have been possible, however, had writing not been developed by the time of Moses and later prophets. The invention of writing, therefore, was of the greatest significance for the history of the Bible. Indeed, without such an invention we could have no Bible. It is only proper, then, that we say something about the development of the alphabets and the materials with which God's revelation came to be recorded.

I. THE DEVELOPMENT OF WRITING

The first stage in the development of writing seems to have been the pictogram. There must have been, to begin with, many individual attempts at the picturization of people or objects. The pictogram is still used widely in modern advertising. TV commercials see to that! One might also call this "semantic" writing (*sema* in Greek means "sign"). It is extremely useful in road signs, especially when these are to be understood internationally. The pictogram communicates a message visually, not phonetically.

An extension of the pictogram is the ideogram, in which not objects but ideas are represented by the pictogram. The symbol of light might be the sun; the symbol of busyness, the bee; and so forth. Chinese script is an outstanding representative of ideographic writing. And we are not surprised to find that Chinese script makes use of an almost unlimited number of characters in order to overcome the ambiguities of the ideogram (the "sun," for example, could also symbolize the day, or heat, instead of light; the "bee" could symbolize honey, or sweetness, instead of busyness).

Once a symbol is used for a sound, we leave behind the universal system of communicating by written or drawn symbols and restrict ourselves to one language. Arabic numeral "4" is understood worldwide, but if I give it a phonetic value by saying "four," I have restricted its meaning to English (the German says *vier*, and the French *quatre*). The symbol of the bee might be understood universally, but when I say "bee," I speak only to those who know English. The picture of the sun is understood if the spoken word "sun" were not used. (It should be added, however, that even in English the phonogram "sun" could be misunderstood if it were not spoken in a given context, since phonetically "sun" is the same as "son.")

In alphabetic writing, such as we have in the English Bible, every sound is given a distinct symbol. This is true in theory; in practice English is one of the worst offenders—as foreigners who seek to learn English quickly discover. Why should "c" (as in car), "ck" (as in knock), "ch" (as in choir), and 'k'' (as in keep), all be pronounced as "k," when in fact there are four different symbols used for the "k" sound? Other examples might be given; nevertheless, the principle of alphabetic writing still holds: one symbol per sound. But who devised the alphabets in which the books of our Bible were written?

II. THE ALPHABET AND SCRIPT OF BIBLICAL BOOKS

Alphabetic writing in one form or another may have been the brainchild of a number of people living in different parts of the world. Egyptian scribes, for example, developed syllabic writing that comes close to alphabetic out of their hieroglyphic writing, but it never developed into an independent alphabet. It may be that the Egyptians, nevertheless, did put the idea of alphabetic writing into someone's head, for it is believed that the basic alphabet used by the biblical writers was devised by Syro-Palestinian Semites.

The word "alphabet" is nothing more than the combination of the names of the first two letters of the Greek alphabet, namely *alpha* and *beta*. Interestingly, these names are not entirely different from those of the Hebrew alphabet (*aleph* and *beth* are the Hebrew equivalents of the Greek *alpha* and *beta*, respectively). This suggests that our Hebrew and Greek alphabets have a common ancestor. Greek tradition attributes the Greek alphabet to the Phoenicians, and this is confirmed by the actual facts of the case.[1]

The Phoenician alphabet can be traced by inscriptions back to at least the eighteenth century B.C. It is called Phoenician because the Phoenicians were the first to use it, as far as is known, but it is the alphabet that before long came into use throughout Syria and Palestine and is known by the more general name of the North Semitic alphabet, to which also the Hebrew alphabet belongs.[2]

---

[1] F. F. Bruce, *The Books and the Parchments*, 3rd rev. ed. (Old Tappan: Revell, 1963), p. 18.
[2] Bruce, *Books and Parchments*, p. 22.

THE HEBREW ALPHABET
The Hebrew alphabet consists of 22 consonants. They are:

Form		Name	Transliteration	Numerical Value
	Finals			
א		'Aleph	'	1
ב	ב	Beth	b	2
ג	ג	Gimel	g	3
ד	ד	Daleth	d	4
ה		He	h	5
ו		Vav	w	6
ז		Zayin	z	7
ח		Heth	ch	8
ט		Teth	t	9
י		Yodh	y	10
כ כ	ך	Kaph	k	20
ל		Lamedh	l	30
מ מ	ם	Mem	m	40
נ נ	ן	Nun	n	50
ס		Samech	s	60
ע		'Ayin	'	70
פ פ	ף	Pe	p	80
צ	ץ	Tsadhe	ts	90
ק		Qoph	q	100
ר		Resh	r	200
ש ש		Sin, Shin	s, sh	300
ת ת		Tav	t	400

A. The Hebrew Alphabet

The Hebrew and Phoenician alphabets were actually two branches of a common stem, from which other scripts such as Moabite, Ammonite, and Edomite evolved.[3] All these language groups in Syria and Palestine used basically the same alphabet.

Through the excavations and research of the last century it is now possible to trace the Hebrew alphabet back to about 1000 B.C. There is, for example, the Gezer Calendar, a small soft stone tablet, discovered in 1908 at Gezer. It contains an enumeration of the agricultural seasons, and is as-signed to about 1000 B.C., the time of Saul or David.[4] The script is like that of Early Hebrew.

The Moabite Stone, discovered in 1868, has a long inscription that goes back to the ninth century B.C. It tells the story of King Mesha's conflict with Omri, Israel's king. This Moabite script is almost identical with the Hebrew script.

From the ninth or eighth century come the Samaritan Ostraca. These are inscribed potsherds, containing receipts and orders of various commodities such as oil, wine, and barley for the capital, Samaria. The script again is similar to biblical Hebrew.

[3]D. Diringer, "The Biblical Scripts," *Cambridge History of the Bible*, eds. P. R. Ackroyd and C. F. Evans (Cambridge: Cambridge University Press, 1970), Vol. 1, p. 13.
[4]Diringer, "The Biblical Scripts," p. 13.

In 1880 a lapidary inscription on the wall of the Siloam tunnel in Jerusalem was discovered. It dates back to the eighth century and tells the story of how Hezekiah's men diverted the waters of Gihon into the walled City of David. This inscription of six lines dates from about 700 B.C.

In 1953–58 the so-called Lachish Letters were discovered. These are inscribed ostraca that describe the condition of the Lachish garrison during the last months of Judah's struggle against Nebuchadnezzar. They give us an example of Hebrew in flowing handwriting from the sixth century. All these inscriptions have basically the same North Semitic alphabet, as do Hebrew, Phoenician, and other languages in that area.

A drawing of the Moabite stone. There are thirty-four lines of writing on the stone that tell of Moabite history and mention a conflict with Israel.

The Gezer Calendar is the earliest known Hebrew inscription. This agricultural calendar dates from the second half of the tenth century B.C.

Several biblical fragments, found among the Dead Sea Scrolls, are written in Early Hebrew script. They probably belong to the fourth or third century B.C. The Dead Sea Scrolls generally, however, are written in the Hebrew Square Script, which developed under the influence of Aramaic and represents a later form of the alphabet. Prior to this discovery, in 1947, relatively few examples of the Hebrew Square Script were known. There was, of course, the square script of the Nash Papyrus, of the second or first century B.C., but the other available manuscripts of the Hebrew OT belong to the ninth or tenth century A.D.—all written in the square script. With the discovery of the Dead Sea Scrolls it has become clear that before the Christian era the earlier He-

The Siloam Inscription. It reads: "(Behold) the excavation. Now this is the history of the excavation. While the workmen were still lifting up the ax, each toward his neighbor, and while three cubits still remained to (cut through, each heard) the voice of the other who called to his neighbor since there was an excess in the rock on the right hand and on (the left). And on the day of the excavation the workmen struck, each to meet his neighbor, ax against ax, and there flowed the waters from the spring to the pool for a thousand two hundred cubits; and . . . of a cubit was the height of the rock over the heads of the workmen."

brew script had changed to the "Square Script"—so-called because of the box-like form of the Hebrew letters.

The Hebrew alphabet consists of twenty-two ancient Semitic letters, all of them consonants (four of them were also used to represent vowels). As time went on, and familiarity with biblical Hebrew declined among the Jews, they also invented vowel signs, but this invention falls into the Christian era and we will have occasion to say more about that later. At this point we are simply underscoring the fact that the Hebrew script in which the OT books were originally written was the North Semitic alphabet, sometimes loosely called Phoenician, which was employed by other Semitic languages in Syria and Palestine.

B. The Greek Alphabet

The Greek tradition that the seafaring Phoenicians gave them their alphabet is generally accepted as a historical fact. The North Semitic origin of the Greek alphabet can be seen from the following observations: (1) the shapes of nearly all the early Greek letters clearly recall their Semitic origin; (2) the phonetic value of the majority of the early Greek letters was the same as that of the Semitic; (3) the order of the Greek letters corresponds rather closely to the other of the Semitic letters; (4) the direction of writing in early Greek was from right to left as in the Semitic; and (5) the Greek letter names are meaningless in Greek, while some of their Semitic equivalents are

ת	ש	ר	ק	צ	פ	ע	ס	נ	מ	ל	כ	י	ט	ח	ז	ו	ה	ד	ג	ב	א	
																						1
																						2
																						3
																						4
																						5
																						6
																						7
																						8
																						9
																						10
																						11
																						12
																						13

A comparison of early Aramaic, Phoenician, and Hebrew scripts. The top line shows the modern Hebrew alphabet, and the lines under it show the alphabet as found on the following inscriptions and scrolls. (1) Ahiram sarcophagus, c. 1000 B.C., Phoenician; (2) Gezer Calendar, late tenth century B.C., Hebrew (3) Mesha stele, mid-ninth century B.C., Moabite; (4) Samaria ostraca, eighth century B.C., Hebrew; (5) Bar-Rekub stele, late eighth century B.C., Aramaic; (6) Siloam inscription, c. 700 B.C., Hebrew; (7) Mezad Hashavyahu ostracon, late seventh century B.C., Hebrew; (8) Saqqara papyrus, c. 600 B.C., Aramaic; (9) Hebrew seals, late seventh—early sixth century B.C.; (1) Lachish ostraca, early sixth century B.C., Hebrew; (11) Elephantine papyrus, late fifth century B.C., Aramaic; (12) Eshmun'azor inscription, fifth century B.C., Phoenician; (13) Exodus scroll fragment, second century B.C., Paleo-Hebrew.

THE GREEK ALPHABET

	Capital	Minuscule	Name of letter	Equivalent in Roman script	Approximate Pronunciation
1	A	α	Alpha	a	father
2	B	β	Beta	b	ball
3	Γ	γ	Gamma	g	gone
4	Δ	δ	Delta	d	dog
5	E	ε	Epsilon	e	met
6	Z	ζ	Zeta	z	adze
7	H	η	Eta	ē	they
8	Θ	θ	Theta	th	throne
9	I	ι	Iota	i	fit, machine
10	K	κ	Kappa	k	king
11	Λ	λ	Lambda	l	long
12	M	μ	Mu	m	men
13	N	ν	Nu	n	new
14	Ξ	ξ	Xi	x	likes, asks
15	O	ο	Omicron	o	log
16	Π	π	Pi	p	pea
17	P	ρ	Rho	r	her
18	Σ	σ: final ς	Sigma	s	sign
19	T	τ	Tau	t	ten
20	Y	υ	Upsilon	y	new (German "ü")
21	Φ	φ	Phi	ph	phone
22	X	χ	Chi	ch	Bach (the composer)
23	Ψ	ψ	Psi	ps	lips
24	Ω	ω	Omega	ō	only

Semitic words[5] (*beth*, the second letter of the alphabet, means "house"). While Greek is not a Semitic language, the alphabet of this European tongue is basically North Semitic.

There has been some debate over when the Greeks took over this Semitic alphabet. Perhaps we are safe in putting the date about 1000 B.C. The Greeks did not invent the alphabet, but they made some changes after they took it over. Like the Semitic scripts, earliest Greek was written from right to left. After about 500 B.C., however, the Greeks wrote from left to right, the way we do. There was, interestingly, an intermediate period in which they wrote in *boustrophedon* fashion (*bous-trophedon* means literally, "as the oxen turns," when plowing the field, alternating the rows from right to left, then left to right).

After receiving it through the Phoenicians, there arose some diversity in the Greek alphabet, but by the late fifth century B.C. the Ionic Greek alphabet of twenty-four letters prevailed—final acceptance coming by edict. In contrast to the consonantal alphabet of the Semitic parent script, the Greek alphabet had vowel letters as well. It should be mentioned also that in addition to the Greek uncial script, in which many of the biblical books were originally written, there was also the flowing hand-

[5]Diringer, "The Biblical Scripts," pp. 18–19.

writing known as cursive.

Through its descendants in western Europe (the Etruscan and Latin alphabets) and in eastern Europe (the Cyrillic alphabet), the Greek alphabet became the progenitor of all European alphabets that have spread all over the world.[6] And since most of us read our Bibles in English, a word should be added about the Latin alphabet.

C. The Latin Alphabet

The link between the Greek and the Latin alphabet that we use is the Etruscan. Greek colonists brought the Greek script to Italy where it was adopted by the Etruscans, and from them it was adopted by Latin speakers. And just as the Greeks had to adapt the Phoenician alphabet (Greek, for example, has no letter for the Semitic "j"), so the Greek script was adapted to Latin (Latin has no equivalent for the Greek *zeta*). Again, there were different forms of Latin script, and English to this day distinguishes between capital and lower-case letters, and between print and flowing handwriting.

Without a script we could not have had a Bible. Fortunately the Bible, both Old and New Testament, was written in a relatively simple alphabetic script. Had the biblical books been written in hieroglyphics they would be accessible to only a few professionals, but with Bibles available in Hebrew, Greek, and above all, in Latin scripts, every schoolboy or girl may read the Bible.

However, a written language is of little use without materials to write on. In God's good providence such materials were at hand when God's Word came to be written.

III. WRITING MATERIALS

A great variety of materials have been used by man for the keeping of records and memoranda. Stone, leaves, bark, skins, wood, metals, baked clay, potsherds, and papyrus have at one time or another served as writing materials. Some of these did not prove satisfactory in the long run; others were used for thousands of years until they, too, were eventually replaced by paper. We are interested here primarily in those materials on which the biblical books were written originally and on which they were later transcribed.

A. Stone

Natural surfaces of rock, the walls of caves and cliffs, offered the most obvious opportunities for the early attempts at pictographs. Later, monumental inscriptions were made. For example, there is the trilingual inscription of Darius the Great, at Behistun, in modern Iran. It was deciphered in the mid-nineteenth century and unlocked the secrets of cuneiform.[7] We have already mentioned the Moabite Stone. There is also the famous Rosetta Stone, discovered in Egypt in 1799, written in three scripts (hieroglyphic, demotic, and Greek).

As far as the OT is concerned, we read only of the Decalogue being written on tables of stone. Obviously there are severe practical limitations to writing on stone.

B. Clay Tablets

Clay tablets were very popular in the ancient Near East, for they were cheap

---

[6]Diringer, "The Biblical Scripts," p. 20.

[7]F. C. Putman, "Key Finds in Archaeology," *Eternity* Vol. 30 (Oct. 1979), p. 35.

and durable. In cuneiform inscriptions (from *cuneus*, meaning "wedge") characters were jabbed rather than drawn upon tablets with a stylus when the clay was still soft. The tablets were then dried or baked and stored on shelves or in boxes. Thousands of such tablets have been unearthed by the archaeologists. At Boghaz-koy (Turkey) 10,000 clay tablets from the ancient Hittite capital were found in 1906. At Nuzi 20,000 clay tablets that have helped to illuminate the patriarchal period were unearthed in 1925. In 1929 the discovery of the Ras Shamra texts in northern Syria added greatly to our understanding of Canaanite culture. Then there are the 22,000 tablets discovered in 1936 at Mari, which cast light on Abraham's journey from Ur to Haran. More recently, in 1974, some 16,000 tablets were unearthed at Ebla in northern Syria, and these promise to open up even further the culture of the Near East between the third and second millennia B.C.

It has at times been suggested that the ten *toledoth* (generations, histories) of Genesis were originally recorded on clay tablets, but that is not certain. The writing tablet, however, is mentioned in Isaiah 30:8 and in Habakkuk 2:2, but it is more likely that a wooden tablet is meant.

C. Wooden Tablets

It is well known that wooden tablets were in use in ancient times. In Greco-Roman times the wax-covered *tabellae* were in common use, sometimes bound together in book form. The Israeli archaeologist, Dr. Yadin,

Clay tablets were widely used for writing in the ancient Near East. This tablet is the eleventh Tablet of the Assyrian version of the Epic of Gilgamesh. It records the Babylonian version of the Flood.

found slats of wood with writing on them in the caves at Murabba'at, at the Dead Sea, dating from the second Jewish revolt (A.D. 130). In Ezekiel 37:15 it is reported that the prophet was told to "take a stick of wood and write on it."

D. Papyrus

We already described the preparations of writing material from this reed plant when we traced the origins of our word for "Bible." It is obvious from such texts as Job 8:11 and Isaiah 18:2 that papyrus was known to the ancient biblical writers. Papyrus as writing material was in use in Egypt as early as the third millennium B.C. and continued to be used well into the first millennium A.D.[8]

Unfortunately we have next to no OT

[8]J. C. Trever, "Papyrus," *Interpreter's Dictionary of the Bible*, ed. G. Buttrick (Nashville: Abingdon, 1962), Vol. 3, p. 649.

papyrus manuscripts; we do have a goodly number of NT papyri. Although papyrus was cheaper than leather it had certain disadvantages. (1) It was not as readily available outside of Egypt; (2) there was the danger of punching it while writing; (3) it was more susceptible to damage from moisture; and (4) when it dried out it became highly fragile.

The sands of Egypt, however, have proved to be the best "library" for papyrus, and great quantities of mostly nonbiblical papyri have been discovered in the last hundred years. Although writings on papyrus were known earlier, the search for papyri began in earnest only about 1870, and soon the libraries of Vienna, Berlin, Paris, and London were procuring papyrus manuscripts. (Some countries got into the game somewhat later.) As recently as 1945 a large jar with forty-nine documents of the Gospel of Thomas were discovered at Nag Hammadi, in Egypt.

These nonbiblical papyri opened up a new era of lexicography and also cast new light on ancient cultures. Among them are bills, tax receipts, and many personal letters. For example, we have a letter of a husband to his pregnant wife, advising her that should she bear a son she is to bring him up; if it should be a girl to do away with her by exposure.[9] We have deeds of divorce, last wills and testaments, marriage contracts, death notices, magical papyri, and so forth.

These discoveries made it clear that the Greek of the NT was not all that different from the Koine spoken elsewhere in the world. In many instances they opened up new meanings of the Greek words in the NT. Adolf Deissmann, in *Light from the Ancient East*, led the way in demonstrating the extreme usefulness of the secular papyri for understanding the Greek of the NT.

It has been the good fortune of biblical scholars to discover also some important papyrus manuscripts of the NT, and we will have more to say about these when we come to discuss the text of the NT.

E. Parchment

Whereas papyrus is writing material made from a plant, parchment is made from animal skins. The procedure of tanning animal skins was known from ancient times, but in the preparation of parchment more was involved than tanning. The skin was soaked in limewater and the hair on one side and the flesh on the other was scraped off. The skin was then stretched, dried, and smoothed with pumice.[10]

Parchment was known as early as 3000 B.C. (as was papyrus), and some of the OT books may have been written on parchment originally. Whether the scroll that King Jehoiakim cut in pieces and burned (Jer. 36) was of papyrus or leather is difficult to determine. The most likely guess would be papyrus.[11] Most of the biblical manuscripts in the Dead Sea Scrolls are of leather. Also, we are informed by the *Letter of Aristeas* (second century

---

[9]C. K. Barrett, *The New Testament Background: Selected Documents* (New York: Harper and Row, 1961), p. 38.

[10]J. Finegan, *Encountering New Testament Manuscripts* (Grand Rapids: Eerdmans, 1974), p. 25.

[11]I. M. Price, *The Ancestry of Our English Bible*, 3rd ed., revised by W. A. Irwin and Allen P. Wikgren (New York: Harper and Row, 1956), p. 17.

B.C.) that the scrolls of the Law which were brought from Jerusalem to Alexandria to be translated into Greek were leather.

The word "parchment" comes from the name of the city of Pergamum in Asia Minor. Pliny tells a story of King Eumenes of Pergamum who wanted to outshine the Egyptian Ptolemy by establishing a better library than Egypt could boast. Ptolemy V, of Egypt, then imposed an embargo on the export of papyrus from Egypt, to handicap the development of the library at Pergamum. To make up for the shortage of papyrus, as the story goes, parchment was invented at Pergamum. Perhaps all the story does is show the preeminence of Pergamum in developing parchment (called *pergamene* in Greek, *Pergament* in German).

Another Greek word used for parchment was *diphthera* (meaning "tanned leather"); in Latin, however, the word is *membrana* (from which we derive the English "membrane"). Greek then borrowed this Latin word, and Paul asks Timothy to bring with him "the books and the *membrana* (parchments)" (2 Tim. 4:13). Refined parchment is called vellum (from the Latin word for "calf," our "veal").

Parchment had the advantage that it was more durable than papyrus. Also, one could more readily make erasures. In fact we have manuscripts which are called palimpsests, in which the original text has been erased and a new text written over it.

To begin with, parchment manuscripts were in the form of scrolls (as were those of papyrus), but eventually the parchment codex prevailed over the scroll. In the codex form both sides of the parchment page could be used for writing, and so in the end parchment won out over papyrus. Most of our manuscripts of the OT, as well as of the NT, are parchment codices.

F. Ostraca

The use of pieces of broken and discarded pottery as writing material was widespread in the ancient world. They were readily available, inexpensive, and could easily be written on with pen and ink. Potsherds are mentioned in the OT (Job 2:8; Ps. 22:15; Isa. 30:14), but no reference is made to their use for writing. Greek ostraca, with portions of our Gospels inscribed on them, have been found in Upper Egypt. Single ostraca may have been used as amulets, but they also served poor Christians as a kind of "Bible."[12]

As time went on all earlier writing materials were superseded by paper. Paper made its way from the East across Central Asia to Egypt about A.D. 900. Here it replaced papyrus, as can be seen from letters in which the writer apologizes for using papyrus, when it would be more stylish to use paper. Papyrus, of course, gave the name "paper" to the new writing material.

Evidently because paper came to Europe from Mohammedan sources, it lay under the displeasure of the church at first. For some time it could be used only for writings that were of little significance. But with the development of printing in the fifteenth century, paper was assured of victory over parchment and papyrus. The first Bible ever to be printed, Gutenberg's

---

[12]A. Deissmann, *Light from the Ancient East* (Sevenoaks, England: Hodder and Stoughton, 1910), pp. 41–52.

Latin Vulgate, was printed partly on parchment and partly on paper.

A writer needs not only materials to write on, but also instruments to write with. The instrument is determined largely by the writing material. For inscriptions on stone or metal, a chisel would be required. Incisions on soft clay would call for a stylus, either of wood, bone, or metal. The OT speaks of an iron tool (Job 19:24; Jer. 17:1). For writing with ink on papyrus, leather, parchment, wooden tablets, or ostraca, reed pens were used (see Jer. 8:8). About the third century B.C. Greek writers in Egypt devised a new type of pen by splitting the point of a reed to form a nib. This true pen is called a *kalamos* ("reed") in Greek, and is mentioned in 3 John 13.

Black ink was made from carbon in the form of soot mixed with a thin solution of gum. This was dried into cakes and then moistened with water for use. The NT word for ink, *melas*, means "black" (2 Cor. 3:3; 2 John 12; 3 John 13). Red ink was also used, especially for headings (our word "rubric" comes from the Latin word *ruber*, meaning "red").

A penknife was used for sharpening pens (Jer. 36:23). A straight edge for ruling lines, pumice stone for smoothing papyrus, and a sponge for making erasures were all part of a writer's equipment.[13]

God in his infinite mercy condescended to make use of such very earthy materials to bestow on us the greatest literary treasure of human history: God's Word written.

SUGGESTED READING

Black, M. "Language and Script," **Cambridge History of the Bible,** eds. P. R. Ackroyd and C. F. Evans. *Cambridge: Cambridge University Press, 1970, Vol. 1, pp. 1–29.*

Bruce, F. F. **The Books and the Parchments,** *3rd rev. ed. Old Tappan: Revell, 1963. See "The Bible and the Alphabet," pp. 15–32.*

Kenyon, F. G. **Our Bible and the Ancient Manuscripts,** *rev. ed. New York: Harper and Brothers, 1958. See "Ancient Books and Writing," pp. 19–46.*

Lambin, T. O. "Alphabet," **Interpreter's Dictionary of the Bible,** *4 vols. ed. G. A. Buttrick. Nashville: Abingdon, 1962, Vol. 1, pp. 89–96.*

Pritchard, J. B., ed. **Ancient Near Eastern Texts Relating to the Old Testament.** *Princeton: Princeton University Press, 1950.*

Snaith, N. H. "The Language of the Old Testament," **Interpreter's Bible,** *12 vols. ed. G. A. Buttrick. Nashville: Abingdon, 1951, Vol. 7, pp. 43–59.*

---

[13]R. J. Williams, "Writing," *Interpreter's Dictionary of the Bible,* ed. G. Buttrick (Nashville: Abingdon, 1962), Vol. 4, p. 919.

Chapter 5

The Old Testament Canon

Anyone who converses with Roman Catholics or with believers from the Orthodox tradition knows that the question of canon is still very much alive. The Protestant canon does not have all the books that are included in the official Bibles of the Roman Catholic and the Orthodox churches. Our topic, therefore, is not simply of antiquarian interest, but is very close to everyday life.

When we speak of the OT canon we are not talking about an instrument of war (spelled "cannon"), but rather about the collection of the books of the OT. The word "canon" is originally a Semitic word (*qaneh* in Hebrew), meaning "reed" or "stalk" (Job 40:21; 1 Kings 14:15). The Greeks took over this Semitic word (*kanon* in Greek), and through the Greek and the Latin (*canna*) it comes into English as "canon."

From its original meaning of "reed," "canon" comes to denote a rule, a measuring stick or an instrument with which to make straight lines. Metaphorically it is then used for any standard, whether of art, music, literature, or morals. Paul wishes those "who follow this rule" (*kanon*) the blessings of God (Gal. 6:16). Some of the early Fathers spoke of "the rule of faith" or the "canon of truth," meaning the standard, authoritative teaching by which all doctrines were measured. Since Christians held the Scriptures to be the final authority for faith and practice, Scriptures were said to be "canonical."

However, the word "canon" was used also for a list or index (a list of saints, for example, who have been "canonized"). The canon of Scripture is the list of books that belong to the Holy Scriptures and that are reckoned as supremely authoritative for belief and conduct.[1]

The formation of the Old and New Testament books into the biblical canon took place over a long period of time. No ancient writer left us an ac-

[1]F. F. Bruce, *The Book and the Parchments*, 3rd rev. ed. (Old Tappan: Revell, 1963), p. 95.

count of the individual steps in this long process of collecting and forming these books into what we now call the Bible, although we have pointers here and there. Before we can speak about the collecting of the biblical books, we must make a few comments on their production.

I. THE WRITING OF THE BOOKS

It should be said at the outset that the books of the OT were written at different times and under various circumstances. We have the good fortune of having at least one description in the OT itself of how a book came to be written. Jeremiah had given his messages orally and decided, then, that he would impress them on the people by having them recorded. His faithful scribe, Baruch, took them down from dictation (Jer. 36).

Baruch then took the finished scroll to the royal house and read Jeremiah's messages in the presence of King Jehoiakim, who objected to the prophet's words and cut the scroll into pieces and burned them in the fire. Naturally Jeremiah was disappointed, but God directed him to take another scroll and write the former words again. Baruch recorded them carefully. But what is significant for us at this point is that the second scroll contained much more than the first. We read, "and many similar words were added to them" (Jer. 36:32). Obviously this case is unique, and we must allow for infinite variety in the manner in which the biblical books were initially composed.

Turning to the books of the OT as a whole, we begin with the Torah. Traditionally the first five books of our Bible are assigned to Moses. Several times we are informed that Moses "wrote" (Exod. 17:14; 34:28). For the material recorded in Genesis, Moses would have had to depend on oral traditions, handed down from generation to generation. Whether the author of Genesis made use of any written documents is hard to say. The record of the creation of the world and of human life must have been given by divine revelation, for no one was present when these events took place. As for the materials for the books of Exodus, Leviticus, Numbers, and Deuteronomy, no one would have been better suited than Moses to give us these accounts. This does not mean, however, that Moses also wrote the account of his own death in the last chapter of Deuteronomy; it was added, no doubt, by another writer. The divine inspiration of the Pentateuch does not rule out the participation of other authors, or of later editors, in the production of the Pentateuch.

Joshua was Moses' successor, and his name became attached to the Book of Joshua since he is the central character in the book. How much of the book Joshua himself may have written is not known. Certain parts claim to have been written by him (see 24:26). Clearly someone else wrote the account of Joshua's death (chap. 24).

The Book of Judges describes the period between the death of Joshua and the rise of Samuel, and gets its title from the "judges" who guided the fortunes of Israel at this time. It was possibly composed in the early days of the monarchy.

Ruth gives us a picture of life during this rather turbulent period of the judges, but again, as in the case of the Book of Judges, we do not really know who wrote the book. The Talmud attributes both Judges and Ruth to Samuel.[2] Since, however, David is already well known (Ruth 4:22), Judges and Ruth must be from a later period.

The Talmud also attributes the two books of Samuel to the prophet Samuel, but the report of his death (1 Sam. 25:1), and some of the events mentioned in the books, demand a later date. The author, no doubt, made use of previously written documents. The books cover the period from the birth of Samuel to the end of the reigns of Saul and David, Israel's first two kings.

The two books of Kings describe the reign of Solomon over the united kingdom of Israel, as well as the period of the divided monarchy until the end of both kingdoms. The author may have been a contemporary of Jeremiah, but the books are anonymous.

The two books of Chronicles cover a much wider period than the books of Kings. The narrative begins with the death of Saul (chap. 10) and continues to the time of the exile. The last verses (2 Chron. 36:22–23) give the decree of Cyrus for the return of the captives to Judah. Chronicles can, therefore, not have been written until after the Babylonian captivity.

Ezra begins where Chronicles ends and tells the story of the return of the exiles, the rebuilding of the temple and the restoration of true worship. The book is named after its principal character. Some parts of the book (see Ezra 7) seem to come from Ezra's own hand, for they were written in the first person. This holds also for the Book of Nehemiah, which forms one book with Ezra in the Hebrew canon. Both Ezra and Nehemiah are obviously postexilic.

Esther belongs to the Persian period and is also postexilic. Its author is unknown. The book casts light on Israel's experiences in exile.

Job is a majestic drama dealing with the timeless problem of human suffering. The chief character of the book, from whom the book derives its name, seems to have lived in Patriarchal times. It is hard to say who the author of the book is and when the book was composed.

The Psalms were a sort of hymnal for Israel. About half of them are attributed to David, but most of the others are anonymous. Their dates probably stretch from the time of David to the exile.[3]

Proverbs is a collection of wisdom sayings, gathered over a long period of time. Some were written by Solomon and copied out by scribes of Hezekiah (25:1) some two hundred years later. The last two chapters are attributed respectively to Agur and King Lemuel.

Ecclesiastes is credited to "son of David, king in Jerusalem" (1:1), but not necessarily to Solomon. Edward Young thinks a postexilic author put these words into the mouth of Solomon. The message of the "preacher" is that life without God is without meaning.[4]

Song of Songs is also attributed to Solomon (1:1), who describes the joys of marital love in typical Oriental fashion.

The rest of the OT consists of the prophetic books. The ministry of Isaiah to the people of Judah is dated from about 740 to 700 B.C. Micah, a fel-

---

[2] *Baba Bathra*, 14b.

[2] R. Earle, *How We Got the Bible* (Kansas City: Beacon Hill, 1971), p. 23.

[3] E. J. Young, *An Introduction to the Old Testament* (Grand Rapids: Eerdmans, 1949), p. 340.

low countryman, prophesied about the same time. A contemporary of Isaiah and Micah was Hosea (750–636 B.C.), who witnessed to the Kingdom of Israel. Amos may be the earliest of the writing prophets. His book may be dated about 760 B.C. These are the four eighth-century prophets. Some would include Joel, Obadiah, and Jonah in this period also.

Jeremiah prophesied during the last forty years of the Southern Kingdom (626–586 B.C.). The Book of Lamentations is attributed to him also.

Ezekiel was the Lord's prophet to his people in the Babylonian captivity (593–586 B.C.). Like Ezekiel, Daniel prophesied in Babylonia (606–536 B.C.). Daniel is largely an apocalyptic book, as are parts of Ezekiel.

Obadiah, possibly an eighth-century prophet, predicts the destruction of Edom and the restoration of Israel. Jonah was called to minister during the reign of Jeroboam II (787–747 B.C.), and became an unwilling messenger to the Assyrian city of Nineveh. Nahum is dated between 663 and 612 B.C. He predicted the destruction of Nineveh, Israel's ancient foe. About 603 B.C. Habakkuk foretold the coming punishment of Judah by the Babylonians. Zephaniah (c. 625 B.C.) blasts the idolatry of Judah.

In the postexilic period, Haggai and Zechariah (520 B.C.) encourage the reestablished Jewish community to rebuild the temple and to walk in the ways of Yahweh. Malachi (c. 450 B.C.) the last of the prophets, predicts a new day for God's people.

Apparently, by the fifth century B.C., all the books of the OT had been writ-ten. The question now is: what happened to these books once they were published?

II. THE PRESENCE OF THE BOOKS

There are references in the OT suggesting that these sacred writings were stored in Israel's sanctuary. The books of Moses, for example, were stored alongside the ark of the covenant (Deut. 31:24–26). We read also of Joshua's words being written and laid up in the sanctuary (Josh. 24:26). Samuel wrote on the rights and duties of kingship and laid the book up "before the Lord" (1 Sam. 10:25). In the days of Josiah a revival broke out when the Law of Moses was found in the temple as it was being repaired (2 Kings 22–23). The first reference to "the Scriptures" as a collection of books that were considered canonical seems to be in Daniel 9:2. However, there are references in other books of the OT to earlier writings. The Book of the Law of Moses, for example, is appealed to again and again in the OT, beginning with Joshua 1:8. The implication is that the books of the Pentateuch were known and held in high regard. Daniel affirms the prophecies of Jeremiah (Dan. 9:2). Ezekiel makes reference to Noah, Daniel, and Job (14:14, 20), although this may have little to do with the books of Job or Daniel as such. "From the fact that one prophet sometimes quotes another it is clear that they ascribed authority to their predecessors."[5]

However, not every book referred to in the OT became part of the biblical canon. There is reference, for example,

---

[5]H. H. Ridderbos, "Canon of the Old Testament," *The New Bible Dictionary*, ed. J. D. Douglas (Grand Rapids: Eerdmans, 1962), p. 188.

to the Book of Yashar (Josh. 10:13), or the Book of the Wars of Yahweh (Num. 21:14), or the Chronicles of the Kings of Israel (2 Chron. 33:18f.), which were not included in the sacred Scriptures. Obviously, then, a selection had to be made.

The question is, what determined whether a book was canonical or not? Evidently those books that possessed special authority were included in the canon, others were not. It was not the inclusion of books in the sacred canon that made them authoritative, but rather, those that had the stamp of divine authority on them in the first place were eventually incorporated in the collection.[6]

Some words of God spoken to Israel by his servants were recognized as authoritative even before they were part of the sacred collection. For example, when Moses read the "book of the covenant" to Israel they recognized that God was speaking to them and promised to do everything he commanded (Exod. 24:7). On the other hand, even after such messages from God had been recorded they were, at times, totally ignored by Israel.

We have at least one story of how the people began to take God's written Word seriously once more, after a time of neglect. The spiritual revival in the days of Josiah came about through the discovery and the reading of the Law in the hearing of the people (2 Kings 22–23).

The exile also seems to have had a profound effect on Israel's regard for the sacred books because the people saw that the words of the prophets had been fulfilled. No doubt this new focus on the Scriptures, when the temple lay in ruins and the land was lost, accelerated the collection and study of the writings. "It was because of the cataclysmic event of the destruction of the First Temple that what we now know as the Law and the Prophets first came to be collected and galvanized into the shape they now have."[7] On their return to Judea we find Ezra, with others, making a deep impact on the people by reading the Book of the Law to them (Neh. 8).

We see, then, that although the OT does not tell us how and when the sacred books were collected into a canon of Scripture, there are many references to the presence of these books in the life and worship of Israel. No doubt it was because these books continued to be the voice of the living God to Israel that they were collected into a corpus.

The first known list of OT books from Christian circles was drawn up by Melito, Bishop of Sardis, about A.D. 170.[8] The Book of Esther is missing, but that may be because he got his information from Syriac informants (the Syriac Church did not have Esther in its canon).[9]

III. THE COLLECTION OF THE BOOKS

From the fourth century B.C. onwards it was the conviction of the Jews that the voice of God had ceased to speak directly. This view is already reflected in passages such as Zechariah 13:3, "And if anyone still

---

[6]Bruce, *Book and Parchments*, p. 95.
[7]J. A. Sanders, *Torah and Canon* (Philadelphia: Fortress, 1972), p. 6.
[8]Eusebius, *Ecclesiastical History*, 26.
[9]Bruce, *Book and Parchments*, p. 100.

prophesies, his father and mother, to whom he was born, will say to him, 'You must die, because you have told lies in the LORD's name.' When he prophesies, his own parents will stab him." It is expressed also by Jewish writers in the intertestamental period. In 1 Maccabees 14:41 we read of Simon who is made leader and priest "until a trustworthy prophet should rise," and earlier he speaks of the sorrow in Israel such "as there has not been since the prophets ceased to appear to them." "The prophets have fallen asleep," complains the writer of 2 Baruch (85:3). Books that were written after the prophetic period had closed were thought of as lying outside the realm of Holy Scripture.

Although we have no accurate information, there are a number of references to the fact that the final collection of the sacred writings was made in the postexilic period.

The Prologue to Ecclesiasticus, written c. 131 B.C., refers to the great things handed down—the writings of the Law and the prophets and of others who have followed in their steps. From this we can gather that the tripartite division of the biblical books was by then established.

In 2 Maccabees 2:13 (c. 165 B.C.), we read that Nehemiah founded a library and collected books about the kings and prophets and the writings of David. At best this points to the fact that the postexilic community, under the leadership of Ezra and Nehemiah, took a great interest in the collection of sacred books. Ezra was the forerunner of a great scribal movement and it would not be stretching the truth if we said that he played an important role in the collection, transcription, study, and teaching of the Scriptures.

It can be seen that all the books of the OT had been collected in pre-Christian times from the fact that the Alexandrian Jews made a Greek translation of the Hebrew OT, known as the Septuagint, and they began this project about 250 B.C. The NT also witnesses to the completed collection of the OT books. Jesus, for example, spoke of "the Law, the Prophets and the Psalms" (Luke 24:44)—again the three divisions of the OT canon. Moreover, he also used the expression: "from the blood of Abel to the blood of Zechariah, who was killed between the altar and the sanctuary" (Luke 11:51). Since the death of Zechariah is mentioned in 2 Chronicles 24:21, this would be like saying, "from Genesis to Malachi."

In the apocryphal book of 4 Ezra (also called 2 Esdras) there is a fictional account of the work of Ezra (chap. 14). In Ezra's time the Law had been lost, and Ezra was called to restore it. For forty days and forty nights he dictated nonstop to five men, producing ninety-four books. Then the Most High said to him: "Make public the twenty-four books that you wrote first and let the worthy and unworthy read them; but keep the seventy that were written last, in order to give them to the wise among your people" (14:44–46). Fourth Ezra was written in the first century A.D. and clearly witnesses to a twenty-four book canon.

Josephus, writing about A.D. 100, says that the Jews, unlike the Greeks who have vast numbers of conflicting and mutually contradictory books, have only twenty-two (he combined Ruth and Judges, Jeremiah and Lamentations). After listing the sacred books he adds: "For although so great an interval of time (since they were written) has now passed, not a soul has ventured either to add or to remove or to alter a syllable; and it is the instinct of every Jew from the day of his birth to consider these books as the teaching of God, to abide by them, and, if need be, cheerfully to lay down his life for them."[10]

With the destruction of Jerusalem in A.D. 70 the Jews experienced a disaster from which they never really recovered. And just as the prophetic writings had taken on new significance at the time of the exile, so now again the survivors of the debacle of A.D. 70 were driven to the Word of God. The Jews became a people of the book. Harrison writes: "In all its essentials the canon was most probably complete by about 300 B.C., and while discussions concerning certain component parts was continued well into the Christian era, the substance of the canon as it existed a century and a half after the time of Ezra and Nehemiah remained unaffected by these controversies."[11]

Shortly after the destruction of Jerusalem, Jochanan ben Zakkai got permission from the Romans to convene a council of rabbis at Jamnia (also called Jabneh), near Jaffa, in A.D. 90. At this council vigorous debates took place on the question of the canonicity of certain books. It would be overstating the case if we said that this council fixed the limits of the Hebrew canon, but it raised questions about the presence of certain books in the canon. Books that the council refused to admit to the canon had not been there in the first place. The primary concern of the council was the right of certain

books to remain in the canon, not the acceptance of new books.

IV. THE CANONICITY OF THE BOOKS

Apparently the council of Jamnia never raised any questions about the Law. There were questions, however, about the propriety of the Book of Jonah in the Hebrew canon. Here was a book that had to do with God's concern for the salvation of a heathen people, the wicked Assyrians—a message hard for postexilic Judaism to swallow. Also, the council expressed concerns about Ezekiel. First of all, there were those chapters that described the chariot of God (the *Merkaba*) with animal images. Some rabbis forbade these passages as synagogue lessons; others forbade their translation into Aramaic; still others did not wish men under thirty to read these chapters (Ezekiel evidently got this vision at thirty years of age). But there was also a problem with the prescriptions for temple worship in Ezekiel 40–48 that did not jibe with those of the Pentateuch, and called for an explanation. There is a story of how Hananja ben Hiskia ben Goran, after long debates on Ezekiel, used up three hundred pots of oil for his night lamp and finally answered the questions regarding Ezekiel.[12]

There were more questions about books in the third division of the canon, the Writings. In the case of Proverbs some seeming contradictions had to be solved. "Do not answer a fool according to his folly," is the advice of the writer in one verse (26:4),

---

[10]*Contra Apion*, 18.

[11]R. K. Harrison, *Introduction to the Old Testament* (Grand Rapids: Eerdmans, 1969), p. 286.

[12]G. F. Moore, *Judaism*, 4 vols. (Cambridge: Harvard University Press, 1927–39), Vol. 1, pp. 238ff.

and "answer a fool according to his folly" in the next (26:5).

Some rabbis evidently had suspicions about the Book of Esther. Here was a book that did not mention the name of God. Also, this book tells of how the Feast of Purim began—a feast that had no warrant in the Law.

The weary pessimism of Ecclesiastes also raised questions about the book. The Song of Songs seemed just a bit too explicit about sexual love. Origen, in his introduction to his commentary on the Song of Songs mentions the Jewish custom of withholding this book (and some sections of other books as well) from those who had not yet reached the age of maturity.

It should be underscored, however, that while questions about these books were raised, there was no thought of removing them from the canon. The discussions at Jamnia dealt not so much "with acceptance of certain writings into the Canon, but rather with their right to remain there."[13]

It bears repeating that no human authority and no council of rabbis ever made an OT book authoritative. These books were inspired by God and had the stamp of authority on them from the beginning. Through long usage in the Jewish community their authority was recognized, and in due time they were added to the collection of canonical books.

In one sense the question of the canon of the OT is easier to answer than that of the NT, for our Lord and his apostles by their high view of the books of the OT endorsed these books as authentic words of God. And when Paul claimed that "all Scripture is God-breathed" (2 Tim. 3:16), he had supremely the OT books in mind. We can do no less than join him in this affirmation.

SUGGESTED READING

Bruce, F. F. **The Books and the Parchments,** 3rd rev. ed. Old Tappan: Revell, 1963. See "The Canon of Scripture," pp. 95–113.

Geisler, N. L. and Nix, W. E. **From God to Us.** Chicago: Moody, 1974. See "The Development of the Old Testament Canon," pp. 74–85.

Harrison, R. K. Introduction to the Old Testament. Grand Rapids: Eerdmans, 1969. See "The Old Testament Text and Canon," pp. 260–88.

Young, E. J. "The Canon of the Old Testament," **Revelation and the Bible,** ed. C. F. H. Henry (Grand Rapids: Baker, 1958), pp. 153–68.

---

[13]A. Bentzen, *Introduction to the Old Testament*, 2 vols. (G. E. C. Gad, 1948), Vol. 1, p. 31.

Chapter 6

Extracanonical Books

The Bible of Jesus and his disciples was the Hebrew Bible of twenty-four books. This Bible had, however, been translated into Greek by Alexandrian Jews prior to Christ's birth. When the gospel left its Palestinian homeland and began to penetrate the Greek-speaking world this Greek translation of the Old Testament, known as the Septuagint, proved to be very helpful to the messengers of the good news.

Since the Septuagint, at least in the manuscripts that have come down to us, contains many books not found in the Hebrew Bible, the question must be asked whether these extracanonical books, known today as the Apocrypha, have any right to be considered canonical. Before we answer that question we must make a survey of this apocryphal literature.

I. THE APOCRYPHA

A. The Meaning and Use of the Term

One of the difficulties in explaining the meaning of the word "Apocrypha" arises from the fact that the word means different things to different people. The word *apocrypha* is a Greek neuter plural of the singular *apokryphon*, and signifies books that are "hidden away."

It was originally a term applied to those books that were held to be so mysterious and profound that in the opinion of some Jews they were to be hidden from ordinary readers. Since only the initiated could understand them, they were to be withdrawn from common use.[1]

We have already referred to the fictitious story in which Ezra is said to have restored all the books after they had been destroyed during the exile, and that he produced ninety-four volumes, twenty-four to be published and seventy to be kept secret from the ordinary person because they were too lofty. This story illustrates the view that "apocryphal," to begin with, described those books that were too deep for the common person.

That, however, is not the way we use

---

[1] B. M. Metzger, *Introduction to the Apocrypha* (New York: Oxford University Press, 1957), p. 5.

the word "apocryphal" today. Nowadays, when something is described as apocryphal, we mean that it is fictitious. An apocryphal story is simply not true. The word is used of legendary tales that tend to gather around distinguished people. In this popular sense of the word, "apocryphal" is really a derogatory term. In fact, early Christians used the term apocryphal for those books that were withheld from general circulation, not because they were so profound but because of doubts about their authenticity.[2]

We use the word "apocryphal" in this chapter to refer to that collection of Jewish books that are not found in the Hebrew Bible. These books are, however, in the Greek Septuagint, and Jerome grudgingly allowed them to slip into the Latin Vulgate in the fourth century A.D., and so they have become part of the Bible of the Roman Catholic Church. Protestants, however, do not accept them as canonical and call them "Apocrypha." Many Protestant Bibles have the Apocrypha in them, but they are not held to be on par with the twenty-four books of the Hebrew Bible.

B. Their Number and Date

Generally speaking there are fourteen or fifteen books, written during the last two centuries before Christ and the first century of the Christian era, that make up the collection of books called the Apocrypha. The Revised Standard Version (in those editions that have the Apocrypha) lists the following titles: (1) 1 Esdras, (2) 2 Esdras, (3) Tobit, (4) Judith, (5) Addi-

tions to Esther, (6) The Wisdom of Solomon, (7) Ecclesiasticus, or the Wisdom of Jesus the Son of Sirach, (8) Baruch, (9) The Letter of Jeremiah, (10) The Prayer of Azariah and the Song of the Three Young Men, (11) Susanna, (12) Bel and the Dragon, (13) The Prayer of Manasseh, (14) 1 Maccabees, (15) 2 Maccabees.

In some previous English editions The Letter of Jeremiah was incorporated into the Book of Baruch, giving us fourteen instead of fifteen Apocrypha. These may be called the "official" Apocrypha. But if we look into a modern printed Septuagint, we notice, for example, that 2 Esdras is not included, while 3 and 4 Maccabees, as well as Psalm 151 are. It does not follow, of course, that the Septuagint always contained the same number of apocryphal books.

In Roman Catholic Bibles the list is considerably shorter. In 1546 the Council of Trent declared Tobit, Judith, Wisdom, Ecclesiasticus, Baruch, 1 and 2 Maccabees, and certain supplementary parts of Esther and Daniel to be canonical and on a par with the books of the OT, among which they are dispersed.[3] Since these ten or eleven books were accepted into the canon at a later time, some Catholic scholars speak of them as deuterocanonical. If Catholic scholars use the word "Apocrypha" they mean those books that others call the Pseudepigrapha, on which we shall comment later. There is, then, considerable confusion on the limits of the OT Apocrypha.

We need not go into detail in the matter of the dates of these books. Sev-

---

[2]R. K. Harrison, *Introduction to the Old Testament* (Grand Rapids: Eerdmans, 1969), p. 1,185.
[3]Metzger, *Apocrypha*, p. 6.

TABLE OF BOOKS OF APOCRYPHA

Type of Book	Revised Standard Version	Catholic Versions
Didactic	1. The Wisdom of Solomon (c. 30 B.C.)	Book of Wisdom
	2. Ecclesiasticus (Sirach) (132 B.C.)	Ecclesiasticus
Religious	3. Tobit (c. 200 B.C.)	Tobias
Romance	4. Judith (c. 150 B.C.)	Judith
Historic	5. 1 Esdras (c. 150-100 B.C.)	3 Esdras* or 1 Esdras‡
	6. 1 Maccabees (c. 110 B.C.)	1 Machabees
	7. 2 Maccabees (c. 110-70 B.C.)	2 Machabees
Prophetic	8. Baruch (c. 150-50 B.C.)	Baruch chaps. 1-5
	9. The Letter of Jeremiah (c. 300-100 B.C.)	Baruch chap. 6
	10. 2 Esdras (c. A.D. 100)	4 Esdras* or 2 Esdras‡
Legendary	11. Additions to Esther (140–130 B.C.)	Esther 10:4–16:24†
	12. The Prayer of Azariah (second or first century B.C.) (Song of Three Young Men)	Daniel 3:24–90†
	13. Susanna (second or first century B.C.)	Daniel 13†
	14. Bel and the Dragon (c. 100 B.C.)	Daniel 14†
	15. The Prayer of Manasseh (second or first century B.C.)	Prayer of Manasseh*

*Books not accepted as canonical at the Council of Trent, 1546.
†Books not listed in Douay table of contents because they are appended to other books.
‡The numbering of these books depends on whether Ezra and Nehemiah are titled 1 and 2 Esdras or Ezra and Nehemiah.

eral of them, such as 1 Esdras, Tobit, The Song of Three Young Men, are pre-Maccabean (c. 300–200 B.C.). Others come from the Maccabean period (c. 200–100 B.C.; Judas Maccabeus died 160 B.C.). Judith, Ecclesiasticus, Bel and the Dragon, and Additions to Esther would belong to this period. Still others are post-Maccabean (c. 100 B.C. to A.D. 100). First and 2 Maccabees, Susanna, The Wisdom of Solomon, Baruch, The Prayer of Manasseh, and 2 Esdras would belong to this latter period.

C. Their Literary Character

Several books of the Apocrypha are (1) historical in character. First Esdras may be viewed as a variant version of Chronicles-Ezra-Nehemiah. (Esdras is simply the Greek form of Ezra.) First Maccabees is our principal source of information on the Jewish struggle for independence under the Hasmoneans. Martin Luther valued this book so highly that he thought it was not unworthy to be reckoned among the books of Scripture. Second Maccabees provides us with glimpses into this same period, but it is not as trustworthy historically as is 1 Maccabees.[4] Some copies of the Septuagint have 3 and 4 Maccabees. These books, which also reflect some aspects of Jewish life during this period, were never part of the official Apocrypha in Western Christendom.

---

[4]F. F. Bruce, *The Books and the Parchments*, 3rd rev. ed. (Old Tappan: Revell, 1963), p. 166.

A number of apocryphal books may be classified (2) as religious fiction. Some of these are moralistic novels. This category would apply to the Book of Tobit—a charming tale that underscores the importance of observing the Law. Judith, by contrast, is a bloodthirsty thriller (a forerunner of the modern detective story).

The Additions to Esther are designed chiefly to compensate for the absence of the name of God or, in the opinion of some, the lack of true religion in the canonical book. The Additions to Daniel include the story of Susanna, in which Daniel rises to the defense of an innocent but maligned girl. In Bel and the Dragon, Daniel exposes the fraudulent conduct of idolatrous pagan priests. A third addition to Daniel is inserted between verses 23 and 24 of chapter 3 of our canonical Daniel. There is first a prayer for deliverance, put into the mouth of Azariah (Abednego), followed by an ascription of praise to God by the three young men who had been thrown into the furnace of fire for refusing to worship the king's image.

There are some apocryphal books that may be called (3) didactic treatises, or wisdom literature. Two of the books are, in fact, called "wisdom" books: The Wisdom of Jesus the son of Sirach (also called Ecclesiasticus—not to be confused with Ecclesiastes), and the so-called Wisdom of Solomon.

Baruch contains, besides a homily on wisdom, a confession of national sin and a promise of deliverance and restoration. The Epistle of Jeremiah, which is sometimes attached to Baruch, contains a warning against idolatry.

The Prayer of Manasseh is a confession of sin and a petition for forgiveness that King Manasseh is supposed to have made in Babylonian captivity. Together with The Prayer of Azariah and The Song of the Three Young Men, it ranks high as devotional literature.

Finally, (4) there is one apocalyptic book (2 Esdras) that is not in the Septuagint but is usually included in the official Apocrypha as they are listed in Protestant Bibles. Martin Luther thought it was so bizarre that he refused to translate it for his German Bible. He says that he had thrown this book into the Elbe. Much of the literature classified as pseudepigraphical is apocalyptic in character.

D. Their Acceptance

1. *By the Jews.* The apocryphal books, many of them written originally in Hebrew or Aramaic and later translated into Greek, were written during those centuries in which the Jewish community experienced much trouble and stress. They are, of course, not the only books written by the Jews during this time. There were other "outside books," as they were known in Judaism. According to statements in the Talmud we learn that the canonical books were said "to defile the hands." This phrase was employed to designate canonical books, although the reason why they were so designated is not clear. The books that we now call apocryphal were said not "to defile the hands." These writings enjoyed considerable popularity at first, as can be seen from the fact that they were translated into Greek or Aramaic.

There is, however, no evidence that they were ever considered as Scripture by the Jews. It has sometimes been argued that Alexandrian Jews did not limit the canon to the twenty-four Hebrew books, since the Apocrypha were translated by them into Greek and were eventually included in the Septuagint. Their presence in the Septuagint, however, does not of itself prove that Alexandrian Jews had more liberal views in the matter of the canon. Philo, who was an Alexandrian Jew (died c. A.D. 50), adhered strictly to the Hebrew canon and ignored the Apocrypha completely.[5] It does not follow, however, that all Alexandrian Jews were equally strict.

Just how these books crept into the Septuagint originally, no one knows. It has been suggested that these book rolls were kept on the same shelves with the biblical books, and that with the change to the codex form of the book, they were incorporated with the canonical books.

After the destruction of Jerusalem and the advent of Christianity, the Apocrypha (as well as the Pseudepigrapha) fell into disuse. The survival of these books can be attributed mainly to the interest that Christians took in them.

2. *By the New Testament.* Since the writers of the NT wrote in Greek, they tended to take their quotations from the Septuagint version of the OT (according to one estimate, 80 percent of all quotations in the NT are from the Septuagint, although their wording is not always exactly the same as in that version). The Septuagint made the Apocrypha available to NT writers. However, these writers never quote from the apocryphal books. Jesus and his apostles evidently did not consider them as canonical, for they ignore them completely. This argument, however, must be used with care, for there is no direct quotation in the NT from Joshua, Judges, Esther, and other OT books, either.

It should be noted, also, that even if the NT writers had quoted the Apocrypha, that would not by itself have made them canonical. After all, Paul can quote pagan authors, such as Epimenides (Titus 1:12) and Menander (1 Cor. 15:33), and Jude can quote the Book of Enoch (Jude, 14–15)—a noncanonical book. Others could be mentioned.

Nestle's Greek NT lists some 132 NT passages that appear to be verbal allusions to paracanonical books, but that is the kind of thing we would expect. Writers living at a given period in history tend to reflect the current language of their day. There is, however, no indication that Jesus or the apostles viewed the Apocrypha as Scripture. Verbal similarities between New Testament writings and apocryphal books does not mean that Jesus and his apostles viewed the Apocrypha as authoritative—something they obviously did not do.

3. *By the Early Church.* The early church felt no particular inclination to proscribe the Apocrypha. In fact, it was the popularity of these books that stimulated Jewish reaction against the Apocrypha. One wonders whether these books, produced by Jews, would have survived had it not been for the church.

The limits of the OT canon were not always clearly drawn in the early church, as can be seen from some of the debates on this matter. Melito of Sardis (A.D. 170) drew up a list of OT

---

[5] R. H. Pfeiffer, "The Literature and Religion of the Apocrypha," *Interpreter's Bible*, ed. G. Buttrick (Nashville: Abingdon, 1952), Vol. 1, p. 393.

books that excluded the Apocrypha. Origen was challenged by the Bishop of Emmaus, Julius Africanus (c. A.D. 240), for his use of Susanna, since that book was not in the Hebrew Bible. Jerome refused to translate these books into Latin for his Vulgate (c. A.D. 391), but yielded to pressure by the bishops and allowed them to be included in their Old Latin form. Augustine felt that ecclesiastical custom favored the inclusion of the Apocrypha in the canon. Cyril of Jerusalem (died A.D. 444), however, exhorted his catechumens to hold fast to the books in the Hebrew Bible and to disregard the Apocrypha.[6]

This vacillation in the attitude of the church to the Apocrypha is reflected in the manuscripts of the Septuagint itself. The Codex Vaticanus (fourth/fifth century A.D.) omits 1 and 2 Maccabees and The Prayer of Manasseh; the Codex Alexandrinus (fifth century A.D.) contains, in addition to the standard Apocrypha, also 3 and 4 Maccabees and The Prayer of Manasseh (among the Odes, supplementing the Psalms).

Only a few scholars in the Latin-speaking church of the early centuries seem to have objected to the use of the Apocrypha, and so by common usage throughout the Middle Ages they took on the same authority that the OT books had.

4. *The Roman Catholic Church.* During the Middle Ages the apocryphal books enjoyed almost undisputed canonicity. With the revival of learning, leading to the study of Hebrew once more, and with the Protestant Reformation and its polemic against Roman Catholic doctrines, the question of the

canon became very acute once again. Martin Luther (c. 1534) translated the Apocrypha into German, but he set them off from the rest of the OT in his German Bible, and wrote in the foreword to them that they were not to be regarded as sacred Scripture, even though they could be read with profit.

The Roman Catholic Church was quick to respond, and in 1546 the Council of Trent declared all the Apocrypha (with the exception of 1 and 2 Esdras and The Prayer of Manasseh) to be canonical, and the Council pronounced every person anathema who did not accept the Apocrypha as canonical. This was the first council of the (Roman Catholic) church to give official approval to the present set of apocryphal books.

The Anglican Church accepted the Apocrypha for instruction in life and manners, but not for the establishment of doctrine (Article VI in the Thirty-Nine Articles). Lectionaries from the Apocrypha have been used in the Anglican liturgy from time to time. Luther valued the books highly, but he did not view them as Scripture. Reformed churches in the Calvinistic tradition took a clear-cut approach. The Westminster Confession (1648) states unequivocally that the Apocrypha are not divinely inspired and therefore have no authority in the church of God and are to be viewed as human books. In contrast to the Roman Catholic Church, no Protestant bodies accepted the Apocrypha as Scripture.

5. *English Bibles and the Apocrypha.* English Bibles were patterned after those of the Continental Reformers by having the Apocrypha set off from the

---

[6]Pfeiffer, "The Literature of the Apocrypha," p. 394.

rest of the OT. Coverdale (1535) called them "Apocrypha." All English Bibles prior to 1629 contained the Apocrypha. Matthew's Bible (1537), the Great Bible (1539), the Geneva Bible (1560), the Bishops' Bible (1568), and the King James Bible (1611) contained the Apocrypha. Soon after the publication of the KJV, however, the English Bibles began to drop the Apocrypha and eventually they disappeared entirely. The first English Bible to be printed in America (1782–83) lacked the Apocrypha. In 1826 the British and Foreign Bible Society decided no longer to print them.

Today the trend is in the opposite direction, and English Bibles with the Apocrypha are becoming more popular again. This has raised the question of their canonicity once more, and we should give some reasons why we believe they ought not to be considered as canonical.

E. Their Place in the Canon

We believe a good case can be made against ascribing canonical status to the Apocrypha by the following observations:[7] (1) The Apocrypha were never part of the Hebrew canon. (2) Although the Septuagint contains apocryphal books, it cannot be proved that the Alexandrian Jews accepted a "wider" canon. (3) The strongest single argument against the canonicity of the Apocrypha is to be found in the NT. Jesus and his apostles obviously did not accept these books as Scripture. (4) Also, the sermons in the Book of Acts indicate how the apostles felt about the Apocrypha. The sermon summaries that Luke gives us in Acts usually span the history of salvation, beginning with Abraham or David, and ending with the fulfillment of God's promises in Jesus Christ. However, they completely ignore the four hundred-year intertestamental period. We appreciate all the information that the Apocrypha supply for this period of Jewish history, but the apostles did not think that the books written in this period were a continuation of divine revelation.

(5) Persistent uncertainty about the apocryphal books also suggests that they did not have the stamp of God on them, as did the canonical books that were eventually recognized as having divine authority. In fact, only by ecclesiastical authority (Augustine is an example), was resistance to these books suppressed. (6) All attempts at compromise, giving the Apocrypha an intermediate position, are inconsistent. One cannot, for example, read them in public worship and at the same time say that they are not authoritative for doctrine.

Enough has been said, we believe, to suggest that a good case can be made for denying canonical status to the Apocrypha. This does not mean, however, that these books are without value. From a historical and cultural point of view they are really invaluable. Also, one can find high points of religious devotion in them. John Bunyan tells us in *Grace Abounding* of how God spoke to him through a passage in Ecclesiasticus (2:1). When he discovered that the passage was in the Apocrypha, he felt very uneasy. He finally resolved the conflict by arguing

---

[7]These and other arguments are developed in greater detail by Floyd Filson in his book, *Which Books Belong in the Bible?* (Philadelphia: Westminster, 1957).

that, although the passage was not canonical, it expressed, even if in different words, what the Bible taught.[8]

Because the Apocrypha were preserved by the church, they have had a profound influence on a number of areas of life and thought. The language of these books has entered Christian hymnody, influenced Christian art, and has penetrated some of the world's great literature. Perhaps such influences have been generally quite positive, but unfortunately the Roman Catholic Church has also based its doctrine of purgatory on 2 Maccabees 12:39–45, and that teaching must be rejected.

It can even be argued that the Apocrypha were responsible for the discovery of America, for Christopher Columbus was persuaded by a passage from 2 Esdras (6:42ff.) that six-sevenths of the earth is land and only one-seventh is sea, and that gave him courage to look for new lands beyond the seas.

Nevertheless, as Bruce Metzger says, "When one compares the books of the Apocrypha with the books of the OT, the impartial reader must conclude that, as a whole, the true greatness of the canonical books is clearly apparent."[9]

II. THE PSEUDEPIGRAPHA

A. Their Designation

Besides the books that we call Apocrypha, Judaism produced a body of literature that has come to be known as the Pseudepigrapha. These books never made a serious bid for canonical status and we mention them only to indicate that there was a vast number of Jewish books in circulation from which the biblical books were set off.

Since the Roman Catholic Church accepts the Apocrypha as canonical, scholars in that tradition at times speak of the Pseudepigrapha as the Apocrypha. One could, however, just as well call some of the apocryphal books pseudepigraphic, for the word simply means that the author of a book writes under a pen name. Moreover, some of the pseudepigraphical books are anonymous, not pseudonymous. Some Protestant scholars, therefore, prefer to speak of the Pseudepigrapha as the "wider Apocrypha." However, the term Pseudepigrapha is used quite generally today, and we use it here to designate those books, composed by Jewish writers between 200 B.C. and A.D. 200, that fall outside the Hebrew canon and the Apocrypha.

B. Their Number

There is no recognized limit to the number of books in this body of literature. Besides, some books that are listed with the Apocrypha are at times listed with the Pseudepigrapha. R. H. Charles, for example, not only listed 2 Esdras with the Pseudepigrapha, but added three works to the standard list: Pirke Aboth, The Story of Ahikar, and Fragments of a Zadokite Work.[10]

Together with these four the official list includes some eighteen titles: The Book of Jubilee, The Letter of Aristeas, The Book of Adam and Eve, The Martyrdom of Isaiah, 1 Enoch, The Testa-

---

[8] J. W. Wenham, *Christ and the Bible* (Downers Grove: InterVarsity, 1973), p. 126.

[9] Metzger, *Apocrypha*, p. 172.

[10] R. H. Charles, *The Apocrypha and Pseudepigrapha of the Old Testament*, 2 vols. (Oxford: Clarendon, 1913).

THE STANDARD COLLECTION OF THE PSEUDEPIGRAPHA*

LEGENDARY:	1. The Book of Jubilee 2. The Letter of Aristeas 3. The Book of Adam and Eve 4. The Martyrdom of Isaiah
APOCALYPTIC:	5. 1 Enoch 6. The Testament of the Twelve Patriarchs 7. The Sibylline Oracle 8. The Assumption of Moses 9. 2 Enoch, or the Book of the Secrets of Enoch 10. 2 Baruch, or The Syriac Apocalypse of Baruch† 11. 3 Baruch, or The Greek Apocalypse of Baruch
DIDACTICAL:	12. 3 Maccabees 13. 4 Maccabees 14. Pirke Aboth 15. The Story of Ahikar
POETICAL:	16. The Psalms of Solomon 17. Psalm 151
HISTORICAL:	18. The Fragment of a Zadokite Work

*Since the discovery of the Dead Sea Scrolls others have come to light.
†1 Baruch is listed in the Apocrypha

ment of the Twelve Patriarchs, The Sibylline Oracles, The Assumption of Moses, 2 Enoch, 2 Baruch, 3 Baruch, 3 and 4 Maccabees, Pirke Aboth, The Story of Ahikar, The Psalms of Solomon, Psalm 151, The Fragment of a Zadokite Work. Today about fifty-two pseudepigraphical books are known.

C. Their Character

For the most part these books were written in conscious imitation of the Hebrew canonical books. Many of them belong to the type of literature called "apocalyptic," for which the canonical Book of Daniel was the prototype. 1 and 2 Enoch, 2 and 3 Baruch, The Testament of the Twelve Patriarchs, The Sibylline Oracles, and The Assumption of Moses, are apocalypses. Such literature was born out of the fires of persecution during the intertestamental period. Although it has its roots in the OT, it came to full bloom during the Maccabean Revolt. This apocalyptic literature presented a theological view of history that sustained the Jews in their time of trouble. These Jewish apocalypses are a great help in understanding the one great Christian apocalypse that we have in the NT, the Revelation.

Besides these apocalypses, there are some legendary books, such as The Martyrdom of Isaiah, that later came to be incorporated in a larger Christian work entitled The Ascension of Isaiah. There are also didactical treatises such as 3 and 4 Maccabees, Pirke Aboth, and The Story of Ahikar. Two books, The Psalms of Solomon and Psalm 151, are poetical in nature, and Fragments of a Zadokite Work is historical.

D. Their Acceptance

At the Jewish Council of Jamnia (A.D. 90) the rabbis banned these "outside books," as they were called. Evidently the fall of Jerusalem made their message meaningless. More important still, Christians had appropriated some of these books and recast them to fit their own views. Consequently Jewish leaders held them to be heretical.

Among Christians they enjoyed considerable popularity, and the NT gives evidence of their circulation at the time of the apostles. Jude, as mentioned earlier, quotes 1 Enoch 1:9 in Jude 14–15. Also, the reference in Jude 9 to the dispute of Michael, the archangel, with the devil about the body of Moses seems to be a direct allusion to The Assumption of Moses.

The question of the canonicity of the Pseudepigrapha, however, never arose in the mainstream of Christianity, just as it had not in Judaism. Nevertheless, most of them, composed originally by Jews in Hebrew, Aramaic, or Greek, have come down to us in the various branches of the Oriental churches in such languages as Syriac, Ethiopic, Coptic, Georgian, Armenian, Slavonic, and others.[11]

With the discovery of the Qumran materials the body of Jewish extracanonical literature has increased considerably. And while all this literature is invaluable in our study of Judaism in the intertestamental and early Christian period, none of these books are, to use Luther's words regarding the Apocrypha, "to be equated with Holy Scripture."

---

[11]C. T. Fritsch, "Pseudepigrapha," *Interpreter's Dictionary of the Bible*, ed. G. Buttrick (Nashville: Abingdon, 1962), Vol. 3, p. 963.

SUGGESTED READING

Bruce, F. F. The Books and the Parchments, 3rd rev. ed. Old Tappan: Revell, 1963. See "The Apocryphal Books," pp. 163–75.

Charles, R. H. ed. The Apocrypha and Pseudepigrapha in English with Introductions and Critical Notes, 2 vols. Oxford: Clarendon, 1913.

Dentan, R. C. The Apocrypha, Bridge of the Testaments. Greenwich: Seabury, 1954.

Filson, F. V. Which Books Belong in the Bible? Philadelphia: Westminster, 1957.

Geisler, N. L. and Nix, W. E. From God To Us. Chicago: Moody, 1974. See "The Extent of the Old Testament Canon," pp. 86–100.

Harrison, R. K. Introduction to the Old Testament. Grand Rapids: Eerdmans, 1969. See "The Apocrypha," pp. 1,173–1,276.

Metzger, B. M. ed. The Apocrypha. New York: Oxford University Press, 1965.

Rowley, H. H. The Relevance of Apocalyptic: A Study of Jewish and Christian Apocalypses from Daniel to Revelation, rev. ed. New York: Harper and Brothers, 1955.

Russel, D. S. The Method and Message of Jewish Apocalyptic. Philadelphia: Westminster, 1964.

Young, G. D. "The Apocrypha," Revelation and the Bible, ed. C. F. H. Henry. Grand Rapids: Baker, 1958, pp. 171–85.

Chapter 7

The Text
of the Old Testament

In the previous chapters we have attempted to describe the formation of the biblical books into a body of literature that came to be called the Old Testament. We must now inquire into the history of the transmission of these biblical books. We would like to know who copied these books and what happened to the text of the Hebrew books from the time they were composed until they were put in print.

It should be stated at the outset that we do not have the original manuscripts of any of the books of the OT (nor of the NT, for that matter), if by original we mean the manuscripts produced by the authors of the books (or their scribes). These original manuscripts are called the *autographa,* and all we have are copies of the *autographa.* The word "manuscript" comes from Latin and means literally "that which is written with the hand." (Today we may also speak of typewritten manuscripts.) What are popularly called the "original manuscripts," are only the copies that later scribes made of the autographs.

Until the discovery of the Dead Sea Scrolls the oldest Hebrew manuscripts at our disposal (other than the Nash Papyrus fragment) were dated no earlier than the ninth century A.D. One can, therefore, appreciate the excitement of scholars when manuscripts of OT books were found in the Judean Desert in 1947. Some of these copies were a thousand years older than those that had been available to biblical scholars up to that point.

These discoveries have cast considerable light on the state of the OT text at the beginning of the Christian era.

I. THE TEXT OF THE
OLD TESTAMENT PRIOR TO A.D. 100

It should not surprise us that the original manuscripts have disappeared. The manuscripts of the biblical books were subject to wear and tear and decay just like other ancient books. Moreover, the calamities that befell Jewry not only when Jerusalem was destroyed in 586 B.C., but again in A.D. 70, explain to some degree why so few manuscripts of OT books have survived. There is, however, another explanation for the scarcity of early copies of the biblical books. The Jewish rabbis had such a high regard for the sacred Scriptures that, when manuscripts began to show signs of wear, they reverently disposed of them. And since they exercised great care in copying the biblical text, they did not think that old manuscripts had an advantage over newer copies.

Before older manuscripts were disposed of, they were kept in the *genizah* (meaning "hidden") of the synagogue. This was a storage room or an extra room in the synagogue. One such genizah, discovered in Old Cairo, at the end of the nineteenth century, yielded a rich supply of manuscripts and fragments, some dating back to the sixth century A.D. Worn and used manuscripts were deposited in these synagogue storage rooms, and were protected in that way from profanation. Once the room or cupboard was full, they were removed and buried with elaborate ceremony.[1]

In our efforts to trace the history of the biblical text we have to plead ignorance about the earliest stages of its transmission. We simply have no Hebrew manuscripts that go back further than 100 B.C., and these were only discovered in 1947. It would not be wrong, however, to make some inferences from later phases of the textual tradition.

Because the sacred books were ac-knowledged as authoritative in Israel and were consequently set apart from other literature, giving rise to the biblical canon, concern for a correct text began to grow.[2] It seems as if variant readings in nonsacred writings in Judaism were regarded as of no consequence.[3] By contrast, Jewish scribes became very concerned that the sacred books be transcribed accurately.

The contact of Jewish scribes with the Greek world of letters in the inter-testamental period probably encouraged greater exactitude in the transmission of the biblical texts. Later the separation of church and synagogue, both claiming the Hebrew books as their Bible, also called for an accurate text. The destruction of the Jewish state (A.D. 70) and the dispersion of the Jews over an ever widening geographical area also called for an exact standard text. Moreover, with the founding of the church the text of the OT was transmitted not only by Jews but by Christians also (the latter mostly in translations of the Hebrew text).

From the Dead Sea Scrolls it has become clear that the text of the Hebrew canonical books was characterized by considerable diversity in the centuries before Christ. Some of the Qumran texts are closer to the Samaritan Pentateuch (of which we will speak later), others have an affinity for the Septuagint, still others reflect the later Masoretic Text that we have in our Hebrew Bibles today.[4] However, there

---

[1]F. G. Kenyon, *Our Bible and the Ancient Manuscripts*, revised by A. W. Adams (New York: Harper and Brothers, 1958), p. 70.

[2]E. Wuerthwein, *The Text of the Old Testament*, trans. E. F. Rhodes (Grand Rapids: Eerdmans, 1979), p. 16.

[3]S. Talmon, "The Old Testament Text," *The Cambridge History of the Bible*, eds. P. R. Ackroyd and C. F. Evans (Cambridge: Cambridge University Press, 1970), Vol. 1, p. 166.

[4]Wuerthwein, *Text of Old Testament*, p. 16.

was a strong move in Judaism to establish a model text, a *textus receptus*, and to banish deviant manuscripts from circulation. By the end of the first century A.D. a kind of standard OT text emerged.[5] The rabbis obviously relied on earlier traditions in establishing such a standard text. From about A.D. 100 on, the transmission of the text was to be governed by strict regulations. "No pains were spared in preventing errors from entering the sacred text, or in discovering and eliminating them if they should creep in."[6]

The following rules for copying the Scriptures, coming from Talmudic times, illustrate with what care the biblical books (at least the official copies) were transcribed. (1) Only parchment from clean animals was allowed; (2) each written column of the scroll was to have no fewer than forty-eight and not more than sixty lines; (3) the page was first to be lined, and the letters suspended from these lines; (4) the ink was to be black in color, prepared according to a specific recipe; (5) no word or letter was to be written from memory; the scribe was to pronounce the words before he wrote them down; (6) he was to wipe his pen before writing the sacred name, Yahweh; (7) the new copy was to be revised within thirty days after completion; if more than three errors were found on any single sheet, the roll was condemned; (8) every word and letter was counted; (9) there were also rules on the form of the letters and the spaces between them.[7]

Some of these rules may seem slightly ridiculous to us, but they do encourage great confidence in the accuracy of such copies.

II. THE MASORETIC TEXT

A. The Masoretes

In the intertestamental period, when the law became the center of Jewish life, there emerged a class of scribes who copied and edited Israel's sacred literature. About the time of Ezra these sopherim ("scribes"), as they were called, emerged as an influential class of teachers and interpreters of the law. We have a classic description of the scribe in Ecclesiasticus 38:24–39:15. In Jesus' day scribes were a well-established order, belonging mainly to the Pharisaic tradition.

The Jewish scribes, beginning with the Christian era, are sometimes called Tannaim ("repeaters," i.e., "teachers"). Under them the Mishnah (Jewish oral traditions) took shape. The collecting of these traditions had gone on for a long time. Rabbi Akiba (c. A.D. 55–137) established the basic structure of the Mishnah (with its six divisions and tractates), and Judah, the Prince, published it toward the end of the second century A.D. With that we have entered the Talmudic period (c. 200–500), in which supplementary materials were added to the Mishnah, out of which grew the Talmud (from the Hebrew *lamad*, "to study"). The scholars who worked on this project were called Amoraim ("expositors"), although these designations were not always clearly distinguished one from the other. Since these scholars were concentrated in both Babylonia and Palestine, two

---

[5]F. G. Kenyon, *The Story of the Bible* (Grand Rapids: Eerdmans, 1967), p. 13.

[6]Wuerthwein, *Text of Old Testament*, p. 19.

[7]Kenyon, *Bible and Manuscripts*, p. 79f.

Talmuds emerged, the Babylonian and the Palestinian. However, not only was the oral tradition put into writing, but also the biblical books were transcribed.

At the end of the fifth century, this long scribal tradition was continued by scholars known as Masoretes (one suggestion is that the name comes from *masar*, "to hand down"). Because of their work on the OT, the text of our Hebrew Bibles today is called the Masoretic Text. The Masoretic period stretches roughly from A.D. 500 to 1000. The Masoretes inherited a Hebrew text on which many scribes had worked before them.

B. Pre-Masoretic Modifications

From about A.D. 100, when a standard text of the biblical books of the OT emerged, the scribes exercised great care in transcribing the text. One of the great contributions of the scribes in the pre-Masoretic period was to make word divisions in the Hebrew consonantal text. To begin with, all the letters of the biblical text ran together, which created the potential for misreading the words. One can illustrate this from English. If, for example, one looks at the letters, GODISNOWHERE, it could be read as "God is now here," or "God is nowhere." In Amos 6:12 the KJV has "will one plow there," but the RSV reads, "will one plow the sea." The difference can be explained by a difference in word division.

The amount of time and labor that went into the exacting discipline of dividing up the text of all the OT books

into words can hardly be sufficiently appreciated today by Bible readers.

Another contribution made by scribes in the pre-Masoretic period was the division of the biblical text into paragraphs for lectionary purposes. The manuscripts from Qumran indicate that such divisions were already known in pre-Christian times. There were, in fact, two kinds of divisions: Parashoth (singular, Parashah) and Sedarim (singular, Seder). In Palestine the Torah was divided into Sedarim, providing a sufficient number of weekly lessons for a three-year cycle. In Babylonia, where the entire Torah was read each year, the division was made into fifty-four (or fifty-three) Parashoth (weekly lessons). The Babylonian system prevailed in the end, and it has been the universal practice in Jewish synagogues from the thirteenth century on to read through the Torah in one year.[8]

These divisions should not be confused with the chapter divisions that were carried over into the Hebrew Bible in the fourteenth century from the chapter divisions that Stephan Langton (1150–1228) made in the Latin Vulgate. Also, although there were verse divisions as early as Talmudic times, the present verse division was fixed by the Masoretes about A.D. 900. The numbering of the verses, however, was not introduced until some time after the chapter divisions were carried over into the Hebrew Bible.[9]

C. Contributions of the Masoretes

As in Talmudic times, so also in the Masoretic period, Babylonia and

[8]I. M. Price, *The Ancestry of Our English Bible*, 3rd ed., revised by W. A. Irwin and Allen P. Wikgren (New York: Harper and Row, 1956), p. 24.

[9]Wuerthwein, *Text of Old Testament*, p. 21.

Tiberias were the centers of activity for the Eastern and Western Masoretes, respectively. When the Babylonian schools lost their significance, the Western Masoretes became determinative for the Hebrew text.

The Masoretes had a high regard for the Hebrew consonantal text that had become standard about A.D. 100. Any text, however, that is transcribed by human hands over several centuries, runs the risk of scribal misreading and miswriting, and the Masoretes were concerned that they preserve and transmit the best text possible.

A common source of error in copying Hebrew texts was the confusion of letters that look alike. Nebuchadnezzar is now a universally accepted English spelling, but the correct spelling is Nebuchadrezzar. The confusion was caused by writing "n" for "r." Also, in copying a word, letters can easily be transposed. Another besetting weakness is to omit a letter (called haplography) or to double a letter (called dittography). Some errors have to be ascribed simply to carelessness on the part of scribes. In 1 Samuel 13:1 we find, "Saul was ... years old." Some copyist neglected to write in the number. The manuscripts available to us give ample evidence for such mistakes.

The Masoretes, in their reverence for the received text, which they called the *Ketib* ("written") text, put what they thought was the better reading in the margin, and indicated this preferred reading by calling it *Qere* ("read"). They did not want to tamper with the received text, but did not want it to be misread either. There are more than 1300 such instances.

It was understood that whenever the sacred name Yahweh occurred in the text, the reader in the synagogue would read it as Adonai. This was *Qere Perpetuum* and was not indicated in the margin; the reader was expected to know this. No doubt it was the reading of Yahweh as Adonai that led to the combining of the consonants of the word Yahweh with the vowels of Adonai, yielding the hybrid of "Jehovah."

Some of the words marked as *Qere* had nothing to do with transcriptional error, but were euphemisms. For example, Baal, Ashtoreth, and Molech were read as *boshet* (the Hebrew word for "shame"). Not only in the matter of idolatry, but also in the area of sexuality and certain bodily functions, euphemisms were preferred in the public reading of Scripture.

In an embarrassing situation, such as Judges 18:30, where a priest of Dan is identified as a grandson of Moses, they suggested reading Manasseh (a wicked king) instead. And since the reader could overlook a Qere in the margin they introduced the letter "N" into the text, but wrote it higher than the other letters to indicate that they had added it. Such corrections are called *Litterae Suspensae*.

In fifteen passages they put special points above the letters of a word that seemed to them to be incorrect, but which they did not dare to correct. One such example is Numbers 3:39, where we find dots over the letters of the name Aaron. Evidently there were manuscripts that did not have Aaron's name.

In some instances, however, they went a step further and actually made corrections in the written text. These corrections were always clearly indicated by marking them as "Tiq soph" (abbreviation of Tiqqune Sopherim, "scribal corrections"). For example, in Genesis 18:22 it is reported that "the Lord remained standing before Abraham." That is an idiom for servanthood, and seemed irreverent. So the Masoretes changed it to "Abraham remained standing before the Lord," but indicated this correction in the lower margin.

On the whole the Masoretes showed the highest regard for the received text, and sought diligently to pass on to the next generation the most reliable biblical text. But they made one very important innovation. They developed a system by which the vowels of the Hebrew words could be indicated in writing. This was of very great significance since the same consonants could be read differently if one did not know the vocalization. If, for example, we saw a word like "BD" in English, we would be hard pressed to read these consonants, because we would not know which vowels to add. It could mean "bad," "bid," "bade," "bud," "bed," "bide," or what have you. Of course, if we saw these two consonants in a sentence such as, "John is a BD boy," we would know immediately it meant "bad," since the other words would not fit. We hear of Jerome struggling with Jeremiah 9:21 where the triliteral word DBR, could be read as *debar* (word) or *deber* (pestilence). The vocalization determines the meaning.

Since Hebrew had no vowel letters (there were four consonants that did double duty, being used both as consonants and vowels), the Masoretes developed a system of indicating the vowels in writing, called "pointing." Different systems of pointing were

A section of the earliest dated Bible manuscript in Maaravic square script, 946 A.D. The markings above and below the letters reflect the work of the Masoretes.

developed in the East and the West. The Babylonian and Palestinian system eventually gave way to the Tiberian. Some rabbis resisted such an intrusion into the sacred biblical text. In fact, it became an occasion for debate during the Reformation, whether or not the vowel points were inspired. Johan Buxtorf the Elder (1566–1629) held that God had not given the Torah in unpointed form to Israel originally.[10] The Masoretes, of course, did not view the vowel points as sacrilegious. All they wanted to do was to preserve the correct pronunciation (and therewith the correct meaning) for future generations. We must be very grateful to the Masoretes for their labor of love that went on for hundreds of years.

The Masoretes also left us their notes, called Masora ("tradition"), found in the margins of the Hebrew printed Bibles today. The Hebrew text to this day is called the Masoretic Text (MT for short).

After the Masoretic schools of

---

[10]Wuerthwein, *Text of Old Testament*, p. 27.

Babylonia became defunct the Tiberian school kept the lamp of textual studies burning. There were two families, Ben Asher and Ben Naphthali, who vied with each other in transcribing and preserving the best Hebrew text on which later printed editions of the Hebrew Bible were to be based. The great Jewish scholar Maimonides (died c. 1204) acclaimed the Ben Asher text to be superior to that of Ben Naphthali, and the former has enjoyed the prestige of textus receptus ever since.

III. MANUSCRIPTS OF THE HEBREW BIBLE

A. Manuscripts in the Masoretic Tradition

Most of the available Hebrew manuscripts, prior to the discovery of the Dead Sea Scrolls, did not go back beyond the ninth or tenth century A.D. The most comprehensive collection of Hebrew manuscripts is in the Russian Public Library in Leningrad. The Russian Jew, Abraham Firkowitsch (1785–1874) collected a great many manuscripts in synagogues in the East and brought them to Russia.

It will suffice to mention only several of the important manuscripts on which our printed Hebrew Bibles were based in the past. These include: (1) the Cairo Codex of the Prophets (both Former and Latter Prophets), dated A.D. 895; (2) the Aleppo Codex of the entire OT from about A.D. 930, which is now in Jerusalem and will be used for a new Hebrew Bible to be published by the Hebrew University; (3) the Leningrad Codex, from A.D. 1008, which formed the base of Kittel's third edition of the Hebrew Bible—until recently the international standard; (4) the British Museum Codex of the Pentateuch, dated about A.D. 950; (5) The Leningrad (formerly Petersburg) Codex of the Prophets (dated A.D. 916); (6) the Reuchlin Codex of the Prophets (c. A.D. 1105), which stands in the Ben Naphthali tradition rather than the Ben Asher, as do the others mentioned here.[11]

There are many other manuscripts, some of them quite fragmentary, but these are the most important Hebrew codices of the OT in the Masoretic tradition. With the discovery of the Hebrew scrolls in the Judean Desert in 1947 and following, we can now look at manuscripts a thousand years older. What is assuring, when one considers all the possibilities of transcriptional errors slipping in, is the fact that the Masoretic Text is substantially the same as that of the Dead Sea Scrolls.

THE CHIEF EXTANT MANUSCRIPTS OF THE HEBREW OLD TESTAMENT
(Prior to the Discovery of the Dead Sea Scrolls)

1. A codex of the Former and Latter Prophets (A.D. 895)
2. The Aleppo Codex of the complete Old Testament (A.D. 930)
3. British Museum Codex of the Pentateuch (A.D. 850)
4. The Leningrad Old Testament (A.D. 1000)
5. Leningrad Codex of the Prophets (A.D. 916)
6. Reuchlin Codex of the Prophets (A.D. 1105)

---

[11]Kenyon, *Bible and Manuscripts*, pp. 84–86.

B. Recent Discoveries

Before the discovery of the scrolls at the Dead Sea, the oldest fragment of the Hebrew OT was the Nash Papyrus from the second or first century B.C., containing the Decalogue and the Shema (Israel's confession of faith). Many fragments of the Hebrew text, the earliest from the fifth century A.D., had been discovered at the end of the nineteenth century in the Cairo

The Qumran Caves, where the Dead Sea Scrolls were found.

The Nash Papyrus, from the first century B.C. contains the Ten Commandments as presented in Deuteronomy 5. Until the discovery of the Dead Sea Scrolls this was the oldest biblical text available to scholars.

Genizah. With the discovery of the Dead Sea Scrolls we have more substantial evidence for the pre-Masoretic text of the OT.

After the chance discovery of the first cave at Qumran in 1947, search parties of archaeologists and Bedouins, between 1952 and 1956, discovered texts in ten other caves. Much of the material discovered is nonbiblical in content, but there are also some important manuscripts of OT books.

The largest copies of OT manuscripts are the two Isaiah scrolls, found in Cave 1. One is complete, the other not. The former is the best preserved and was written in the second century B.C.[12] Also, a commentary on Habakkuk (including the biblical text of that book) was found in Cave 1. Cave 11 yielded a Psalm scroll of forty-one

---

[12]O. Betz, "Dead Sea Scrolls," *Interpreter's Dictionary of the Bible*, ed. G. Buttrick (Nashville: Abingdon, 1962), Vol. 1, p. 795.

A detail of the Thanksgiving Scroll from the Dead Sea Scrolls, photographed under infrared light in order to make the text legible.

canonical, as well as some apocryphal, psalms.

Fragments of over a hundred scrolls of OT books have been discovered.

Every book of the OT, except Esther, has been found in some fragment form. The favorite books of the Qumran community seem to have been

Deuteronomy, Psalms, Isaiah, and Genesis.

The texts from Qumran suggest that there was some diversity of readings in the Hebrew books prior to the time of Christ. The discoveries of manuscript materials at Murabbaat, which belong to the second century A.D., have shown the trend toward a standard text. Such a text emerged about A.D. 100 and is essentially the text that the Masoretes have handed down to us, and that was put in print after movable type printing was discovered.

IV. THE PRINTED HEBREW BIBLE

Jewish scholars faithfully transcribed the Masoretic Text during the Middle Ages. Generally the Christian Church showed little interest in the Hebrew Bible during this period. The Latin Vulgate was the Bible of Medieval Europe. With the Renaissance, however, interest in manuscripts and in other languages was stimulated afresh. The man who carried Hebrew studies forward as a Christian scholar was Johannes Reuchlin (1455–1522). By the time the Protestant Reformation got under way, some Christian scholars once again began to take the Hebrew Bible seriously. By then printing had been discovered, and so the Hebrew Bible was published in print.

The first portions of the Hebrew OT were printed by Jewish printers in Italy. The psalms were published at Bologna, in 1477, and the entire Bible at Soncino, in 1488. The Soncino Jewish publishers elicited the parody, "Out of Zion shall go forth the law, and the word of the Lord from Soncino" (it should be "Jerusalem," Isa. 2:3).

There were other printings at Naples (1491–93) and Brescia (1494).

Martin Luther used the latter edition for his work on the German Bible. Also, the Jews published Rabbinic Bibles, which had not only the biblical text but rabbinic Targums (Aramaic paraphrases) and commentaries. The first Rabbinic Bible was published by Daniel Bomberg in 1416–17, in four volumes, and these volumes served as the basis for the second Rabbinic Bible of Jacob ben Chayyim in 1524–25. Bomberg's Bible had the Christian chapter divisions, as these were found in the Vulgate. This text enjoyed almost canonical status up to 1929, and the first two editions of Kittel's Biblia Hebraica (1906 and 1912, respectively) were still based on this edition.

About 1520 Christian scholars were beginning to publish the so-called Polyglot Bibles, in which the Hebrew text was included as one column among others. The Complutensian Polyglot, published in 1522, was prepared by Cardinal Ximenes and published in Spain. Tyndale and his helpers made use of this printed Hebrew text in their work on the English Bible. Other polyglots followed. The most massive was the London Polyglot (1654–57), which not only had the Hebrew text, but the Samaritan Pentateuch, a Targum, the Septuagint, the Vulgate, the Peshitta, and other versions, besides a lexicon and a grammar.

One of the early editions of the Hebrew Bible by a Christian scholar was prepared by a Pietist from Halle, J. H. Michaelis, in 1699. Benjamin Kennicott, an Oxford theologian (1718–1783), published a collection of variant readings, as did the Italian scholar de Rossi (in 1784–88). Baer and Delitzsch published a Hebrew Bible a hundred years later. About the same time C. D. Ginsburg prepared several editions

The title page from the London Polyglot of 1657 edited by Brian Walton. This work included many ancient versions of Scripture and represents a pioneering attempt at comparative semitics which stimulated interest in textual criticism.

(1894, 1908, 1926) of the Hebrew Bible. The British and Foreign Bible Society published his 1926 edition.[13] In 1958 this society published a new edition prepared by Norman Snaith.

In 1937 Rudolf Kittel and Paul Kahle (completed by A. Alt and O. Eissfeldt) had their third edition of the Biblia Hebraica published by the Württemberg Bibelanstalt. This edition broke new ground for it had better manuscripts as its base. The seventh edition of this Bible (1951) included readings from the Dead Sea Scrolls.

This was for years the kind of international standard Hebrew Bible. Recently the Biblia Hebraica Stuttgardensis was published. It has made few changes in the text itself, but has an improved textual apparatus. The Hebrew University in Jerusalem is now in the process of preparing a new edition of the Hebrew Bible that, besides having an elaborate textual apparatus, will make use of the Aleppo Codex, making its text available for the first time. The United Bible Societies are also preparing a new publication of the Hebrew Bible.

It is hard for anyone to comprehend fully the vast amount of labor that has gone into the preservation of the biblical text of the OT. After giving full credit to the thousands of faithful scribes and printers who played a part in giving us a trustworthy OT, we are reminded of God's promise to Jeremiah, "I am watching to see that my word is fulfilled" (Jer. 1:12).

[13] B. J. Roberts, "The Old Testament Text," *Interpreter's Dictionary of the Bible*, ed. G. Buttrick (Nashville: Abingdon, 1962), Vol. 4, p. 589.

יחזקאל EZECHIEL.

1 יַיְהִי ׀ בִּשְׁלֹשִׁים שָׁנָה בָּרְבִיעִי בַּחֲמִשָּׁה לַחֹדֶשׁ וַאֲנִי בְתוֹךְ־
הַגּוֹלָה עַל־נְהַר־כְּבָר נִפְתְּחוּ הַשָּׁמַיִם וָאֶרְאֶה מַרְאוֹת אֱלֹהִים:
2 בַּחֲמִשָּׁה לַחֹדֶשׁ הִיא הַשָּׁנָה הַחֲמִישִׁית לְגָלוּת הַמֶּלֶךְ יוֹיָכִין:
3 הָיֹה הָיָה דְבַר־יְהוָה אֶל־יְחֶזְקֵאל בֶּן־בּוּזִי הַכֹּהֵן בְּאֶרֶץ כַּשְׂדִּים
עַל־נְהַר־כְּבָר וַתְּהִי עָלָיו שָׁם יַד־יְהוָה: 4 וָאֵרֶא וְהִנֵּה רוּחַ סְעָרָה
בָּאָה מִן־הַצָּפוֹן עָנָן גָּדוֹל וְאֵשׁ מִתְלַקַּחַת וְנֹגַהּ לוֹ סָבִיב וּמִתּוֹכָהּ
כְּעֵין הַחַשְׁמַל מִתּוֹךְ הָאֵשׁ: 5 וּמִתּוֹכָהּ דְּמוּת אַרְבַּע חַיּוֹת וְזֶה מַרְאֵיהֶן
דְּמוּת אָדָם לָהֵנָּה: 6 וְאַרְבָּעָה פָנִים לְאֶחָת וְאַרְבַּע כְּנָפַיִם לְאַחַת
לָהֶם: 7 וְרַגְלֵיהֶם רֶגֶל יְשָׁרָה וְכַף רַגְלֵיהֶם כְּכַף רֶגֶל עֵגֶל וְנֹצְצִים
כְּעֵין נְחֹשֶׁת קָלָל: 8 וִידֵי אָדָם מִתַּחַת כַּנְפֵיהֶם עַל אַרְבַּעַת רִבְעֵיהֶם
וּפְנֵיהֶם וְכַנְפֵיהֶם לְאַרְבַּעְתָּם: 9 חֹבְרֹת אִשָּׁה אֶל־אֲחוֹתָהּ כַּנְפֵיהֶם
לֹא־יִסַּבּוּ בְלֶכְתָּן אִישׁ אֶל־עֵבֶר פָּנָיו יֵלֵכוּ: 10 וּדְמוּת פְּנֵיהֶם פְּנֵי
אָדָם וּפְנֵי אַרְיֵה אֶל־הַיָּמִין לְאַרְבַּעְתָּם וּפְנֵי־שׁוֹר מֵהַשְּׂמֹאול
לְאַרְבַּעְתָּן וּפְנֵי־נֶשֶׁר לְאַרְבַּעְתָּן: 11 וּפְנֵיהֶם וְכַנְפֵיהֶם פְּרֻדוֹת
מִלְמָעְלָה לְאִישׁ שְׁתַּיִם חֹבְרוֹת אִישׁ וּשְׁתַּיִם מְכַסּוֹת אֵת גְּוִיֹּתֵיהֶנָה:
12 וְאִישׁ אֶל־עֵבֶר פָּנָיו יֵלֵכוּ אֶל אֲשֶׁר יִהְיֶה־שָּׁמָּה הָרוּחַ לָלֶכֶת יֵלֵכוּ
לֹא יִסַּבּוּ בְּלֶכְתָּן: 13 וּדְמוּת הַחַיּוֹת מַרְאֵיהֶם כְּגַחֲלֵי־אֵשׁ בֹּעֲרוֹת
כְּמַרְאֵה הַלַּפִּדִים הִיא מִתְהַלֶּכֶת בֵּין הַחַיּוֹת וְנֹגַהּ לָאֵשׁ וּמִן־הָאֵשׁ

Cp 1, 1 ᵃ 𝔊ᴹˢˢ 'ΑΘΣΔ מראת ΖΓΛ𝔘 ‖ 3 ᵃ⁻ᵃ Ζ𝔊Λ𝔘 הָיָה 𝔊 ‖ ויהי 𝔊 ‖ ᵝ > 𝔊ᴮ (✳) ‖ 4 ᵃ 𝔊𝔘 וְעֵ ‖ ᵝ⁻ᵝ 𝔊 trsp ante וְאֵשׁ ‖ 7 ᵃ 𝔊'Α עָגְלָה ‖ 12 ᵃ nonn MSSᴷᵉⁿ 𝔊Σ𝔘 וְלֹא ‖ ᵝ > 𝔊Σ ‖ 13 ᵃ MSᴷᵉⁿ Kᴼʳ Eb 10 הוא, > 𝔊.

Cp 1, 1 ᵃ ? ‖ ᵇ prps שָׁנֵי vel ins לְחַיֵּי ‖ 3 ᵃ 1? אֵלָי אֶל־ vel אֵלַי אֲנִי אֶל־ ‖ ᵇ 1 c 13MSS 𝔊ΣΑ עֲלָי ‖ 4 ᵃ⁻ᵃ add ‖ 6 ᵃ⁻ᵃ 1 c 𝔊𝔏Σ𝔘 לְאֶחָת (cf 10,14) vel c pc MSS לְאַחַת מֵהֶם ‖ 7 ᵃ hic et in vs sqq pr הֵם et 𝔇 suff MSS 𝔖 הֵן et וְ ‖ ᵇ 1? ונצצות ‖ 8 ᵃ 1 c Q MSS Edd וִידֵי ‖ ᵇ 1 תַּחַת cf 10,8 ‖ ᵉ 1 עֶבְרֵיהֶם, prb conjg c sq ‖ ᵈ prb 1 פִּ ‖ ᵉ > 𝔊ᴮ, add ‖ 9 ᵃ⁻ᵃ > 𝔊ᴮ (✳), add ‖ 11 ᵃ > 𝔊𝔏, add ‖ ᵇ 1 אִשָּׁה אֶל־אֲחֹתָהּ cf 9. 23 ‖ 13 ᵃ 1 c 𝔊𝔏Α לָפִּ ‖ ᵇ 1 מַרְאֵה c 𝔊 ‖ ᶜ 1 c 𝔊 וּבֵינֹות vel וּמִתּוֹךְ.

A page from the Biblia Hebraica, edited by Rudolf Kittel. This is the Hebrew text used in most modern translations of the Old Testament. Masoretic notations are written around the text, notes relating to textual matters are placed at the bottom of the page.

SUGGESTED READING

Kenyon, F. G. **Our Bible and the Ancient Manuscripts**, *rev. ed. New York: Harper and Brothers, 1958. See "The Hebrew Old Testament," pp. 61–88.*

Price, I. M. **The Ancestry of Our English Bible**, *3rd rev. ed. New York: Harper and Row, 1956. See "The Hebrew Bible: Writing, Text, and Manuscripts," pp. 13–39.*

Roberts, B. J. **The Old Testament Text and Versions.** *Cardiff: University of Wales Press,* 1951. See pp. 1–100.

_____. "The Hebrew Text," **Interpreter's Dictionary of the Bible,** *4 vols. ed. G. A. Buttrick. Nashville: Abingdon, 1962, Vol. 4, pp. 580–94.*

Wuerthwein, E. **The Text of the Old Testament,** *trans. P. R. Ackroyd. Oxford: Blackwell,* 1957.

Chapter 8

Ancient Versions of the Old Testament

In the previous chapter we attempted to trace the transmission of the text of the OT. We may have found it a bit discouraging that, until the discovery of the Dead Sea Scrolls, the manuscripts on which our printed Hebrew Bibles were based did not go back beyond the tenth century A.D. There was, however, another source of evidence supporting the text of the OT, in addition to the Dead Sea Scrolls, that has greatly encouraged confidence in the Masoretic Text. Several ancient versions, that is, translations of the Hebrew OT into other languages, are available in manuscripts that take us back to the fifth and fourth centuries A.D. The Hebrew books were translated into Greek prior to the time of Christ. Also, there were translations into Syriac and Latin. Moreover, the Samaritans had taken over the Hebrew Pentateuch, writing it in Samaritan letters. Besides, the Jews eventually put the Aramaic paraphrases, which were made of the Hebrew text when Hebrew became defunct as the language of conversation, into writing. These paraphrases are known as Targums. All this literature throws light on the text of the OT, and we must look at several of these literary productions.

I. THE SAMARITAN PENTATEUCH

A. The Samaritans

When Omri, king of Israel, made Samaria his capital, the name of the capital was extended to the country as a whole, which was then called the Kingdom of Samaria. When the Northern Kingdom fell to the Assyrians (722 B.C.), thousands were taken into exile, and colonists from the East took the place of the deportees. These newcomers from the East intermarried with the people left in the land. In time these foreigners accepted the worship of Israel's God.

The Southern Kingdom also went to the dust (587 B.C.), and the inhabitants were taken into exile. When some seventy years later they were finally allowed to return to their homeland, the Samaritans offered to cooperate with them, but their offer was turned down.

Sometime in the fourth century B.C. this rift became complete. The Samaritans then built their own temple on Mount Gerizim. When the Hasmoneans established an independent Jewish state, John Hyrcanus (d. 104 B.C.) overran the province of Samaria and demolished the temple. Hatred between Jews and Samaritans was still intense at the time of Jesus, but under the Romans the Samaritans at least were free from Jewish domination and continued to worship at Nablus, near ancient Shechem. These Samaritans accepted the Pentateuch as their Bible, and they preserved a text of these five books that is independent of the Masoretic Text.

B. The Character of the Text

The Samaritan Pentateuch is written in a script derived from the Old Hebrew script, which was superseded by the Aramaic or Square Script about 200 B.C. Strictly speaking, then, this is not a "version" (i.e., a translation), but simply the Hebrew Pentateuch in "Samaritan" script.

Since the Samaritan Pentateuch comes from a time before the Hebrew text was standardized—even before the writing of the Dead Sea Scrolls—it is an important witness to the early form of the text of the OT.

The Samaritan text differs from the Masoretic Text in about 6000 places, but most of the variations are trifling, having to do with grammar and spelling. In many of these variations the Samaritan Pentateuch agrees in approximately 2000 places with the Greek Septuagint. For example, in Exodus 12:40 we are told that Israel was in Egypt "and in Canaan" for 430 years. The addition, "and in Canaan" is not in the Hebrew text.

The Samaritan Pentateuch is definitely biased in favor of the Samaritan center of worship. "The place which the Lord your God shall choose" (Deut. 12:5), is identified as Gerizim. And in a number of places the Samaritan Pentateuch reads, "the place which the Lord has chosen," meaning Gerizim. In Deuteronomy 27:4, where the Hebrew has "Ebel" the Samaritan Pentateuch has "Gerizim."

The oldest Samaritan scroll.

Also, it differs from the Masoretic Text in several places in chronology. The Samaritan text, for example, gives information on Abraham's journey to Canaan (Gen. 11:26–32) that agrees with Stephen's statement in Acts 7:4. Also, it has different ages for the patriarchs mentioned in Genesis 5 and 11. The age of Methuselah, for example, was reduced considerably, for the editors wanted to make sure he had died before the flood came. In a number of instances the Samaritan Pentateuch agrees with readings in the Dead Sea Scrolls, rather than the Masoretic Text, and since it represents an independent textual tradition the Samaritan text has to be taken seriously. Also it is a text that goes back to the fourth or fifth centuries B.C., and therefore precedes the Masoretic Text in time. Moreover, the Samaritan community has lived in relative isolation through the centuries and so it is not likely that its Scriptures were affected to any degree by the standard Hebrew text.

C. The Discovery of the Samaritan Pentateuch

The Samaritan Pentateuch was known to some of the church fathers, such as Eusebius and Jerome.[1] No copy of this text, however, had become available to European scholars until A.D. 1616, when a copy from Damascus was brought to Paris. Today many copies of the Samaritan Pentateuch are available to Western scholars (the largest collection in Europe is in Leningrad). The first time the Samaritan Pentateuch was published in print was in 1632, in the Paris Polyglot Bible.[2]

The most important copy of the Samaritan Pentateuch is the Nablus Scroll, which is in the hands of the Samaritans. The oldest known codex (as distinct from the scroll) is in the Cambridge University Library. There are other copies in European libraries and in the hands of the Samaritans. Few of these manuscripts go back earlier than the thirteenth century A.D.[3] The standard printed edition of the Samaritan Pentateuch was published at Giessen by A. von Gall in 1914–18, based on some eighty manuscripts. It was reprinted in Berlin in 1963.

Scholars do not all agree on the significance of the Samaritan Pentateuch for establishing the best text of the first five books of the Bible. But as an independent witness to the Hebrew text of the Torah the Samaritan Pentateuch serves as important function. The Revised Standard Version of the English Bible frequently has readings from the Samaritan Pentateuch and indicates this in the footnotes.

II. THE ARAMAIC TARGUMS

A. Their Origin

Aramaic, traditionally the language of Syria, became the lingua franca of most of the peoples from Mesopotamia to the Mediterranean coast in OT times. By the time the Jews returned from exile to Judea, they had pretty nearly made the switch from Hebrew to Aramaic, as their language of communication.

Meanwhile the ancient Hebrew remained as the language in which the sacred books were written, and in which they were read in public worship. Jewish scholars continued to study the Hebrew, but the common folk became less and less familiar with it. It became necessary, therefore, to translate the biblical text into Aramaic for those who attended the synagogue, where the lessons were read in Hebrew.

At first these paraphrases were

---

[1]F. F. Bruce, *The Books and the Parchments*, 3rd rev. ed. (Old Tappan, Revell, 1963), p. 127.

[2]F. Kenyon, *Our Bible and the Ancient Manuscripts*, revised by A. W. Adams (New York: Harper and Brothers, 1958), p. 91.

[3]E. Wuerthwein, *The Text of the Old Testament* (Grand Rapids: Eerdmans, 1979), p. 44.

given by word of mouth, extemporaneously. These verse by verse "translations" into Aramaic differed from place to place, since they were not prepared in advance and were not put into writing.[4] The reason the paraphrases were not written down in advance was to prevent people from confusing them with the canonical books that were written in Hebrew.[5]

This practice of paraphrasing the synagogue readings in Aramaic was begun in pre-Christian times (cf. Neh. 8:8), and by the time of Christ some of these oral paraphrases had been put into writing, called Targums (meaning "translation" or "paraphrase").[6] Ironically, once the Targums were put in written form they ceased to be used in the synagogue, for eventually the Jews lost the use of Aramaic as the language of conversation.[7]

Unofficial Targums circulated in Palestine in various forms beginning in pre-Christian times. Eventually official Targums emerged. For this we have to give credit to the Babylonian schools.

B. The Written Targums

Only a fraction of the written Targums has survived and those available reflect either a Palestinian or Babylonian provenance. The Palestinian Targums are earlier and show greater diversity, for they were never officially edited. They were revised in Babylon and these then became the official Targums whose definitive wording was established in the fifth century A.D.,

after a long history of development.[8]

There are several Targums representing the three divisions of the Hebrew canon. Let us mention first those of the Pentateuch. There is an Old Palestinian Targum of the Pentateuch. Although many manuscript fragments of this Targum had been discovered in the Cairo Genizah in the late nineteenth century, a complete manuscript of this Palestinian Pentateuch was discovered in the Vatican Library as recently as 1957, and is called Neofiti I. It seems to be as old as the first century A.D. At the moment, it is in the process of being published by A. Diez Macho.

Then there are the Jerusalem I and II Targums of the Pentateuch, wrongly ascribed to Jonathan and known, therefore, also as the Pseudo-Jonathan Targums.

The official Targum of the Pentateuch took shape in Babylonia and is called Targum Onkelos. This Aramaic version stands much closer to the text of the Hebrew Pentateuch, and dates from the third or second century A.D.

Several Targums of the Prophets are also available. These Targums originally circulated in different forms in Palestine, but they were finally replaced by an authorized version in Babylonian. This official Babylonian Targum of the Prophets is known as Targum Jonathan bar Uzziel. It was published in Leiden by A. Sperber (the Former Prophets, 1959; the Latter, 1962).

The Targums of the third division of

---

[4]Kenyon, *Bible and Manuscripts*, p. 94.

[5]Bruce, *Books and Parchments*, p. 133.

[6]Targums discovered at Qumran have proved this.

[7]B. M. Metzger, "Ancient Versions," *Interpreter's Dictionary of the Bible*, ed. G. Buttrick (Nashville: Abingdon, 1962), Vol. 4, p. 749.

[8]Wuerthwein, *Text of Old Testament*, p. 78.

the Hebrew Bible, the Writings, reflect an even greater diversity in style. There are Targums for most of the books in this division, with the exception of Ezra, Nehemiah, and Daniel. Some of the Targums of the Writings can hardly be called paraphrases, let alone translations; they are more like commentaries. Since these Targums of the Writings are (with some exceptions) no older than the fifth century A.D., it is unlikely that they were prepared for use in the synagogue or school.

C. The Character of the Targums

The Targums range from Aramaic translations of the Hebrew text to a free retelling of the biblical narrative. Only those that are reasonably close to the Hebrew text are of significance in establishing the correct biblical text. Targums that have extraneous material are an important index of Jewish life and thought during the centuries when the Aramaic Targums took shape.

One tendency of the Targums is to avoid the direct reference to the name of God. Instead, they use the word *Memra* ("the Word"). Instead of God walking in the garden (Gen. 3:8), it is the "Word of God." Instead of God being with Ishmael, it is the "Word of God" (Gen. 21:20). "Shekinah" and "Glory" are other substitutes in the Targums for the name of God. Could that be the reason John speaks of the "Word"(*Memra*)that"dwelt among us" (*Shekinah* means "dwelling") and whose "glory" the early witnesses beheld (John 1:1, 14)?

The translators of the Targums

seem to have been embarrassed by the many anthropomorphisms for God in the Hebrew text, and consequently they do away with them in many instances. Some include longer or shorter stories that serve to illustrate the Scripture text.[9]

To give a few snatches from these Targums, Pseudo-Jonathan gives Genesis 3:21f. in this way: "And the Lord God made unto Adam and his wife garments of honour, from the skin of the serpent which He had stripped from it, on the skin of their flesh, instead of the beauty which they had cast off; and He clothed them."[10]

The Targum of Ruth is even more enterprising. "And Ruth said: Do not urge me to leave you, to turn back from following you, for I wish to become a sojourner (meaning a 'proselyte'). Naomi said: We are commanded to keep the sabbaths and the holy days, so as not to walk more than 2000 cubits. Ruth said: Wherever you go, I will go. Naomi said: We are commanded not to lodge together with the Gentiles. Ruth said: Wherever you lodge, I will lodge. Naomi said: We are commanded to keep the 613 precepts. Ruth said: Whatever your people observe, I myself will observe...."[11] We can see that this Targumist is concerned that the biblical story be brought in line with later Jewish tradition, and so he does not hesitate to leave the text far behind.

These Targums seem to have left their mark on the NT. For example, the quotation of Isaiah 6:9–10 in Mark 4:12, is not like the Greek Septuagint nor the Hebrew Masoretic Text, but is closer to the Targum of Jonathan. Another

---

[9]Metzger, "Ancient Versions," p. 750.

[10]Bruce, *Books and Parchments*, p. 139.

[11]Bruce, *Books and Parchments*, p. 142.

example is found in Ephesians 4:8, where Paul quotes Psalm 68:18 with the words, "He . . . gave gifts to men," whereas the Masoretic and Septuagint texts have, "Thou hast received gifts among men." The form in which Mark gives Jesus' cry of dereliction, *"Eloi, Eloi, lama sabachthani,* suggests a Targumic version of Psalm 22:1.

The Targums thus provide a valuable background for the study of the NT besides witnessing to the text of the OT, and open up for us windows on Jewish life and thought.

III. THE GREEK TRANSLATIONS OF THE OLD TESTAMENT

The Samaritan Pentateuch is basically the Hebrew text written in Samaritan letters. The Targums are translations, paraphrases, and expansions of the Hebrew text. We now turn to a version of the OT in Greek that can be truthfully called a translation. Repeatedly we have had occasion in the previous chapters to mention this important version, and we must now say something about its origin, its nature, and its significance.

A. The Septuagint Version

1. *The Need for a Greek Version.* With the fall of Jerusalem in 587 B.C. the Jewish Diaspora began. Even though a great many returned to Judea after the exile in Babylonia, the majority of Jews continued to live in lands around the Mediterranean, outside the Holy Land. Shortly after Jerusalem was destroyed by Nebuchadnezzar's armies, a large number of Jews moved to Egypt. Actually Egypt had never been without a

Jewish colony, and about the time this remnant went down to Egypt with Jeremiah, the Egyptian king settled a garrison of Jews at the first cataract of the Nile. Here at Elephantine they built a temple some time before 525 B.C.[12]

When Alexander the Great founded the city of Alexandria in 332 B.C., Jews formed an important element in the population right from the beginning. The Ptolemies, who fell heir to Alexander's kingdom, favored the Jews and eventually two of the five wards of the city were known as Jewish districts. It is estimated that almost a million Jews lived in Alexandria and other parts of Egypt.

Alexandria was a Greek-speaking city, and the Jews there had to speak Greek to carry on their business. Soon Greek replaced their Palestinian vernacular, and we have a large Greek-speaking Jewish community that wanted to retain and pass on to future generations its spiritual heritage.

Since the Hebrew Scriptures were no longer understood by those who spoke only Greek, it was necessary that they be translated into Greek. In a sense, then, the same situation that gave rise to Aramaic Targums demanded a Greek version of the biblical books.

Those who undertook to translate the OT into Greek could hardly have guessed how significant this undertaking would be. This so-called Septuagint Version was to become the Bible of Diaspora Judaism and the Bible of the early church. When the writers of the NT, who write in Greek, quote the OT, they prefer to quote from the Septuagint. Also this Greek version became the base for translations into several

---

[12]Bruce, *Books and Parchments,* p. 147.

other languages. Moreover, it was now possible for non-Jews to read the Jewish Scriptures.

2. *The Story of the Translation.* Actually very little is known about the first attempts of the Alexandrian Jews to put the OT into Greek dress. We can glean some information from the *Letter of Aristeas* (one of the pseudepigraphical books), which purports to be written about the middle of the third century, but probably is no older than 100 B.C. In this letter, Aristeas, an official at the court of the Ptolemy who ruled 285–246 B.C. wrote to his brother about Demetrius, the librarian who aroused the interest of Ptolemy Philadelphus in the Jewish writings. A delegation was then sent by the king to the high priest in Jerusalem who, in response, chose six men from each of the twelve tribes and sent them to Alexandria with a beautiful copy of the Hebrew Torah. These seventy-two men were received very graciously and were allowed to stay on the island of Pharos, where in seventy-two days they completed the translation of the Pentateuch into Greek.

Other versions of this story add interesting details. One has it that the translators lived in separate cells, where they worked independently of each other, and in the end found that the seventy-two translations were identical—a sign of divine inspiration![13] The Greek version of the Law was then put into Alexandria's famous library, after receiving approval from the Jewish community.

This Greek translation got the name Septuagint, meaning "seventy." Perhaps because seventy elders accompanied Moses up the mountain to receive the Law, it was only appropriate that the number should later be rounded off to seventy.[14] (From here on we will use the Latin numerals "LXX" for the Septuagint.)

The legendary character of the Aristeas tradition has long been recognized. However, there is sufficient evidence that the LXX was made in Alexandria, not by Palestinian translators, however, but by Alexandrian Jews. The Hebrew text from which they translated may well have been a parchment scroll from Jerusalem.

The Aristeas story is limited to the Pentateuch. What about the rest of the OT? The other books seem to have been translated in stages as time went on. It is to be expected that the Torah would be translated first.[15] This means that the LXX is not the work of a single translator or group of translators. The fact that the books are not uniform translations would bear this out. We can be quite certain, however, that by the time of Jesus ben Sirach (late second century B.C.) the LXX was completed, for he refers to the Law, the Prophets, and the other books, which are the three divisons of the Hebrew canon. It may be that there were several Greek versions of OT books in circulation, and that our LXX, completed prior to the first century B.C., emerged as the official version.

3. *The Character of the LXX.* The LXX contains not only the books of the Hebrew Bible, but it has the Apocrypha as well. These are mixed in with the canonical books and are not set off from

---

[13]Bruce, *Books and Parchments,* p. 147.

[14]J. H. Reumann, *The Romance of Bible Scripts and Scholars* (Englewood Cliffs: Prentice-Hall, 1965), p. 13.

[15]Wuerthwein, *Text of Old Testament,* p. 51.

them as happened later in Protestant editions of the OT. Our manuscripts of the LXX, however, do not all list the same number of apocryphal books.

Also, there are a number of passages in the Hebrew Bible that have been transposed in the LXX. The Psalms are hopelessly scrambled; chapter 9 and 10, and 114 and 115 appear as single units in the LXX, and chapter 116 is split up. This throws out the numbering for most of the Psalms and explains why quotations from the OT in the NT books often have both the Hebrew and the LXX chapter and verse reference. The LXX places the chapters of Jeremiah 46–51 after 25:13, with the omitted chapters following chapter 51.

The translation varies greatly, from a close literal rendering of the Hebrew in

BOOKS IN THE SEPTUAGINT VERSION TODAY

THE PENTATEUCH:	Genesis Exodus Leviticus Numbers Deuteronomy
HISTORICAL BOOKS:	Joshua Judges Ruth 1 and 2 Kings (our 1 and 2 Samuel) 3 and 4 Kings (our 1 and 2 Kings) 1 and 2 Chronicles 1 Esdras 2 Esdras (our Ezra-Nehemiah)
POETICAL AND DIDACTIC BOOKS:	Psalms Proverbs Ecclesiastes Song of Songs Job Wisdom of Solomon Ecclesiasticus (or Wisdom of Sirach)
STORY BOOKS:	Esther (containing additions) Judith Tobit

PROPHETICAL BOOKS:	The Twelve Prophets (Hosea, Amos, Micah, Joel,
	   Obadiah, Jonah, Nahum, Habakkuk, Zephaniah,
	   Haggai, Zechariah, Malachi)
	Isaiah
	Jeremiah
	Baruch
	Lamentations
	Epistle of Jeremiah
	Ezekiel
	Daniel (including The Song of the Three Children,
	   The History of Susanna, Bel and the Dragon)

THE BOOKS OF THE MACCABEES:	1 and 2 Maccabees (to which were sometimes added 3 and 4 Maccabees)

some places to a very free translation in others. Where the LXX differs from the Masoretic Text we should perhaps not always blame the translators, but allow for the fact that their Hebrew copies may have been different from the current standard text we now possess. The scrolls from Qumran would point in that direction.

4. *The Acceptance of the LXX.* One can surmise that there must have been considerable resistance among Alexandrian Jews to the suggestion of translating the Holy Scriptures into a pagan tongue. Once the Torah had been translated, however, and read to the Jewish community, they were favorably impressed, according to Aristeas. Indeed, a curse was pronounced on anyone who would add to it, delete from it, or alter it in any way.

The LXX was eventually accepted by Jews throughout the Diaspora, and when the gospel spread in the lands around the Mediterranean, the missioners found a Bible in the language of the people wherever they went. It became the Bible not only of the Greek-speaking Jews, but also of the early church. This can be seen from Acts 15:16–18, where James argues for the acceptance of the Gentiles on the grounds that the LXX of Amos 9:11–12 predicts that "the rest of men may seek the Lord," whereas the Hebrew text of Amos has, "that they may possess the remnant of Edom."

When the Jews saw that the Christians had accepted a Jewish translation of the OT, they lost interest in the LXX. Christians used the LXX freely in witnessing to both Jew and Gentile. We have records of Jewish-Christian debates in which Christians argued from the LXX and the Jews objected because the Hebrew text was different from the LXX. In Justin's *Dialogue with Trypho the Jew* (c. A.D. 135), Justin sees a prophecy of the Cross in Psalm 96:10, where his Greek text reads, "Say among the nations that the Lord reigns from the tree." Trypho objects on the grounds that the Hebrew does not have this. Justin then retorts that the Jews have erased this reading. Trypho finds that incredible. And, in this case, Trypho was right; the phrase, "from the tree," was not omitted by the Jews, but added by the Christians.[16]

Another reason the Jews eventually rejected their own version, the LXX, lay in the fact that about A.D. 100 a kind of standard Hebrew text emerged, and it would be expected that a Greek version of the biblical books should conform more closely to this established text. In the end the rejection of the LXX by the Jews was so complete that they called it a work of Satan.

The preservation of the LXX must then be credited to the Christian church, not to the Jews, and it is found in the great codices of the Christian Bible that stem from the fourth and fifth centuries (Vaticanus, Sinaiticus, Alexandrinus). Alfred Rahlfs, who edited the LXX that was published by the Württemberg Bible Society in 1935, knew of 1,500 complete and fragmentary manuscripts of the LXX. Several more have been discovered since, with papyrus fragments pushing the LXX text back almost to its beginnings.[17] A very ambitious project of publishing a new edition of the LXX is

---

[16]Justin, *Dialogue*, chap. 73.

[17]Wuerthwein, *Text of Old Testament*, p. 68.

the Goettingen Septuagint, of which a number of OT books have already been printed, and others are to follow.

B. Revisions and Rival Versions

1. *Later Greek Versions.* Once the LXX had been renounced by the Jews, the Greek-speaking Jewish community faced the need for a version to replace it. Several efforts were made to meet this need.

Aquila of Sinope in Pontus, who had become a proselyte to Judaism and a disciple of Rabbi Akiba, produced a slavishly literal translation of the Hebrew text into Greek, about A.D. 130. The Greek of this version suffered greatly under his attempt to imitate the Hebrew words and syntax so closely. By changing *parthenos* (virgin), in Isaiah 7:14, to *neanis* (young woman)— something the Hebrew text allows— he attempted to weaken the argument for the virgin birth of Christ, which some Christian apologists based on this OT passage when arguing with Jews. This became the official version of Greek-speaking Jews.

At the end of the second century A.D. another proselyte to Judaism, Theodotion, produced a very free translation of the Hebrew books into Greek. It became so popular that the church preferred his version of Daniel to that of the LXX. Rahlfs printed both versions in his publication of the LXX. The Book of Job in Theodotion's version is closer to the Hebrew and fills in gaps left by the LXX, which is one-sixth shorter than the Hebrew text.

About this same time (c: A.D. 170), Symmachus, an Ebionite Christian, prepared a Greek version of the OT for Jewish Christians. Symmachus tried to produce an idiomatic and accurate translation. It is Greek in style and represents a principle of translation that is the opposite of the slavish literalism of Aquila.

2. *The Hexapla of Origen.* In the process of its transmission the LXX underwent several major changes beyond the usual amount of alteration that copying by hand brings with it.[18] The first of these modifications was made by the famous Christian scholar Origen at the beginning of the third century. His monumental work, on which he worked for some twenty years, is known as the Hexapla—a six-fold version of the OT. It was completed about A.D. 240. Origen stated that the chief purpose of the undertaking was to equip Christians for their discussion with Jews.

This great Alexandrian scholar, who later transferred to Caesarea, prepared a massive volume in which the OT was laid out in six parallel columns: (1) the Hebrew text, (2) the Hebrew text written in Greek letters, (2) Aquila's Greek version, (4) Symmachus' version, (5) a revision of the LXX, (6) the Greek translation of Theodotion.

The whole work ran to nearly 7,000 pages, and only fragments of the entire volume are known. Origen's fifth column (i.e., the LXX), however, was recopied several times. Jerome, at the end of the fourth century, consulted this massive work, which was kept in the Christian library at Caesarea. Although no manuscript of Origen's Septuagint has survived, there are manuscripts that represent the text of Origen more or less closely. The LXX column of the Hexapla was translated

---

[18]Metzger, "Ancient Versions," pp. 750f.

THE FORM OF ORIGEN'S HEXAPLA

Hebrew	Hebrew Transliterated	Aquila	Symmachus	LXX	Theodotion
למנצח	λαμαναασση	τῷ νικοποιῷ·	ἐπινίκιος·	εἰς τὸ τέλος·	τῷ νικοποιῷ·
לבני קרח	λαβνηκορ	τῶν υἱῶν Κόρε	τῶν υἱῶν Κόρε	ὑπὲρ τῶν υἱῶν Κόρε	τοῖς υἱοῖς Κόρε
על עלמות	αλ αλμωθ	ἐπὶ νεανιοτήτων	ὑπὲρ τῶν αἰωνίων	ὑπὲρ τῶν κρυφίων	ὑπὲρ τῶν κρυφίων
שיר	σιρ	ᾆσμα.	ᾠδή.	ψαλμός.	ᾠδή.
אלהים לנו	ελωειμ λανου	ὁ θεὸς ἡμῶν	ὁ θεὸς ἡμῶν	ὁ θεὸς ἡμῶν	ὁ θεὸς ἡμῶν
מחסה ועז	μασε ουζ	ἐλπὶς καὶ κράτος,	πεποίθησις καὶ ἰσχύς,	καταφυγὴ καὶ δύναμις,	καταφυγὴ καὶ δύναμις,
עזרה	εζρ	βοήθεια	βοήθεια	βοηθὸς	βοηθὸς
בצרות	βασρωθ	ἐν θλίψισιν	ἐν θλίψεσιν	ἐν θλίψεσι	ἐν θλίψεσιν
נמצא מאד	νεμσα μωδ	εὑρέθη σφόδρα.	εὑρισκόμενος σφόδρα.	ταῖς εὑρούσαις ἡμᾶς σφόδρα.	εὑρέθη σφόδρα.
על כן	αλ χεν·	ἐπὶ τούτῳ	διὰ τοῦτο	διὰ τοῦτο	διὰ τοῦτο
לא נירא	λω νιρα	οὐ φοβηθησόμεθα	οὐ φοβηθησόμεθα	οὐ φοβηθησόμεθα	οὐ φοβηθησόμεθα
בהמיר	βααμιρ	ἐν τῷ ἀνταλλάσσεσθαι	ἐν τῷ συγχεῖσθαι	ἐν τῷ ταράσσεσθαι	ἐν τῷ ταράσσεσθαι
ארץ	ααρς	γῆν,	γῆν	τὴν γῆν	τὴν γῆν
ובמוט	ουβαμωτ	καὶ ἐν τῷ σφάλλεσθαι	καὶ κλίνεσθαι	καὶ μετατίθεσθαι	καὶ σαλεύεσθαι

into Syriac before Origen's Greek Hexapla was lost in the Moslem conquests of the seventh century.[19]

3. *Other Recensions of the LXX.* In the century following Origen, three editions or recensions of the LXX were published. Eusebius of Caesarea supplied Constantine with fifty copies of the Bible when the persecution of Christians ceased, and these Bibles contained the fifth column of Origen's Hexapla, namely the LXX. Also, Lucian of Samosata, who died a martyr's death in A.D. 311, undertook a revision of the LXX. A third edition of the LXX was prepared by Hesychius of Egypt.

So it happened that by the fourth century three different forms of the LXX circulated in the Christian church. The edition of Eusebius was generally used in Palestine; that of Lucian in Asia Minor; while the Hesychian recension was popular in Egypt.[20] In the centuries that followed, readings from these different versions often intermingled, so that it is very difficult today always to know exactly which readings were present in the LXX originally.

There is perhaps no version of the Bible that has been so significant in the history of Bible translation as the LXX. Whatever its value may be in seeking to establish the best text of the OT, its influence on the NT, and, con-

sequently, on Christian life and thought, has been enormous. The apostolic writers of the NT did not need to invent a Greek theological vocabulary; such a vocabulary existed in the LXX. Many of the great Greek words of the NT no longer have the same meaning which they had in secular society. As translations of Hebrew OT words, they had taken on new meanings.[21] For example, the Greek word *eirēnē* means "peace" in the sense of absence of strife, but as a translation of the Hebrew *shalom*, *eirēnē* in the NT means much more; it now conveys the Hebrew meaning of health, wholeness, salvation, and fulness of life and blessing.

In conclusion to this chapter on the ancient versions of the OT it may be added that a Syriac translation of the OT was prepared probably by the Jews by the beginning of the Christian era, so that Syriac-speaking Jews could read or hear the Scriptures in their own tongue. Since, however, this version came to be combined with the Syriac NT at an early stage, we will reserve our comments on this version until we get to the ancient versions of the NT. Also, we will comment on the Latin OT at that point. But before we say anything about NT versions, we have to tell the story of the formation of the NT canon.

---

[19]F. C. Grant, *Translating the Bible* (Greenwich: Seabury, 1961), p. 26.

[20]I. M. Price, *The Ancestry of Our English Bible*, 3rd ed., revised by W. A. Irwin and Allen P. Wikgren (New York: Harper and Row, 1956), p. 79.

[21]Bruce, *Books and Parchments*, p. 159.

SUGGESTED READING

On the Samaritan Pentateuch see:

Bruce, F. F. The Books and the Parchments, 3rd rev. ed. Old Tappan: Revell, 1963. See "The Samaritan Pentateuch," pp. 125–32.

Price, I. R. The Ancestry of Our English Bible, 3rd ed., revised by W. A. Irwin and Allen P. Wikgren. New York: Harper and Row, 1956. See "The Samaritan Pentateuch," pp. 40–49.

Roberts, B. J. The Old Testament Text and Versions. Cardiff: University of Wales Press, 1951. See "The Aramaic Targumim," pp. 197–213.

On the Aramaic Targums see:

Bruce, F. F. The Books and the Parchments, 3rd rev. ed. Old Tappan: Revell, 1963. See "The Targums," pp. 133–45.

McNamara, M. Targum and Testament. Grand Rapids: Eerdmans, 1972.

Roberts, B. J. The Old Testament Text and Versions. Cardiff: University of Wales Press, 1951. See "The Aramaic Targumim," pp. 197–213.

On the Septuagint see:

Bruce, F. F. The Books and the Parchments, 3rd rev. ed. Old Tappan: Revell, 1963. See "The Old Testament in Greek," pp. 146–61.

Price, I. R. The Ancestry of Our English Bible, 3rd rev. ed. New York: Harper and Row, 1956. See "The Greek Bible: The Septuagint," pp. 50–71; "Rival Greek Bibles and Revisions of the Septuagint, pp. 72–81.

Roberts, B. J. The Old Testament Text and Versions. Cardiff: University of Wales Press, 1951. See "The Septuagint and the Greek Versions," pp. 101–87.

Chapter 9

The Beginnings of the New Testament

About the time when the text of the OT books assumed a standard form, the apostles were writing books that were later to form the NT. When the church was born on the first Christian Pentecost it had the same Bible as the Jewish synagogue. As the apostolic writings began to circulate, they too were read in the worship services of the church.

The reading of the Scriptures held an important place in the church's worship, just as it did in the synagogue which also served the church as a model in other respects. In what may be Paul's earliest known letter (1 Thessalonians), Paul charges the church "to have this letter read to all the brothers" (5:27). To the Colossians he writes that when this letter is read they shall see to it that the Laodicean church also gets to read it, and that the Colossians read the letter he wrote to the Laodiceans (Col. 4:16). "Until I come," he writes to Timothy at Ephesus, "devote yourself to the public reading . . ." (1 Tim. 4:13). The one who reads the Scriptures to the congregation is given a special beatitude by John the apostle (Rev. 1:3).

Private copies of the biblical books were hard to come by, and so the reading of the Scriptures in the meetings of the believers played an important role. To begin with, however, only the books of the OT were read, interpreted in the light of Christ's coming, death, and exaltation. The NT books were not available to the church during the first few decades of its existence. The earliest of our four Gospels (probably Mark) was not written until thirty years after our Lord's ascension to glory. It can be seen that the sayings of Jesus were valued equally highly with the OT Scriptures, for example, from 1 Timothy 5:18, where Deuteronomy 25:4 is quoted together with a saying of Jesus. For an entire generation after Christ's death the teachings of Jesus were transmitted orally. We should, therefore, say a few things about the period of oral tradition that preceded the writing of the NT books.

I. THE PERIOD OF ORAL TRADITION

A. The Delay in Publishing New Testament Books

We may ask today, Why the delay in the writing of the apostolic books? The early church may have asked, Why the hurry? How can we explain this delay?

First, the apostles were living books. As long as the apostles were present in the church, there was no great need for written records of the life and sayings of Jesus. They were the eyewitnesses who knew not only the facts but they could also give the interpretation of the facts. The important place eyewitnesses had in establishing the truth of the gospel can be seen, for example, from 1 Corinthians 15:6, where Paul mentions some five hundred witnesses to Christ's resurrection, most of whom were still alive. The second-century bishop, Papias, writes: "I do not think that I derived so much benefit from books as from the living voice of those that are still surviving."[1]

Moreover, as already mentioned, the church had the OT. Jesus had spoken with high regard of God's Word in the Jewish Scriptures. The apostles preached from these inspired books of the OT. So it wasn't that the church had no Bible—albeit a Bible that came from the age of preparation and that was now understood in the light of its fulfillment in Christ.

A third reason, perhaps, why the writing of the NT books was delayed was the Oriental practice of passing on tradition orally. Printing was still a long way off, and the production of scrolls or codices was laborious and costly. Moreover, there was much illiteracy among the common folk. When Jesus taught the multitudes, he would frequently say, "You have heard!" (e.g., Matt. 5:27). They heard the Scriptures read in the synagogue, but there was little private reading. The matter was different, of course, among the scribes whom Jesus asked upon occasion, "Have you not read?" (e.g., Mark 2:25).

Jewish traditions had been handed down orally for centuries, and some of the rabbis had a dislike for writing. The oral law was not written down until about A.D. 200, and the Mishnah in the English translation of Danby runs to some eight hundred pages. All of this material had to be memorized and passed on from teacher to student. Some rabbis boasted of students who had memories like well-plastered cisterns that never lost a drop. There would, then, be nothing unusual about transmitting the teachings of Jesus by word of mouth.

There are those who argue that the strong belief in the imminent return of Christ in the first-century church did little to encourage the writing of books for future generations, but that is hard to prove.

B. The Need for Written Records

We should not think of the oral tradition of Jesus' words and works as a confused legacy. It was what A. M. Hunter call "guarded tradition."[2] We all know that when children hear the same story several times they will immediately notice when the storyteller, the tenth time round, changes some details. In a simliar way "the story of

---

[1]Eusebius, *Ecclesiastical History*, iii, 39.3.

[2]A. M. Hunter, *Paul and His Predecesors*, rev. ed. (London: SCM Press, 1961), p. 22.

Jesus," as it was told and retold, took on fixed forms.

Paul exhorts the Thessalonians to hold the traditions that they were taught, whether by *word* or epistle (2 Thess. 2:15). The Corinthians are commended for maintaining the traditions Paul had delivered to them (1 Cor. 11:2). He himself had received his information about what Jesus did and taught from eyewitnesses. Repeatedly he stresses the fact that he had "received" the gospel (e.g., 1 Cor. 15:3).

Trustworthy though this oral tradition may have been, the need for written records must have become more pressing as time went on. The apostles, who were founding churches all over the empire, found it necessary to write letters to these churches, to instruct, correct, encourage, and admonish the young converts. This missionary outreach of the church must have made the apostles aware of the need for written Gospels also. New converts needed written records of the sayings and deeds of Jesus; the Gentile churches often had no access to eyewitnesses. To this day one of the first tasks of the pioneer missionary is to learn the language of the tribe, reduce it to writing, and put at least one Gospel into writing. The missionary intent of our canonical Gospels seems to be quite obvious. John, for example, writes that "these are written that you may believe that Jesus is the Christ, the Son of God, and that by believing you may have life in his name" (20:31).

Moreover, as the gospel spread in the Graeco-Roman world, it entered a literary society. Publishing books was no small business. Bookshops in Rome were covered with advertisements of new books as they are today. A reading public looks for written materials; the written Gospels met that need.

The need for written Gospels and other apostolic books was underscored also by the danger of heresy. False prophets claimed special insights into divine truth. By what norm was the church to determine whether a doctrine was apostolic or not? Written records of the teachings of Jesus and his apostles proved to be a bulwark against the invasion of heresies.

There were also pastoral reasons why a church should have written records of Jesus' teachings. How important it must have been to know what Jesus had said about divorce, the sabbath, food laws, fasting, and many other issues that the church faced in the first century! When Paul writes to the Corinthians about the matter of divorce he seems to be glad that he can quote a word of Jesus on that question (1 Cor. 7:10). On the question of mixed marriages Jesus had evidently not said anything, and so Paul has to speak on his own apostolic authority (1 Cor. 7:12). Without the written Gospels, the record of the early church's founding and growth, the many letters to the young churches, and the book of comfort for suffering saints (the Revelation), the churches would have been at a loss concerning their life and mission once the apostles passed off the scene. And so in God's good providence these Christian writings became part of the church's Bible. We should remind ourselves that no account of the writing and the collection of these apostolic books is adequate if it fails to reckon with the inspiration and witness of the Holy Spirit.[3]

---

[3]F. F. Bruce, *Tradition: Old and New* (Grand Rapids: Zondervan, 1970), p. 71.

Once the NT books were written, they were collected, and eventually these twenty-seven books comprised the NT. However, by the time the limits of the NT canon were being drawn, a great many other Christian books were circulating in the churches. Also, the oral tradition of Jesus' deeds and sayings continued. And so a distinction between canonical and noncanonical books had to be made.

In order that we might be more aware of this mass of Christian literature surrounding the apostolic writings, we should mention some of these extracanonical books.

II. EXTRACANONICAL LITERATURE

A. The Agrapha

Luke tells us in his prologue (1:1-4) that many others had taken it in hand to write "gospels"—other than our four. John informs us that Jesus did many other "signs" not recorded in the Fourth Gospel (John 20:30). In fact, he goes so far as to say that if everything Jesus did were to be recorded the world could not contain the books that would be written (John 21:25).

Outside of the apocryphal gospels, where an attempt is made to supplement the record of Jesus' deeds in our four Gospels, there is little tradition of what Jesus did (beyond that recorded in our canonical Gospels). It is otherwise with what Jesus said.[4] Many sayings of Jesus were known in the early church that are not recorded in the Gospels. These are called *Agrapha* (meaning, "not written" in our canonical Gospels).

We have a few Agrapha within the NT itself. Paul, for example, in speaking to the elders of the Ephesian church recalls a saying of Jesus, not in our Gospels, "It is more blessed to give than to receive" (Acts 20:35). Some Agrapha are found in variant texts in the manuscripts of the NT. Codex Bezae, for example, has a saying of Jesus, at Luke 6:5, to a man whom he found working on the sabbath: "Man if you know what you are doing, you are blessed; but if you do not know, you are cursed and a transgressor of the law." Joachim Jeremias argues for the authenticity of this saying.[5] In other words, if the man was doing something good in obedience to Jesus' teachings on the sabbath, he was blessed; if he was violating the sabbath out of impudence, he was cursed. In the literature of the early church, references to sayings of Jesus not recorded in the Gospels are not at all uncommon. Some of these are recorded by Eusebius, the church historian, others are in the writings of the Fathers (Justin Martyr, Tertullian, Clement of Alexandria, Origen, Jerome, Augustine, and others). One saying that is frequently mentioned is Jesus' exhortation to be good moneychangers, and some see the vocabulary of that saying reflected in Paul's command to test everything and to hold fast what is good (1 Thess. 5:21).

In 1959, a second-century work, the Gospel According to Thomas, was published. This was one of forty-nine documents discovered at Nag Hammadi in 1945 in Egypt, and this is a compilation of 114 sayings of Jesus, translated into Coptic from Greek.

---

[4]Bruce, *Tradition*, p. 87.

[5]J. Jeremias, *Unknown Sayings of Jesus*, trans. Reginald Fuller (London: SPCK, 1958), p. 51.

Some of these sayings were already known from other literature. Several of them are parallels to words of Jesus in our canonical Gospels; in other cases authentic words of Jesus have been amplified or conflated. However, there are also new sayings, to which there are no parallels in our Gospels. There are beatitudes, fables, and sayings on fasting, circumcision, marriage, and other subjects.[6]

Many of these sayings are very gnostic in orientation, but there are others that seem to be authentic words of Jesus. We mention the Agrapha only to point out that there were sayings of Jesus that came to be recorded but that are not a part of our canonical Gospels. Also, we must constantly be aware of the fact that before the Gospels took on written form they were transmitted orally.

B. Parallel Literature

The vibrant faith of the early church gave birth to what became virtually a flood of Christian literature. Much of these early writings were modeled after the canonical writings. Letters, Gospels, Acts, and Revelations (the four types of literature we have in the NT) were being written, some of which were held in such high regard that several noncanonical books were included in some of the early manuscripts of the NT.

One such letter was that of Clement of Rome, who wrote to the Corinthian church about A.D. 95. It is still found in the fifth-century Codex Alexandrinus. Early in the second century Ignatius, the martyr/bishop of Antioch, wrote

seven letters to churches in Asia Minor and to the church of Rome. Polycarp, bishop of Smyrna, wrote to the Philippians about the middle of the second century. The Letter of Barnabas illustrates how some Christians allegorized the OT. It was held in such high regard that it got into the Codex Sinaiticus. About the middle of the second century a Greek Christian of Asia wrote a letter in the name of all the apostles, called the Epistle of the Apostles, providing the churches with a kind of compendium of Christian doctrine. The account of Justin Martyr's martyrdom has been preserved in the form of court records, but the Martrydom of Polycarp is in the form of a letter. This is true also of the account of the persecution of the churches in Lyons and Vienne in A.D 177, whose sufferings are reported in the Letter of the Gallican Churches. A delightful but anonymous Letter to Diognetus is a defense of the Christian faith and could be classified as an apology—another form of literature that emerges in the early second century.[7]

In imitation of the Book of Revelation—a type of literature very popular in Judaism at one time—several Christian writers produced apocalypses. The one best known is the Shepherd, written by Hermas, a Roman Christian. Published about the end of the first century A.D., it became very popular and is included with the Epistle of Barnabas in the Codex Sinaiticus. About the middle of the second century a Greek Christian wrote the Revelation of Peter. Revelations of Paul, James, Stephen, Thomas, John, Philip, and the Virgin Mary are also known, and with

---

[6]Bruce, *Tradition*, pp. 87–107.

[7]For a review of early Christian literature, see E. J. Goodspeed, *A History of Early Christian Literature*, revised by R. M. Grant (Chicago: University of Chicago Press, 1966).

these books we have crossed over into the area of apocryphal literature.

As this Christian apocryphal literature emerged, the Gospels were also imitated. These apocryphal gospels have a greater biographical interest and often seek to supplement our canonical Gospels. There is much legendary material in them and some of it is strongly Gnostic in coloring. From the second century there comes, for example, the Gospel According to the Egyptians, which evidently was but another name for the Gospel According to the Hebrews. The former circulated among Christians in Egypt and the latter among Jewish Christians. From the same century comes also the Proto-Evangelium of James, the Gospel According to Peter, the British Museum Gospel, the Gospel of the Ebionites, the Infancy Gospel of Thomas, and several others.

Also, we have several apocryphal parallels to our canonical Acts. One is the Acts of Paul, from the latter half of the second century; another is the Acts of John, from about the same time. Somewhat later are the Acts of Peter, the Acts of Andrew, and the Acts of Thomas (the latter, from the Syriac church). For the complete text of these and the following extracanonical books one might consult the two volume *New Testament Apocrypha* by Edgar Hennecke, edited by Wilhelm Schneemelcher.[8]

C. Other Christian Writings

There are a great many Christian writings from the time when the NT was gaining shape that were modeled after the NT books. But others are not. With the founding of the church came the birth of Christian hymns. Tidbits of such hymns are found in the NT (e.g., 1 Tim. 3:16). While no collection of early Christian hymns has survived, a group of Christian hymns, called *Odes to Solomon*, stemming from the late first- or second-century Syriac church, were discovered at the beginning of our century.

Sermons also were published. One that has found its way together with Clement of Rome's letter into the Codex Alexandrinus is called 2 Clement. A good many other sermons by men such as Melito of Sardis, Clement of Alexandria, Origen, and others are known. Also, exegetical works, such as those of Papias, bishop of Hierapolis, appeared as early as the second century.

A special kind of literature, in which Christian writers defend the Christian faith against attacks by its calumniators, also emerged. The earliest of a number of such apologetic works is the Preaching of Peter. It was written about the beginning of the second century. The *Apology of Quadratus*, the *Apology of Aristides*, the *Apology of Athenagoras*, and the *Apology* of Justin (who died a martyr in Rome about A.D. 165), are examples of this kind of literature. These works were addressed to non-Christian readers in an effort to show that the evil rumors spread by the enemies of the Christian faith were unfounded. The *Letter to Diognetus* is called a letter, but is in fact an apology. Perhaps Justin's *Dialogue with Trypho*, as well as Tatian's *Address to the Greeks*, could

---

[8]E. Hennecke and W. Schneemelcher, *New Testament Apocrypha*, 2 vols., trans. R. Mcl. Wilson (Philadelphia: Westminster, 1963).

also be classified as apologies.

With the end of the second and the beginning of the third century, Christian books in great numbers continued to appear. Writers such as Irenaeus, Clement of Alexandria, Origen, Tertullian, Hippolytus, and others enriched the churches with all sorts of books. Nor should it be overlooked that this great body of Christian literature was being produced in difficult times, for up to the beginning of the fourth century the church was often under fire. We should remember, then, that as the limits of the NT canon were being fixed, the twenty-seven books of the NT had to be set off from a vast number of Christian books, some of which were extremely popular in the early centuries of the Christian era.

III. COLLECTING THE CANONICAL BOOKS

A. The Letters of Paul

Among the earliest books that now constitute our NT are the letters of Paul. When Paul wrote to the various churches he was conscious, no doubt, that he was writing under the inspiration of the Holy Spirit. However, he can hardly have known in advance that the letters he wrote—some of them quite chatty and casual—would one day belong to the canon of Holy Scripture. When Luke wrote his second volume, the Acts, he made no mention of the fact that his hero, Paul, had ever written a letter. That means, perhaps, that when Acts was written these letters had not yet been collected. Professor E. J. Goodspeed has suggested that the publication of Acts may have stimulated the collection of the letters of this great church planter, Paul.[9] Be that as it may, there is considerable evidence that by the end of the first century the letters of Paul had been collected.

1. *Witnesses to a Pauline Corpus.* It can be shown from the NT itself that Paul's letters were being collected. Peter refers to the letters of Paul as if they were perfectly familiar to his readers (2 Peter 3:16), and confesses that there are difficult passages in them, which heretical teachers twist to their own ends. Also, Clement of Rome, writing to the Corinthians (c. A.D. 95) can say: "Take up the letter of the blessed Apostle Paul" (1 Clem. 46:1), assuming that his readers have it in their possession. Clement's letter reflects his knowledge of other letters of Paul. Ignatius (c. A.D. 110) can write to the Ephesians, reminding them that Paul remembers them in every letter.[10] Polycarp, writing to the Philippians, reminds his readers that Paul in his absence wrote letters to them.[11] By the middle of the second century Marcion's truncated canon of one Gospel and ten letters of Paul makes its appearance. "It is clear that by A.D. 100 Paul's letters had been collected and were widely known and widely accepted."[12]

From a strictly human point of view this is a bit surprising, to say the least. Paul wrote to deal with local and temporary situations. Heresies threatened; there was the danger of falling back into pagan ways; persecu-

---

[9]E. J. Goodspeed, *The Formation of the New Testament* (Chicago: University of Chicago Press, 1926), p. 21.

[10]Ignatius, *Ephesians*, 12:2.

[11]Polycarp, *Philippians*, 3:2.

[12]W. Barclay, *The Making of the Bible* (New York: Abingdon, 1961), p. 65.

tions discouraged the saints; enthusiasts went off on tangents; cultural differences among members of the churches threatened to divide the body of Christ—all such matters and more had to be addressed in writing when Paul could not be present in person.

There were times when Paul was not even sure that the church would read the letter addressed to it. "I charge you before the Lord," he writes to the Thessalonians, "to have this letter read to all the brothers" (1 Thess. 5:27). So little attention was paid to some of his letters that they are now lost. We do not have the first letter he wrote to the Corinthians, which the readers had badly misunderstood (1 Cor. 5:9). Nor do we have his letter to the Laodicians (Col. 4:16).

It does not follow, of course, that something that is temporary and local cannot attain to universal immortality. The music of Bach has become almost universal, yet it was written, we are told, for the Sunday by Sunday performances of Bach's choir in Leipzig. Also, the collection of Paul's letters had precedent in the collection of the letters of great men, such as Cicero. Could the collection of the seven letters in the Revelation of John also have been a precedent?

In any case, outside the reference in 2 Peter, there is hardly a reference to the letters of Paul prior to A.D. 90. After that, however, they are mentioned frequently. William Barclay makes the observation that "not long after A.D. 90 there was a veritable epidemic of letter writing and something must have given it its impetus."[13] He is of the opinion that the emergence of a

Pauline corpus provided this impetus.

We have no record of how they were collected; nor were the limits of the collection clearly defined from the outset. All we can do is suggest some theories on how the letters of Paul were collected.

2. *Theories of Collection.* Basically there are two theories on how the letters of Paul were collected. One has it that it was a process that went on over a period of time; the other, that there was some historical occasion that led to the collection of all of Paul's letters at once.

The fact that Paul's letters stand in different orders in the manuscripts that come from the early centuries, suggest that collections of Pauline writings were made at various centers of the Christian church. Churches like Corinth, for example, that had received letters from Paul, eventually may have procured letters that the apostle had written to other churches also. This process may have gone on for years in places like Ephesus, Corinth, and Rome. Perhaps Paul himself encouraged such a collection when, for example, he asked the Colossians to exchange letters with the Laodiceans (Col. 4:16).

Those who argue that Paul's letters were all collected at one time are not agreed on what provided the occasion for such a collection. Adolf von Harnack thought Paul's writings were immediately recognized by the church as having permanent value and that all his available letters were promptly collected. Professor Goodspeed held to a "lapsed interest" theory, and that, as already mentioned, the publication of Acts pro-

---

[13]Barclay, *Making of the Bible*, p. 65.

vided the impetus to collect all of Paul's writings.[14]

Another form of this theory of a "complete collection" is that some individual took upon himself the task of making a collection of Paul's writings. One candidate for such an undertaking might be Onesimus, the converted slave, for, as some scholars argue, it is hard to see how the little Philemon epistle would have been included in the Pauline Corpus if the central character of the letter, Onesimus, had not done the collecting. If we are going to look for candidates, perhaps Timothy, who was charged by Paul to commit to faithful men what he had heard (2 Tim. 2:2), should be given first place.

Since we have no records of how the letters of Paul were collected, we have to content ourselves with theories. Of the two just mentioned, it seems more likely that the collecting of Pauline writings was a process that went on over a period of time. Whether Paul's letters already formed a complete corpus when the four Gospels were collected, is hard to say. It appears as if the formation of the fourfold Gospel, as we now have it in the NT, took place about the same time as the collection of Paul's letters.

B. The Gospels

Luke informs us that many writers before him had undertaken to compile a narrative "of the things that have been fulfilled among us" (Luke 1:1). How many such accounts of Jesus' life

and death were circulating is not known; outside of our four, no gospels have survived. The earliest of our canonical Gospels cannot be dated earlier than about A.D. 60, which indicates that for at least thirty years the gospel was transmitted orally.

The first reference to one of our canonical Gospels is to be found in the *Didache*, a little manual of church discipline from the end of the first century A.D. Here the writer warns the churches not to pray like the hypocrites "but as the Lord commanded in his Gospel" (8:2)—a reference to the Lord's Prayer. It can be seen that the Gospel of John had been written by the end of the century from the fact that a papyrus fragment of this Gospel, the John Rylands Papyrus, dating from perhaps as early as A.D. 130, was found in the sands of Egypt. Ignatius, in his letter to the Philadelphians, knows of people who will not believe what is in the gospel if they do not find it in the OT[15]—another witness to the written gospel. Papias, in the beginning of the second century, mentions Gospels, such as Matthew, by name.[16]

A reference to gospels in the plural is found in Justin's *Apology* (c. A.D. 150), where the "memoirs of the apostles" are called "gospels."[17] By about A.D. 180 Irenaeus finds it necessary to defend the fourfold Gospel.[18] Evidently there had been attempts to reduce the four to one. Marcion, for example, had only the Gospel of Luke in his canon (c. A.D. 140). Tatian had prepared a Gospel harmony (c. A.D. 160), called the Diatessaron, in which he had blended the

---

[14]Barclay, *Making of the Bible*, p. 68.

[15]To the *Philadelphians*, 8:2.

[16]Eusebius, *Eccl. History*, iii, 39.16.

[17]Justin, *Apology*, chap. 66.

[18]Irenaeus, *Adv. Haer.* iii, 2.8.

four Gospels into one. Irenaeus defends the fourfold Gospel by arguing that the number lay in the nature of things: there were four points of the compass, there were four covenants, and there were four living creatures.

The attempts to reduce the Gospels to one, as well as the defense of the fourfold Gospel, indicate that the early church was not sure why there should be four. If the Gospels had been strictly narratives or biographies, one might have been enough; but gospels are good news, and the good news about Jesus Christ can be proclaimed in different ways. In fact, the gospel of Christ is so rich it can never be exhausted.[19]

What does all this have to do with the collecting of our Gospels into a fourfold Gospel? Such questions and debates clearly witness to the presence of a fourfold gospel by the beginning of the second century. However, where and by whom our four Gospels were published for the first time as a Tetraevangelium is not known.

C. The Other Books

When the four Gospels were gathered into one collection, Luke's two-volume work, Luke-Acts, was split up; the Gospel went with Matthew, Mark, and John, and Acts was left standing as a single volume. In the process of collecting the twenty-seven-book canon, the most natural place for Acts was between the Gospels and the Epistles. "Acts played an indispensable part in relating the two collections to each other," writes F. F. Bruce.[20] And, as most early lists indi-

cate, Acts did become the connecting link between these smaller collections.

It stands to reason that Acts should follow the Gospels. We want to know what happened after the death, resurrection, and ascension of our Lord. Acts provides that sequel. On the other hand, if we read the Epistles, we ask for the background of these letters. Were it not for Acts, we would know very little about the founding of the churches to whom Paul wrote. Acts, then, performs double duty: it continues the story of the Gospels and also provides the setting for the Epistles. Thus Acts found a secure place in the NT canon.

If one reads Acts one discovers quickly that Paul is not the only apostle who preached the gospel and established churches. In the early chapters of Acts, Peter and John work together. James dies by the sword. About the other disciples of Jesus (except Judas, who was replaced by Matthias) Luke is silent, and we must rely on extrabiblical traditions for information on their ministry. In any case, Peter and John also wrote letters, as did James and Jude, our Lord's brothers. John also wrote the Revelation. Marcion did not accept their books into his canon, and it may well be that Luke's account of the activity of these apostolic men in Acts, helped to secure a place for the General Epistles and Revelation in the canon.

No one can deny that there were questions about the limits of the NT canon, and the next chapter will give a survey of what the NT canon looked like in the early centuries and how it came to be closed.

---

[19]O. Cullmann, *The Early Church*, trans. A. J. B. Higgins (London: SCM Press, 1956), p. 52.

[20]F. F. Bruce, *Commentary on the Book of the Acts* (Grand Rapids: Eerdmans, 1955), p. 15.

SUGGESTED READING

Barclay, W. The Making of the Bible. Nashville: Abingdon, 1961.

Bruce, F. F. The New Testament Documents: Are They Reliable? 5th rev. ed. Grand Rapids: Eerdmans, 1970.

———. Jesus and Christian Origins Outside the New Testament. Grand Rapids: Eerdmans, 1974.

———. Tradition: Old and New. Grand Rapids: Zondervan, 1970.

Geisler, N. L. and Nix, W. E. From God To Us. Chicago: Moody, 1974. See "The Extent of the New Testament Canon," pp. 113–25.

Jeremias, J. Unknown Sayings of Jesus, trans. R. H. Fuller. London: SPCK, 1958.

Martin, R. P. New Testament Foundations, 2 vols. Grand Rapids: Eerdmans, Vol. 1, 1975. See chapter 3, "How the Gospels Came to Be Written."

General ①

I + II Thess.

written: 2nd Miss. tour
Eschatology. - coming
of Christ

General ②

Gal.

I + II Cor.

Rom.

written: 3rd miss. tour.
soteriology.
cross of christ

Prison

Col.
Philemon
Eph.
Phil.

1st mp.
Christological
character of Christ.

Pastoral

I Tim.
Titus
II Tim.

before 2nd mp.
Ecclesiology
church of Christ

Chapter 10

The New Testament Canon

It has often been observed that the question of the NT canon is more problematic than that of the OT. The OT was endorsed by Jesus and the apostles, and so we can rest assured that "the law, the prophets, and the psalms," as Jesus called our tripartite OT, is for us the Word of God. No body of literature ever had its credentials confirmed by a higher authority.[1]

This does not mean, however, that the NT has less authority than the OT. The apostles clearly interpreted the OT in the light of the NT. The Christ who authenticated the OT has also imparted his authority to the NT. On the eve of his crucifixion he promised to send his disciples the Holy Spirit, his Other Self, who, he said, "will teach you all things and will remind you of everything I have said to you" (John 14:26). The NT is the written deposit of the special fulfillment of these words of Jesus.[2]

His Spirit not only inspired the writers of the NT books but he also witnessed to the authenticity of their message. The church was guided in affirming our twenty-seven-book NT canon by the Spirit. We may say this in retrospect, for if we look at the process by which the NT canon became fixed it strikes us as being very human. God, however, was at work in the church and watched over his word. How then, was the NT canon formed?

I. SHAPING THE NEW TESTAMENT CANON

The threat of heretical teachings did not disappear with the death of the apostles. Throughout the second century the church had to face not only attacks from without, but threats from within its own ranks. These attacks made the need for an authoritative collection of apostolic books all the more urgent. Since this need was felt by churches in different geographical

---

[1] F. F. Bruce, *The Books and the Parchments*, 3rd rev. ed. (Old Tappan: Revell, 1963), p. 127.
[2] Bruce, *Books and Parchments*, p. 105.

areas there were, to begin with at least, some differences in these churches in the matter of the limits of the canon. For practical purposes we may speak of the Western church, which was slowly becoming Latin-speaking, the Eastern or Greek-speaking church, and the Syriac church.

A. The Western Church

Irenaeus, the bishop of Lyons, about 185, wrote a book *Against Heresies.* In it he acknowledges twenty-one or twenty-two of our twenty-seven books: Four Gospels, Acts, Epistles of Paul (Philemon is missing, but that may be accidental), 1 Peter, 1 and 2 John, of the General Epistles, and the Revelation of John. The fact that he omits Hebrews, James, Jude, 2 Peter, and 3 John, does not necessarily mean, however, that he rejected these books altogether. But he does not appear to have accepted the Shepherd of Hermas as Scripture.

From about the same time comes the Muratorian Fragment (named after the Italian who discovered it in 1740), which has the Four Gospels, Acts, the Epistles of Paul, Jude, 1 and 2 John, of the General Epistles, and two Revelations, those of John and Peter (some did not want the latter to be read in the church, he says). He recommends the reading of the Shepherd of Hermas in private, and lists the Wisdom of Solomon. Missing are 1 and 2 Peter, Hebrews, 3 John, and James.[3]

Hippolytus (170–235) was a pupil of Irenaeus, and his NT closely resembles that of his teacher. He was the last Roman Christian writer to write in Greek. He accepted the Four Gospels, Acts, and the thirteen Epistles of Paul (Hebrews is not among the Paulines in the Western church). He accepted also three General Epistles (1 and 2 Peter, 1 John). Together with the Revelation he had a canon of twenty-two books. What is new in this list is that 2 Peter is included. He knows the Shepherd of Hermas, the Revelation of Peter, the Acts of Paul, and many more, but does not include them.

Tertullian represents the Western church in North Africa at the close of the second century. He accepts the Four Gospels, Acts, the thirteen Epistles of Paul, 1 Peter, 1 John, and Jude, of the General Epistles, and the Revelation of John. Missing are Hebrews (which he ascribes to Barnabas), 2 Peter, 2 and 3 John, and James. He condemned the Shepherd of Hermas in unmeasured terms.[4]

Generally speaking, then, twenty-two books of the NT were accepted in the Western church by A.D. 200. The Epistle to the Hebrews had not yet found a place, and this does not change much in the West until the fourth century. The other great gap is in the General Epistles (also called "Catholic," meaning "universal"). There is still some ambivalence about how many apocalypses belong to the NT. The Revelation of John is secure, but the Revelation of Peter is also accepted by some, and the Shepherd of Hermas (coming from Rome) is still very popular in the West.

B. The Greek Church

The Greek-speaking church has much in common with the Western

---

[3]E. J. Goodspeed, *The Formation of the NT Canon* (Chicago: University of Chicago Press, 1926). The Muratorian canon list is given on pp. 188f.

[4]Goodspeed, *Formation of NT Canon*, p. 159.

church in the matter of the canon. There are, however, some differences. Clement of Alexandria (died 215) knew many gospels, but he gave the highest place to our four canonical Gospels. Acts is accepted, as are the Pauline Epistles. What is new in the Alexandrian church is that Hebrews is included with the Paulines. As in the West, Clement accepted several of the General Epistles (1 Peter, 1 and 2 John, Jude). Several of the General Epistles, however, are still missing. Strangely, he seems to attribute apostolic authority to the Epistle of Barnabas and the Letter of Clement of Rome. Also, he accepted three apocalypses, that of John, Peter, and the Shepherd of Hermas. It looks as if he also ascribed apostolic authority to the Preaching of Peter. Obviously in Clement of Alexandria the limits of the canon are not yet clearly drawn.

Clement's pupil, Origen, the great Alexandrian scholar (d. 254), took a more scholarly approach to the question of the canon, but essentially he agrees with Clement. Those books accepted by all, of which there were twenty-two, he calls *homologoumena* ("confessed by all"). Seven or eight books he calls *amphiballomena* ("things thrown both ways").

In contrast to the sects that have many gospels, says Origen, the church has only four Gospels.[5] Like Clement, Origen has fourteen letters of Paul. Although he has difficulty in accepting the Pauline authorship of Hebrews, he still ascribes it to Paul. Origen evidently accepted also the Epistle of Barnabas as canonical. The Acts has a firm place in his "acknowledged" list. However, only two General Epistles

(1 Peter and 1 John) are in that list; the others are still in the disputed category. The Revelation of John is accepted together with the apocalyptic Shepherd of Hermas. Although Hebrews was insecure in the West, the Revelation of John was insecure in the East, especially after Dionysius of Alexandria argued that it was not Johannine and, therefore, not apostolic.

Origen, then, has a NT of twenty-nine books, of which only twenty-two are acknowledged by all and seven are disputed. It does not follow, however, that Origen himself disputed every one of these seven.

Eusebius (260–340) became bishop of Caesarea and is best known for his *Church History*. His NT begins with the Four Gospels, followed by Acts and the Pauline Epistles (including Hebrews). Then follow 1 John and 1 Peter and, with considerable reservations, the Revelation of John. These twenty-two are for Eusebius the "acknowledged" books, as they were for Origen.

Among the "disputed" books are James, Jude, 2 Peter, 2 and 3 John. These are, however, not necessarily noncanonical for Eusebius, and when these are added to the former twenty-two we have exactly the books of the NT today.

The "disputed" books that Eusebius rejects are the Acts of Paul, the Shepherd, the Revelation of Peter, the Letter of Barnabas, the Didache. In addition, there are plainly heretical books, such as the Gospel of Peter, the Acts of Andrew, and others, that have no claim to canonicity at all. Eusebius draws a sharper line than Origen. Origen still accepted Barnabas and the

---

[5]Goodspeed, *Formation of NT Canon*, p. 91.

Shepherd, but Eusebius did not.

In the Codex Claromontanus, which comes from the sixth century, there is a list of biblical books that seems to represent the canon in Egypt about 300. In the NT section the codex lists the Four Gospels, the Letters of Paul, eight General Epistles, three revelations—the Revelation of John, the Shepherd, the Revelation of Peter, and two Acts—the Acts of the Apostles and the Acts of Paul. Included also is the Letter of Barnabas, but there is a dash before it and others that we do not consider canonical today.[6] In the third and early fourth century the exact boundaries of the NT continued to fluctuate in Egypt and Palestine.

Athanasius, who became bishop of Alexandria shortly after the Council of Nicaea in 325, wrote an Easter letter to the churches in his diocese, as was the custom among the bishops at that time. This letter, written in 367, is famous for its comments on the books of the Bible. His NT begins with the Four Gospels; these are followed by Acts and the General Epistles (James; 1 and 2 Peter; 1, 2, and 3 John; Jude), and the fourteen letters of Paul (including Hebrews). His list ends with the Revelation of John. While he permits the Didache and Hermas to be used in instructing catechumens, he does not accept them as Scripture. He totally rejects the sectarian apocryphal books. Of the OT books and our twenty-seven NT books he writes: "In them alone is the good news of the teaching of true religion proclaimed: let no one add to them or take away anything of them."[7]

Since Athanasius' letter has a list of twenty-seven books like our own, it may appear as if the story of the canon was now ended. This was not the case, however. Some of the major manuscripts of the fifth century still include extracanonical books: Codex Sinaiticus has the Epistle of Barnabas and the Shepherd of Hermas, and Codex Alexandrinus has 1 and 2 Clement, and the Psalms of Solomon.

There is yet another part of the Eastern church that we need to pay attention to. In the Syriac-speaking church the canon had a somewhat different form than in the churches just mentioned.

C. The Syriac Church

The Syriac church is not the church of Syria, which was largely Greek-speaking, but the church in the land of the two rivers. Missionary zeal brought the gospel to the East, just as it had carried it to the West. Syriac is essentially a form of Aramaic.

About A.D. 170 the Syrian, Tatian, who had been the pupil of Justin Martyr in Rome, returned to his native land, having combined the four Gospels into a Diatessaron, meaning "four-ply." Tatian combined distinctive phrases preserved by only one Evangelist with those preserved by another and arranged the several sections of the Gospels into a single narrative. Omitting a few sections, Tatian managed to preserve practically the entire contents of the separate Gospels woven into one. Although this gospel harmony was very popular, it was replaced eventually by the four canonical Gospels.

From the Teaching of Addai (A.D. 35)

---

[6]Goodspeed, *Formation of NT Canon*, p. 104.
[7]Goodspeed, *Formation of NT Canon*, p. 108.

THE NEW TESTAMENT CANON

it appears that the Syriac church had, at the outset at least, a shorter canon than did the other churches. A Syriac canon of the Old and New Testaments from about A.D. 400 indicates that the four Gospels, the Acts, and fourteen letters of Paul (including Hebrews) were generally accepted. "This is all," adds the writer of the list.[8]

With the publication of the Peshitta NT (c. A.D. 425) the standard Syriac version, we get a canon of: the Four Gospels, the Acts, fourteen letters of Paul, James, 1 Peter and 1 John. When this Peshitta version was revised in 508 it had all seven General Epistles (Hebrews going with the Paulines), and so it actually had the twenty-seven books of our NT. However, this and a later revision by Thomas of Harkel (in 616), never proved as popular as the original Peshitta, which had only three General Epistles and no Revelation.

The question that needs to be addressed now is, on what grounds did churches determine which books were to be included or excluded from the canon? But before we speak of that, we must say something about conciliar decisions with respect to the NT canon.

II. THE AGE OF THE COUNCILS

It should be said straight off that no council ever made a book of the NT canonical. They simply affirmed those books that the church through long usage had found to speak with the voice of the living God.

The Synod of Laodicea, which met in 363, forbade the reading of nonca-

nonical books. From this decision it may be inferred that everyone knew which books were canonical and which were not.

The Council of Hippo in Africa in 393 laid down our present NT list as Scripture. The Synod of Carthage in 397 declared that nothing should be read in the churches as divine Scripture except the canonical books. It then proceeds to give a list of Old and New Testament books—the latter just as we have them today.

This canon was reaffirmed at the Council of Carthage, in 419, except that Hebrews, which had been listed separately from other Pauline letters in 397, is now included among them.[9] When Jerome was working on his Latin Vulgate version, he mentions repeatedly that the Latins do not accept Hebrews.

Through the interaction of Eastern and Western churches, however, the two branches of Christendom drew even in the matter of the disputed books. In the West Hebrews came to be accepted, and in the East the Revelation of John found a secure place. The seven General Epistles were also accepted eventually.

While there may have been uneasiness about several of the NT books for a long time, the major writings were accepted by almost all Christians by the middle of the second century.[10] In fact, the Gospels and the Epistles of Paul were accepted by the end of the first century. What guided the church in establishing the limits of the NT canon?

---

[8]Goodspeed, *Formation of NT Canon*, p. 120.
[9]Goodspeed, *Formation of NT Canon*, p. 127.
[10]R. M. Grant, "The New Testament Canon," *The Cambridge History of the Bible*, eds. P. R. Ackroyd and C. F. Evans (Cambridge: Cambridge University Press, 1970), Vol. 1, p. 308.

III. THE CANONS OF COLLECTION

A. The Apostolicity of the Writings

The apostles were regarded as men who had been uniquely in the confidence of Jesus. They were eyewitnesses; they had established and guided the early church by the teachings of Jesus. Their writings, therefore, were looked on as authoritative. Clement of Rome writes: "The apostles have preached the gospel to us from the Lord Jesus Christ; Jesus Christ [has done so] from God. Christ therefore was sent forth by God and the apostles by Christ."[11] Irenaeus tells us that Polycarp "always taught the things which he had learned from the apostles, which the church has handed down, and which alone are true."[12] Ignatius writes to the Romans, "I do not give you orders like Peter and Paul. They were apostles; I am a convict."[13] Clearly, here we can see how important the apostolicity of the books was in determining the canonicity of books.

The reason some of the apocryphal books were so popular was that the authors often wrote in the name of an apostle. One reason Hebrews was widely accepted in the East was because it was grouped with the Paulines. Revelation, on the other hand, was insecure, because Dionysius had argued against its apostolic authorship. Apostolicity, however, must not be understood simply as a knowledge of who the author of a book was. Anonymous books (such as the Gospels and several epistles) were ac-cepted because they were apostolic in content. The apostolic content of books was known from the apostolic teaching that was well established in the churches—sometimes called "the canon of truth."

B. The Canon of Truth

Church fathers occasionally speak of the canon of faith or truth (in Latin it is known as *Regula Fidei* or *Veritatis*). This "rule of faith" was more or less the same in the various geographical areas of the empire, and was regarded as a key to the interpretation of the Scripture. It was not a document, but a kind of digest of apostolic teaching. Von Campenhausen speaks of it as "the essential content of the Christian faith."[14] The biblical books were the authoritative *source* of the Christian faith, one might say, and the "rule of faith" was the authoritative *substance*. Such a rule of faith was very helpful, not only in combating heresy, but also in determining whether a book was apostolic in content or not.

We are told of a second-century bishop of Antioch, Serapion, who visited the Syrian town of Rhossos and found the church divided over the use of the Gospel of Peter. At first Serapion, not suspecting heresy, said a work of an apostle might be read. Then when he discovered its Docetic character (even though it claimed to be apostolic) he suppressed the book. Obviously this gospel did not measure up to the rule of faith.

It can be seen that this standard

---

[11]Clement, *First Epistle*, 42, 1–2.

[12]Irenaeus, *Against Heresies*, 3, 4.

[13]Ignatius, *To the Romans*, 4, 3.

[14]H. Von Campenhausen, *The Formation of the Christian Bible*, trans. J. A. Baker, (Philadelphia: Fortress, 1968), p. 288.

could not by itself cover every situation from the fact that 1 Clement is not heretical in content, and yet it was not accepted as canonical in the end. In establishing the canonicity of the NT books a number of factors were at work.

C. Catholicity

Another criterion for the canonicity of a book is its universal (i.e., catholic) acceptance. A document acknowledged only in a small corner of Christendom was unlikely to win canonical status. F. F. Bruce writes, "My personal experience of the inward witness of the Spirit, my personal awareness of the self-authenticating quality of Scripture, is important for my personal religious life, but what is important in relation to the canon is the witness of the Spirit in the total Christian community—not only in the total Christian community of the world today but the total Christian community from the first generation onwards."[15]

The interaction of the Greek and Latin churches finally gave both Hebrews and the Revelation a fixed place in the canons of both of these communities. And the interchange of scholars and ideas between the Syriac church and the churches in the West eventually got the General Epistles into the Peshitta.

D. Chronology of Composition

Oscar Cullmann has pointed out that only the tradition that comes from the "period of the incarnation" can be accepted as authoritative for the church.[16] This comprises the period from the birth of Christ to the death of the last apostle. The church is built on the foundation of the apostles (Eph. 2:20), and once they pass off the scene we have no more direct revelation, one might say. Apostles can appoint bishops, but they cannot appoint other apostles to succeed them.

In the Muratorian Canon, the Shepherd of Hermas is excluded from use in the church's worship, and the reason given is: "Hermas wrote the Shepherd only recently, in our time in the city of Rome . . . . Therefore, it must indeed be read, but cannot be publicly recited to the people in the church. . . ." In other words, the apostolic age is past, and no books can be added to the writings of the apostles.

It is, then, not a question of whether Jude is more interesting than Bunyan's *Pilgrims' Progress*, but Jude is an apostolic witness while Bunyan is not. All Christian literature coming from the postapostolic period must be judged by those books that come from "the period of the incarnation." Insofar as they accurately reflect apostolic teaching they can be extremely useful for the life of the individual and the church.

E. The Self-Evidencing Quality of the Books

In retrospect, we can say that besides several external canons of selection there was something about the NT books that made them canonical in the first place. They had the stamp of God on them from the beginning. To

---

[15]F. F. Bruce, "New Light on the Origins of the New Testament Canon," *New Dimensions in New Testament Study*, eds. R. N. Longenecker and M. C. Tenney (Grand Rapids: Zondervan, 1974), p. 17.
[16]O. Cullmann, *The Early Church* (London: SCM, 1956), p. 77.

read them was to hear the message of God and to be drawn into his presence. Many converts to the Christian faith from the first century to the twentieth can testify to the inspiration of the NT books; they found them "alive" when first they began to read them with an open ear.

This canon of selection must, however, not be viewed in isolation. John Calvin stressed the importance of the internal witness of the Holy Spirit in determining canonicity, but this principle must again be seen as operating in conjunction with others. One of these is the public worship of the church.

F. Public Worship

Few early Christians owned a complete collection of NT books. First, these were not yet available; second, it was costly to obtain copies of all the biblical books; and, third, many Christians in the early centuries could not read. But the writings of the apostles were read in the churches and the believers heard them. True, several non-canonical Christian books were read in the worship of the church from time to time before the canon was closed, but the hearers often felt quite ambivalent about them. In the Canon of Muratori there is the comment after the Revelation of Peter, "Some will not read it in the church." Of the Shepherd of Hermas the same writer says it may be read in private but not in public.

Eventually, then, good as some books may have been, if they were not apostolic and did not come from the period of the incarnation, they were excluded from the canon. Floyd Filson observes: "These writings were preserved in living touch with the church, and they received their unique place only because they proved in continued practice and throughout the entire church that they could bring home the gospel with every new appeal and power."[17]

This does not mean that other inspirational literature may not be quite suitable for reading in church, but it cannot claim to be authoritative. In the words of F. F. Bruce, "In those title deeds [the NT books] we hear the Spirit speaking to the churches of the first century, but at the same time we hear him speaking to the church of the 20th century."[18]

Quite apart from these principles that appear to have guided the church in defining the limits of the canon, there were several historical events which forced the church to take a position on the question of the canon. One of these was the truncated canon of Marcion, and the other was the open canon of the Montanists.

IV. AFFIRMING THE LIMITS OF THE CANON

A. The Truncated Canon of Marcion

By the middle of the second century A.D. the books of the NT had circulated in the churches for a long time. Through these books the risen Lord continued to speak to the churches by his Spirit. Apparently the need for defining the limits of the canon in any official sense had not yet arisen. This was to change with the coming of Marcion of Sinope. This man of wealth,

---

[17]F. V. Filson, *Which Books Belong to the Bible?* (Philadelphia: Westminster, 1957), p. 128.
[18]Bruce, "New Light on the Origins," p. 18.

who had come to Rome from Pontus about 140, came to the conclusion that Christianity had been Judaized, and set himself the task of bringing the church back to what he thought was true Pauline Christianity. When he failed to enlist the Roman church in his cause, he left it and began to organize his followers into a church of his own, with considerable success. Justin, his contemporary, writes that in every race of men Marcion has won many to his views.[19]

Marcion, as we have learned earlier, rejected not only the OT, in which he found a God quite different from the God of the NT, but he also rejected more than half of the books of the NT. His canon consisted of the Gospel of Luke (after lopping off those parts that he considered too Jewish) and ten letters of Paul, excluding the Pastoral Epistles.

Marcion was the first man, to our knowledge, who definitely set out to form a Christian canon of Scripture. The books he chose were, of course, highly valued in the church before his time; had this not been so, he would not have been so successful. Marcion did hardly more than define and regulate what was already the practice of many churches.[20]

He was not able, however, to make the churches give up the OT or the other Gospels and apostolic books. But he drove home to the churches the idea that Christianity must have its own Scripture, if Christianity was not to be divided into innumerable sects. This led the orthodox churches to define the limits of the biblical canon. The end result of this defining was that the twenty-seven books of our NT were acknowledged as canonical.

Marcion had reduced the Christian canon by rejecting a number of authentically apostolic writings. Another movement in the second century, Montanism, tended to go beyond the revelation of God in the apostolic books.

B. The Open Canon of Montanism

The opening years of the second century were overshadowed by the heresy known as Docetism; the middle years by the activities of Marcion and other Gnostics; the closing years by the Montanists. Montanus was a charismatic leader who sought to revitalize the church. He might have done the Christian cause a lot of good, had he had a proper conception of his calling and a more modest perception of himself. But he had come to the conclusion that he was the promised Paraclete, and together with two prophetesses, Prisca and Maximilla, he went about prophesying in the name of the Spirit and predicting the imminent return of Christ. His followers thought of themselves as elite spiritual Christians. He claimed to be the mouthpiece of the Holy Spirit, and this raised the question of whether God had spoken his final word in Christ, as found in the NT, or whether revelation was ongoing.

Somewhere about A.D. 180 the church realized that such an open-ended attitude toward divine revelation held the potential for great mischief, and it was pushed into taking a clearer position on the limits of the

---

[19]Justin, *Apology*, 26.5.

[20]Goodspeed, *Formation of NT Canon*, p. 46.

canon. The apostolic books were being read in the churches and served as authoritative guides in deciding what constituted genuine Christianity. New insights and understandings of these books might come to Christian readers or hearers again and again, but God's final revelation has been given in the apostolic writings. Any person claiming revelations from God, contrary to what is written in the NT, opens the door to heresy. The canon is closed!

In sum we might say that the grounds of canonicity are to be found in an interplay of subjective and objective factors overruled by divine providence.[21] We conclude this chapter with some pertinent observations by Dr. John Wenham:

This was not a collection of books blown together by chance; nor was it a collec-tion that "forced itself" upon the church. In the gentlest way it quietly and unhurriedly established itself in the church's life. There was no noticeable change of attitude before and after the Festal Letter of Athanasius, no flourish of trumpets at Hippo or Carthage.... Neither the decree of Carthage nor that of Trent, nor the Thirty-Nine Articles, nor the Westminster Confession is infal-lible, but in the case of the NT canon they unite in testifying to the collective witness given by the Spirit to the church, thereby giving an immense presump-tion in favor of the NT canon as we have it. We have not here a proof of mathematical precision, but we have evidence of weight and authority, more than sufficient to justify us in humbly taking up the books that God has put into our hands and receiving their teaching as his truth.[22]

SUGGESTED READING

Bruce, F. F. "New Light on the Origins of the New Testament Canon," **New Dimensions in New Testament Study**, eds. R. N. Longenecker and M. C. Tenney, Grand Rapids: Zondervan, 1974, pp. 3–18.

Geisler, N. L. and Nix, W. E. **From God To Us**. Chicago: Moody, 1974. See "The Develop-ment of the New Testament Canon," pp. 101–12.

Goodspeed, E. J. **Formation of the New Testament Canon**. Chicago: University of Chicago Press, 1926.

Grant, R. M. "The New Testament Canon," **The Cambridge History of the Bible**, eds. P. R. Ackroyd and C. F. Evans. Cambridge: Cambridge University Press, 1970, Vol. 1, pp. 284–307.

Ridderbos, H. "The Canon of the New Testament," **Revelation and the Bible**, ed. C. F. H. Henry. Grand Rapids: Baker, 1958, pp. 187–201.

Souter, A. **The Text and Canon of the New Testament**, rev. by C. S. C. Williams. London: Duckworth, 1954.

Tenney, M. F. **The New Testament**. Grand Rapids: Eerdmans, 1953. See chapter 23, "The Canon of the New Testament."

Wenham, J. W. **Christ and the Bible**. Downers Grove: InterVarsity, 1973.

---

[21]J. W. Wenham, *Christ and the Bible* (Downers Grove: InterVarsity, 1973), p. 126.

[22]Wenham, *Christ and the Bible*, p. 163.

Chapter 11

The New Testament in Manuscript Form

By the year A.D. 100 all the books of the NT had been written, and the majority of them had been in existence several decades before this. This can be said with confidence today, for a fragment of John's Gospel that circulated in Egypt prior to A.D. 125 nearly closes the gap between the autographs and our manuscripts.

A century ago critics such as F. C. Baur of Tübingen, and his school, rejected the first-century dates of some of the NT books, thereby robbing them of their apostolic authority. With this came a loss of respect for the Bible with disastrous spiritual consequences.

It must be understood, of course, that we do not have the original manuscripts of the apostolic books. These books were probably written on papyrus in ink (as 2 John 13 states), and only copies of these autographa have been preserved—most of them not earlier than the fourth century. Fortunately, our century has witnessed the discovery of some papyrus manuscripts that have pushed the text of the NT back to about A.D. 200.

The copying of the original documents must have begun as one church asked another for a letter or gospel that the latter evidently had received. The alternative to borrowing such a book from a church was to make a copy of it. It can be seen that this was actually done, for example, from the fact that Clement of Rome, writing to the Corinthians about the end of the first century, asks them to pay attention to Paul's letter. This means that Clement knew not only the letter that Paul had addressed to the Romans, but also the first Corinthian letter, to which he refers.[1] Paul had, in fact, encouraged the exchange of letters between churches (Col. 4:16), and this must have led to the copying of the autographa. In this way collections of copies of the original books of the apostles were being built up in the various centers of early Christianity.

---

[1] 1 Clement, 47. 1–3.

Early Christian literature is completely silent about these apostolic originals. Evidently no one was perturbed about their decay or loss, since there were plenty of copies around. Copying was done for both private and public use. A person might make his own copy or else hire a professional scribe to make a copy of one or more of the sacred writings. Private copying was not supervised, and whenever anyone copies a piece of literature errors are made in transcription. Errors were made even when copies were made by professional scribes in a scriptorium. If it happens today when manuscripts are printed, with all the proofreading that printing calls for, how much more when handwritten copies are made! Not long ago an English Bible appeared in print with some apocryphal material in the Book of Leviticus, and the publisher had to recall the sold copies. (One clergyman did not bother to return it for, as he said, he didn't read Leviticus anyway.)

Since we have thousands of copies of the NT books, we have considerable information on the shape and the form of these early copies.

I. THE CHARACTER OF NEW TESTAMENT MANUSCRIPTS

A. Rolls and Codices

As for writing materials, we have noted earlier that papyrus eventually gave way to more durable material made of leather, called parchment. Some of our earliest manuscripts are of papyrus, but from about the third century on parchment or vellum was used, and this remained the standard writing material until the age of print-ing when paper replaced other writing materials.

Writing on papyrus or parchment was done "with pen and ink," as John says (3 John 13). The ink was normally black or brown, although deluxe codices were at times written with silver or gold letters. Red ink was not uncommon for titles, headings, and initial letters or lines.[2]

The form of the NT books originally was that of a roll. A short letter such as Philemon, of course, would take no more than a sheet of papyrus. Books such as Matthew would represent about as much writing as could conveniently go on a papyrus scroll of normal length (about thirty-five feet).

The writing on such rolls was arranged in a series of columns. A reader had to use both hands, unrolling the scroll with one hand and rolling it up with the other as the reading proceeded. Finding a specific passage on a scroll is not very convenient, and so about the beginning of the second century the codex, or leaf form of book, came into use in the church. Even when the biblical books were published in codex form, the writing on each page continued to be arranged in several columns. Codex Sinaiticus, for example, has four columns on each page.

B. Styles of Writing

Two basic types of writing style were in use. The cursive or "running" hand, which could be written rapidly, with one letter being connected with the other without lifting the pen was used for everyday nonliterary kind of writing. Literary works, on the other hand,

---

[2]J. Finegan, *Encountering New Testament Manuscripts* (Grand Rapids: Eerdmans, 1974), p. 31.

A sample of uncial script taken from an Egyptian scriptorium. This fragment is a palimpsest and contains Matthew 26:57–65.

question mark does not appear until the ninth century. This style of writing could occasionally lead to an error in reading, if one made the word division at the wrong place.

Also, the scribes developed a system of abbreviations for words that occur frequently, particularly the sacred names, such as "Jesus," "Christ," "God," "Spirit," "cross," and the like. Often only the first and last letters were written and a line drawn over the word to alert the reader to the contraction.

Scribes, hired to prepare copies of biblical books, were paid according to the number of lines they wrote. The standard line was called a _stichos_. Stichometry turned out to be an aid in the accuracy of copies of manuscripts, for by counting the _stichoi_, one could

were written in a more formal style, and were called "uncials," resembling somewhat our capitals.[3] Some of our early NT manuscripts, from the third to the sixth century, are in this kind of writing. As time went on, the running hand became dominant and a smaller script, called "minuscule," was used in the production of books. This kind of handwriting not only increased the speed of writing but made it possible to pack much more material into one page, making books more economical. It should not surprise us that the minuscule manuscripts by far outnumber the uncials.

In the earlier manuscripts no spaces were left between words or sentences, and until about the eighth century punctuation was used sparingly. The

A sample of minuscule script. This parchment is a lectionary from the monastery of St. Laurentii Escurialensis and contains the Gospel of John 1:1–12.

---

[3]B. M. Metzger, _The Text of the New Testament_, 2nd ed. (New York: Oxford University Press, 1968), p. 9.

tell whether omissions or additions had been made. The information that has come down to us about the price charged per line for preparing official copies leads to the conclusion that few Christians could have afforded entire New Testaments, let alone whole Bibles.

C. Palimpsests

Since parchment was costly the original writing was at times scraped and washed off, the surface re-smoothed, and then used for new literary material. Such books are called palimpsests (from two Greek words meaning "rescraped"). Several NT manuscripts are of this type. Codex Ephraemi had the NT text written on its pages in the fifth century, but in the twelfth this text was erased and sermons of Ephraem, a Syrian Church Father, were written over it. Fortunately it became possible to decipher the original text. Of the 250 uncial manuscripts of the NT today, fifty-two are palimpsests.[4]

D. Helps for Readers

Some manuscripts of the NT provide helps for readers. There are, for example, chapter divisions. Codex Vaticanus divides Matthew into 170 sections. One scribe divided the Book of Revelation into twenty-four sections, because of the twenty-four elders before God's throne (Rev. 4:4). Reflecting further that these elders each had body, soul, and spirit, he subdivided the twenty-four larger sections into seventy-two (three times twenty-four). These chapter divisions bear little rela-

tion to our present chapters.

The chapter divisions were given headings, called *titloi*, describing the content of the chapters. Also, an ingenius system was devised by Eusebius of Caesarea to aid the reader in the locating of parallel passages in the Gospels. It must have served a useful purpose, for this system is found in a great many manuscripts.

Eventually scribes introduced prologues to the biblical books, or information about the life of the evangelists. Also, titles were added to the books of the NT themselves, and difficult words were explained in the margins of the manuscripts or between the lines (called "glosses").

In addition to an ornamental headpiece at the beginning of a book, some manuscripts have pictures of various kinds. Portraits of Christ and his apostles or pictures of scenes from the NT are not uncommon. In deluxe codices such pictures are often painted in various colors and are a rich source for the study of early Christian art.

Following the custom of the synagogue of reading the Scriptures in the worship service, a regular system of lessons from the Gospels and the Epistles was developed. Scribes at times marked the beginning and end of the lesson for Sundays or holy days, so that the lector knew where to begin and where to stop. Lectionary manuscripts, which gave these lessons in proper sequence (beginning with Easter), were also prepared for the convenience of the reader. These manuscripts are called "lectionaries."

With the establishment of monasteries, the copying of manuscripts was often done by monks in the scriptoria

---

[4]Metzger, *Text of New Testament*, p. 12.

of the monasteries. This was an arduous task (for scribes stood at writing desks), and some manuscripts have footnotes or marginal comments in which the scribes express their feelings about their work. One can find expressions such as, "the end of the book; thanks be to God." One monk complains about his stiff fingers because a snowstorm is raging outside. Another describes the physiological effects of the labor of copying: "Writing bows one's back, thrusts the ribs into one's stomach, and fosters a general debility of the body."[5] Some footnotes (called "colophons") give the name of the scribe, and occasionally the place and date of the writing—information that is of great value today. Approximate dates for the manuscripts can also be established by the science of paleography. Experts in ancient scripts can usually tell from which period a manuscript comes by the style of the handwriting in it.

Some scribes write blessings on the readers in the footnote, others warn readers not to add or subtract from the Word of God. These and many other features make the study of manuscripts very interesting. Questions that naturally come to us when we think of the early manuscripts of the NT are, Where are these manuscripts today? How many are there? Who keeps a record of them? Let us give some answers to such questions.

II. THE CLASSIFICATION OF NEW TESTAMENT MANUSCRIPTS

A. The Abundance of Manuscripts

Perhaps we can appreciate the wealth of NT manuscript material if we compare it with manuscripts of non-biblical ancient books. For example, Caesar's *Gallic War* (about 54 B.C.) is found in only nine or ten good manuscripts, and the oldest is some 900 years later than Caesar's day. Of the 142 books of the Roman History of Livey (49 B.C.–A.D. 17) only thirty-five have survived. No manuscript is older than the fourth century. Of the fourteen books of the *Histories* of Tacitus (c. A.D. 100) only four and a half survive; of the sixteen books of his *Annals*, ten survive in full, two in part; none is older than the ninth century.[6] Of the writings of Plato the earliest manuscript available comes from a date some 1300 years after Plato; of Demosthenes no manuscript is earlier than 1200 years after he lived.

How different is the picture when we turn to the NT manuscript materials! Not including the thousands of quotations in the church fathers, we have around 5000 complete or partial manuscripts of the NT books. But this is not all, for besides these copies of the Greek NT, we have thousands of copies of translations into various languages made in the early centuries of the Christian era.

Although the number of NT manuscripts is overwhelming, the age of some of them enables scholars to see what the NT text looked like in the third and even the second centuries A.D. When one compares this with the big gap between the autographs and the available copies of classical books, the gap in the textual tradition of the NT is infinitesimal. Indeed, it is an embarrassment of riches, for the work of the

---

[5]Metzger, *Text of New Testament,* pp. 17f.

[6]F. F. Bruce, *The New Testament Documents: Are They Reliable?* 5th rev. ed. (Grand Rapids: Eerdmans, 1960), p. 16.

textual scholar would be reduced considerably if he had less material.

B. Listing New Testament Manuscripts

Before standard lists were universally accepted, it was often difficult to know where some of the manuscripts were located. Different systems of labelling or numbering manuscripts added to the confusion.

The Swiss scholar, Johann Wettstein, took the first step in standardizing the nomenclature for manuscripts in 1751–52. The system now in general use was elaborated at the end of the nineteenth century by C. Gregory, a native of Philadelphia, who became professor at the University of Leipzig in 1889. The list was kept up to date by Ernst von Dobschuetz, who was succeeded by Walter Eltester. Today, Kurt Aland, of Muenster, Germany, is responsible for the listing of manuscripts and ascribing *sigla* to any newly discovered materials.

This system of listing manuscripts has now been accepted universally, so that printed Greek New Testaments, wherever they are published, use more or less the same nomenclature for the Greek manuscripts and versions in the footnotes of the text (these footnotes are called the "critical apparatus").

The manuscripts are divided on the basis of writing material. The manuscripts made of papyrus are all listed separately from those made of parchment. The papyrus manuscripts are identified by a "P", followed by a small superior numeral (P^{45}, for example, is a codex belonging to the Chester Beatty Papyri).

Moreover, the uncial manuscripts,

of which there are fewer than minuscules, are commonly designated by the capital letters of the Latin and Greek alphabets. Since, however, the number of uncials came to exceed the number of letters in the Latin and Greek alphabets, they also have an Arabic number assigned to each of them, preceded by a zero. Several of the more important uncials also have names as, for example, the Alexandrinus (numbered A, 02). The minuscule manuscripts are referred to simply by Arabic numerals.

A subsidiary class of Greek manuscripts (whether uncial or minuscule) is devoted to lectionaries. These are reading selections for the ecclesiastical year. They are designated by the letter "l," followed by an Arabic numeral.

This may be the place to say something about several of the more important manuscripts of the NT. Some manuscripts contain the entire Bible (with the OT in Greek); others again contain only parts of the NT, sometimes only fragments of single books.

III. SIGNIFICANT MANUSCRIPTS OF THE NEW TESTAMENT

A. Important Uncials

Heading the list is the Sinaiticus. This codex was discovered after other uncials had already been assigned letters of the alphabet, and since it would have caused confusion if the letters that had established themselves had been changed once again, Sinaiticus received the first letter of the Hebrew alphabet.

This codex was discovered by Constantin von Tischendorf in the middle of the nineteenth century. It is called Sinaiticus because he found it in the

SOME IMPORTANT UNCIAL MANUSCRIPTS OF THE GREEK NEW TESTAMENT

Manuscript		Content	Location	Date
ℵ	01	complete	London: Sinaiticus	4th century
A	02	complete	London: Alexandrinus	5th century
B	03	last books missing	Rome: Vaticanus	4th century
C	04	some pages missing	Paris: Ephraemi Rescripturs	5th century
D	05	Gospels and Acts	Cambridge: Bezae (bilingual)	5/6th century
D	06	Pauline Letters	Paris: Claromontanus	6th century
W	032	Gospels	Washington: Freer Gospels	5th century

monastery of St. Catherine on Mount Sinai. In 1844 he was in the Near East in search of biblical manuscripts. While at St. Catherine he was able to retrieve some leaves of the Septuagint version of the OT, written in early Greek uncial script. The monks had been using similar material to make fires. He warned them not to use such precious material again, and left.

In 1853 he revisited St. Catherine in the hope of finding more manuscripts, but he got nothing. In 1859 he was back under the patronage of the Czar of Russia, official head of the Greek church. Almost by accident a monk directed him to a manuscript in his cell. Tischendorf was allowed to take it to his room for the night, and he stayed up all night examining the codex, so great was his excitement. Here was a manuscript of most of the Bible from the fourth century, in excellent condition.

The next morning he tried to buy the manuscript, but to no avail. Eventually he got permission to transport it to Cairo, where he began to copy it. In the end he got it as a gift for the Czar, who rewarded the monks in Cairo and at St. Catherine. In 1862 it was published for the first time.

After the Bolshevik Revolution in Russia, it became known that the Sinaiticus might be for sale. An American syndicate was greatly interested, but the manuscript went to the British Museum in 1933, for the price of a half million dollars.

The codex contains most of the OT in Greek, and all the NT with two additional books, the Shepherd of Hermas and the Epistle of Barnabas. The text is written on vellum, with four columns

Lobegott Friedrich Constantin von Tischendorf (1815–1874), the famous German Protestant theologian and textual critic who discovered the Codex Sinaiticus. During his lifetime he published more manuscripts and critical editions of the Greek New Testament than any other scholar.

The beginning of the Gospel of Luke in the Codex Alexandrinus. In 1624 the codex was given by Cyril Lucar, patriarch of Constantinople, to the British ambassador for presentation to James I. James died before the manuscript arrived and it was presented to Charles I in 1627.

to the page. The date is late fourth (or early fifth) century.

From the middle of the fifth century comes the Codex Alexandrinus. Today this codex lies side by side with the Sinaiticus in the British Museum. In 1627 Cyril Lucar, patriarch of Constantinople, offered this manuscript to the English ambassador to Turkey, Sir Thomas Roe, as a gift to King James I. It came to England in 1627 after King James had died. Cyril Lucar had earlier been patriarch of Alexandria and he evidently brought it to Constantinople. That explains why it is called "Alexandrinus."

Originally it contained all of the OT (in Greek) and the NT, together with 1 and 2 Clement. Most of Matthew, however, is now missing. It has two columns per page, written on vellum with black ink. It was the first of the

great uncials made accessible to scholars.

Codex Vaticanus gets its name from the fact that it has been in the Vatican library so long. Although its presence was known since 1475, the Vatican discouraged work on it. The codex was carried off to Paris by Napoleon together with other manuscripts as a prize of war. After 1815 it had to be returned, but again the Vatican kept it under wraps. Tischendorf finally got enough of its readings that he published an edition in 1867. The Vatican then published its own edition at the end of the century.

The Vaticanus comes from the fourth century, as does the Sinaiticus, and originally contained all the books of the Bible. Today some parts are missing; missing are the NT books from Hebrews 9:14 onwards (including the Pastorals).

Each page has three columns of text, written on fine vellum. Unfortunately, a corrector has spoiled it somewhat by going over the original writing. Together with the Sinaiticus it is one of the finest manuscripts of the NT.

Codex Ephraemi is the fifth-century palimpsest. Someone erased the text of the NT in the twelfth century and wrote the sermons of Ephraem, the Syrian church father, over it. It has been said, somewhat facetiously, that this is not the first nor the last time that a text of the NT was "covered up" by a sermon. Today this codex is in the National Library in Paris, but it came originally from the Near East.

Several scholars had tried to decipher the NT text behind the sermons, but with little success. In 1841 Tischendorf set himself the arduous task of deciphering the text. By 1843 he had completed the task, and in 1845 it was published. Treatment with chemicals and better photography later showed that Tischendorf had made relatively few errors.

Only sixty-four leaves of the OT in Greek are left. Of the NT there are 145 leaves, containing portions of every book of the NT except 2 Thessalonians and 2 John. The codex has only one column of text per page.

While the codices just mentioned vary in numerous details, none of them differ so much from each other as does, for example, Codex Bezae. First of all, it is a bilingual manuscript, with the Greek page on the left, facing the Latin page on the right. Moreover, the Gospels are in the so-called Western order (Matthew, John, Luke, Mark). Also, the text is written in "sense lines," which means that some are short and others are long. It contains only the four Gospels and Acts, and the first three lines of each book are in red ink.

It was presented to Cambridge University by Theodore Beza, the successor of John Calvin at Geneva, and so it is also called "Codex Cantabrigiensis." The codex comes from the fifth (possibly the sixth) century, and has a remarkable number of variations from what is usually taken to be the normal NT text. In Acts 19:9, for example, we are informed that Paul preached in the hall of Tyrannus "from eleven o'clock to four." That is the time of day when not even Tyrannus (probably a nickname given to him by his students) could conduct school lessons because of the heat.

We cannot describe all the uncials and we will have to leave it at that, and make a few comments on several of the minuscules.

B. Minuscule Manuscripts

Certain minuscule manuscripts have such striking similarities of text-type as to suggest a close "family" relationship. In 1868 Professor Ferrar, of Dublin University, found several manuscripts that were very closely related. Others belonging to the same text-type have been added since, and so the entire family is called the "Ferrar" family. Since the first manuscript in this family is minuscule number 13, the family is also called "family 13." Somewhat later (about 1902) Kirsopp Lake identified another group of minuscules that belonged to the same family. Minuscule number one stands at the head of the list and so the family is called either the "Lake family" or "family 1." What is interesting about family 13 is that all of the manuscripts belonging to this family have the story of the adulterous woman (John 7:53–8:11) not in John's Gospel, but after Luke 21:38.

The minuscule manuscripts now number 2,792, and are generally from a later period than the uncials. It does not follow necessarily, however, that a late manuscript always has a less trustworthy text than an early one. A late manuscript may have been copied from a very early parent manuscript and so, although the manuscript is late, the text of the manuscript is early. One such minuscule is number 33, which has received the nickname "Queen of the cursives." It contains the entire NT except the Revelation and comes from the ninth or tenth century, but the text of the manuscript resembles that of the great uncials described earlier. It is in the National Library in Paris.

Minuscule 81 was written in the

year A.D. 1044, but it has a text that resembles that of number 33, and that of the great uncials. It is now in the British Museum and is considered to be one of the most important manuscripts.

Minuscule 565, now in the public library at Leningrad, is a deluxe copy of the Gospels, written in gold letters on purple vellum during the ninth or tenth century. The text of this manuscript belongs to a different family than numbers 33 and 81. This holds true for minuscule 700, an eleventh- or twelfth-century codex of the Gospels, now in the British Museum. It has the remarkable reading in the Lucan Lord's Prayer, "May thy Holy Spirit come upon us and cleanse us" (Luke 11:2), instead of "Thy kingdom come."

Minuscules 1 and 2 are mainly of historical significance for they were the main manuscripts used for the first printing of the Greek NT. Erasmus had given minuscule 2 and several other twelfth-century manuscripts to the printer, and number 1 was used for proofreading. Minuscule 1 has a text that agrees very much with the older uncials, but Erasmus was suspicious of its supposedly erratic readings.

We cannot comment on the hundreds of minuscules available today. Quite aside from their text, some have a unique format. For example, number 16 is a copy of the four Gospels in Greek and Latin, and is written in four colors. The narrative generally is in vermillion; the words of Jesus and of angels is in crimson; OT words and words of disciples are in blue; the words of the Pharisees, the centurion, Judas Iscariot, and the devil are in black.

Although the minuscules represent the last stage of the manuscript tradition, the papyri represent the earliest, and to these we now turn.

C. Biblical Papyri

A great many secular papyri had been discovered in the sands of Egypt before any biblical texts on papyrus came to light. In 1931 Frederic Kenyon announced in the *Times* of London that twelve such manuscripts had been discovered in jars in a Coptic graveyard in Egypt. They were sold for a high price by Egyptian dealers to an American, Chester Beatty, who lived in Dublin. These Chester Beatty Papyri, as they are now called, pushed the text of the NT back to about 200 to 250. These papyri included also OT portions, but we are interested here only in the NT codices.

Ephesians 1:1–11 of the Chester Beatty Papyri in the collection at the University of Michigan. These papyri were important in showing that the codex form was used before the fourth century.

P⁴⁵ comprises portions of thirty leaves of a papyrus book that originally had about 220 leaves and contained all four Gospels and Acts. Matthew and John are the least well preserved in this codex. P⁴⁶ comprises eighty-six leaves of the Pauline Epistles. Portions of several epistles are lacking and the Pastoral Epistles apparently were not included in the first place. P⁴⁷ comprises ten leaves of the Book of Revelation. Here, then, we have manuscripts that carry the NT text back almost 200 years beyond that of our early uncials. One can readily grasp the significance of such a discovery.

We have mentioned P⁵², the John Rylands Fragment, earlier, not because there is much on it, but because of its age. It contains a few verses from John's Gospel in uncial script and was in the John Rylands library at Manchester, where it was discovered in 1934. Not only does it show that John's Gospel was circulating in Egypt not later than A.D. 125, but it also confirms the fact that the codex form of books was already in use.[7]

There is another collection of biblical papyri named after a Swiss business man, Martin Bodmer, of Geneva. In 1956 the discovery of Bodmer II, written about A.D. 200, was announced. P⁶⁶ contains a major portion of the Gospel of John. A corrector (perhaps the copyist himself) has gone over it and made numerous corrections. P⁷² was edited in 1959, and contains among other things, the Epistle of Jude and the two Epistles of Peter.

This Bodmer manuscript comes from the third century and has provided us with the oldest text of these epistles. Included also in this manuscript are such writings as: The Nativity of Mary, the apocryphal correspondence of Paul to the Corinthians, a Passover sermon by Melito of Sardis, and several other literary works. P⁷⁵ is another early manuscript of Luke and John, dated between A.D. 175 and 225. This is then the earliest copy of the Gospel according to Luke and one of the earliest of John. At John 10:7, instead of the traditional text, "I am the gate for the sheep," this manuscript has, "I am the shepherd of the sheep." In the parable of the Rich Man and Lazarus (Luke 16), the rich man is given the name *Neues*. The Sahidic version calls him "Nineveh," the symbol of dissolute riches, and *Neues* is probably an abbreviation of Nineveh.[8]

These brief sketches of the rich collection of manuscript materials are sufficient, we believe, to demonstrate that there is no ancient book so well attested as are the books of the NT. In our next chapter we will have to say more about the textual variations found in these hundreds, indeed, thousands, of NT manuscripts, and how textual scholars handle these variant readings. And lest this should sound unsettling to any Bible reader, we should add that these thousands of variant readings in our manuscripts do not affect any basic teaching of the NT.

---

[7]Finegan, *Encountering Manuscripts*, p. 86.
[8]Metzger, *Text of New Testament*, p. 42.

SUGGESTED READING

Birdsall, J. N. "The New Testament Text," Cambridge History of the Bible, 3 vols. eds. P. R. Ackroyd and C. F. Evans. Cambridge: Cambridge University Press, 1970, Vol. 1, pp. 308-76.

Finegan, J. Encountering New Testament Manuscripts. Grand Rapids: Eerdmans, 1974.

Kenyon, F. G. Our Bible and the Ancient Manuscripts, rev. ed. New York: Harper and Brothers, 1958. See "The Text of the New Testament," pp. 155-78; "The Manuscripts of the New Testament," pp. 185-219.

Metzger, B. M. The Text of the New Testament, 2nd ed. New York: Oxford University Press, 1968.

Parvis, M. M. "The Text of the New Testament," Interpreter's Dictionary of the Bible, 4 vols. ed. G. A. Buttrick. Nashville: Abingdon, 1962. Vol. 4, pp. 594-614.

Price, I. M. The Ancestry of Our English Bible, 3rd ed. revised by W. A. Irwin and Allen P. Wikgren. New York: Harper and Row, 1956. See "Writing and Manuscripts in General," pp. 153-60; "The Greek Manuscripts of the New Testament," pp. 161-76.

Williams, C. S. C. "The History of the Text and Canon of the New Testament to Jerome," The Cambridge History of the Bible, 3 vols. ed. G. W. H. Lampe. Cambridge: Cambridge University Press, 1969, Vol. 2, pp. 27-53.

Chapter 12

The Printed Greek New Testament

Prior to the Renaissance and the Protestant Reformation the Bible of western Europe was the Latin Vulgate, prepared initially by Jerome in the fourth century. With a renewed interest in the classics, beginning in the fourteenth century, there came a revival of interest in ancient manuscripts, including those of the Greek NT.

The manuscripts of the NT books that were known at the time were generally no older than the eleventh or twelfth century. Since it was held that they all had basically the same text, textual criticism, in which manuscripts are compared in an effort to establish the most trustworthy readings, was not yet practiced. When Erasmus published the first Greek NT in print, in 1516, he simply printed the "received text" as he found this in several late manuscripts that he used.

The work of Erasmus, the Renaissance scholar, may be a convenient point to begin our survey of the development of the science of textual criticism, but before we talk about that, we must say a word about the invention of printing.

I. THE FIRST PRINTED GREEK NEW TESTAMENT

A. The Discovery of Printing

Just who first discovered the art of printing is a matter of debate. It appears as if the Chinese were experimenting with print several hundred years before Gutenberg, who is credited with this invention in the Western world. The story goes that an apprentice of his accidentally dropped a woodcut of a page of the Bible, breaking it into many pieces. After boxing the apprentice's ears and giving him a scolding, Gutenberg sat over the pieces and pondered how he might repair the broken plate. Then it occurred to him: if these broken pieces can be put together again, why not put every page together? And so, we are told, the notion of movable type was born.

Gutenberg's real name was Hans Gensfleisch, who took on the name Gutenberg from his father's estate where he was born (c. 1400). He lived in Mainz for a time, then in Strasbourg, but in 1445 he was back in Mainz, printing calendars, a Latin grammar, and other materials. Johannes Fust helped Gutenberg recover from these projects that were financial disasters, and in 1452 Gutenberg published the first Bible ever to be printed. The type was made of wood blocks and Gutenberg had to prepare some 46,000 of them to keep the setters working. He used both parchment and paper. About thirty copies were on parchment, and he had some 170 calves slaughtered to supply him with the leather for each copy; about 120 copies were paper.

This two-volume printed Latin Bible cost an enormous sum of money to produce, and Gutenberg suffered much from financial embarrassment. But the Bible sold immediately, and in 1457/58 another edition appeared. The day of printing had arrived and printing houses sprang up everywhere. During the next fifty years at least one hundred editions of the Latin Bible were published. The Greek NT,

Johann Gutenberg (1398–1468), the inventor who published the first Bible.

however, had to wait. One reason was that the type for the Greek letters was more expensive to produce. The more basic reason was the prestige of the Latin Vulgate. A printed Greek text would question the supremacy of the Vulgate.

With the invention of printing a new era dawned in the history of the transmission of the biblical text. The practice of copying manuscripts was discontinued and the guilds of copyists were put out of business. Paper replaced parchment as writing and printing material. The Renaissance and the Reformation revived interest in the Greek and Hebrew Bible. Biblical scholars began to look beyond the Latin Vulgate to the original languages of the Bible. The scholar who ventured to put the Greek NT into print was Erasmus.

B. Erasmus's Greek New Testament

Cardinal Ximenes was actually the first to put the Greek NT into print in the so-called Complutensian Polyglot Bible. This massive four-volume work came off the press in Spain in 1514, but ecclesiastical authorities delayed its publication. So it happened that Erasmus of Rotterdam (1469–1536) had the honor of publishing the first Greek NT.

Erasmus, whose Dutch name was Gert, was born in the Netherlands and entered a monastery early in life. However, the monastic life did not agree with him and he was released from his vows. After studies in Paris, he went to England, where John Colet and Thomas More impressed him with the New Learning. Having learned Greek, Erasmus came away from England in 1515 determined to publish a Greek NT

NOVVM IN

ftrumentũ omne, diligenter ab ERASMO ROTERODAMO
recognitum & emendatum, nõ folum ad græcam ueritatem, ue-
rumetiam ad multorum utriufq; linguæ codicum, eorumq; ue-
terum fimul & emendatorum fidem, poftremo ad pro-
batiffimorum autorum citationem, emendationem
& interpretationem, præcipue, Origenis, Chry
foftomi, Cyrilli, Vulgarij, Hieronymi, Cy-
priani, Ambrofij, Hilarij, Augufti,
ni, una cũ Annotationibus, quæ
lectorem doceant, quid qua
ratione mutatum fit.
Quifquis igitur
amas ue-
ram
Theolo,
giam, lege, cogno
fce, ac deinde iudica.
Neq; ftatim offendere, fi
quid mutatum offenderis, fed
expende, num in melius mutatum fit.

APVD INCLYTAM
GERMANIAE BASILAEAM.

CVM PRIVILEGIO
MAXIMILIANI CAESARIS AVGVSTI,
NE QVIS ALIVS IN SACRA ROMA,
NI IMPERII DITIONE, INTRA QVATV
OR ANNOS EXCVDAT, AVT ALIBI
EXCVSVM IMPORTET.

The title page from the Greek New Testament of Erasmus.

Also, he began publishing books to combat the ignorance and bigotry of his age.[1]

The conviction that theology was in the final analysis the "handmaiden of grammar," persuaded him to have the Greek NT printed. In 1515 he made his way to Basel, where with the help of the printer Froben, he completed this project in 1516. Theologians had tried to dissuade him. In a letter from the University of Louvain, Erasmus was told: "What if it be contended that the sense, as rendered by the Latin version, differs indeed from the Greek text? Then, indeed, adieu to the Greek. I adhere to the Latin because I cannot bring my mind to believe that the Greek are more correct than the Latin codices."[2] But Erasmus argued that one cannot blame the Holy Spirit for errors that spring from ignorance.

Erasmus's printed Greek NT was really a diglot, for he put the Greek column alongside his own translation of the Greek text into Latin. (He was severely criticized for this presumption, when his diglot was published.) To his vexation he found only a few late Greek manuscripts in Basel, and he had to correct some of them before he gave them to the printers. For the Book of Revelation he had borrowed one twelfth-century manuscript from his friend Reuchlin, but the last leaf was missing, so he supplied the Greek text by retranslating the Latin Vulgate back into Greek. Even in other places Erasmus occasionally inserted Vulgate readings. For example, he introduced into Acts 9:6 the question, "Lord, what will you have me do?" This question is found in Acts 22:10, but not in the Greek manuscripts of Acts 9:6. If we find it in some older English Bibles, we have no one to blame but Erasmus and his proofreader.

The printing was done in a remarkably short time, in an effort to get the volume on the market before Ximenes's Polyglot could appear. As a result there were many errors in the text. Perhaps if Erasmus had realized that his printed Greek NT would be the standard text for many generations, he would have paid greater attention to accuracy.

The response to this printed Greek NT varied. Some were suspicious and even hostile; Cambridge and Oxford students were forbidden to read Erasmus's writings; others accepted his NT enthusiastically. Within three years another edition was printed, and the total number of copies of the 1516 and 1519 editions was 3,300. Luther made his translation into German from this second edition.

One criticism of Erasmus was that he had omitted 1 John 5:7–8—a passage he had not found in any Greek manuscripts. When pressed, he promised to include these verses in future editions, if a Greek manuscript could be found that had this passage. One Greek manuscript finally turned up that had this passage (some suspect that it was specially prepared to confound Erasmus), and he inserted it into his 1522 edition.[3]

---

[1] D. Ewert, "Erasmus," *A Cloud of Witnesses*, ed. J. C. Wenger (Harrisonburg, Va.: Eastern Mennonite Seminary, 1981), pp. 74–77.

[2] Quoted in H. G. G. Herklots, *How Our Bible Came to Us* (New York: Oxford University Press, 1954), p. 24.

[3] B. M. Metzger, *The Text of the New Testament*, 2nd ed. (New York: Oxford University Press, 1968), p. 100.

A fourth and definitive edition of Erasmus's NT appeared in 1527. This edition had three parallel columns on each page, the Greek, the Latin Vulgate, and Erasmus's own Latin version. By now the Polyglot of Ximenes had been published and Erasmus carried over some readings from this version to his own. The fifth edition (1535) is basically like the fourth, only that the Latin Vulgate column was deleted.

Although the Complutensian Polyglot had a superior text, Erasmus's edition was first on the market. Also, because it was cheaper, it attained a much wider circulation and exercised a greater influence than its rival.[4] The text of Ersamus came to be called the Textus Receptus, and this "received text" was published again and again during the next 400 years.

II. PRINTINGS OF THE "RECEIVED TEXT"

The famous Parisian printer and publisher, Robert Estienne, latinized as Stephanus (1503–1559), issued four editions of the Greek NT (1546, 1549, 1550, and 1551).[5] The fourth edition is noteworthy in that it had the text divided into numbered verses for the first time. It has sometimes been said that some of the less fortunate verse divisions were made by Stephanus while riding on horseback from Paris to Lyons. The jogging of the horse presumably bumped his pen into the wrong place.

Theodore Beza (1519–1605), successor of John Calvin, published no fewer than nine editions of the Greek NT between 1565 and 1604. He made relatively little use of a famous manuscript in his possession, Codex Bezae, and his editions in essence continue the textual tradition established by Erasmus. In 1624 two Elzevir brothers of Leiden published a Greek NT, the text of which was taken mainly from Beza's 1565 edition.[6] In the preface to their second edition (1633), they made the boast that the reader now had a text that was received by all. The Latin words *textum receptum* ("received text") worked like magic and have given us the term "Textus Receptus."

This Greek text was essentially that of Erasmus, Stephanus, and Beza, and this continued to be the standard Greek text until almost the end of the nineteenth century. It established itself so firmly that to question its readings bordered on sacrilege.

This "received text" has other names as well—names that reflect the history of this textual tradition. Through repeated copying and re-copying of the NT manuscripts in the early history of the church, variant readings slipped in. In an effort to combat confusion, a standard text emerged. Sometimes Lucian of Antioch (died 312) is given credit for this text,[7] and so it has been called "Lucianic." Since this standard text emanated from Antioch of Syria, it is also known as the "Antiochian" text, and Westcott and Hort called it the "Syrian" text. This Greek text became well established in the Greek-speaking church and so is known also as the

---

[4]Metzger, *Text of New Testament*, p. 103.

[5]Metzger, *Text of New Testament*, p. 104.

[6]Metzger, *Text of New Testament*, p. 107.

[7]J. N. Birdsall, "The New Testament Text," *The Cambridge History of the Bible*, eds. P. R. Ackroyd and C. F. Evans (Cambridge: Cambridge University Press, 1970), Vol. 1, p. 320.

"Ecclesiastical" text. Since Byzantium became the center of the Greek church, it is also known as the "Byzantine" text. This text was so common in the Greek-speaking church that some prefer to call it the "Koine," meaning the "common" text.

The majority of the late manuscripts have this text, and so it happened that Erasmus put it into print; other printed editions also had this standard text. With the discovery of new manuscript material, particularly in the nineteenth century, serious questions were raised about the quality of this standard Greek text. Older manuscripts have shown that this common Greek text is in error in a great many places. The errors were not the kind that affect any major doctrine, but there were hundreds of places where the "received text" needed correction. How did such errors creep in, and how can they be corrected?

III. IN SEARCH OF THE MOST TRUSTWORTHY TEXT

A. The Causes of Variant Readings

As anyone who has copied literary material knows, it is next to impossible to produce a copy that is identical with the master copy. And since many of the NT manuscripts were produced privately, without the advantage of careful supervision or proofreading, we should not be surprised to find a certain amount of diversity in the manuscripts. Copyists make mistakes quite unintentionally. Some variant readings were introduced intentionally when scribes felt that the text

needed correction or improvement. Let us look first at some examples of unintentional changes.

1. *Unintentional Changes.*[8] (a) One cause of error in copying manuscripts is the failure of the scribe to distinguish between letters that look alike. In 1 Timothy 3:15 the Received Text has, "God was manifested in the flesh." The preferred reading is, "Who was manifested in the flesh." The abbreviation of the word "God" in Greek looks very much like the relative pronoun "who," when written in uncials. And so through an error of the eye a variant slipped in. In some manuscripts of 2 Peter 2:13 we have "love feasts" *(agapais)*; others read "deceptions" *(apatais)*. An error of the eye has caused the transposition of letters.

When two lines of the exemplar from which a scribe is making a copy end with the same word, his eye might skip a line. For example, in Codex Vaticanus, John 17:15 lacks one line, enclosed here in square brackets: "I do not pray that thou shouldst take them *from the* [world, but that thou shouldst keep them *from the*] evil one." The eyes of the scribe jumped from the first "from the" to the second. This error is called *parablepsis* (a looking by the side) and happens easily where we have *homoeoteleuton* (a similar ending of lines).

(b) Some errors arose from faulty hearing. When scribes made copies from dictation, they could not always distinguish the words by their sound. If an English teacher should dictate words to a class of students to test their spelling skills, they would not be able to distinguish between "their"

---

[8]Although the writer has drawn on many sources, the best summary of the causes of error in transmission of the text of the Greek NT is to be found in Bruce Metzger's *The Text of the New Testament,* chapter 8, where much more material on this topic can be found.

and "there." Similarly, if the Greek text of Romans 5:1 is dictated, one could hardly distinguish between *echomen* and *echōmen*, but one is indicative and means, "we have peace with God," the other is subjunctive and reads, "let us have peace with God."

In Revelation 1:5 the King James Version states that Christ "washed *(lousanti)* us from our sins," but modern versions have, he "freed *(lusanti)* us from our sins." The words in Greek are hardly distinguishable in sound. This error is called "itacisim," because it so often involves the confusion of the vowel *iota*.

But, not only are vowels easily confused, consonants too can be misunderstood. For example, we are not quite sure whether Paul in 1 Thessalonians 2:7 said, "we become babes" *(egenēthēmen nēpioi)*, or, "we become gentle" *(egenēthēmen ēpioi)*. If the "n" before *ēpioi* (gentle) was omitted, we have an example of haplography (omission of a letter), if, on the other hand, the second "n" was added, giving us *nēpioi* (babes), then we have an example of dittography (repetition of a letter, word, or phrase).

(c) Scribes also make errors of the mind. If a copyist reads a line and then writes it down from memory, he may introduce a wrong word, change the sequence of words, and the like. Such alterations can produce utter nonsense. In John 5:39 Jesus says of the Scriptures that they "bear witness" *(marturousai)* about him, but the scribe of Codex Bezae wrote "they sin" *(hamartanousai)* about him. When the RSV was first published, some readers failed to find the phrase "through his blood" in Colossians 1:14, and immediately accused the translators of denying the blood of Christ. The fact is

that a scribe by mistake carried Ephesians 1:7, "in whom we have redemption through the blood," over into Colossians 1:14. The better texts have it in Ephesians, but not in Colossians. The scribe had too good a memory! Some variant readings in the manuscripts were introduced deliberately, although it is not always possible to say which are intentional and which are unintentional.

2. Intentional Changes. Scribes who thought too deeply while copying were often tempted to improve the text, or to write comments in the margin that were later incorporated into the text. Most modern English versions do not have verse 4 in John 5. It is the explanation for the moving of the waters of the Pool of Bethesda. Some scribe must have explained in the margin that an angel came down at certain times to trouble the waters. A later scribe incorporated that into the text and so it got into the Textus Receptus. The better manuscripts do not have this explanation. And with this illustration we have come to another class of textual alterations.

In the margin of Codex Vaticanus at Hebrews 1:3 a later scribe noticed that a corrector had changed a word in the text. After restoring the original reading, he wrote in the margin, "Fool and knave, can't you leave the old reading alone and not alter it"—clear evidence that alterations were being made. Scribes were at times offended by real or imagined errors in the text and sought to improve it.

(a) Some changes involved the spelling of words. In Revelation 1:4 we have the nominative case after the preposition *apo* (from), something that is not done in Greek. This very ungrammatical construction may have come from the apostle who hesitated to inflect the title for the Deity. In any case, later copyists patched up the text in several ways in an effort to improve on John's grammar.

(b) Very often scribes correct a text in the synoptic Gospels because they want to bring one Gospel in line with the other. These are called "harmonistic" corruptions. Luke has a shorter form of the Lord's Prayer than Matthew, and so some scribes have carried over some elements of Matthew's into the Lucan version. OT quotations are often given loosely by the NT writers. Later scribes brought this into line with the Greek translation of the OT, the Septuagint. For example, John 2:17 reads, "The zeal for thy house will consume me." This is a quotation from Psalm 69:9, which reads (in the Septuagint), "The zeal for thy house has consumed me." Later scribes, accordingly, introduced the past tense into John 2:17 and so brought it into line with their OT text.

(c) Scribes were tempted to add some items to the text they were copying, when they remembered a parallel text that had a fuller form. According to Matthew 9:13 Jesus said, "I came not to call the righteous, but sinners." Since Luke 5:32 has this saying with the addition, "unto repentance," later scribes added this to the Matthean text also. Paul, writing to the Colossians (1:23), calls himself a "minister," that is, a "servant." Later scribes felt that was too lowly a designation and changed the word to "preacher and apostle." Some manuscripts now read "preacher and apostle and minister"; another has "minister and apostle"; still another, "preacher and minister."

(d) Sometimes copyists wanted to clear up a difficulty in the text for the reader. Mark begins his Gospel with a quotation from Malachi 3:1, which is conflated with a verse from Isaiah 40:3. "Behold I send my messenger . . . ," is from Malachi; "the voice crying in the wilderness . . . ," is from Isaiah. The entire quotation is introduced thus: "As it is written in Isaiah the Prophet." The later scribe recognized that the first half of the quote is from Malachi and so he omitted Isaiah and made "prophet" a plural, "As it is written in the prophets."

There has been considerable debate over whether Paul wrote: "If I give up my body to be burned" (as KJV has it), or "in order that I may boast" (1 Cor. 13:3). The two words look very much alike and we may in fact have an error of the eye in this case (*kauthēsōmai* is to "burn," *kauchēsōmai* is to "boast"). The manuscript evidence is divided over which reading is to be preferred, and modern translators do not agree. The Greek text of the United Bible Societies has "boast." One reason for that choice is that, given the church's situation, in the early centuries where martyrdom was not uncommon, it is easier to see why a scribe would prefer to read "burn" rather than "boast," and therefore "boast" is the original. But a deliberate change from the original "boast" to "burn" is also possible.

(e) The alterations made out of doctrinal considerations are somewhat easier to detect if one is familiar with the theological tendencies at the time the scribe wrote. Marcion, for example, made a number of corrections that betray his anti-Jewish attitude. Instead of salvation coming from the "Jews," he made it come from "Judea." In Luke 2:41 and 43 the Evangelist speaks of Jesus' "parents." Later scribes, fearing that expression could undermine the doctrine of the virgin birth, changed "parents" to "Joseph and Mary."

A scribe, remembering Jesus' cry of dereliction on the cross, "My God, my God, why have you forsaken me," found it hard to understand how the writer to the Hebrews could say that he tasted death "by the grace of God" (Heb. 2:9). Therefore, he changed *charis* (grace) to *choris* (without), and made the verse say that he tasted death for every man "without God."

The radical saying of Jesus that he who is angry with his brother shall be in danger of judgment was apparently considered overly demanding by some enterprising scribe, and so he changed it to read (as King James Version has it), "whosoever is angry with his brother without a cause shall be in danger of the judgment."

(f) Some changes grew out of the church's liturgy. The Lord's Prayer in Matthew originally had no doxology, and ended with the petition, "and lead us not into temptation but deliver us from evil" (6:13). Since the church used this prayer, and since it was Jewish custom to attach a doxology to one's prayer, it was added later. The older manuscripts do not have this doxology and the Latin Vulgate did not have it either—which explains why Roman Catholic English versions do not have it. There is nothing unbiblical about this doxology and the church can feel free to use it, but it was not in the Lord's Prayer originally.

Similarly, Acts 8:37, present in the King James Version but absent in modern English versions, is absent in the earlier manuscripts of the NT. It probably arose out of the baptismal liturgy of the early church, in which the baptized was asked whether he

believed that Jesus Christ was the Son of God. Later scribes put that into the mouth of Philip who baptized the Ethiopian official.

Enough has been said to illustrate what happened to the original apostolic documents in the hands of copyists. The question now is, how does one know which is the original reading and which the later alteration?

B. Helps in Establishing the Correct Reading

There are three lines of evidence for the original form of the text: (1) the Greek manuscripts, (2) the early translations into other languages, and (3) the quotations of the NT text in the writings of the church fathers.

1. *The Greek Manuscripts.* We have already described some of the early manuscripts, discovered in the past hundred years or so, that enabled scholars to see the form of a much earlier Greek text than that printed by Erasmus. Here we mention in particular the great uncials such as the Sinaiticus and Vaticanus, and also the great papyrus manuscripts in the Chester Beatty and Bodmer collections—some of which take us back to the third and second century. While the rule doesn't always hold, in general it is obviously true that the later a manuscript, the more scribal changes have been made; the earlier a manuscript, the less possibility there was for copyists to introduce variants. The older manuscripts, therefore, carry more weight, as a rule.

2. *The Early Translations Into Other Languages.* Early in the history of the Christian church the Greek NT was translated into other languages, such

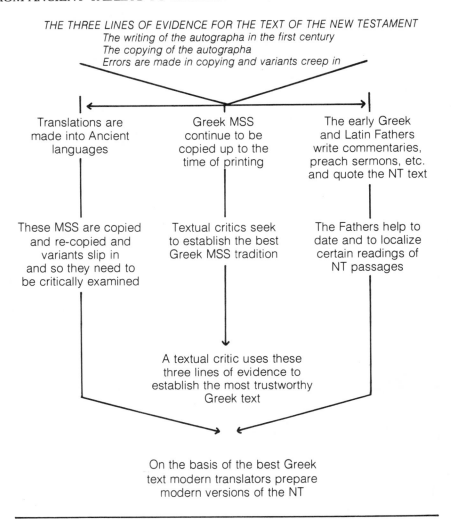

THE THREE LINES OF EVIDENCE FOR THE TEXT OF THE NEW TESTAMENT

The writing of the autographa in the first century
The copying of the autographa
Errors are made in copying and variants creep in

Translations are made into Ancient languages

Greek MSS continue to be copied up to the time of printing

The early Greek and Latin Fathers write commentaries, preach sermons, etc. and quote the NT text

These MSS are copied and re-copied and variants slip in and so they need to be critically examined

Textual critics seek to establish the best Greek MSS tradition

The Fathers help to date and to localize certain readings of NT passages

A textual critic uses these three lines of evidence to establish the most trustworthy Greek text

On the basis of the best Greek text modern translators prepare modern versions of the NT

as Syriac, Latin, Coptic, Armenian, and so forth. Copies of these ancient versions have come down to us, and by studying the text of these versions one can discover what kind of Greek text they used. Some manuscripts of these early versions are as old or older than some of our great uncials themselves, and therefore make an important contribution to Greek readings at an early period. Moreover, the versions come from widely scattered geographical areas that enable the scholars to see what readings were circulating in different parts of the empire. It must be remembered, however, that the manuscripts of the versions were subject to the same kind of alterations by scribes as were the manuscripts of the Greek NT.

3. *The Quotations of the NT Text in the Writings of the Church Fathers.* A third strand of textual evidence are the writings of the church fathers. In the sermons and commentaries of the Greek and Latin Fathers the NT is

quoted profusely. From these quotations one can discover what kind of Greek text a particular expositor had at hand. Also, these quotations help us to localize certain readings, as well as date them. If, for example, Origen quotes Matthew 27:17 in the form, "Whom do you want me to release for you, Jesus Barabbas or Jesus who is called the Christ?" we know that this reading was known in Caesarea prior to Origen's death in A.D. 253. We should then not be surprised to find "Jesus Bar-Abbas" in the New English Bible, particularly since this reading is supported by a major uncial (Theta), family 1 of the minuscules, and the Sinaitic Syriac and Armenian versions. Of course, we do not always know whether a church father is quoting from the Greek text, from some version, or whether he is giving the text in his own words. Nevertheless, the writings of the Fathers are an invaluable source of information on the state of the NT text in the early centuries. Obviously, the writings of the later Fathers are of less significance than the writings of Athanasius of Alexandria; Augustine of Hippo; Clement; Origen of Alexandria; Cyprian of Carthage; Ephraem the Syrian; Eusebius of Caesarea; Hippolytus of Rome; Irenaeus, bishop of Lyons; Justin Martyr; Tatian; Marcion; Tertullian; and Jerome. It has been said that if all the manuscripts of the NT should be lost, the NT could be restored from the quotations of the Fathers alone.

The scholars who bring all this evidence from the Greek manuscripts, the ancient versions, and the Patristics to bear upon the text of the NT for the purpose of establishing the best readings are called textual critics. A textual critic is not one who sits in judgment over the teachings of the Bible, but one who is seriously concerned to determine precisely what the correct text of the NT is.

IV. THE DEVELOPMENT OF TEXTUAL CRITICISM

A. Pioneers in the Field

Textual criticism began when scholars became aware of the fact that the manuscripts of the NT did not agree in innumerable places. John Mill (1645–1707) of Oxford published a Greek text before his death, in which he listed some 30,000 variant readings. For some people this seemed very threatening, but more and more scholars began to compare the Greek manuscripts with the versions and the Fathers, and to publish new editions of the Greek NT. Richard Bentley and Daniel Mace deserve credit for publishing such new editions.

On the Continent, Johann Bengel (1687–1752) had been greatly disturbed in his pietistic faith when he discovered that there were thousands of variant readings in the Greek NT, and with great devotion he collected all the evidence he could, to establish the best text possible. Some of the rules of textual criticism that he established are valid to this day. He published a new edition of the Greek text in 1734, and although he was a man known for his personal piety, there were those who now treated him as an enemy of the Holy Scriptures because his edition departed in so many places from the Textus Receptus.

Not all textual critics were orthodox in doctrine, but all of them had one major concern: to establish the most trustworthy text of the NT. Johann Wettstein (1693–1754) published the

Elzevir text in a new edition, but in the margin he listed those readings that he held to be correct. Many other scholars published new editions of the Greek NT, and we can mention only a few.

With Johann Griesbach (1745–1812) came a breakthrough, for he divided all the textual evidence into three large families: Alexandrian, Western, and Byzantine. He had discovered that the Greek manuscripts, the versions, and the Fathers, seemed to fall into three basic text types. Also, he laid down some fifteen rules of textual criticism, many of which hold even today. Scholars such as Karl Lachmann, the famous Count von Tischendorf in Germany, and Tregelles in England, tended to discount all later manuscripts of the NT and based their editions primarily on the older manuscripts.

The most noteworthy edition of the Greek text, published in 1881, was that of the Cambridge scholars B. F. Westcott (1825–1901) and F. J. A. Hort (1828–1892). By examining the relationships of the Greek manuscripts, the versions, and the Fathers, they came to the conclusion that there were four principal types of text, which they called Syrian, Western, Alexandrian, and Neutral. They had such a high regard for the Sinaiticus and Vaticanus that they classified them as "neutral," meaning that they had remained relatively free from scribal corruptions. The Syrian family was Griesbach's Byzantine type, and Westcott and Hort rejected this family.

As scholarly studies continued into the twentieth century, and as the NT papyri were recovered, pushing the text of the NT farther back than did the great uncials, Westcott and Hort's theory was modified somewhat. It was found that there is no such thing as a "neutral" text, and instead of the neutral text other scholars have suggested a text type called Caesarean, but not all agree.[9] To give an illustration of what is meant by a textual family let us look at some of the features of the three main families.

B. The Textual Families

1. *The Byzantine Family*. Most of the later uncials and nearly all the minuscules (which are generally late) support this text type. Among the versions the Syriac Peshitta is Byzantine, as are all of the later Fathers, beginning with the fourth century.

A feature of this family is to replace difficult readings with easier ones. For example, instead of saying that John's disciples disputed with "a Jew," it has "the Jews." Also, it tends to improve the Greek style by eliminating many "ands." Semitisms, which Greek readers would not understand, are replaced by readings that appeared more sensible to the scribes. Instead of saying, "Take heed lest you do your 'righteousness' before men" (Matt. 6:1), it has "alms." Also, it has the doxology in the Lord's Prayer, and the baptismal formula in Acts 8:37. The Byzantine texts tend to be longer. Where the Alexandrian family in Matthew 8:26 reads, "Do not enter the village," and the Western has, "Do not speak to anyone in the village," the Byzantine has, "Do not enter and do

---

[9]I. M. Price, *The Ancestry of Our English Bible*, revised by W. A. Irwin and Allen P. Wikgren (New York: Harper and Row, 1956), p. 216.

FAMILIES OF MANUSCRIPTS, VERSIONS, AND FATHERS

ALEXANDRIAN WITNESSES

(1) Proto-Alexandrian:

P45 (in Acts) P46 P66 P76 א B Sahidic (in part), Clement of Alexandria, Origen (in part), and most of the papyrus fragments with Pauline text.

(2) Later Alexandrian:

Gospels: (C)[11] L T W (in Luke 1:1 to 8:12 and John) (X) Z Δ (in Mark) Ξ Ψ (in Mark; partially in Luke and John) 33 579 892 1241 Bohairic.
Acts: P50 A (C) Ψ 33 81 104 326.
Pauline Epistles: A (C) H I Ψ 33 81 104 326 1739.
Catholic Epistles: P20 P23 A (C) Ψ 33 81 104 326 1739.
Revelation: A (C) 1006 1611 1854 2053 2344; less good, P47 א.

WESTERN WITNESSES

Gospels: D W (in Mark 1:1 to 5:30) 0171, the Old Latin (syrs and syrc in part), early Latin Fathers, Tatian's Diatessaron.
Acts: P29 P38 P48 D E 383 614 1739 syrhmg syrpalms copG67 early Latin Fathers, Ephraem.
Epistles: the Greek-Latin bilinguals D F G, Greek Fathers to the end of the third century, Old Latin mss. and early Latin Fathers, Syrian Fathers to about A.D. 450.

It will be observed that for the Book of Revelation no specifically Western witness have been identified.

CAESAREAN WITNESSES

(1) Pre-Caesarean: P45 W (in Mark 5:31 to 16:20) f1 f12 28.

(2) Caesarean proper: Θ 565 700 arm geo Origen (in part), Eusebius, Cyril-Jerusalem.

BYZANTINE WITNESSES

Gospels: A E F G H K P S V W (in Matt. and Luke 8:13—24:53) Π Ψ (partially in Luke and John) Ω and most minuscules.
Acts: H L P 049 and most minuscules.
Epistles: L 049 and most minuscules.
Revelation: 046 051 052 and most minuscules.

not speak to anyone in the village."

2. *The Alexandrian Family.* This family is supported by most of the early uncials and a few outstanding minuscules, such as numbers 31 and 81. It has the support of most of the papyri in the Chester Beatty and Bodmer collections. Also, several early versions, such as the Bohairic and the Vulgate, support this family, as do most of the early Greek Fathers.

All the manuscripts and versions of this type end the Gospel of Mark at 16:8. They all omit the story of the adulterous woman from John 8. This does not mean that this is not an authentic account, but it probably doesn't belong in John 8. All these texts omit the verse in John 5:4 about the angel who troubled the waters. Also, none of these texts has the address "to the Ephesians" in Ephesians 1:1. It may be that Ephesians was an encyclical that came to rest in Ephesus and so had this address attached to it later. All the texts belonging to this family have "men of his pleasure," in Luke 2:14, instead of "men of good will." We can see, then, how families of manuscripts are determined, namely, by common readings.

3. *The Western Family.* This family has the support of such uncials as Codex Bezae and Codex Claromontanus. It has the support of several minuscules and is the text most frequently quoted by the early Latin and Syriac Fathers.

It has interesting details not found in the other textual families. For example, in Luke 23:53, it adds that "twenty men could not move the stone." In Luke 22:19, 20, it omits the reference to the second cup, the bloody sweat, and does not have Jesus' prayer on the cross, "Father forgive them."

In the Acts the Western text makes Luke an Antiochian, for Acts 11:28 reads, "when we were gathered together," that is, Luke and the others. The conversion of the Ethiopian official ends with the comment: "And the Spirit of the Lord fell on the eunuch" (Acts 8:39). It appears to be somewhat antifeminist, for in several passages in which Priscilla's name precedes that of Aquila, the Western text turns that around and puts Aquila's name first.

The Alexandrian family used to be given first place, and the Byzantine last, if one had to choose between variant readings. This was found to be too simple an approach, and while the Textus Receptus, that is, the Byzantine family, is a later text type generally, and the Alexandrian represents an earlier tradition, today each reading, regardless of family, is treated with respect. External and internal probabilities are weighed in the case of every important variant reading. This method is known as the eclectic method of textual criticism.

C. An Example of the Eclectic Method

In 1 Corinthians 15:51 Codex Vaticanus reads, "We shall not all sleep, but shall all be changed." Codex Sinaiticus reads, "We shall all sleep, but we shall not all be changed." Codex Bezae has, "We shall all be raised, but we shall not all be changed." The Chester Beatty Papyrus (P[46]) reads, "We shall not all sleep, and we shall not all be changed."

The first question that a textual critic asks is: How well are these different readings supported by the Greek manuscripts, the versions, and the Fathers? Vaticanus is of the Alexandrian family and is supported also by the Byzantine family. Besides, the Syriac Peshitta, the Sahidic and the Bohairic, the Armenian, the Ethiopic, and the Gothic versions all support it. Moreover, the church fathers such as Cyril of Jerusalem, Tertullian of Africa, and Chrysostom of Antioch support that reading.

Codex Sinaiticus has the support of Codex Alexandrinus and Codex Ephraemi (all of the same family). Codex Bezae has only the Old Latin version, Marcion, and the Old Latin Fathers to support it.

From external evidence alone it is clear that what we have in our English Bibles today is the best supported and most widely distributed ancient text. Also, one can see why scribes would want to change it. Paul says, "We shall not all sleep," but he did fall asleep (i.e., died). So, an enterprising scribe switched the "not" from the first clause to the second—"we shall all sleep, but we shall not all be changed." Also, that fits in with the notion that only those who are perfect enough will be transformed. Codex Bezae probably wanted to give the Gnostics a blow and reads, "We shall all be raised." P⁴⁶ stands all alone and represents a compromise by putting the "not" in both clauses.

Since Vaticanus is best attested, most widely known, and is the most difficult reading (no one wants to have Paul make a wrong observation—which, of course he really did not), we must prefer that reading. Moreover, the reading of Vaticanus best explains how the three variant readings emerged. It would be hard to see how the reading of Vaticanus could be derived from the other readings. There is, then, no doubt that the reading, "We shall not all sleep, but we shall all be changed," is the correct text.

If one can imagine all the work that goes into establishing the correct reading in hundreds of passages in the NT, one learns to appreciate the devoted service of the textual critics to the church. Fortunately, through long experience several guidelines for establishing the best text have emerged, and these help the student in his search for the best text: (1) The age of the text is more important than the age of the manuscript, since it can happen that a late manuscript was prepared from an early exemplar. (2) Readings supported by ancient witnesses, especially when these come from a wide geographical area, are generally preferred. (3) The quality, not the quantity of manuscripts, is the determining factor in choosing a reading. If, for example, ten manuscripts have the same reading, and one does not, then the ten are equal in value to one. Manuscripts, in other words, must be "weighed" not "counted." (4) The

shorter reading is generally preferable, since scribes tend to add, rather than eliminate. (5) Readings that bear the marks of stylistic improvement are suspect. (6) The more difficult reading is generally preferable, since scribes tend to "ease" difficult readings. (7) Readings that reflect an author's characteristic tendencies are favored. (8) In parallel texts (e.g., in the synoptic Gospels) differences in readings in the individual Gospels tend to be preferred because scribes have a penchant for harmonizing them. (9) The reading that best accounts for variant readings is likely to be correct.

These rules overlap and no single rule is a safe guide, but taken together with a good dose of common sense, coupled with a knowledge of the ancient languages, and an intimate knowledge of early church history and Christian thought, the textual critic is able to provide for us a most dependable text of the NT.

John Wenham summarizes the history of NT textual studies in these words:

> It is thus roughly true to say that in the fifteenth century we had no Greek text in use; in the seventeenth century we had a late medieval Greek text; by the end of the nineteenth century we were firmly established upon a good fourth-century Greek text; now we are finding our way about the early third-century (some would even say late-second-century) texts with growing confidence.[10]

In 1966, after a decade of work by an international committee, five Bible Societies (American, British, Scottish, Dutch, and Württemberg) published an edition of the Greek NT for Bible

---

[10]J. W. Wenham, *Christ and the Bible* (Downers Grove: InterVarsity, 1973), p. 174.

translators and students.[11] The third edition of this United Bible Societies text was published in 1975, and is at present the best Greek text available.

What Sir Frederic Kenyon, famous British textual scholar, wrote in 1936, can still be repeated fifty years later in spite of all the new material that has come to light and in spite of all the progress that has been made in recovering the original text: "It is reassuring at the end to find that the general result of all these discoveries and all this study is to strengthen the proof of the authenticity of the Scriptures, and our conviction that we have in our hands in substantial integrity, the veritable Word of God."[12]

SUGGESTED READING

Finegan, J. Encountering New Testament Manuscripts. *Grand Rapids: Eerdmans, 1974.*

Geisler, N. L. and Nix, W. E. From God to Us. *Chicago: Moody, 1974. "The Development of Textual Criticism," pp. 159–73.*

Greenlee, J. H. An Introduction to the New Textual Criticism. *Grand Rapids: Eerdmans, 1964.*

Metzger, B. M. The Text of the New Testament, *2nd ed. New York: Oxford University Press, 1968.*

Price, I. M. The Ancestry of Our English Bible, *rev. ed. New York: Harper and Row, 1956. See "Textual Criticism and the Printed Text," pp. 202–11; "Textual Criticism Since Westcott and Hort," pp. 212–22.*

Twilley, L. D. The Origin and Transmission of the New Testament: A Short Introduction. *Grand Rapids: Eerdmans, 1959.*

Wegener, G. S. 6000 Years of the Bible, *trans. M. Shenfield, London: Thames and Hudson, 1963. See "Printing Takes Over," pp. 187–200; "Count Tischendorf," pp. 275–94.*

---

[11]Metzger, *Text of New Testament,* p. 146.

[12]F. G. Kenyon, *The Story of the Bible,* revised by F. F. Bruce (Grand Rapids: Eerdmans, 1967), p. 113.

Chapter 13

Early Eastern Versions
of the Bible

In our previous chapter we underscored the significance of the early versions of the NT for establishing the best text. One can tell from a translation whether a word or phrase was present in the Greek text that the translator used. And like the Greek manuscripts, the versions fall into textual families that are designated in the same way as the various types of text found in the Greek manuscript tradition: Byzantine, Western, Alexandrian, or Caesarean. These early versions also cast considerable light on the life, the mission, and the theology of the churches within and beyond the borders of the Roman Empire in the centuries following the founding of the church.

The next two chapters will be devoted to these early translations of the Greek NT into other languages. In some cases translations of the entire Bible were made, but our primary interest at this time is in the early versions of the NT.[1] For the purpose of our brief discussion we divide these translations into Eastern and Western versions. Let us begin with the Eastern.

I. THE SYRIAC VERSIONS

A. Syriac Christianity

Among the visitors at Pentecost were Parthians, Medes, Elamites, and the dwellers of Mesopotamia. These were Jews who lived in territories beyond the Euphrates, outside the limits of the Roman Empire. There were probably several million Jews in these territories by the first century.[2]

Whether any of these Eastern Jews who heard Peter speak in Jerusalem at Pentecost brought the Gospel back home with them cannot be determined. Legend has it that the gospel

---

[1]Although there are many scholars who have written on the early versions of the NT, there are two that stand out. Some thirty years ago Professor Arthur Vööbus published his *Early Versions of the NT: Manuscript Studies* (Stockholm, 1954). More recently Professor Bruce Metzger published *The Early Versions of the New Testament* (Oxford: Clarendon, 1977).

[2]F. F. Bruce, *The Books and the Parchments*, 3rd rev. ed. (Old Tappan: Revell, 1963), p. 191.

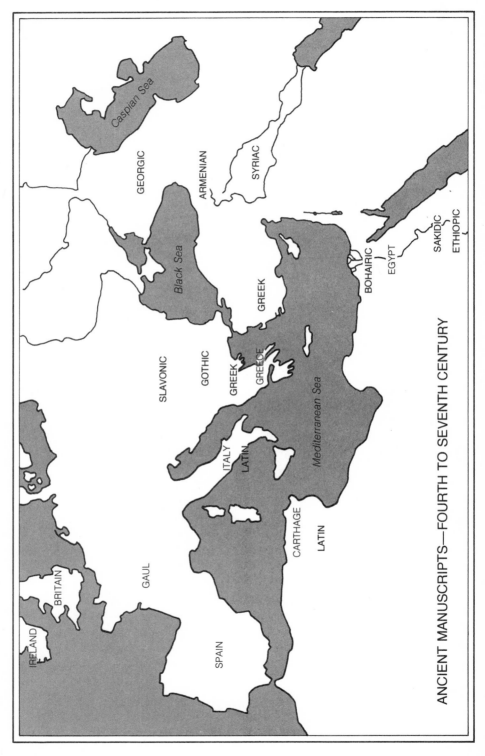

ANCIENT MANUSCRIPTS—FOURTH TO SEVENTH CENTURY

was preached in the Land of the Two Rivers by apostolic missionaries, but little is known of first-century Syriac Christianity. What is known is that the Christian faith was introduced to such centers as Arbela, east of the Tigris, and Edessa, east of the Euphrates, by the end of the first century. Luke tells the story of how Paul and his associates brought the gospel to the West. It is not unlikely that the gospel moved to the East in similar fashion.

Once the church was firmly established it rose to the challenge of proclaiming the gospel to the ends of the earth. The Syriac church took the good news as far as China. Syriac missionaries penetrated India and established the church on the Malabar coast—a church that has survived to this day. Eusebius reports that Pantaenus, head of the catechetical school in Alexandria, went to India as a missionary about A.D. 180, and reportedly found a Gospel of Matthew, which Bartholomew, a disciple of Jesus, had left there. Indian tradition ascribes the founding of the Mar Thoma Church to the evangelistic efforts of the Apostle Thomas. The official Bible and the ecclesiastical language of this church is still the Syriac.

When we speak of Syriac Christianity we do not mean the Christianity of Antioch in Syria, which was Greek-speaking. But east of Antioch, in the Land of the Two Rivers where Aramaic was widely spoken, there developed a large and dynamic church that spoke Syriac. Syriac may be defined as Christian Aramaic; the Syriac script, however, is distinct from Aramaic.

Since so many Jews lived in the lands beyond the Euphrates it is quite possible that they, like the Alexandrians who translated the Bible into Greek, had already translated the Bible for Syriac-speaking Jews. This Syriac translation of the OT was very likely taken over by the Christians. As for the NT, the first effort to render the Greek Gospels into Syriac was that of Tatian.

B. Tatian's Diatessaron

Tatian, who came from Mesopotamia, traveled to Rome about A.D. 150. Here he was converted and became a pupil of Justin Martyr. After Justin's death, Tatian was charged with heresy on account of his extremely ascetic views, and returned to his native land, where he became the founder of the Encratites, an ascetic Christian movement, perhaps around A.D. 170.

Either before he left Rome or after his return to his homeland, Tatian (C.A.D.170) provided the Syriac-speaking Christians with a Gospel Harmony called Diatessaron (literally "through four," but in the sense of a "harmony of four parts"). There has been some debate on whether Tatian wrote this Harmony originally in Greek or in Syriac. Or, did he write it in Greek first and then translate it into Syriac?

This Diatessaron was not simply a translation of the four Gospels published in four parallel columns, but rather Tatian tried to weave all four Gospels together into one continuous gospel account. It came to be known in the East as the "mixed" gospel. Tatian began with the first verses of John's Gospel, followed by Luke's narrative of the nativity of John the Baptist. Generally he followed the Markan order, into which he fitted the material from the other Gospels. The whole work had some fifty-five chapters and that suggests that the Diatessaron was designed to be read in the churches.

His ascetic tendencies seem to have affected his translation. In Matthew 1:19, Tatian avoided referring to Joseph as Mary's husband. He reduced Anna's connubial bliss from seven years to seven days (Luke 2:36). Since the Encratites did not drink wine, the words, "When men have drunk freely," in the story of the Wedding at Cana, is omitted (John 2:10). His anti-Jewish attitude is reflected in his rendering of Luke 2:10, where the good news of the Savior, proclaimed by the angels, is for "all the world," instead of "all the people," since people could mean the Jewish people.

In spite of these tendencies Tatian's Diatessaron became extremely popular; so popular that it was translated into a number of languages. Ephraim in the fourth century wrote a commentary on the Diatessaron, in Syriac. A Persian and Arabic translation of this Harmony witness to its popularity throughout the Near and Middle East. Latin, Dutch, Medieval German, Old Italian, and Middle English translations speak of its great popularity in the West.

In 1933 a fragment of the Diatessaron in Greek was discovered at Dura-Europos, on the Upper Euphrates, a former Roman army outpost, captured by the Persians in A.D. 256. This seemed to prove that the Diatessaron was originally written in Greek and then translated. However, scholars such as Arthur Vööbus, of Chicago, hold that this is a Greek translation of an original Syriac.

So popular was the Diatessaron that it appears as if church leaders made conscious efforts to replace this Harmony with the fourfold Gospel. On the other hand, the replacement of the Diatessaron by the Old Syriac version of the four Gospels may have been a natural process. In fact, the Old Syriac version and the Diatessaron may have been two quite independent efforts to give Syriac-speaking Christians the gospel in their mother tongue. With that we turn to the Old Syriac version.

C. The Old Syriac Version

The Diatessaron was not the only attempt to translate the NT into Syriac. A century ago little was known about other early Syriac versions, but in 1842 a mass of Syriac manuscripts reached the British Museum from a monastery in Egypt. In this collection was a beautiful but fragmentary codex of the Four Gospels from the fifth century. Dr. Cureton of the Museum edited this codex and found it to be an Old Syriac version of the Gospels.

In 1892 two enterprising Cambridge women, Mrs. Agnes Smith Lewis and Mrs. Margaret Dunlop Gibson, visited the monastery of St. Catherine on Mt. Sinai, and came away with, among other things, a photographic copy of a palimpsest manuscript that also has the Four Gospels in Old Syriac. The earlier copy is now called the Curetonian Syriac and the latter the Sinaitic Syriac.[3]

While both manuscripts are in Old Syriac they are not completely identical. The origin of this "unmixed" Gospel (Tatian's is the "mixed") is shrouded in darkness, but the text comes from the late second or early

---

[3]F. G. Kenyon, *Our Bible and the Ancient Manuscripts*, revised by A. W. Adams (New York: Harper and Brothers, 1958), p. 226.

third century. Some scholars have suggested that this Old Syriac version was prepared prior to the Diatessaron, but that does not seem to be the majority opinion.

There are some interesting readings in these two manuscripts, which apparently are two forms of an original Old Syriac version. For example, the Sinaitic Syriac has it that "Joseph, to whom was betrothed Mary, the virgin, begat Jesus, who is called the Christ" (Matt. 1:16). In Matthew 27:16 Barabbas is given the added name "Jesus." It omits the reference to the bloody sweat (Luke 22:43–44) and the prayer, "Father forgive them" (Luke 23:34), which the Curetonian retains. Both manuscripts omit "first born" in Matthew 1:25. Both have the longer text on the second cup in the words of institution in Luke 22:17–20. Both omit the story of the woman caught in adultery (John 8:1–11). In Matthew 6:13 the Curetonian has the doxology in the Lord's Prayer, omitted by the Sinaitic and the great uncials. In Luke 23:48 both manuscripts add, "saying, Woe to us, what has befallen us! Woe to us for our sins."

Unfortunately no manuscript of the Old Syriac version for Acts and the Epistles has survived, although we have quotations from these books in Syriac Church Fathers. As time went on the Old Syriac version was superseded by the Peshitta versions.

D. The Peshitta Versions

The word "Peshitta" means that which is simple and clear. It is used much like the word "Vulgate," in the sense of widely-used, current, or

A page from the Syriac Peshitta. This easy-to-read version dates from the fifth century, and, in spite of tradition that relates it to the Bishop Rabbula, it appears to have the marks of multiple authorship.

common. The Peshitta is the great standard version of the ancient Syriac church, in use from the fifth century onwards. This version was long believed to have been prepared by Rabbula, bishop of Edessa from A.D. 411 to 435, but that is no longer certain. It antedates the division of the Syriac church into Nestorians and Jacobites, for both communities made use of the Peshitta, and so it must have been generally accepted before A.D. 431. In its official form it includes only twenty-two books of the NT; the four minor General Epistles (2 Peter, 2 and 3 John, and Jude) and the Revelation are absent.[4]

More than 350 Peshitta manuscripts of the NT are available to scholars in

---

[4]Metzger, *Early Versions*, p. 48.

the Western world. The Peshitta is a smooth and scholarly version, copied so carefully that the manuscripts exhibit relatively few variants.[5]

In the year 508, Philoxenus, bishop in eastern Syria, felt that the Peshitta was not sufficiently close to the original Greek and had a certain Polycarp revise it, since Philoxenus did not know Greek. It is called the Philoxenian Syriac. Then, in 616, this version was itself revised by Thomas Harkel, with the help of some Greek manuscripts from Alexandria, and this is now called the Harclean Syriac. This version is so close to the Greek that scholars can usually tell what Greek reading lay behind the Syriac. Besides, it has some very interesting variant readings in the margin. The Harclean version, for example, has it that Stephan was "full of faith," rather than "full of grace" (Acts 6:8). Jesus' cry on the cross is "My God, my God, why have you taunted me?" Presumably the translator or a later scribe could not reconcile his knowledge of God with the fact that God forsook his son on the cross. These revised versions of the Peshitta included also those five NT books that were absent from the Peshitta.

There is yet another Syriac version, which we mention only in passing, namely the Palestinian Syriac, stemming from about the fifth century. The language of this version is the Aramaic dialect used in Palestine during the early Christian centuries. It is called Syriac only because it uses the Syriac script.[6] It has some unusual readings; the following are but a few examples: "Men must give account of every good

word which they do not speak" (Matt. 12:36); "all have sinned and lack the knowledge of the glory of God" (Rom. 3:23); "God's end of the law is Christ" (Rom. 10:4).

The Syriac version of the NT (at least of the Gospels) has the honor of being the first translation of the Greek NT into another language. This version was born in an area of Christendom about which relatively little is known, but that represents one of the bright spots of early Christianity.

II. THE COPTIC VERSIONS

A. Christianity in Egypt

The date when Christianity was introduced into Egypt is not known. According to Acts 2:10 there were Jews from Egypt in Jerusalem at Pentecost. It appears as if the gospel had reached Alexandria by the middle of the first century. A great amount of Christian literature (not always orthodox) originated in Egypt in the second century. Besides, we have NT papyrus manuscripts that come from the second century and were discovered in Egypt.

Alexandria and its environs was Greek-speaking and so there was no need to translate the NT for the residents of Alexandria. Even the Jews here spoke Greek and they had already translated the OT into Greek before the time of Christ. But, as the Christian faith spread to the countryside, where various Coptic dialects were spoken, translations were called for. By the end of the third century, monasticism had already made its appearance in Egypt, and the NT was available in Coptic prior to this time.

---

[5]Kenyon, *Bible and Manuscripts*, p. 231.

[6]Metzger, *Early Versions*, p. 76.

Coptic represents the last phase of the development of ancient Egyptian, and has assumed a half dozen dialects, such as Sahidic, Bohairic, Fayyumic, and others, in the valley of the Nile. In Upper Egypt, around Thebes, Sahidic was spoken, and in the Delta area, Bohairic. Two important early translations of the NT into Egyptian tongues are Sahidic and Bohairic.

B. The Sahidic Version

This version was not known until the end of the eighteenth century, but enough manuscript material is now available to establish the fact that the Sahidic goes back, possibly to the third century. The Sahidic has preserved some interesting readings. It has a binary doxology at the end of the Lord's Prayer: "For thine is the power and the glory forever" (Matt. 6:13). In the parable of the Rich Man and Lazarus (Luke 16:19), the rich man is called "Nineve." In Acts 15, the Apostolic Decree is given with four prohibitions, followed by the negative form of the Golden Rule.

C. The Bohairic

Of the several Coptic dialects, Bohairic is the only one that continues to be used today in the liturgy of the Coptic Church,[7] which has its seat in Cairo. Although Sahidic may be a slightly earlier version, Bohairic has become the standard Coptic version. It should be added that the OT was also translated from the Greek Septuagint into Sahidic and Bohairic.

Both Sahidic and Bohairic lack the

reference to the strengthening angel (Luke 22:43), the prayer of Jesus on the cross, "Father forgive them" (Luke 22:34), the reference to the angel who troubled the waters (John 5:4), the story of the woman caught in adultery (John 8:1–11), and the reference to "fasting" in Mark 9:29. The Sahidic has "for they had not received the Spirit," instead of "for as yet the Spirit had not been given" (John 7:37–39). Perhaps the translator (or a later scribe) could not accept the fact that there was no Spirit yet.

The Coptic versions are the product of the missionary ventures of Egyptian Christianity in the early centuries, as it reached out to its non-Greek speaking neighbors. This is the case also with the Armenian version and, indeed, with nearly all of these early versions.

III. THE ARMENIAN VERSION

The missionary activity of the Syriac church in the early centuries of the Christian era was responsible, so it appears, for several secondary translations of the Scriptures—translations made not from the original Hebrew or Greek, but from the Syriac version, which was itself a translation. North of the region where the Syriac churches flourished lived the Armenians, in a territory lying between the Roman and Persian empires, north of Mesopotamia. Christianity came here in the third century, and in time the entire country became officially Christian. One of the great Christian leaders was Gregory the Illuminator (c. 257–331), who was of royal lineage and, after studying in Cappadocia, returned as a missionary to his native land.

---

[7]Metzger, *Early Versions*, p. 120.

Before this time all books were written in Greek or Syriac, since the Armenian alphabet had not yet been invented. In the early part of the fifth century an Armenian alphabet had been invented by Mesrop. This scholar and churchman then collected manuscripts of the Bible and began to translate the Bible into Armenian.

No version of the NT, other than the Latin Vulgate, is available in so many manuscripts as is the Armenian version. Because of this it is sometimes called "the Queen of the Versions." What is unique about the Armenian version is that the NT includes the Epistle of the Corinthians to Paul and a Third Epistle of Paul to the Corinthians. Also, the NT text has some peculiar readings. For example, the lame man at the Pool of Bethesda complains, "while I drag myself, another steps in before me" (John 5:7). Acts 20:28 has "Lord" instead of "God," in an attempt to ease the problem that Paul created for us by speaking of the "church of God, which he bought with his own blood." In Revelation 22:14 instead of the beatitude on "those who wash their robes," the Armenian has "those who keep his commandments."

In the Armenian manuscripts the General Epistles are always placed immediately after the Book of Acts. Most of the Armenian manuscripts omit the last twelve verses of the Gospel of Mark. One manuscript has these verses, but the heading states that these verses were written by an elder, named Ariston.

The standard Armenian version seems to be a revision of an Old Armenian version by the use of the standard Greek text. The Old Armenian was probably based on an Old Syriac text and is a secondary translation.

IV. THE GEORGIAN VERSION

Georgia lies north of Armenia, in the Caucasus. This territory, between the Black and the Caspian Sea, is now within the Soviet Union. After Armenia had been evangelized, the gospel came to the Georgians also, about the middle of the fourth century. Before the NT could be translated into Georgian, an alphabet had to be created, just as it had in the case of the Armenians. How soon after the earliest evangelization of Georgia a translation of the Scriptures was made in the native tongue is not known exactly, but there is evidence that the Gospels at least were translated before the middle of the fifth century.[8]

Opinion differs as to which language the Georgian version was based on. Some hold that it was prepared on the basis of the Syriac; others, that the translation was made from the Greek. A third view is that the Georgian translation was made from the Armenian version and represents a tertiary version (a translation of a translation). This appears to be the majority opinion.[9] Whatever its base may have been, the Georgian version, like others from that period, was revised later and brought into greater conformity to the Greek NT.

Like the Armenian, the Georgian was a missionary version. It is good to know that the goal of modern missionary organizations such as that

---

[8]Metzger, *Early Versions*, p. 190.

[9]Bruce, *Books and Parchments*, p. 213.

of the Wycliffe Translators, to reduce spoken languages to writing and to translate the Scriptures in the language of the people, was part of the church's vision in its early centuries.

V. THE ETHIOPIC VERSION

The early history of Ethiopia, or Abyssinia, is shrouded in mystery. It was assumed by some early church fathers that the Ethiopian official who was baptized by Philip had brought the Christian faith to this land, but it is not certain that Candace, whose servant he was, ruled over the territory now called Ethiopia. There are traditions that one or the other of the twelve apostles brought the gospel to Ethiopia, but these cannot be confirmed. There is evidence, however, that the Christian faith was in Ethiopia by the end of the fourth century. One story has it that Frumentius and Aedesius, who were on a ship that was attacked on the Ethiopian coast, survived the ordeal and stayed in Ethiopia. After winning the confidence of the people they preached the gospel and the royal house became Christian. Frumentius, so the story goes, after getting help from the Alexandrian church, became the bishop of the Ethiopic church. Presumably by the end of the fifth century Ethiopia was Christianized.

Ethiopia had an alphabet long before Christ. It is a South Semitic script, even though it is read from left to right and now has vowel characters. Just when the first translations of the biblical books into Ethiopic (or Ge'ez, as the Old Ethiopiac is called) were made is not known, but by the fifth or sixth century at least parts of the Bible were available in the language of the people.

The translation of the Bible into Ethiopic is connected with the coming of Syriac Christians from the eastern parts of the empire. Monophysite monks (who held that Christ had but one nature) were persecuted by the Byzantine rulers and made their way to Ethiopia, and this may explain the Syriac elements in the Ethiopic version. The Coptic and Ethiopic churches are Monophysite. The Ethiopic Bible contains some books (such as First Enoch and Jubilees) not found in our canon. It is available in a great many manuscripts, but most of them are from a rather late date.

The Arabic NT also belongs to the eastern branch of translations. Translations into Arabic prior to the seventh century are not known, and there is no uniformity of versions. Some were translated from the Greek, others from the Syriac, and still others from Coptic. Since the Arabic versions are so late they are not useful as witnesses to the original text of the NT; they are, of course, exceedingly useful for the mission of the church to Arabic-speaking peoples.

As for the Christians who lived in Persia in the early centuries, they read the Scriptures in Syriac. However, there is evidence for a translation of at least some biblical books into Persian as early as the beginning of the fifth century.[10] There are modern versions in Persian, but these do not provide evidence for the form of the text of the NT in the early centuries.

We must now turn to some of the early versions that were published in the western parts of the empire.

---

[10]Metzger, *Early Versions*, p. 277.

SUGGESTED READING

Kenyon, F. G. **Our Bible and the Ancient Manuscripts,** *rev. ed. New York: Harper and Brothers, 1958. See "The Ancient Versions of the New Testament," pp. 220–49.*
Metzger, B. M. **The Early Versions of the New Testament.** *Oxford: Clarendon, 1977.*
———. *"A Survey of Recent Research on the Ancient Versions of the NT,"* **New Testament Studies,** *Vol. 2 (1955), pp. 1–16.*
———. *"Ancient Versions,"* **Interpreter's Dictionary of the Bible,** *4 vols. ed. G. A. Buttrick. Nashville: Abingdon, 1962, Vol. 4, pp. 749–59.*
Price, I. M. **The Ancestry of Our English Bible,** *3rd ed. revised by W. A. Irwin and Allen P. Wikgren. New York: Harper and Row, 1956. See "The Syriac and Other Eastern Versions," pp. 189–201.*

Chapter 14

Early Western Versions of the Bible

The Book of Acts tells the story of how the gospel spread from Jerusalem westward, until it reached the heart of the empire, Rome. The apostles had no insurmountable language barriers to overcome in the first century, since Greek was spoken in all the great centers of the Roman world. When Paul wrote his letter to the Romans in the middle of the first century, he could write it in Greek. And when Clement of Rome at the end of the first century wrote to the Corinthians, he wrote in his readers' native Greek. Ignatius, bishop of Antioch, wrote a letter to the Romans about A.D. 110, and again it was in Greek.

About the middle of the second century Hermas of Rome wrote his famous *Shepherd* in Greek. A little later Polycarp of Smyrna visited Rome because of the controversy over the date of Easter, and he was asked by the Roman church to lead in the celebration of the Eucharist in Greek. Greek remained the language of Roman theologians until the beginning of the third century.

However, the official language of the Roman government, of the army, and the law courts, was Latin, and gradually the West became Latin speaking. The last Roman theologian to write his works in Greek was Hippolytus (died 236). Although Pope Victor (c. 190) wrote in Latin, his writings have not survived, and the first Christian writer of repute to write in Latin was Novatian (c. 250). The change from Greek to Latin in everyday life came perhaps around A.D. 150, although many ordinary folk had probably never learned to speak Greek. By 250 Latin had become the language of Christian writers and theologians. Since the liturgy of the church is usually last to change, it is estimated that some Greek continued to be used for another hundred years; by then the West was Latin. Nevertheless, the publisher of Codex Bezae, at the end of the fifth or beginning of the sixth century, for some reason or another still thought it worth the effort to publish a Greek/Latin bilingual codex of the Gospels and Acts.

As the West became Latin in speech the need for a Latin Bible arose. And this led to various efforts to render the Bible into Latin. These early versions that preceded the work of Jerome are called Old Latin versions.

I. THE OLD LATIN VERSIONS

A. The Origin of Old Latin Versions

It appears that the need for a Latin Bible arose first in the Roman province of Africa, covering the territory now represented by Tunisia, Algeria, and Morocco. Some of the most flourishing churches of early Christianity were located here, before Islam snuffed out the light of the gospel in the seventh century. Several of the great teachers of the church came from North Africa; one might mention Tertullian, Cyprian, and the famous Augustine. Students of the history of Christian missions have observed that in territories such as Egypt and Syria, where the Bible was translated into the languages of the common people at an early stage, the Muslim conquest was unable to wipe out Christianity. In North Africa, however, where no translations into the languages of the Berber peoples were made, hardly a trace of Christianity is left.

The official language of the Roman province of Africa was Latin, although indigenous people had their own languages. This was particularly the case in the great city of Carthage. And it was here that the need for a Latin version came to the surface.[1]

In A.D. 180 there was an outbreak of persecution in Numidia (modern Tunisia). A record of the trial of Christians in a town named Scillium has come down to us. This account, drawn up in Latin, identifies those who were beheaded for their faith. When the proconsul asked Speratus what he had in the box that he carried, he replied: "Books and letters of a just man, one Paul."[2] It is generally assumed that if Paul's letters were available in Latin in A.D. 180, then Latin Gospels must have been available also, since the Gospels are usually translated first.[3]

Since the earliest evidence for a Latin NT comes from North Africa, we may have to conclude that the first attempts to render the Greek NT into Latin were made in Africa. On the other hand, there may have been parallel efforts to make Latin translations of the Greek NT in Italy. The fact is that the Old Latin version is not the product of one man; nor was it, as far as we know, an official project of the church. Rather, individuals in different parts of the Western Empire took it in hand to prepare Latin versions for those who could not speak Greek. Augustine in his day complained that "in the early days of the faith, every man who happened to gain possession of a Greek manuscript and who imagined he had any facility in both languages, however slight that might have been, dared to make a translation."[4]

The NT books were translated a number of times and no single translator did all twenty-seven books. Perhaps the first translations were made orally. Just as the Jews, when they could no longer understand the

---

[1] F. F. Bruce, *The Books and the Parchments*, 3rd rev. ed. (Old Tappan: Revell, 1963), p. 202.

[2] B. M. Metzger, *The Early Versions of the New Testament* (Oxford: Clarendon, 1977), p. 289.

[3] A. Vööbus, *Early Versions of the New Testament* (Stockholm, 1954), pp. 35–37.

[4] Metzger, *Early Versions*, p. 290.

Hebrew Bible, had translators who gave synagogue audiences an Aramaic paraphrase, so the Greek Scriptures were probably translated orally into Latin in those churches of the West where Greek was not understood. Finally, instead of translating into Latin orally, written versions were prepared in advance. This resulted in a great multiplicity of translations, and Jerome later complained that there were almost as many Latin versions as there were manuscripts.[5]

We know that the Bible was available in Latin by the time of Tertullian, for this great jurist/theologian quotes the NT in Latin (died c. 220). Also, Cyprian, bishop of Carthage, who died about 258, quotes copiously from a Latin version of both Old and New Testaments.[6] It is even possible that in the case of the OT, African Jews had already translated the OT into Latin, just as Alexandrian Jews had a Greek version prepared, and that Christians took over this Latin OT, just as they had adopted the Septuagint.

In any case, we are not dependent on the quotations of the early Latin Fathers for our knowledge of Old Latin, even though these quotations are extremely important in establishing the best Old Latin text; we have a number of manuscripts that have retained for us the Old Latin text.

B. Old Latin Manuscripts

As compared with the more than 10,000 manuscripts of Jerome's Latin Vulgate, the manuscripts of the Old Latin versions are few in number, and often quite fragmentary in form. The Gospels are represented by about thirty-two mutilated manuscripts. A few brief comments on several of the most important codices is in place.

Representing the African family there is Codex Palatinus, a fifth-century copy of the Gospels, now at Trent. It is written with silver and gold ink on purple vellum. The text contains the Gospels in the Western order (Matthew, John, Luke, Mark). More important, and also belonging to the African family, is Codex Bobiensis, now at Turin. Although it is rather fragmentary it is a fourth-century manuscript that has preserved the Old Latin text for us better than any other manuscript.

Of the European family the most outstanding is the fourth-century Codex Vercellensis. It has been held in such high regard that the kisses of the faithful over the centuries have damaged the text. It is now under glass at Vercelli in northern Italy. It is also written in gold and silver letters on purple vellum, and has the Gospels in the Western order. Codex Veronensis, stored at Verona, Italy, is a purple parchment manuscript written in the fifth century with silver and gold ink. It represents the type of text Jerome used as the basis for the Vulgate. Codex Colbertinus comes from the twelfth century but has the Gospels in Old Latin. It is also a representative of the European family.

One of the largest manuscripts in the world is appropriately called "Gigas" (giant), requiring two men to lift it. Its pages are twenty by thirty-six inches and besides some other writings, it contains the whole Bible in

---

[5]Metzger, *Early Versions*, p. 290.

[6]F. G. Kenyon, *Our Bible and the Ancient Manuscripts*, revised by A. W. Adams (New York: Harper and Brothers, 1958), p. 140.

Latin. Formerly it was in Prague, but it was moved to Stockholm, Sweden, in 1648. It is sometimes called the Devil's Bible because it contains a huge painting of this potentate in garish colors. Actually only Acts and the Book of Revelation are in Old Latin, elsewhere Gigas is Vulgate.

The Old Latin versions contain some interesting readings. In the parable of the Barren Fig Tree (Luke 13:7), several manuscripts have: "I will throw on a basket of dung." They have the comment on the descent of the angel to trouble the waters (John 5:3–4) and the story of the woman taken in adultery. When Jesus was baptized "a great and tremendous light flashed forth from the water, so that all who were present feared" (Matt. 3:15). In Luke 23:5 it is reported that Jesus was charged with alienating "both our sons and our wives from us, for he does not baptize as we do." The Resurrection account in Mark 16:3 is expanded; Jesus "rose in the brightness of the living God, and at once they (the angels) ascended with him, and immediately there was light." And the bystanders, instead of saying that Jesus was calling Elijah as he hung on the cross, say, "He calls the sun" (Mark 15:34).

The Old Latin Bible was printed in several volumes at Oxford, beginning in 1883, and another series was begun in Rome, in 1912. At the moment an ambitious project is under way at the Monastery of Beuron in Württemberg Germany, in an effort to publish the most trustworthy Old Latin Bible to date.

Since various people at various times and places, with greater or lesser degree of success, had attempted to render the Bible into Latin in the early centuries of the Christian era, the result was chaos. Hardly two manuscripts could be found that agreed in detail. Accordingly Pope Damasus (366–384) undertook to remedy the situation, and the man he chose to create order out of this confusion was the great biblical scholar, Sophronius Eusebius Hieronymus, known to us as Jerome.

II. THE LATIN VULGATE

A. Jerome, the Reviser/Translator

Jerome was born about 346 at Stridon, on the borders of Dalmatia and Pannonia, not far from Trieste. His parents were fairly well-to-do Christians and gave their son the opportunity to study. Soon after the Emperor Julian died in 363 Jerome went to Rome to study under the famous grammarian Donatus. Jerome began building up his library by copying every book he could lay his hands on. He attended some disreputable places at this time, but on Sundays he often visited the catacombs. It was during this time that he made a formal profession as a Christian, was baptized, and embarked on the study of Greek.[7]

From Rome Jerome and a friend moved to Gaul, where his interests shifted from classical to biblical and theological studies. As often happened in those days, he developed serious conflicts in his mind between classical and Christian studies. From Gaul he moved to Aquileia, in Italy, and in 373 Jerome set out for the East. At

---

[7]H. F. D. Sparks, "Jerome as Biblical Translator," *The Cambridge History of the Bible,* eds. P. R. Ackroyd and C. F. Evans (Cambridge: Cambridge University Press, 1970), Vol. 1, p. 510.

Antioch he had a major spiritual crisis. While suffering from a fever he had a dream in which he was summoned before the Judge of all the earth who asked him to state who he was. Jerome answered: "I am a Christian!" But the Judge answered, "You lie; you are a Ciceronian, not a Christian. For where your treasure is there will your heart be also." He was then taken away for punishment, but Jerome begged for mercy and promised never to read a pagan book again. Evidently Jerome did not take his oath, made in a feverous condition, too seriously, for he always did treasure the classics.

Nevertheless, it was a turning point in his life. He now sought seclusion and joined the hermits in the desert east of Antioch for four or five years, devoted to sacred studies. He got a converted Jew to teach him Hebrew and so he added a third tongue to his equipment as translator.

Jerome had already published several works when he went to Rome in 382, where he became the secretary and confidant of Pope Damasus. It was here that Damasus commissioned him to revise the Latin versions in the light of the Greek. With this he launched on his life's work. He realized, scholar that he was, that the task of a Bible reviser/translator can be a very thankless one. Moreover, Jerome was by nature quite sensitive to criticism. He asks Damasus in his preface to his revision of the Four Gospels:

> Is there a man, learned or unlearned, who will not, when he takes the volume in his hands, and perceives that what he reads does not suit his settled tastes, break out immediately into violent lan-

guage and call me a forger and a profane person for having had the audacity to add anything to the ancient books, or to make any changes or corrections therein?[8]

When Damasus died in 385 there were those who would have been glad to see Jerome become his successor. But that did not happen, and the new pope did not hold him in such high esteem as had Damasus. Jerome, therefore, left Rome and went to the East, settling finally in Bethlehem. A wealthy high-born woman, Paula, established three convents for women there, of which she was the Superior. Jerome directed the monastery for men. Here they spent the remainder of their lives. Jerome wrote a great number of scholarly works here in Bethlehem, but it is his revision and translation of the Bible that has made him world renowned.

B. Revising and Translating the Scriptures

Before Jerome left Rome he had already revised the Gospels and the Psalter; this is known as the "Roman Psalter." At Bethlehem he prepared a more thorough revision of the Psalter that, because it was first adopted in Gaul, is called the "Gallican Psalter." Both of these had been done on the basis of the Greek OT and Jerome soon realized this would not do. So, finally, he produced the "Hebrew Psalter," by translating the Hebrew into Latin.

Meantime he was improving his Hebrew and translating other OT books. Jerome's productivity did not cease with the completion of his translation of the Bible into Latin. In spite of fail-

---

[8]Metzger, *Early Versions*, p. 333.

ing eyesight he continued to put out scholarly works. The feared criticism of his version was not slow in coming either and he defended himself sharply against his critics, whom he called "two-legged asses." He confesses that it would have been easier to weave mats out of palm leaves than to be a translator, for, as he wrote in the prologue to his version of Kings and Samuel, "If I correct errors in the Sacred Text, I am denounced as falsifier; if I do not correct them, I am piloried as disseminator of error."

As one might expect, Jerome's version of the Bible was not immediately accepted everywhere. People had become used to the Old Latin versions and weren't about to give them up without a struggle. Jerome thought it was like refusing to drink from a pure fountain and keep on drinking at muddy streams. Some Bible readers recognized the merits of Jerome's version and so his version circulated side by side with Old Latin versions for some time. He got a measure of satisfaction from observing that many of those who criticized his version in public read it in private. Eventually Jerome's version won out over all others and got the name "Vulgate" (in the sense of common or popular). Although he had had the joy of seeing his revised Gospels accepted in his day, he did not live to see his Bible become the Vulgate of the Latin-speaking church. The sack of Rome in 410 shocked him severely, and in 420 he died, leaving the commentary on Jeremiah, which he was writing at the time of his death, incomplete.

The Latin Vulgate was to become the Bible of Western Europe for a thousand years. With the dawn of the Reformation it was realized once again that people needed the Bible in their mother tongue, and a number of translations of the Latin Vulgate into other languages were produced. In the history of Bible translation no version, other than the Septuagint, has had such a profound influence on Christianity. The influence of the Latin Vulgate was obvious in some renderings of biblical terms in the early English versions. "Do penance," "our super-substantial bread," instead of "our daily bread" (or "our bread for the morrow") came into English via the Vulgate.

C. Jerome as Bible Translator

Jerome had a flair for languages. In his day the linguistic cleavage between the Latin West and the Greek East had become rather pronounced, and there were few scholars who handled both languages well. Jerome was able to bridge this gap and more: he also knew the Hebrew. Moreover, through his training in the Latin classics he had become a master of style and thus was able to render the Hebrew and Greek of the biblical books into good Latin.

He had, of course, not trained as a translator; he was set on this course by Damasus, and he accepted the assignment only because there was a great need for a standard Latin text, and he looked upon his task as a holy calling. Damasus had not really asked for a fresh translation of the Bible, but simply a revision of the Old Latin versions. As time went on, however, Jerome became less and less a reviser and more a translator of the original Hebrew and Greek.

Jerome admits that the art of translation is difficult to master. Languages vary in the order of their words, their metaphors, their idioms. The translator must therefore choose between a word-for-word rendering or a freer translation that exposes the translator to the charge of unfaithfulness to the original. Jerome decided to translate sense for sense, not word for word.[9] Fidelity to Scripture does not mean "pestilent minuteness" in transcribing the words, argued Jerome.

Jerome's Vulgate is not uniform throughout. That may be due in part to the fact that he began as reviser but then became translator. Yet even as translator he was slavishly literal in some places and free in his rendering of the sense in others. Martin Luther later thought his version would have been better if he had had others to help him, rather than translating all alone. After all, as Luther put it, our Lord promised to be present only "where two or three are gathered" in his name.

Early Christians had taken over the Jewish Septuagint, which included the Apocrypha. Although the Jews later rejected this version the church continued to use it. Jerome realized that the Apocrypha were not part of the Hebrew canon and insisted that these books not be used to establish Christian doctrine. But Jerome's contemporaries looked with even less favor on his championship of the "Hebrew" canon than they did on his new "Hebrew" translation.[10] Augustine particularly opposed Jerome on this point and argued that long tradition demanded that they be retained in the canon. Jerome had an appreciation for apocryphal literature, but he did not want them to be treated as Scripture.

Nevertheless, they were included in his version (mostly in their Old Latin form) and it was left to the Reformers of the sixteenth century to revive Jerome's view of the canon.

So completely did Jerome's Vulgate eventually conquer all rival versions that later, when church councils were held, the Vulgate was carried in triumph in a golden reliquary (a repository for relics). The tragedy was that the Bible was left too much in the reliquary, and while medieval writers knew their Vulgate well, and priests knew at least those parts that were included in the service books, the common people seldom read the Bible.

D. Revisions of the Vulgate

Just as the Old Latin versions had become corrupt through repeated copying, so the Vulgate copies also differed considerably one from another as time went by. Attempts were made by Cassiodorus in the sixth century to revise the Vulgate. Again, about A.D. 800 Charlemagne had the famous British monk, Alcuin, carry out a revision. In the thirteenth century scholars at the University of Paris revised it, and it was this edition that formed the basis of the first printed Bible by Gutenberg in 1456. One scholar who participated in this project was Stephanus who introduced a standardized set of chapter divisions into the Vulgate.

When Protestant Reformers advocated the principle of *sola scriptura*, which included among other things the rejection of the Apocrypha as Scripture and a return to the original

---

[9]Sparks, "Jerome," p. 523.
[10]Sparks, "Jerome," p. 534.

languages, the Council of Trent in 1546 decreed that the Latin Vulgate was to be held as authoritative in lectures, disputations, sermons, and expository discourses. When the Council made this decree not only were the many copies of the Vulgate quite diverse, but others, such as Erasmus, had already taken it in hand to make fresh Latin translations. In a sense, then, the decree of Trent was meaningless, since the Vulgate manuscripts were no longer uniform. And so along with this decree it was also decided that the Vulgate would need to be edited and printed as accurately as possible.[11]

This work was entrusted to a papal commission, but after forty years the task was far from complete. The reigning Pope, Sixtus V, then took the matter in his own hands and his edition appeared in 1590. He then forbade any questioning of this authoritative edition. Soon after he died, however, his successor, Gregory XIV (1590–91), made a start with a drastic revision of the Sixtine edition, and this was completed in the reign of Clement VIII, and published in 1592. This revised edition is commonly known as the Sixto-Clementine Vulgate, and has remained the "authorized version" of the Roman Catholic Church.

A critical edition of the Vulgate was begun in 1889 by Wordsworth and White and was completed at Oxford in 1953. In 1907 a critical edition was begun by papal authority and is now being prepared by a community of the Benedictine Order.

There are thousands of manuscripts of the Latin Vulgate extant. Some of them are deluxe copies, written on purple parchment with gold and silver ink. The influence of the Latin Bible on the language and thought of Western Christianity can hardly be overestimated.

During the Middle Ages several Bible versions that made their appearance in Europe were made from the Latin Vulgate, including the translation into English made by Wycliffe in the fourteenth century.

III. THE GOTHIC VERSION

A. The Christianization of the Goths

The ancient Goths founded an extensive empire north of the lower Danube and the Black Sea. Gothic warriors occasionally made forays into lands that lay within the Roman Empire, and by the third century, Christians, captured on such raids, had begun to propagate their faith among their captors.

About A.D. 264 the grandparents of Ulfilas, who was to give the Bible to the Goths in their mother tongue, were deported from Asia Minor to what is today Rumania. Ulfilas was probably the son of a Gothic father and a Cappadocian mother. The name Ulfilas is Gothic for "little wolf." Although Christianity had already come to the Goths, Ulfilas has been rightly nicknamed "Apostle of the Goths." Born about 311, he labored faithfully until his death (381 or 383) as bishop.

For years he labored north of the Danube. Resistance to his work led him to take his flock across the river into what is now Bulgaria. Consequently he is known also as "the Moses of the Goths." When the Goths in 410 sacked Rome, Augustine was thankful they had been Christianized,

---

[11]Bruce, *Books and Parchments*, p. 208.

else Rome's fate would have been much worse.

B. Ulfilas's Translation

Ulfilas's greatest accomplishment was the creation of an alphabet— primarily from Greek and Latin characters, but also some Gothic runes—and the translation of the Scriptures into his native tongue. Since he translated the OT from the standard Greek version and not from the Hebrew, the Gothic OT is a secondary version. We are told that he left the two books of Kings untranslated, for the warring Goths did not need the war stories of these books to spur them on.[12]

For the NT Ulfilas followed the Greek text that had established itself at Byzantium, and so the Gothic version is of limited value in establishing the best text of the NT. Since, however, he translated almost word for word, it is possible, as a rule, to detect the Greek words that lie behind the Gothic. The Gothic Bible is of historical significance, for it is not only the oldest Bible, but the oldest written literature in a Germanic tongue.

There are several fragmentary manuscripts of the Gothic Bible available: the most famous is known as Argentius, that is, "the Silver Codex." It is written in silver letters on purple vellum, and is now in Uppsala, Sweden.

We do not know whether Ulfilas ever completed the translation of the entire Bible, but twenty years after his death his helpers were in correspondence with the famous Jerome about translation problems. It was a pleasant sur-prise when a parchment leaf of a bilingual codex, with Gothic on one side and Latin on the other, came to light in Egypt in 1908. Ulfilas was a forerunner of the modern Bible translator's movement.

IV. THE OLD CHURCH SLAVONIC VERSION

In the ninth century there was but one Slavic language in Eastern Europe, of which the various Slavonic languages of the present day were but dialects. About the middle of the ninth century a Moravian Empire was formed in Eastern Europe that professed Christianity. Rostislav, the founder of the empire, in order to check the growth of Frankish influence from the West, asked in 863 that Slavonic priests be sent from Byzantium.[13]

In response to this request the Eastern Emperor, Michael III (842–867), sent two brothers, Constantine and Methodius, to preach in the Slavonic language. The brothers came from Thessalonica where masses of slaves had settled, and so they knew the language. Constantine, who later assumed the name Cyril when he entered the monastic life, devised a Slavonic alphabet and translated the Scriptures from Greek into Slavonic. After Cyril's death Methodius, with two or three helpers, continued the translation work begun by Constantine. The version is naturally too late to be of any great use in establishing the best text of the NT, but it is of historical significance. Like the Gothic it grew out of the missionary concern of the church.

---

[12]G. S. Wegener, *6000 Years of the Bible*, trans. M. Shenfield (Harper and Row, 1963), p. 170.

[13]Bruce, *Books and Parchments*, p. 217.

In the three hundred years between A.D. 150 and 450 the missionary fervor of the church gave birth to numerous versions of the Bible. The second great epoch of Bible translation is the period of the Reformation. The third great age of Bible translation began with the massive missionary movements of the nineteenth century, and continues unabated into the period of modern missions.

Prior to A.D. 1000 there were several attempts to render portions of the Bible into Anglo-Saxon, and that is a good starting point for our survey of the history of the English Bible that will be our subject in the next few chapters.

SUGGESTED READING

Kenyon, F. G. **Our Bible and the Ancient Manuscripts,** *rev. ed. New York: Harper and Brothers, 1958. See "The Vulgate in the Middle Ages," pp. 250–64.*

Metzger, B. M. **The Early Versions of the New Testament.** *Oxford: Clarendon, 1977.*

———. **The Text of the New Testament,** *2nd ed. New York: Oxford University Press, 1968.*

Price, I. M. **The Ancestry of Our English Bible,** *3rd ed. revised by W. A. Irwin and Allen P. Wikgren. New York: Harper and Row, 1956. See "The Old Latin and the Vulgate," pp. 177–88.*

Vööbus, A. **Early Versions of the New Testament: Manuscript Studies.** *Stockholm, 1954.*

Chapter 15

English Bibles Prior to 1611

Christianity came to England in the days of Roman rule. With the coming of the Angles and Saxons from the Continent in the fifth century, the Christian faith was nearly blotted out. In 597 the monk Augustine and his helpers arrived to establish the Roman Catholic faith in "Angleland." Until this time English Christians had no Bible, and the one that the Roman missionaries brought was the Latin Vulgate, which Englishmen could not read.

About 670, Caedmon, a cowherd attached to the monastery at Whitby, rendered some biblical passages into Old English poems, making it easy for people to memorize and to sing biblical paraphrases. The first known person who actually translated parts of the Latin Vulgate into Old English was Aldhelm, bishop of Sherborne. He is reported to have translated the Psalter into Anglo-Saxon about A.D. 700.

A man whose reputation for learning was known throughout Western Europe was Bede, the monk of Yarrow. This scholar had a concern for his less learned countrymen and translated portions of the Bible from Latin into Old English. He was engaged in the translation of the Gospel of John when he died in 735.[1]

King Alfred the Great (871–901) promoted literacy and culture in a day in which these features were sadly lacking in English life. He himself translated several historical works into Old English and introduced his code of laws with a translation of extracts from Exodus and parts of the Book of Acts.

Some clergymen took it in hand to prepare interlinear glosses of parts of the Bible by writing the Anglo-Saxon words between the Latin lines. The Lindisfarne Gospels (c. 687) are representative of such interlinears. Towards the end of the tenth century the abbot, Aelfric, produced a translation of several books of the OT.

With the coming of the Normans in

---

[1]F. C. Grant, *Translating the Bible* (Greenwich: Seabury, 1961), p. 50.

1066, the Anglo-Saxon period of the English language comes to an end, for the Normans spoke French, and with them we enter the Middle English period. A few efforts were made to render portions of the Bible into Middle English, the language of Chaucer, but often these translations were for the monks and nuns only; the common man did not have a Bible. It is staggering to think that for a thousand years of Christianity in England English Christians had no Bible. All this changed with John Wycliffe (c. 1330–1384).

I. THE BIBLE OF WYCLIFFE

A. John Wycliffe

Wycliffe was an Oxford theologian who became deeply involved in the ecclesiastical issues of his day. The prestige of the papacy had fallen to a very low ebb, and the life of the clergy left much to be desired. Wycliffe became a severe critic of this corrupt church and sought to call people back to a more biblical kind of Christianity. He realized that this was impossible unless the people had the Bible in their language.

Wycliffe's views were propagated throughout the country by travelling preachers, many of them Oxford scholars like himself. This got him into trouble with the hierarchy. His followers were denounced as "Lollards" (derived from "Low landers," but used in the sense of "heretics"), and Wycliffe himself was pronounced heretical. Archbishop Arundel called him a "son of the old serpent, forerunner and disciple of Antichrist." He found it hard to see why people got so upset

John Wycliffe (c. 1329–1384), the first person to translate the Bible into English. Because of his emphasis upon the authority of the Bible and his criticism of clergy who abused their positions, he is often called "The Morning Star of the Reformation."

about his teachings, which were simply the teachings of the Bible, he thought, but to use his words "every sparrow twittereth about it."[2] He was forced to retire to his rectory at Lutterworth, where he died a year and a half later.

B. The Translation

Just how much translating Wycliffe himself did is hard to say, for he had good friends and able assistants. The first version of the Bible in Middle English was published in 1380, while Wycliffe was still alive; the second version of 1384 appeared after his death.

Most of the first edition of the OT, it seems, was prepared by Nicholas of Hereford before the storm broke at Ox-

---

[2]Grant, *Translating the Bible*, p. 56.

ford in 1382 and Wycliffe had to leave. It is an extremely literal rendering of the Latin original. The second edition shows a greater feeling for English idiom, and although it is still a secondary version (a translation of a translation), it gave the common person a Bible in his native tongue.

Wycliffe died in 1384, but he left ardent disciples behind, and it is to these that the credit for the second edition must go. Outstanding among them was John Purvey, who undertook the revision of Wycliffe's earlier version, and who (c. 1388), replaced the earlier word-for-word rendering of the Vulgate with native English idiom.

In order to produce a good English Bible, Purvey had to find a good Latin text. The Vulgate was still being copied by hand and so one manuscript might differ from another in innumerable details. First of all, then, by comparing Latin manuscripts, Purvey and his helpers established the best text possible. Then they rendered it into good English. Purvey had come to see that a word-for-word translation failed to transfer the sense of the original properly. Besides, Jerome's Vulgate was itself a free rendering of the Hebrew and Greek, and that was the principle of translation espoused by Purvey.

Interestingly, the "Epistle of Paul to the Laodiceans," was inserted in the second edition of the Wycliffe Bible. Paul had indeed written such a letter, but it is lost and the one inserted in the Wycliffe Bible is an apocryphal epistle from the fourth century. The fact that so many Wycliffe Bibles have survived indicates its widespread acceptance.

The following is a sample of the English of Wycliffe's Bible:

> The kyngdom of hevenes is made like to a kyng thad made weddingis to his sone / and he sente hise servantis for to clepe men that weren beden to the weddyngis (Matt. 22:2f.).[3]

C. The Reception

In his preface to the second edition Purvey had prayed: "God grante to us alle grace to kunne wel and kepe wel holi writ, and suffre ioiefulle sum peyne for it at the laste"—and suffer he did. Wycliffe's Bible was frowned on in high places. Both Purvey and Hereford endured prison terms; some of their friends died at the stake, some with Bibles tied around their necks. A synod of clergy at Oxford, in 1408, forbade the reading of Wycliffe's Bible, but the version made such an appeal to the hearts and minds of Englishmen that it could not be suppressed, in spite of the severe penalties attached to its circulation. But people paid a good price if only they could obtain a few sheets of Wycliffe's Bible. It is said that the price for an hour's loan of it every day for a course of reading was a load of hay.[4] And now that England had a Bible—albeit a forbidden one—people were eager to learn how to read, and so Wycliffe's Bible not only gave people the Word of God, but it also helped greatly in combating illiteracy.

In 1415, the Council of Constance, which condemned John Huss to burn at the stake, also condemned the writings of Wycliffe and ordered Wycliffe's bones to be dug out of the ground and

---

[3]Grant, *Translating the Bible*, p. 57.
[4]G. MacGregor, *The Bible in the Making* (New York: Lippincott, 1959), p. 109.

to be burned. The ashes were cast in the River Swift and, as has often been said, they were carried out to sea, and Wycliffe's teachings spread to other lands. He is called "the Morning Star of the Reformation."

Although Wycliffe has the honor of being the prime mover in giving England its first complete English Bible, the true Father of the English Bible is not Wycliffe, but Tyndale. Wycliffe's Bible is a translation of Jerome's Latin Vulgate, Tyndale's went back to the Hebrew and Greek. Moreover, Wycliffe's Bible was still a hand-copied manuscript Bible; Tyndale's was printed. Also, Wycliffe translated into Middle English; Tyndale belongs to the Modern English period.

II. TYNDALE'S BIBLE

A. The New Day

Fifty years after the "Constitutions of Oxford" (1408), which condemned the writings of Wycliffe, Gutenberg printed the Latin Bible for the first time (1456). Without the printing press it is hard to imagine the success of the Protestant Reformation. The complete Hebrew OT was printed at Soncino, Italy, in 1488. Erasmus's Greek NT was printed in Basel, in 1516. One of Erasmus's editions was used by William Tyndale to translate the NT into English. England had the printing press by 1474, but it was too dangerous to print Wycliffe's Bible in England, and Tyndale had his Bible printed on the Continent.

Johann Gutenberg began to use movable type one year after the fall of Constantinople, and with the development of printing went the revival of

learning. When Constantinople fell in 1453 Greek scholars migrated to the West and brought ancient manuscripts with them, giving impetus to the study of the Greek NT. In England, John Colet (c. 1467–1519), Thomas More (1480–1535), and the visiting scholar, Erasmus (1466–1536), fostered the new learning. Shortly after Erasmus left Cambridge, William Tyndale arrived there.

When Tyndale came to Cambridge Martin Luther was preparing to nail his theses on the Wittenberg church door (1517), after expounding Romans to his students at the University of Wittenberg. This sparked the Protestant Reformation on the Continent, and this movement is closely tied to the many attempts to give people the Bible in the vernacular. By 1471 there were two independent versions in Italian. In 1477 the NT was printed in French, and in 1487 the whole Bible. There was a Spanish translation in 1478, and in the Netherlands, between 1480 and 1507, the Psalms were published seven times. Luther did not begin his famous translation into German till 1521, and by then there had already been nineteen editions of a German version.[5]

B. William Tyndale

Tyndale was born in Gloucestershire in 1494 or 1495. He went to Oxford at a very early age and received his Master of Arts in 1515. After lecturing at Oxford for a year he moved on to Cambridge, the home of the new learning, where he took up the study of Greek, and where he also imbibed Protestant sympathies.

In 1522 he took employment as pri-

---

[5]MacGregor, *Bible Making*, p. 111.

William Tyndale (1494–1536). In spite of adverse conditions—ship wrecks, police raids, being sought by secret agents, and betrayal by friends—Tyndale was able to produce a translation known for its literary quality.

vate tutor in the home of Sir John Walsh. Here he became convinced that the cause of much of the confusion in his day stemmed from an ignorance of Scripture, and the clergy, he discovered, were often as ignorant as the laity. In debate with one such cleric Tyndale vowed that if God should spare his life he would see to it that the plowboy would know more Scripture than ignorant priests. Erasmus had expressed a similar sentiment in the preface to his Greek NT: "I wish that the farm worker might sing parts of them (the Scriptures) at the plough, that the weaver might hum them at the shuttle, and the traveller might beguile the weariness of the way by reciting them."[6]

Perhaps the publication of Luther's German NT in 1522 also stimulated Tyndale to give Englishmen a Bible in their tongue. Luther's name, however, was anathema in English ecclesiastical circles by now, and the laws prohibiting Wycliffe's Bible remained in effect. Tyndale, therefore, had to have episcopal permission to translate the Bible into English. He asked Tunstall, bishop of London, for such a license, but found little support for his project. Fortunately, Humphrey Monmouth, a wealthy cloth merchant, took him into his house and Tyndale began his work. Soon he realized, however, that England was not a congenial place to prepare a new English Bible, and so he left for Hamburg in 1524.

C. Tyndale's First New Testament

Tyndale spent a good part of the year at Wittenberg, and then made his way to Cologne about August 1525, where he hoped to get his NT printed. When this became known, the authorities forbade the printing, and Tyndale escaped to Worms, having rescued the 6000 copies of Matthew 1–22 already printed. At Worms the first printing of a NT in English was completed in 1526, and in a month copies were beginning to reach England.

Tyndale had written a fourteen-page prologue to this NT that resembled Luther's prologue to his NT. This prologue had been printed in Cologne, and since the project was aborted the Worms edition did not have this prologue. The Worms NT, however, has a short epistle at the end, exhorting the reader to come to this text with a pure mind and single eye, and not to be

---

[6]F. F. Bruce, *History of the Bible,* 3rd rev. ed. (Oxford: Oxford University Press, 1978), p. 29.

overcritical, since it is the translator's first attempt. Tyndale promised to improve upon this first edition in the future if God would grant him opportunity.

Tyndale's NT was smuggled into England in bales of cloth or barrels of other merchandise, and Bishop Tunstall of London was furious. He took steps to gather up all the copies in his diocese and to burn them publicly. In 1530, in the presence of Cardinal Wolsey, a great bonfire of these NTs was kindled in old St. Paul Cathedral. When this did not accomplish what he had hoped, he decided to buy up all the copies on the Continent and to dry up the source, what he called a "pestiferous and most pernicious poison."

He made an agreement with an Antwerp merchant, Packington, to buy all of Tyndale's remaining copies. Tyndale knew the bishop wanted to burn them, but he was happy to sell them for at least two reasons: one, he would then have the money to publish a new edition, and, two, such a holocaust would elicit outrage at the burning of God's Word and help to publicize the availability of an English Bible.

However, burning the NT was not the only form of attack. Thomas More, a leading humanist and a representative of the New Learning, attacked "the pestilent sect of Luther and Tyndale" in writing, and called Tyndale a "devilish drunken soul." The bitter irony of this controversy was that both More and Tyndale were to suffer death for the sake of their conscience. Tyndale's NT, said More, "was not worthy to be called Christ's testament, but either Tyndale's own testament or the testa-ment of his master Antichrist."[7] It is strange that More would have such an appreciation of Erasmus's Greek NT, and yet be so critical of its translation into English.

More's criticism was grossly unfair, but he was irritated by Tyndale's translation of certain ecclesiastical terms. Instead of "church" he had "congregation," "senior" for "priest," "repentance" for "penance," and so forth. Also Tyndale's NT had the Lutheran arrangement of the books and the last four (Hebrews, James, Jude, and Revelation) were set off from the rest in the index.

D. Translation and Retranslation

Because Tyndale took such an active part in the theological disputations of his day, he was not able to complete the translation of the entire Bible. He had, however, completed and published the translation of the Pentateuch and several other parts of the OT by 1530.

His translation is bold and idiomatic. The serpent says to Eve, "Tush, ye shall not dye" (Gen. 3:4); Pharaoh's "jolly captains" are drowned in the Red Sea (Exod. 15:4). Some of the marginal notes were quite caustic and did not help his translation to gain acceptance. In the margin of Exodus 32:35, where it is reported that many Israelites died because they had worshiped the gold bull/calf, Tyndale wrote, "The Pope's bull slayeth more than Aaron's calf." When Israel collected more than enough for the building of the tabernacle, the people are told to stop the contributions (Exod. 36:5–7). Tyndale wrote in the margin,

---

[7]Bruce, *History of Bible*, p. 40.

"When will the Pope say 'Hoo!' and forbid an offering for the building of St. Peter's church? ... Never until they have it all."

But, not only did he translate major portions of the OT, he also revised his published NT. Tyndale was anxious to get another edition of his NT into circulation because the climate in England was changing. Henry VIII was quarreling with the Pope, and Cromwell, who favored Bible reading in the vernacular, was gaining influence. Another factor that spurred Tyndale on to revise his earlier NT and publish a new edition was the fact that pirate printings, in which deliberate changes were made in Tyndale's NT, were being published as Tyndale's own version. One of the chief offenders was George Joye, a former associate of Tyndale. For this reason Tyndale asked in the prologue of the second edition (1534) that Joye and others make their own translations of the Bible, but not to take his, make changes in it, and then publish it in Tyndale's name. If they made changes and then published it in their own name, he did not mind.

The 1534 revision was very carefully done. He went over the earlier translation with great devotion and published it under the title: "The Newe Testament dylygently corrected and compared with the Greke by Willyain Tindale." This was Tyndale's definitive version, even though he did not stop revising his translations. It is estimated that nine-tenths of the King James Version of 1611 is Tyndale, and where the Authorized Version departed from Tyndale, later re-

visers often returned to it.

This new edition of the NT was printed at Antwerp. It had fewer controversial notes in the margins; introductions were prefixed to each book; and at the end were appended extracts from the OT for reading as "Epistles" in the church services for certain days of the year.[8]

This was Tyndale's crowning work. As long as Tyndale stayed in Antwerp he was safe, for Antwerp was a free city. But the Emperor, Charles V, held Tyndale to be a heretic, and one day, in 1535, Tyndale was treacherously kidnapped and imprisoned near Brussels. In August 1536 he was found guilty of heresy and condemned to be executed. When the tragic moment arrived Tyndale was tied to the stake, strangled by the hangman, and then burned. His last words were: "Lord, open the King of England's eyes."

What Tyndale did not know was that just before his death Henry VIII had granted permission for an English Bible to circulate among the people—a Bible that was largely Tyndale's version.

III. COVERDALE'S VERSION

A. Miles Coverdale (1488–1569)

Coverdale was an Augustinian friar and a graduate of Cambridge. After coming under the influence of the Reformation he left his order. In 1528 he fled to the Continent for refuge, and here he worked with Tyndale for a while. He returned to England under the patronage of Anne Boleyn and Cromwell, but when their fortune ended, he returned to the Continent

---

[8]F. Kenyon, *Our Bible and the Ancient Manuscripts*, revised by A. W. Adams (New York: Harper and Brothers, 1958), p. 288.

again and remained there until Henry VIII died in 1547. With the accession of Edward VI he returned to England once more, but when Mary Tudor came to the throne he barely escaped death at the stake, and fled once more to the Continent. He returned to England for the last time in 1559.

Coverdale was not the scholar that Tyndale was, but he devoted most of his life to giving the English a Bible in their own tongue.

B. The Coverdale Bible

Coverdale had translated the entire Bible while in exile on the Continent. It was published in 1535 (probably at Marburg, Germany) and copies quickly made their way to England. It was dedicated to Henry VIII. The dedication denounces the Pope, who is compared to Caiphas—something that must have pleased Henry greatly.

Evidently Archbishop Cranmer had petitioned King Henry to allow the Scriptures in English to circulate among the populace, and the King had responded by asking Cranmer to prepare such a version. The bishops who were to assist Cranmer dragged their feet, and when Coverdale's version, with the flattering dedication to King Henry appeared, Cromwell drew the King's attention to it. The bishops were asked to check it and when they could not find any heresies in it, Henry reportedly said, "Then in God's name let it go abroad among our people."

Coverdale explained in the title page that he felt inadequate for the task of translation, for he was no expert "in tongues," as he put it. But since others who were more able had not been able

to finish what they began (no doubt a reference to Tyndale's uncompleted OT), he had been bold enough to make this translation. Therefore, he leaned heavily on the work of others, such as the Latin Vulgate, the Zürich version, Luther's German Bible, and, above all, on Tyndale's English version. F. F. Bruce says that Coverdale's version was "basically Tyndale's version revised in the light of the German versions, and not noticeably improved thereby."[9] It can be seen that he used the German versions from the Germanized English expressions: "Unoutspeakable" (Rom. 8:26) is hardly English, but is good German *(unaussprechlich)*. Luther's *Handreichung* (gift) becomes a "handreaching"—a translation that cannot possibly convey the meaning of the Greek text to an English reader.

What was new in Coverdale's Bible was that the OT Apocrypha were segregated from the canonical books, rather than being scattered all over the OT as they are in the Septuagint and the Latin Vulgate. Also, he has a note advising the reader that they are not found in the Hebrew Bible and are not of the same authority as the canonical books. Most English Bibles followed Coverdale's example for years to come. Eventually this practice was discontinued and the Apocrypha were omitted altogether. Today, however, one can buy many English versions with or without the Apocrypha.

Although Coverdale leaned heavily on Tyndale, he made some innovations. When we pray, "Forgive us our debts," in the Lord's Prayer, we get that from Coverdale; Tyndale had, "Forgive us our trespasses." He substituted

---

[9]Bruce, *History of Bible*, p. 59.

"murderers" for Tyndale's "thieves" in the parable of the Good Samaritan. No doubt it was Luther's *"fiel unter die Moerder"* that led him to this translation. Some of Coverdale's renderings are rather quaint. For example, God's promise to the godly person is, "Thou shalt not nede to be afrayed for eny bugges by night" (Ps. 91:5).

Although Coverdale's version was reprinted twice in 1537, once in 1550, and once again in 1553, it was never fully accepted by the hierarchy. With the death of Anne Boleyn in 1536, all chances for Coverdale's Bible to become an "authorized" version were lost. However, in 1537 there appeared another Bible that had in its title the words, "truly and purely translated into Englysh by Thomas Matthew."[10]

IV. MATTHEW'S BIBLE

Fresh revisions of the Bible followed Coverdale's in rapid succession. The first of these is Matthew's Bible, which is in fact the completion of Tyndale's work.[11] Tyndale had never completed the OT, and it was left to John Rogers, a disciple of Tyndale, to complete his mentor's work. Rogers took the pen name Matthew. When England reverted to Romanism under "Bloody Mary," Rogers was the first to be burned at the stake in 1555.

Interestingly, Matthew's Bible claims on the title page to be "Set forth with kinges most gracyous lycence." Archbishop Cranmer, as we have said, had been charged by Henry VIII with revising the Bible. Meantime Coverdale's version had been allowed to circulate. Then, when Matthew's appeared, Cromwell used his influence with the king to obtain the royal license for this new version to "be sold and read of every person . . . until such a time that we, the bishops, shall set forth a better translation, which I think will not be till a day after doomsday."[12]

The royal license was procured not only for Matthew's Bible, but also for the second 1537 edition of Coverdale's. So there were two versions circulating freely in England one year after Tyndale's death. Both of these versions were heavily indebted to Tyndale, but it was not yet advisable to associate Tyndale's name with these versions publicly.

Matthew's Bible was still printed on the Continent. It was dedicated to Henry VIII, was promoted by Cranmer, and was presented publicly to the king by Cromwell. The King then gave permission that it be read in public.

V. THE GREAT BIBLE

The English Bible had been licensed, but it had not yet been commanded to be read in churches. That honor was reserved for a new revision that Cromwell asked Coverdale to make on the basis of Matthew's Bible.[13] Printing was begun in Paris in 1538, but the Inquisition caught up with Coverdale, and so the project (printers, presses, and type) was transferred to London. The printing was completed in 1539, and because of the size of its pages (16½ by 11 inches) it is called the Great Bible. The clergy were then ordered to place a copy in a con-

---

[10]Bruce, *History of Bible*, p. 64.

[11]Kenyon, *Bible and Manuscripts*, p. 293.

[12]E. H. Robertson, *The New Translations of the Bible* (Naperville: Allenson, 1959), p. 13.

[13]Kenyon, *Bible and Manuscripts*, p. 294.

Title page from the Great Bible of 1539. The inscription reads: "The Bible in English, that is to say the content of all holy Scriptures, both of the old and new testament, truly translated after the best of the hebrew and greek texts, by the diligent study of diverse excellent learned men, expert in the foresaid tongues."

venient place in every church. So popular did the reading of these Bibles by the public become that the king had to issue a proclamation forbidding the reading of the English Bible aloud during divine service. Some parishioners evidently found the reading of the Bible in their mother tongue more interesting than listening to the parson. From the complaints registered by bishops that people read the Bible during the sermon, it is clear that the king's command was not always taken seriously.

The Great Bible had a finely engraved title page, in which the Almighty is pictured blessing Henry, who hands out copies of the Bible to Cranmer and Cromwell to his right and left. These in turn distribute copies to the clergy and the laity respectively, while the bottom of the page is filled with a crowd of people shouting *Vivat Rex!* ("Long live the King!").

This Bible spread throughout the land and became so popular that it even replaced popular romances as the favorite reading of the people. To this day the Book of Common Prayer has the Psalms from the Great Bible.

The Lutheran order of the books of the NT was discontinued in the Great Bible, and the order that we now have in our English Bibles was established. By mistake the Apocrypha, which again are set off from the canonical books, are called "Hagiographa" ("holy writings")—a term which properly denotes the third division of the Hebrew canon.

The title of the Great Bible suggests that it was the product of a consultation between "divers excellent learned men." It was in fact Coverdale's revision of Matthew's Bible, and the latter was a revision of Tyndale's (as far as Tyndale went). The "divers excellent learned men" are simply the translators, editors, and other scholars whose works Coverdale consulted.[14] Coverdale, not satisfied with the first edition of the Great Bible, revised it again, and a second edition was published in 1540. This edition has the words of Cranmer in the preface: "This is the Byble apoynted to the use of the churches." Because of this preface it is sometimes called the "Cranmer Bible." Five further editions were published between 1540 and 1541.

Probably a short time before the appearance of the Great Bible, in 1539, another revision of Matthew's Bible began to circulate in England, that of Richard Taverner. Taverner was a good Greek scholar and had done a creditable piece of work but his edition was completely eclipsed by the Great Bible, and, consequently Taverner's version has had little influence on the English Bible.

VI. THE GENEVA BIBLE

A. Political Changes

The closing years of Henry VIII were years of reaction, as far as the principles of the Reformation were concerned. Parliament in 1543 made it a crime for unlicensed people to read or expound the Bible publicly and even forbade the private reading of the Bible by those belonging to the lower classes. Henry VIII himself went further in 1546, making it illegal for anyone "to receive, have, take, or keep, Tyndale's or Coverdale's New Testa-

---

[14]Bruce, *History of Bible*, p. 70.

ment." Bibles were again ceremoniously burned in London.

Actually these decrees were absurd, for as long as the Great Bible was the officially accepted Bible, the readers had essentially the literary products of Tyndale and Coverdale. This had been recognized earlier by leading ecclesiastics, who decided in 1542 to have it revised and brought more in line with the Latin Vulgate, the official Bible of the Roman Catholic Church. But neither the bishops nor the university showed much enthusiasm for such a project.

With the death of Henry VIII in 1547, and the accession of Edward VI, the trend was reversed, and during his reign all the previous translations were frequently reprinted. It is estimated that some forty editions of Tyndale's, Coverdale's, Matthew's, the Great Bible, and even Taverner's, were issued in the course of Edward's short reign.[15]

On the accession of Mary in 1553, Edward's Reformation policy was again reversed. Some of the men who helped to give England a Bible, like John Rogers and Thomas Cranmer, were executed, and Coverdale sought refuge on the Continent. But, while there was a lot of Bible burning in Mary's reign, the Great Bible was not put out of existence, and when Elizabeth I reversed the pro-Roman policies of Mary, it was still the English standard version.

B. An English Bible From Geneva

During Mary's reign Protestant fugitives from persecution in England gathered in various Protestant centers, including Geneva, the home of Calvin and Beza. Among them were learned scholars, such as William Whittingham, who had taught at Oxford and had produced a version of the English NT in 1557. Together with scholars like himself, Whittingham undertook the revision of the entire Bible, which appeared in 1560 and is known as the Geneva Bible.

It had a dedicatory epistle to Queen Elizabeth, with a prayer that she might "build up the ruins of God's house to his glory." The Apocrypha appear as an appendix to the OT, with a note saying that they may be read for the advancement and furtherance of knowledge and for instruction in godly manners, but they are not to be expounded as Scripture.

The marginal notes are clearly Calvinistic in doctrine, yet they are not nearly as polemical as were Tyndale's. Anti-Roman sentiment, however, is obvious. The beast that ascends from the pit (Rev. 11:7) is identified as "The Pope which hath his power out of hell and cometh hence."

The Geneva Bible is divided into verses. Words that have no equivalent in the original text are printed in italics—a practice continued by the translators of the 1611 Authorized Version. This Bible was printed in Geneva in Roman type, not Gothic, as had been the case with former editions of the English Bible. This type was more legible, and that was of considerable importance, for the invention of printing had promoted a flourishing trade in spectacles, even though the optical prescriptions were rather simple. The cost of the printing was born by the English-speaking colony of that city.

---

[15]Kenyon, *Bible and Manuscripts*, p. 298.

The Geneva Bible immediately became popular in England and was for years the household Bible of English Protestants. While it was not appointed to be read in the churches of England, it was the Bible of Scotland. John Knox naturally preferred the Geneva Bible, prepared by his friends and fellow exiles at Geneva. Even after the King James Version was authorized, the Geneva Bible held its own for some time in Scotland. It was the Bible of Shakespeare, the Bible of the Puritans, and the Bible of the Pilgrim Fathers. Since it was published and spread without hindrances in the reign of Elizabeth, it is also known as the "Elizabethan Bible." Sometimes it was called the "Breeches Bible," because, according to Genesis 3:7, Adam and Eve made breeches for themselves, when they discovered that they were naked. One edition is known as the Placemaker's Bible for instead of "peacemakers" in Matthew 5:9, the printer made it speak of "placemakers." Another edition had "Jesus Church" instead of "Jesus Christ" in John 5:20, and was known as the "Jesus Church Bible."[16] It went through 160 editions, and, next to Tyndale, the Geneva Bible had the greatest influence on the Authorized Version.

VII. THE BISHOPS' BIBLE

With the Geneva Bible's increasing popularity it was impossible to keep on using the Great Bible. However, the Geneva Bible, with its Calvinistic marginal notes, hardly commended itself for the same use in English churches as it obviously did in the Scottish. When Elizabeth I ascended the throne all churches were ordered to have a copy of the Great Bible placed in their churches. But the superior quality of the Geneva Bible pointed up the weaknesses of the Great Bible.

Matthew Parker, the archbishop of Canterbury, initiated a project in 1563, by which a number of scholars working separately on assigned portions of the Bible were to revise the Great Bible. Parker himself was a competent scholar and acted as editor-in-chief. In seven years the work was complete and the version was published in 1568. It became known as the Bishops' Bible.

Although many explanatory notes were carried over from the Geneva Bible, there were no controversial notes in its margins, and those passages, such as genealogies, that were considered unedifying were marked so that they could be omitted in public reading. It aimed at accuracy, but often failed in this respect. "Lay thy bread upon wet faces" is hardly an improvement on the Great Bible's, "Cast thy bread upon the waters" (Eccl. 11:1).

Although the Bishops' Bible became the official English version by law, and thus superseded the Great Bible as the authorized version of the Church of England, it was never given preferential treatment. It had the disadvantage of having to contend with rival versions that it was unable to dislodge.

---

[16]MacGregor, *Bible Making*, p. 135.

SUGGESTED READING

Bruce, F. F. **History of the Bible in English,** *3rd ed. New York: Oxford University Press, 1978. See pages 1–91.*

Hargreaves, H. "The Wycliffite Versions," **The Cambridge History of the Bible,** *3 vols. ed. G. W. H. Lampe. Cambridge: Cambridge University Press, 1969, Vol. 2, pp. 387–415.*

Kenyon, F. G. **Our Bible and the Ancient Manuscripts,** *rev. ed., New York: Harper and Brothers, 1958. See "The English Manuscript Bibles," pp. 265–81; "The English Printed Bible," pp. 282–319.*

MacGregor, G. **The Bible in the Making.** *New York: Lippincott, 1959. See pages 97–139.*

Partridge, A. C. **English Biblical Translation.** *London: Andre Deutsch, 1973. See pages 1–104.*

Price, I. M. **The Ancestry of Our English Bible,** *3rd ed. revised by W. A. Irwin and Allen P. Wikgren. New York: Harper and Row, 1956. See "The Early English Manuscripts," pp. 225–31; "Wycliffe's Version of the Bible," pp. 232–39; "Tyndale's Version of the Bible," pp. 240–51; "Versions Close to Tyndale's," pp. 252–59.*

Shepherd, G. "English Versions of the Scriptures Before Wyclif," **The Cambridge History of the Bible,** *3 vols. ed. G. W. H. Lampe. Cambridge: Cambridge University Press, 1969, Vol. 2, pp. 362–87.*

Chapter 16

The Authorized Version and Its Revisions

Before we speak of the publication of the Authorized Version of English Protestants, a few comments should be made on the English Bible of Roman Catholics. While Protestant scholars left England under the reign of the Roman Catholic Queen Mary, Catholic scholars left for the Continent under Elizabeth I. William Allen, an Oxford Fellow and a Roman Catholic who left England, had established an English College at Douai, France, in 1568. The college was moved to Rheims in 1578, and back to Douai in 1593.

During the years that the college had its headquarters in Rheims, Gregory Martin, another Oxford scholar, translated the Bible from the Latin Vulgate into English. Martin's NT was published in 1582, when the college was still at Rheims, but the OT was not published until the college had moved back to Douai, and so it was called the Douai-Rheims Bible.

This English Bible was to replace the "false translations" by Protestants, as the preface had it. The translation is very stiff and awkward, since the trans-

lators adhered closely to the Latin, yielding such strange renderings as "Give us today our supersubstantial bread," in the Lord's Prayer. In the parable of the Good Samaritan the good Samaritan tells the innkeeper, after giving him two pence, "whatever thou shalt supererogate, I, at my return will repay thee." Readers no doubt were thereby reminded of the Roman doctrine of supererogation. The translators prefer "do penance" to "repent," and Paul and Barnabas ordain "priests" in every church, rather than "elders."

As might be expected the Apocrypha were not gathered together in an appendix, as in Protestant versions beginning with that of Coverdale, but appear in the positions they have in the Vulgate. Also, the Douai-Rheims Bible had a full apparatus of annotations in which the sacred text was interpreted in conformity with Roman Catholic doctrine.

The Douai-Rheims had no general success, and its circulation was not large. It was slightly revised from time to time, but the most radical revision was made by Bishop Richard Challoner of London (1691–1781). The stilted style of the original version had become almost unintelligible in the course of a century, and Challoner made it more readable. Challoner was a convert from Protestantism and was well familiar with the Authorized Version. In this way the Protestant AV influenced the Roman Catholic Douai-Rheims-Challoner Bible. But in 1611, the influence was the other way round, for the translators of the King James Version had the Douai-Rheims at hand, and this explains in part why so many Latinisms got into the AV, for the Douai-Rheims was a translation of the Latin Vulgate.

Having just mentioned the King James Version, it is now time that we turn to this rather major revision of the English Bible that represents a watershed in the history of English Protestant versions.

I. THE AUTHORIZED VERSION OF 1611

A. The Hampton Court Conference

In 1603 Elizabeth I died and the crown of England passed to James I, who had already been king of Scotland for thirty-six years, as James VI. On his way to England he was presented with the Millenary Petition (so called because it had a thousand signatures), in which the grievances of the Puritan party in the English Church were set forth.[1] In response to their petition a

conference was called at Hampton Court, in 1604, to hear complaints about the state of the church. Nothing much came of this conference except a notable resolution: "That a translation be made of the whole Bible, as consonant as can be to the original Hebrew and Greek; and this to be set out and printed, without any marginal notes, and only to be used in all churches of England in time of divine service."[2]

The attempt on the part of the Elizabethan bishops to provide a universally acceptable Bible had failed. The Bishops' Bible had replaced the Great Bible for use in the churches and that was all.[3] In private use the Geneva Bible still held the field.

At the Hampton Court Conference Dr. John Reynolds, an Oxford scholar and a leader of the Puritan side in the Church of England, raised the subject of the imperfections of the current Bibles. Bancroft, the bishop of London, supported Reynolds, but the conference itself arrived at no conclusions on this or any other subject. But King James was interested in a new translation of the Bible that would be done by university scholars and reviewed by the bishops and ratified by the king. He did not like the Geneva Bible for he thought it undermined the divine right of kings. If such a version was to be acceptable to all English Protestants it would have to be without marginal notes, for the Geneva Bible was a good translation, but its notes made it unacceptable to church leaders.

---

[1] G. MacGregor, *The Bible in the Making* (New York: Lippincott, 1959), p. 146.

[2] F. F. Bruce, *History of the Bible in English,* 3rd rev. ed. (New York: Oxford University Press, 1978), p. 96.

[3] F. Kenyon, *Our Bible and the Ancient Manuscripts,* revised by A. W. Adams, (New York: Harper and Brothers, 1958), p. 303.

James I, who astonished the clergy with his theological learning at the Hampton Court Conference of 1604. Although he failed to understand the concerns of the Puritans at this conference, he did play a role in planning the Authorized Version.

B. The Translation Policies

King James took a leading part in organizing the translation project. Six panels of translators (about fifty in all) were given the responsibility to revise and translate assigned portions of the Bible. Three panels worked on the OT (Genesis to 2 Kings, 1 Chronicles to Ecclesiastes, Isaiah to Malachi), one panel did the Apocrypha, and two panels worked on the NT (one did the Gospels, Acts, and Apocalypse, the other did all the Epistles). Two of the panels met at Oxford, two at Cambridge, and two at Westminster.

When the panels had finished their task, the entire work was reviewed by a smaller group of twelve men, two from each panel, and then the work was sent to bishops and leading churchmen for approval.

The rules that guided the translators were sanctioned, if not drawn up, by James himself. The Bishops' Bible was to be used as the basis for the revision/translation, but it was to be examined in the light of the Hebrew OT and the Greek NT. All the available English versions were naturally consulted, as well as German, Italian, Spanish, and Latin versions. Also, to prevent the English from being too stilted, there was to be variety in the rendering of Hebrew and Greek words. For example, in 1 Corinthians 13:8–13, where the same Greek word *katargeō* occurs four times in succession, the AV has four different renderings: "fail," "vanish away," "done away," and "put away." In Romans 5 the Greek word *kauchaomoi* is translated "rejoice" (v. 2), "glory" (v. 3), and "joy" (v. 11). *Parakletos* was translated as "comforter" in John 14:16, but as "advocate" in 1 John 2:1.

Also, it was agreed that italics would be used for words not present in the Hebrew and Greek. Unwary readers of the AV today may be led to think that the words in italics are important, but they have been added in the interests of English style.

The names of Bible characters were to correspond as closely as possible to those in common use. In the Bishops' and Geneva Bibles the names were conformed to the original form. "Isaac," for example, is "Isahac" in the Bishops' Bible, which is reasonably close to the Hebrew. Such Hebraic spellings were now to be avoided.

Old ecclesiastical words, however, were to be retained. Where Tyndale had rendered *ekklesia* as "congregation," the AV revisers returned to "church." Unfortunately they also reversed Tyndale's translation of *agape* by "love," and returned to the Latinized "charity."

As already mentioned, there were to be no marginal notes, other than explanations of Hebrew and Greek words. The existing chapter and verse divisions were to be retained, but new headings were to be supplied for the chapters. In these headings the scholars occasionally went beyond factual statements and entered the field of exegesis. The love scenes in the Song of Songs, for example, are explained to be exchanges between the church and Christ. The heading over the story of the beheading of John the Baptist reads: "The Inconvenience of Dauncing."

The names of all the revisers were approved by the King. Among them were some of the finest scholars of that day. One of them, Lancelot Andrews, Dean of Winchester, was a painstaking scholar who had mastered fifteen languages and who, it was mused, might have been Interpreter General at the Tower of Babel. Perhaps the most illustrious of all was Dr. Reynolds, one of the instigators of the project. He gave himself so wholeheartedly to the work that he died prematurely. Even while lying on his deathbed, members of the committee would bring him samples of their translations and seek his advice.

Those who have learned to love and appreciate the AV should, however, not think that all the revisers were paragons of piety. One of them, Richard Thomson, born in Holland of English parents, and famous for his linguistic skills, was known as the "Drunken Dutchman."[4]

The translators/revisers were given free board and room, but did their work gratis. From the preface to the AV of 1611, we can tell how the translators viewed their holy calling: "Translation it is that openeth the window to let in the light; that breaketh the shell, that we may eat the kernel; that putteth aside the curtain, that we may look into the most holy place; that removeth the cover of the well, that we may come by the water."[5]

C. Early Printed Editions of the AV

The work of revising and translating began in earnest in 1607, and in 1611 the new Bible came from the presses of Robert Barker, King's Printer. The 1,500 pages were printed in double columns. Although there is no record of any decree ordaining its use, by either king, Parliament, or Convocation, the words, "Appointed to be read in Churches" appear on its title page. The title forms the center of an engraving, showing the figures of Moses and Aaron, with the four Evangelists in the corners. At the top is the name of God in Hebrew, beneath it is the sacred Dove (the Spirit), and farther down is the Lamb. At the foot of the page is the pelican, wounding herself with her beak to feed her young with her own blood—the symbol of Christ's redeeming work.

The AV was dedicated to King James,

---

[4]For biographical comments on the translators of the AV see G. S. Paine, *The Learned Men* (New York: Crowell, 1959).

[5]MacGregor, *Bible Making*, p. 162.

Title page from the original Authorized Version showing the four evangelists, Moses, Aaron, Peter, and Paul, and symbols representing the trinity.

and in America the 1611 version is commonly referred to as the "King James Version" (KJV). Also, there is a preface in which the translators pay respect to their predecessors who laid a good foundation on which this new edition is built. Those readers who would find imperfections in the version are reminded that perfection is never attainable to man. They confess that there are words in the original that occur only once and whose meanings, therefore, cannot be known with certainty.

The AV was printed three times in the year of its publication. The earliest edition is known as "the great He edition" and the other two as "the great She editions," because the first renders the closing words of Ruth 3:15, "and he went into the city," while the others have "she went into the city."

There were quite a number of misprints and variations in wording and spelling in the early editions. One misprint has been perpetuated in AV editions: "strain at a gnat" instead of "strain out a gnat" (Matt. 23:24). In an edition of 1631 the "not" in the seventh commandment was omitted. The King's printers were fined 300 pounds by the archbishop for the error and the edition got the opprobrious nickname, "Wicked Bible," for it commanded people to commit adultery. An Oxford edition of 1717 is known as the "Vinegar Bible," because the chapter heading had "The Parable of the Vinegar" (instead of "vineyard") in Luke 20. A 1795 edition has Mark 7:27 in the form: "Let the children first be killed" (instead of "filled"), and came to be known as the "Murderers' Bible."

One careless typesetter inadvertently summed up the abuse the Bible has suffered at the hands of printers, by making Psalm 119:161 read, "Printers [not 'Princes'] had persecuted me without a cause."

In the course of time the spelling in the earlier editions was modified, the chapter summaries were reduced, and the marginal references expanded. In 1701 dates were introduced into the margin, based on the calculations of Archbishop Ussher.[6]

Like its predecessors, the AV included the Apocrypha, something the Puritans disapproved of.

D. The Reception of the AV

This version quickly became the "authorized" version. It easily replaced the Bishops' Bible as the official version for public service. Against the Geneva Bible it had a harder struggle, and the two versions existed side by side for half a century. Eventually, however, the AV won out over all others because of its superior merit and its freedom from party or sectarian spirit.[7]

It should not be assumed that the current King James Version is exactly like the original in 1611. Only two years after its publication over three hundred variations were introduced in a new edition. Another revision came out in 1629 and still another in 1638. But it was the revision made at Cambridge in 1762 and at Oxford in 1769 that modernized its spelling so that it can be read with ease in our day. This is essentially the version we now have.[8]

---

[6]Bruce, *History of Bible*, p. 109.

[7]Kenyon, *Bible and Manuscripts*, p. 306.

[8]Paine, *Learned Men*, p. 106.

Also, it should not be overlooked that the AV did not get by without severe criticism. Dr. Hugh Broughton, a biblical scholar of great eminence and erudition, had been omitted from the list of the revisers on account of his rather violent disposition. As one might expect, he was extremely critical of the 1611 version. He condemned the whole thing as idle words for which the translators would have to answer on the day of judgment. As for himself, "he had rather be rent in pieces by wild horses than any such translation by [his] consent should be urged upon poor churches."[9]

Critics accused the translators of blasphemy and modernism, and called them "damnable corrupters." The AV was denounced as being unfaithful to the original, and one London clergyman thought it denied the deity of Jesus Christ. Dr. Broughton remarked that "the cockles of the sea shores, and the leaves of the forest, and the grains of the poppy may as well be numbered as the gross errors of this Bible, disgracing the ground of our own hope."

The Dissenters who fled to America took the Geneva Bible with them, since in their view, the AV reminded them too much of the divine right of kings. Attacks on the AV continued almost to the end of the seventeenth century, but eventually this version won out over all others.

So popular did it become that an Ulster Protestant might say: "If the AV was good enough for the apostle Paul, then it is good enough for me."[10] While we can't fault the man for his high opinion of Paul, the gross ignorance

betrayed in such a statement hardly does him credit. On occasion, whether by accident or from ignorance, it was called the "Saint James" instead of the "King James Version." For some 250 years, when English Protestants spoke of the Bible, they usually meant the AV of 1611.

E. The Supremacy of the AV

The AV was able to displace other English versions because the Greek and Hebrew scholarship it represented had made great advances in England during the forty years since the Bishops' Bible was published in 1568. Admittedly, the Greek text of the NT was still the Byzantine text first printed by Erasmus, and the great uncials of the fourth and fifth century were not yet available, but we are now speaking only of the excellent translation of the available Hebrew and Greek text into English.

What made it a trustworthy revision was the fact that it was done by a company of scholars and divines and not by one individual. This version represented no minority point of view, and the absence of controversial marginal notes also helped to make the version acceptable to readers of different persuasions. Moreover, these scholars were able to build on the labors of many generations of Bible translators.

Also, in the half century previous to 1611 there had been great growth in English literature. Writers such as Spenser, Marlowe, Shakespeare, and others, had raised the standards of literary taste. The revisers of the AV en-

---

[9]R. Earle, *How We Got Our Bible* (Kansas City: Beacon Hill, 1971), p. 75.

[10]A. M. Hunter, *Jesus—Lord and Saviour* (Grand Rapids: Eerdmans, 1976), p. 19.

tered into this rich heritage and left us with a monument of Elizabethan prose. Kenyon observes that "the English of the Authorized Version is the finest specimen of our prose literature at a time when English prose wore its stateliest and most majestic form."[11] In a sense it was a far greater *literary* work than are the books of the NT in the original Greek.

The influence of the AV on the language and literature of English-speaking people everywhere is inestimable. There is hardly a book or newspaper to this day which does not consciously betray an acquaintance with the language of the AV. One can think of expressions such as "lick the dust," "skin of his teeth," "salt of the earth."[12] I recall taking an English course at the University of British Columbia, where several biblical books of the AV were required reading, not for religious reasons, but for examples of excellent English prose.

But much more important than the literary value of the AV has been its religious significance. It has been the literature of millions who have read little else, and it has been the source of the knowledge of salvation and the guide of conduct for countless millions for several hundred years.[13]

"As time went on the Authorized Version acquired the prescriptive right of age; its rhythms became familiar to the ears of all classes; its language entered into our literature; and Englishmen became prouder of their Bible than of any of the creative works of their own literature."[14]

However, for all its merits, the AV could not remain unchallenged forever. Not only did the English language continue to change, but scholars were plowing new furrows in biblical scholarship. Even more important was the recovery of early manuscripts of the Bible that led to great improvements in the biblical texts, especially in the Greek NT.

Sixteen years after the publication of the AV, the fifth-century Codex Alexandrinus came to the British Museum from Constantinople. Although it is not as good as the Sinaiticus and Vaticanus, it represented a much better text than the revisers of the AV had used. But it had come too late. Between 1611 and 1800 at least a thousand editions of the AV were published and up to the end of the nineteenth century it reigned supreme.

F. Attempts to Improve on the AV

Throughout the eighteenth and nineteenth centuries private ventures in Bible translation sought to incorporate the new textual information that was coming to light. Some tried to revise the AV, others made independent translations. As early as 1703 Daniel Whitby published his Paraphrase and Commentary on the New Testament. Edward Wells produced a revised text of the AV in The Common Translation Corrected (1718–24). Daniel Mace in 1729 published a Greek text of the NT with a corrected AV alongside it. William Whiston of Cambridge, when

---

[11]Kenyon, *Bible and Manuscripts*, p. 307.

[12]A Wikgren, "The English Bible," *Interpreter's Bible*, ed. G. Buttrick (Nashville: Abingdon, 1952), Vol. 1, p. 95.

[13]Kenyon, *Bible and Manuscripts*, p. 307.

[14]Kenyon, *Bible and Manuscripts*, p. 308.

he was seventy-eight years of age, published his Primitive New Testament in 1745, in which he brought the AV into line with the so-called "Western Text," such as is found in Codex Bezae.

In 1755 John Wesley issued a revision of the NT of the AV. He had made some 12,000 changes, divided the text into paragraphs, and added explanatory notes. A Quaker by the name of Antony Purver in 1764 issued a NT in very florid languages. "Hallowed be thy name," in the Lord's Prayer, read "sacredly reverenced be thy name." (A Quaker Bible published in 1828 had all those passages unsuitable for mixed audiences in the footnotes.)[15]

Edward Harwood's Liberal Translation of the New Testament (1768) is a literary curio. In this classical and biblical scholar's version, the Lord's Prayer began thus: "O Thou great governour and parent of universal nature—who manifest thy glory to the blessed inhabitants of heaven. ..." The Prayer turns out to be three times as long as it is in the Greek NT. As one can imagine, the work was not well received.

The Unitarian, Samual Sharpe, in 1840, issued a NT translated from the Greek text of Johann Griesbach. He followed this up with the OT in 1865.

Dean Alford published a Greek NT with a copious commentary. Then, in 1869, he issued a revision of the NT of the AV, and so paved the way for the publication of the English Revised Version of 1881 and 1885.

Another private version was issued by John Darby, a leader in the Brethren movement (NT, 1871; OT, 1890). He had already translated the Bible into German (Elberfelder) and into French (Pau). What his English version had in accuracy, it lacked in style.

Robert Young wanted to put English Bible readers as clearly as possible within reach of the Hebrew and Greek text and consequently produced his Literal Translation of the Bible (1862). Such word for word translations never commend themselves to readers. How does this sound? "Already also the axe to the root of the trees is laid, every tree, therefore, not bringing forth good fruit is cut down, and into the fire cast" (Luke 3:9). That may be literal, but it is hardly good English. His *Analytical Concordance* to the Bible did him more credit. Rotherham's The Emphasized Bible (NT, 1872; OT, 1902) was also a fairly literal translation. In 1876 Julia Smith published a Bible that was little more than a matching of English with Hebrew and Greek words, which ends up in complete nonsense.

Some new translations of the English Bible were incorporated in commentaries to the Bible. One of the best known is Conybeare and Howson's *The Life and Epistles of Paul* (1864).

There were also several attempts on this side of the Atlantic to improve on the AV, but sufficient examples have been given to show that Bible translation did not stop with the publication of the AV in 1611. In fact, between 1611 and 1881 at least seventy "private" versions of the Bible in English were published.[16] A major version of the AV of 1611 was undertaken at the end of the nineteenth century.

---

[15]MacGregor, *Bible Making*, p. 199.
[16]MacGregor, *Bible Making*, p. 316.

II. THE ENGLISH REVISED VERSION

About the year 1855 several scholars and churchmen had published revised versions of portions of the NT that gave readers a taste of what a revised version of the Bible might look like.[17] With the discovery of older manuscript materials in the middle of the nineteenth century, especially that of the Codex Sinaiticus and Vaticanus, it became obvious that the time had come for the publication of a new Greek text of the NT. For all the merits of the King James Version it was based on a Byzantine text, as this was found mainly in late manuscripts. The climax of all this textual study came in 1881, with the publication of a Revised NT by Westcott and Hort, based on a new Greek text that was published almost simultaneously with the revised English NT. Shortly after, in 1885, the revised OT was completed. The entire work is known as the English Revised Version (ERV).

A. The Initiation of the Project

In 1870, Dr. Wilberforce, Bishop of Winchester, recommended to the Convocation of the Province of Canterbury that a revision of the NT of the AV be undertaken—a recommendation that was expanded later to include the OT. After some discussion a committee of sixteen was appointed to supervise this revision project. A revision committee of fifty-four members was formed, which divided itself into two companies, one for each Testament. The scholars belonged both to the Church of England and to nonconformist denominations, such

as the Church of Scotland, Baptists, Methodists, Congregationalists, and others. Even a scholar who had turned Roman Catholic, John Henry Newmann, was invited, but could not accept. There was also a Unitarian on the committee, Dr. Vance Smith, and his presence among the revisers caused considerable misgivings among orthodox Bible readers.[18]

Among the English NT committee were scholars such as Westcott, Lightfoot, Hort, Alford, and Trench; on the OT committee were men such as A. B. Davidson, C. D. Ginsburg, J. J. S. Perowne, and E. H. Plumptre—all of them competent scholars.

Philip Schaff was a brilliant student of theology and history. Born in Switzerland, he came to America in 1844 to teach at the theological seminary of the German Reformed Church at Mercersburg, Pennsylvania. In 1870 he became a professor at Union Theological Seminary, and during this period he chaired the American Committee for the Revised Version.

---

[17]Kenyon, *Bible and Manuscripts*, p. 310.

[18]Bruce, *History of Bible*, p. 136.

American participation was also invited and Dr. Philip Schaff was chosen to chair the committee of thirty men on this side of the Atlantic. The committee was divided into an Old and a New Testament company, and these two American companies met in New York for committee work one session every month, except July and August. During the first three years, 1872 to 1875, a workable scheme was finally developed between the Americans and their British counterparts.

The English revisers promised to send their revision in its various stages to the American revisers and to take all the American suggestions into special consideration before the final draft was sent to the printers. Those suggestions that the English revisers could not accept were to appear in an Appendix to the revised Scriptures. The Americans were asked to pledge their moral support to this new version and had to promise not to issue an edition of their own for a term of fourteen years.

B. Policies of the Revisers

It was agreed that the revisers would introduce only such changes into the text of the AV that would bring it more closely in line with the original Hebrew and Greek. Also, they were not to modernize the English of the AV unduly.

Each company was to go over the revised portions twice. Any changes made after the second screening had to have two-thirds of the votes of the company; otherwise, the majority decided where there were questions.

The revisers introduced changes such as (1) alterations due to the adoption of a different Greek text from that of the AV; (2) improvements where the AV was ambiguous; (3) correction of errors in the AV; (4) alterations where the AV was inconsistent in the rendering of the Greek by different English words.[19]

Since the NT revisers were using a somewhat different Greek text as their base than had the revisers in 1611, the AV had to be changed where the new Greek readings demanded this. (As it turned out this called for some six thousand changes.)

The headings of chapters, pages, paragraphs, italics, and punctuation in the AV were also revised.

In the case of special problems the committee felt free to call on experts at home or abroad.

Oxford and Cambridge University Presses were willing to assume the expenses of printing this revised version on condition that they retain the copyright for fourteen years. The revisers did their work gratis.[20]

C. The Revised New Testament

The work was begun in 1870, and after eleven years, in 1881, the NT was published. On May 17 the Revised New Testament was published in England and on May 20 it was on sale in the United States. The pressure for copies in New York and Philadelphia began early on May 20. It is estimated that three million copies of the Revised New Testament were sold in England and America within less than a year of its publication. In addition, there were various periodicals and papers that

---

[19]MacGregor, *Bible Making,* p. 210.
[20]Bruce, *History of Bible,* p. 137.

published either a part or the whole of the new volume. Both the *Tribune* and the *Times* of Chicago published the entire book in their issues of May 22, 1881. The Gospels, Acts, and Romans were telegraphed from New York, and the remainder of the book was set up from copies received in Chicago on the evening of May 21. Sales were brisk, and so were the debates on its merits.

Many Bible readers were shocked at the new readings in this Revised Version. The fiercest criticism came from Dean Burgon. He reviewed the ERV of the NT in a series of articles in which he argued that the older manuscripts were not necessarily the better ones. He found nothing good to say about the revised NT.

> How it happened that, with so many splendid Scholars sitting round their table, they should have produced a Translation which, for the most part, reads like a first-rate schoolboy's *crib*,—tasteless, unlovely, harsh, unidiomatic;—servile without being really faithful;—pedantic without being really learned;—an unreadable Translation, in short; the result of a vast amount of labour indeed, but of wondrous little skill;—how all this has come about it were utterly useless at this time of day to enquire.[21]

The passage about the angel troubling the water of the pool of Bethesda (John 5:3f.) was in the margin, as was Acts 8:37. The omission of the reference to the three witnesses (1 John 5:7), caused considerable consternation, and the revisers were charged with undermining Trinitarian teaching (But there's hardly a Greek manuscript that has this verse.)

Although the revised NT had a better Greek text as its base, the English of the translation left much to be desired, even though it reflected some improvements over the AV. In their efforts to be as faithful to the Greek as possible the revisers paid too little attention to English style. Had the version been in more readable English it would have replaced the AV; as it was, this did not happen.

One of the marks of the AV is that it renders the same Greek word by a variety of English equivalents, depending on the context. For example, in Mark's Gospel the word *euthus* ("immediately") occurs some forty times, and the AV had translated it as "straightway," "immediately," "forthwith," and "anon." The ERV now rendered it consistently as "straightway." The revisers knew what was meant when they rendered Matthew 5:29, "if thy right eye causeth thee to stumble," but to the ordinary reader, stumbling over one's eye did seem a bit monstrous. But this is the problem the translator encounters when he wants to do it literally.

Several changes no doubt were for the better: "charity" once more became "love," and "Hades" was substituted for "hell" (where the Greek calls for it; "hell" is the correct translation of "Gehenna"). On the whole, however, the English of the Revised Version was too close to the original languages, and so it never became very popular. In spite of initial sales of three million copies of the Revised NT within the first year (two million within the first few days) this version failed to enjoy continued popularity.[22]

---

[21]Bruce, *History of Bible*, p. 150.
[22]MacGregor, *Bible Making*, p. 211.

D. The Entire Bible

As the OT is longer than the NT, it took fourteen years to complete, and it was published in 1885. The Apocrypha were not part of the project originally, but in 1895 they were also published. Great strides forward had been made in Hebrew studies since the publication of the AV, and even though fewer changes in the Hebrew text were called for than in the New, more changes in the English translation were made. However, readers were not surprised so much by the new readings in the OT as they were in the NT where the translation was based on a different Greek text.

The ERV departed from the practice of printing every verse as a separate paragraph. It retains the verse numbers, but prints the text in sense paragraphs—a practice that a number of modern versions have followed.

The ERV is an accurate version, and was widely used as a study Bible, but it never replaced the AV in popular esteem. Few parish churches in England adopted it for regular use. Spurgeon, the most renowned popular preacher at that time, called the new version "strong in Greek, weak in English."[23]

E. The American Revised Version

The American committee had suggested a number of changes to the British revisers in the interests of modernizing the language. They wanted "Jehovah" instead of "Lord," "patched" instead of "clouted," "astonished" instead of "astonied," "turned away" instead of "eschewed," "spirit" instead of "ghost," "covenant" instead of "testament," and the like. The English revisers, however, were rather more conservative than the Americans and clung to these archaic expressions. They did the Americans the honor of putting some three hundred of their suggestions in an appendix with an apology to their American friends on the other side of the Atlantic, with whom they were prepared to agree to a friendly difference of opinion.

The American committee remained intact after the publication of the ERV in 1881–1885, and when the English copyright ran out they were ready with their version of the ERV. They had wanted a more extensive elimination of archaic words and phrases than the English revisers felt inclined to allow. Also, they wanted a version that would take account of American usage. Moreover, some unauthorized editions of the New Testament were published in America that included some of the American suggestions that had been relegated by the English revisers to the appendix. For these reasons it was decided by the American Committee to publish a separate American edition of the Revised Version. In August, 1901, this new edition was published by Thomas Nelson and Sons and it came to be known as the American Standard Version.

This version had a more readable style than did its English counterpart and became much more popular in America than did the ERV in England. It was used widely by students of the Scriptures who had not had the advantage of studying Greek and Hebrew.

In 1971 a New American Standard Bible was published, and we will have more to say on that in a later chapter.

---

[23]MacGregor, *Bible Making,* p. 212.

III. KING JAMES II VERSION

In America the AV had become every bit as popular as it had in Britain. More commonly it is known as the King James Version. In 1971 the King James II Version was published by Associated Publishers and Authors. This is the work of Jay Green who evidently has no appreciation for the many excellent English versions that have been published of late. He is confident that God's people don't want a new Bible, just the old one, and that means the AV of 1611. Other versions, he claims, reflect the translator's theology; they have paraphrased, interpreted, deleted, and added to God's Word. The Living Bible, he thinks, should rather be called the "Dying Bible." In his view it is profane and is not a Bible at all. He calls it a "rewrite job" that shows what a poor job man would do if God-breathed words were not directly given to him. To that one might say that while translators do experience the help of God's Spirit in their work they do not claim divine inspiration for themselves.

In the view of Armerding and Gasque, Jay Green's King James II, is hardly an improvement over what it was designed to replace.[24] Are the AV's "swaddling clothes" not superior to KJ II's "naval-band?" And surely KJ II's "shepherd men" is no improvement over the AV's "shepherds" (Luke 2:7, 15)—to give only two examples. Robert Bratcher recommends that readers who prefer the King James, stay with the original, not with this substitute.[25]

IV. THE NEW KING JAMES BIBLE

In 1979 Thomas Nelson and Sons, publishers of the ASV of 1901 and the RSV of 1952, published the NT part of the New King James Bible (NKJB). This reversion from twentieth-century versions to a Bible published in 1611 was due to the fact that Thomas Nelson and Sons was purchased by an American corporation whose policies differ considerably from that of the 180-year-old British firm.[26]

A group of some 119 scholars, representing various denominations, have done a moderate revision of the 1611 KJV. In the introduction the publishers declare that the NKJB seeks "to produce a revised English edition which will unlock the spiritual treasures found uniquely in the King James Version of the Holy Scriptures." One must ask immediately, of course, what "spiritual" treasures the KJV has that other translations do not have. And if not other English versions, what spiritual treasures can there "legitimately" be found in the KJV that are not in the Hebrew and the Greek?

The entire project was completed in 1982, and cost some 3.5 million dollars. Sam Moore, who heads the new corporation, hopes not only to retrieve that investment, but to make a good profit, for he is of the firm conviction that a vast majority of English Bible readers still prefer the KJV. It is hard to understand, however, how a revised KJV can still be advertised and sold as a KJV, even if it is a new KJV. The publisher's claim that the NKJB is "the first major revision of the KJV since 1867" is

[24]C. Armerding and W. Gasque, "The Bible as a Whole," *Christianity Today* Vol. 16 (February 18, 1972), p. 8.

[25]R. Bratcher, "Old Wine in New Wineskins," *Christianity Today* Vol. 16 (October 8, 1971), p. 16.

[26]J. P. Lewis, *The English Bible/From KJV to NIV* (Grand Rapids: Baker, 1981), p. 330.

simply not true. The ERV (1881–85), the ASV (1901), and the RSV (1946–52) were all efforts at revising the KJV.

Moreover, by a moderate updating of the KJV this Bible is no longer the KJV of 1611, nor is it a modern version. It is a mixture of Jacobean English and twentieth-century style.[27] In one respect the NKJB is like its 1611 counterpart, namely it puts little stock in the progress made in manuscript studies since 1611, and turns the clock of textual studies back to the seventeenth century.

We should not be surprised if the sales of the NKJB are quite brisk. Those who were brought up on the KJV may gladly turn to a version that is not quite so archaic and yet appears to be like the original. One should always remember, however, that God's revelation was given to us originally in Hebrew, Aramaic, and Greek, and not in Jacobean English.

There is really no need to go back to the KJV of 1611, for as we will see in the following chapters, we now have excellent modern versions of the English Bible.

SUGGESTED READING

Bruce, F. F. **History of the Bible in English**, 3rd ed. *New York: Oxford University Press, 1978. See pages 96–112.*

Carson, D. A. **The King James Version Debate**. *Grand Rapids: Baker, 1979*

Lewis, J. P. **The English Bible/From KJV to NIV**. *Grand Rapids: Baker, 1981. See, "Doctrinal Problems in the King James Version," pp. 35–38; "The New King James Bible," pp. 329–62.*

Paine, G. S. **The Learned Men.** *New York: Thomas Y. Crowell Co., 1959.*

MacGregor, G. **The Bible in the Making.** *New York: Lippincott, 1959. See pages 140–215.*

———. **A Literary History of the Bible.** *Nashville: Abingdon, 1968. See the "King James Version," pp. 170–242.*

Partridge, A. C. **English Biblical Translation.** *London: Andre Deutsch, 1973.*

Price, I. M. **The Ancestry of Our English Bible**, 3rd ed. *revised by W. A. Irwin and Allen P. Wikgren. New York: Harper and Row, 1956. See, "The King James Version of 1611," pp. 268–77; "The Revised Version," pp. 278–91.*

Robertson, E. H. **The New Translations of the Bible.** *Naperville: Allenson, 1959. See, "The Authorized Version," pp. 11–24; "The Revised Version," pp. 25–38.*

---

[27]Lewis, *English Bible*, p. 350.

Chapter 17

English Bibles in the First Half of the Twentieth Century

At the turn of the century a quiet revolution went on in the field of lexicography. The secular papyri that the archaeologists were discovering in Egypt illuminated many a Greek NT word so that the dictionaries of the Greek NT had to be revised. Also, the discovery of vast bodies of Semitic literature, such as the Canaanite tablets at Ugarit, gave Hebrew scholars new understandings for the vocabulary of the OT.

Moreover, with the discovery of the papyri it was recognized that the NT was written in everyday speech. This meant that the Bible could (indeed, should) be published in modern vernaculars. It is then not irreverent to translate the Hebrew and Greek testaments into everyday English; the Bible was not designed to be a masterpiece of prose or poetry, but to communicate God's message to man.

With the discovery of biblical papyri, such as Chester Beatty and Bodmer, it became even clearer than it had already been that the text on which the AV was based called for considerable improvement. So then, better lexicons and a sounder Hebrew and Greek text, combined with the recognition that the Bible should be translated into everyday speech, caused a shift in Bible translation. Let us now turn to some of these modern speech versions.

I. THE TWENTIETH CENTURY NEW TESTAMENT

One of the pioneer modern speech versions was The Twentieth Century New Testament. No one knew who had done the translating until some fifty years later when the names of some twenty men who worked on this project came to light. In 1933 the records of the secretary of this group of translators were deposited in the John Rylands Library in Manchester. Without this information no one would ever have known the names of these people who devoted approximately fourteen years of labor to produce this NT.[1]

---

[1]S. Kubo, and W. Specht, *So Many Versions?* (Grand Rapids: Zondervan, 1975), p. 23.

Evidently it grew out of a concern to make the Bible plain to young people. Some of the translators were ministers, others were lay people, but none of them were what one might call linguistic experts. Devotion to their task somehow made up in part for their lack of expertise. They did, however, consult experts at a number of points.

The translators worked at home and collaborated by mail. The committee was divided into five groups, each with an assigned portion of the NT to translate. Each person's translation was circulated among the group members for examination. Each of the five groups elected one of its members to the revision committee that prepared the final draft. Changes could be made only by a two-thirds vote. Before printing, a committee went over the translation once more to check for English idiom.

This version was published in parts between 1898 and 1901, and after another revision, the final edition appeared in 1904 both in London and New York. The preface states that the purpose of the translation was "to enable Englishmen to read the most important part of the Bible in that form of their own language which they themselves use."

There are some very vivid phrases in this version. Paul is accused of being a "public pest" (Acts 24:5); judgment is described as "the Bar of God" (Rom. 14:10); rudimentary teachings are described as "the very alphabet of the Divine Revelation" (Heb. 5:12). The rendering of "saints" by the phrase "Christ's people" anticipates the New

English Bible. Even alliteration occurs: "dulled by debauches or drunkenness" (Luke 21:34).[2]

What was novel about this NT was that the books were arranged in chronological order with brief introductions. I recall as a youth purchasing this NT at Eatons for twenty-five cents and being struck by the odd arrangement of the books.

Moody Press issued a reprint of this version in 1961 and restored the books to the traditional order, omitted the introduction to the books, and made numerous changes, presumably for the benefit of the American readers.

This English Twentieth Century New Testament was a pioneer in the movement to translate the Scriptures into current speech.[3]

II. WEYMOUTH'S NEW TESTAMENT

One of the scholars who was consulted from time to time by the translators of the Twentieth Century New Testament was Richard Weymouth (1822–1902), a distinguished classical scholar. He was a British Baptist layman who had published an edition of the Greek NT in 1862. His many years of teaching had impressed on his mind the need for giving people a Bible in current English, and when he retired he decided to translate his Greek NT into modern English.

He died before The New Testament in Modern Speech came off the press in 1903. In the preface he explains that he has no desire to supplant the standard English versions, nor to produce a version to be used for public

---

[2]J. H. P. Reumann, *The Romance of Bible Scripts and Scholars* (Englewood Cliffs: Prentice-Hall, 1965), p. 181.

[3]For the story of how the Twentieth Century New Testament was produced, see Reumann, *Romance of Bible*, pp. 163–83.

reading in church. Rather he hoped to supplement other versions, by giving the sense of the Greek as accurately and naturally as he could in present-day English. Present-day English for Weymouth meant the avoidance of colloquialisms on the one hand, and "society" classical English on the other.[4] As a scholar he naturally tried to be as precise as possible in transferring nuances of the Greek to the English. Extensive footnotes explain some of his renderings.

Several editions were published in the years following 1903. The first major overhaul was made in the fourth edition, published in 1924. The fifth and final edition was prepared by James Robertson of Aberdeen, and published in 1929. It was also published in the United States in 1943.

The familiar petition for forgiveness in the Lord's Prayer reads, "Forgive us our shortcomings, as we also have forgiven them who have failed in their duty towards us." Interestingly, the Twentieth Century translators gave the two *denaria* of the Good Samaritan as "four" shillings, but Weymouth reduced it to "two" shillings. (Monetary terms are notoriously difficult to translate because their buying power changes from time to time.) Instead of the AV's, "In whom we have redemption by his blood," (Eph. 1:7), Weymouth has, "It is in Him, and through the shedding of His blood, that we have deliverance." Perhaps Weymouth failed to appreciate fully the Semitic background of many of the Greek words of the NT. This seems obvious in his rendering of eternal life by "the life of the ages." In a later edition this was changed.

Several other attempts were made at the beginning of the century to translate the NT into modern English, in fact Ferrar Fenton published the entire Bible in modern English in 1903. All these versions, however, were eclipsed by the translation efforts of the Scotsman, James Moffatt.

III. THE MOFFATT VERSION

James Moffatt (1870–1944) was a brilliant Scottish scholar who was born and educated in Glasgow. During the fifteen years of his parish ministry he continued his scholarly pursuits and in 1901 published The Historical New Testament, for which St. Andrews

James Moffatt, the Scottish educator who taught in Glasgow and at Union Theological Seminary in New York. He is known for his translation of the Moffatt Bible and his work on the RSV.

---

[4]Kubo and Specht, *So Many*, p. 6.

University awarded him a Doctor of Divinity degree. He held professorships at Oxford, Glasgow, and from 1927 to 1939, at Union Theological Seminary, New York.

While at Oxford, in 1913, he published his first edition of The New Testament: A New Translation. This was not a revision of his earlier work, but a new translation. By the time Moffatt had done the OT, in 1924, he was professor at Glasgow. In 1928, after he moved to America, the one-volume edition of his version appeared, A New Translation of the Bible.[5]

So popular did Moffatt's version become that generally in the years between the two world wars when people spoke of a modern speech translation they had Moffatt in mind. Even in America his version became so popular that on one occasion when he was scheduled to give a lecture in a certain city a billboard announced, "Author of Bible to lecture tonight."

Moffatt realized the complexity of his task. He knew that he would have to translate for two kinds of readers: those who knew the original languages and those who did not. Also, he was aware of the fact that a translator appears more dogmatic than he really is. A preacher or commentator can suggest alternatives, but the translator has to decide on one rendering and thereby lay himself open to criticism.

Moffatt gives three reasons why the AV was no longer satisfactory: (1) its archaic language, (2) the advance made in the study of the vocabulary and syntax of the NT since 1611, (3) new manuscript evidence.

In his attempt to provide a new translation he deliberately avoided the use of other English versions, although he confesses that his memory of other versions did play tricks on him at times.

What made the Moffatt Bible so popular was the freshness of its language. Let us pick out a few examples. The mother of Moses put the babe into "a creel made of papyrus reeds ... daubed over with bitumen and pitch" (Exod. 2:3). Noah's ark becomes a "barge." The wealthy of Samaria are described as "lolling on their ivory divans, sprawling on their couches, dining off fresh lamb and fatted veal, crooning to the music of the lute, lapping wine by the bowlful ... with never a single thought for the bleeding wounds of the nation" (Amos 6:4ff.).

Some renderings betray a Scottish background. Among the musical instruments played at the dedication of Nebuchadnezzar's image are the bagpipes (Dan. 3:10), and when David danced before the Lord he wore a linen kilt (2 Sam. 6:14).

In the NT, too, there are some striking readings. While Martha is troubled about many dishes, Mary is said to have chosen "the better dish." Titus is enjoined by Paul to give Zenas "a hearty send-off," and a bishop must not be "addicted to pilfering" (Titus 1:7).

First Corinthians 13 catches the readers' eye in almost any version, but Moffatt gives it a new lustre: "Love makes no parade; gives itself no airs; is never rude, never selfish, never irritated, never resentful; love is never glad when others go wrong, love is gladdened by goodness, always slow to expose, always eager to believe the

---

[5]F. F. Bruce, *History of the Bible in English*, 3rd rev. ed. (New York: Oxford University Press, 1978), p. 7.

best, always hopeful, always patient."

Moffatt's Bible became so popular that the Moffatt Bible Commentary was later based on this version. He participated in the early stages of the RSV project, and when on one occasion he objected to a certain rendering, he was reminded that it came straight from the Moffatt version. He still refused to accept it, because the RSV, as he explained, had a different purpose to achieve.[6]

However, Moffatt's version also has its weaknesses. In the OT he frequently "improved" on the Hebrew text, and here and there throughout the Bible he rearranged verses and adopted readings which were not well-established. For example, he took Genesis 2:4a, which he translated, "This is the story of how the universe was formed," and made them the opening words of Genesis. Paul's advice to Timothy to take a little wine for the sake of his stomach is put into the footnotes. The sacred name Yahweh is rendered as "The Eternal"; the Word that was in the beginning is left in Greek, so that John's Gospel begins, "The Logos existed in the very beginning."

Some readers thought Moffatt was just too colloquial. The Song of Songs reads at 1:3, "The girls are all in love with you," and Proverbs 22:6, "Train a child for his proper trade"—a rendering that lacks the moral overtones of the Hebrew text. One critic thought that there were plenty of good Christians to be found who would dislike Moffatt as undignified and otherwise unwelcome. However, judged by the sales, it was eminently popular. It invaded Sunday schools, youth clubs, and even church services.

The story is told of a young minister in Scotland who visited an aged member of his flock and read to her from Moffatt's Bible. "That is very nice," she said, "but now, won't you read a bittie of the Word of God before you go?"[7]

Many editions of Moffatt's Bible came from the press after its first publication in 1926. In 1935 Moffatt put out his revised and final edition. He was translating the Apocrypha in 1944 and had just completed the Wisdom of Solomon 3:1, "But the souls of the righteous are in the hand of God, and no torment will ever touch them," when he passed away. In 1949 a concordance of the Moffatt Bible was published.

IV. AN AMERICAN TRANSLATION

Edgar J. Goodspeed (1871–1962)[8] was one of the most eloquent advocates of modern speech versions. He had begun the study of Greek as a boy and after attending Chicago, Yale, and European universities, he became professor of NT at the University of Chicago. In 1920 he presented a paper at the New Testament Club of the University in which he criticized the three leading modern speech versions of the time: The Twentieth Century New Testament, Weymouth, and Moffatt. In the discussion that followed, Dr. Chase, one of Goodspeed's colleagues, suggested that since he found so many flaws in these versions perhaps he

---

[6]G. MacGregor, *The Bible in the Making* (New York: Lippincott, 1959), p. 241.

[7]Bruce, *History of Bible*, p. 8.

[8]The story is told in greater detail in Goodspeed's autobiography, *As I Remember* (New York: Harper and Brothers, 1953).

Edgar J. Goodspeed was a leading scholar in the study of Greek papyri. He translated the New Testament into the American idiom and served on the original RSV New Testament Committee.

when called on to speak at the divinity school chapel.

He called his new version An American Translation. It was published by the University of Chicago Press in 1923. Also, it appeared in serial form in the Chicago Evening Post and in twenty-four other newspapers throughout the United States and Canada.

Although it was a very smooth translation there was considerable criticism of it at the beginning—if for no other reason that that Goodspeed taught at the University of Chicago, known for its liberal theology. The Chicago Tribune came out with the headline: "Monkeying With the Bible." The New York Times criticized him for substituting "lamp" for "candle" and "peck-measure" for "bushel," and so forth. It even suggested that if he had gone "the whole hog he would have written electric light instead of lamp." Actually Tyndale was the culprit, for he introduced "candle" into the English Bible, since that's what England burned in Tyndale's day. "Lamp" is in fact the correct rendering.

The London Telegraph prayed, "Heaven preserve us from Chicago professors." The St. Louis Globe-Democrat volunteered: "It is as much of an anachronism to put the gospels in colloquial American terms today as it would be to put pants on the twelve apostles." The Columbia Record also objected to the elimination of "candles" from the Bible and thought that Goodspeed might as well have given Ruth a McCormick Harvester in place of a scythe (the critic did not know that she had a sickle, not a scythe).

The Indianapolis Star had this: "Nothing stops his devastating pen. He has even abbreviated the Lord's Prayer" (the critic had read Good-

should produce one of his own. Amid the laughter that followed a representative of the University of Chicago Press took the suggestion seriously, with the result that Goodspeed was invited to translate the NT into modern English. He was reluctant at first, but on the encouragement of his wife he finally consented. It was time, he thought, that American readers who had depended so long on versions made in Great Britain, have a version that was truly American in English.

Like Moffatt, Goodspeed found his familiarity with existing versions an obstacle, since he did not wish simply to reproduce what others had already done. Remembering that the NT books were written to be read in public, he wanted his translation to serve a similar purpose, and so on occasion he would read a few pages of his version

speed's translation of the Lucan version of the Lord's Prayer, which is shorter than Matthew's). This critic went on to suggest that Chicagoans, if they ever thought of praying, didn't have time to pray anyway. He concluded: "It is a petition that in its present wording has been held sacred for nearly 2000 years, for the King James translators are said to have made no changes" (as if the King James Version were the original).

Within a matter of weeks after the publication of the NT, the University of Chicago Press asked Goodspeed to do the OT also. Goodspeed, however, handed this assignment over to a colleague in the OT Department, J. M. P. Smith. Smith, then, with the help of several graduates of the University, published the OT in 1927. In 1931 the two were combined in one volume to form: The Bible—An American Translation. Eventually the Apocrypha were also added.

By now English-speaking Bible readers were getting accustomed to modern speech versions, and it would take us too far if we were to mention all the independent efforts to translate the Bible into current English. Not only Protestants but Roman Catholics also caught the vision of letting God's Word speak in today's English. Ronald Knox was such a translator.

V. THE KNOX TRANSLATION

English-speaking Roman Catholics generally used no other English Bible but the Douai-Rheims-Challoner version, which by the beginning of the twentieth century was full of archaisms.

In 1939 the Catholic hierarchy granted Ronald Knox, an Oxford don, permission to translate the NT from the Latin Vulgate into modern English. Knox was born into an Anglican family and was educated at Eton and Oxford. He was a brilliant student of the classics and a writer of vigorous prose and detective novels.[9] At age twenty-nine he converted to Catholicism, and in 1939 he began to apply his literary skills to the translation of the NT into English. This new translation was published in 1945. He then went on to do the OT also, and it was published in 1949. Later he quipped that this period of translation had involved a sentence of nine years at hard labor. He confesses that during these years the Bible was his sole occupation: he "ate, lived, and breathed the Bible."

Knox had a great flair for words and his translation has received great acclaim. His approach to the biblical text was to ask: "How would an Englishman have said this?" Knox wanted to translate in such a fashion that readers would not even be aware of the fact that they were reading a translation. In Job 7:15 the AV reads, "And so my soul chooseth hanging"; Knox has, "the rope for me." "He leadeth me by still waters," becomes, "leads me out to the cool water's brink." The Song of Songs in the AV begins: "Let him kiss me with the kisses of his mouth; Knox reduces that to a few terse words, "A kiss from the lips!" First Corinthians 13:12 reads: "At present, we are looking at a confused reflection in a mirror; then, we shall see face to face."

Because he translated from the Vulgate, this Latin version has affected his style. And since he did not translate

---

[9]Kubo and Specht, *So Many*, p. 55.

from the Hebrew and the Greek, one cannot go to Knox's version for help in determining the precise sense of the original.[10] Even the names of the books are in their Vulgate form: Chronicles is Paralipomena (which is really what the Greek Septuagint has), Hosea is Osee, and so it goes.

The footnotes are generally explanatory, although some emphasize Catholic doctrine. In Matthew 12:46–50, where Jesus' brothers are mentioned, the footnote explains: "Since it is impossible for anyone who holds the Catholic tradition to support that our Lord had brothers by blood, the most common opinion is that these 'brethren' were his cousins." A footnote to 1 Corinthians 3:10–15 endorses the Catholic doctrine of Purgatory.

While Knox did a brilliant piece of translation work, his version suffers from the fact that it is a translation of a translation. And since Catholics, about the time when Knox finished his work, were given the freedom to translate from the original Hebrew and Greek, versions such as the Jerusalem Bible and the New American Bible have eclipsed Knox's Bible, particularly in America.

While we are on the other side of the Atlantic, let us look at another modern speech version published in England, done in this case not by a Catholic scholar, but by an Anglican priest.

VI. PHILLIPS'S VERSION

During World War II, J. B. Phillips was in charge of a flourishing group of young people in southeast London. In the terrible days of the German Blitz he used to read selections from Paul's epistles at the close of their meetings at Youth Club. To his great disappointment he noticed that these young people couldn't make head or tail of the AV. These were young people who were not familiar with "Bible English" because they had not been brought up in the church, and to whom "I couldn't care less" was a more familiar expression than "the Lord is my Shepherd."[11]

Phillips's passion to make biblical truths comprehensible to these young people stimulated him to make fresh translations of Paul's letters and read these to them. He was richly rewarded when he noticed the positive response to his translations.

This might have remained a parochial experiment had not C. S. Lewis entered the picture. Phillips had written him and enclosed a copy of his newly translated letter to the Colossians, and Lewis replied: "Thank you a hundred times. I thought I knew Colossians pretty well, but your paraphrase makes it far more significant. It was like seeing a familiar picture after it's been cleaned . . . I hope very much you will carry out your plan of doing all the epistles."[12]

Phillips followed his advice and in 1947 there appeared Letters to Young Churches, with an introduction by C. S. Lewis, In 1952 he completed the Gospels, and in 1955 Acts (The Young Church in Action), and in 1957 the Book of Revelation. The entire NT was published in 1958 and a revised version of it in 1972.

Phillips laid down five principles that were to guide him in his transla-

---

[10]Bruce, *History of Bible*, p. 208.

[11]E. H. Robertson, *The New Translations of the Bible* (Naperville: Allenson, 1959), p. 102.

[12]Robertson, *New Translations*, p. 103.

tion: (1) the language must be that which is commonly spoken; (2) the translation should expand, if necessary, to preserve the original meaning; (3) the letters should read like letters, not theological treatises; (4) the translation should "flow"; (5) the value of the version should lie in its "easy-to-read" quality. The format was to be that of a modern book, without verse and chapter divisions.

Phillips confesses that he himself was transformed in the process of translating the NT, for the material was strangely alive. When he did Acts he felt "like an electrician re-wiring an old house, without being able to turn the mains off."[13]

While the version is what may be called a paraphrase, it is supreme among the modern English para-

The late Canon J. B. Phillips, known for his translation of the New Testament.

phrases of the NT. Just when a translation should be called a paraphrase is hard to say, for all translation is in one sense a paraphrase. And so "gird your loins" becomes "tighten your belts," "utterly astounded" becomes "scared out of their wits" (Mark 6:51). "To hell with your money" (Acts 8:19) sounds a bit vulgar, but that is in fact what Peter said. "O you dear idiots of Galatia," is striking, to say the least (Gal. 3:1). At times Phillips seems to overstep the bounds of translation and to invade the field of interpretation too deeply. When the command to greet one another with a holy kiss, becomes a "handshake all round," and when "to give over to Satan" becomes "to expell from the church," we wonder whether that should not have been left to the interpreter.

At first blush we may get the impression that Phillips's style is colloquial, but on further reading we find that it is in fact a literary style. There are expressions that the man of the street would not understand. What are "palpable frauds" (Titus 1:6) and "invidious distinctions" (James 2:9)? Would the average reader know what it means to be "dilatory" (2 Peter 3:8)? There is also a Britishism here and there that American readers may find strange (Jesus and his disciples walk through the "cornfields," instead of "grainfields," Matt. 12:1).

Phillips did not anticipate the favorable reception his version would get and for this reason he revised it in 1972, when he noticed that some readers were taking his translation to be authoritative. In this revision, he explains, he has curbed his youthful enthusiasms and has brought the Eng-

---

[13]Robertson, *New Translations*, p. 104.

lish into closer conformity with the Greek text. Also, in this revised version, he switched over from the Greek text of Westcott and Hort to that of the United Bible Societies. Perhaps it is not always as spicy as the first edition, but it is a bit more accurate.

For people who haven't grown up with the church and who are interested in reading the NT, PHILLIPS is certainly one of the best. Such readers may come to confess with C. S. Lewis: "If this book had come into my hands when I first seriously began to try to discover what Christ was, it would have saved me a great deal of labor."

Phillips went on to do the OT, but only Four Prophets (1963) were published before his death.

By the middle of the twentieth century, organizations and denominations took it in hand to provide the churches with revisions of former versions or with new translations. The private modern speech versions had paved the way for such major undertakings but, as we will see, such major revisions and translations did not discourage private individuals from attempting to put God's Word into man's language.

Suggested Reading

Bruce, F. F. **History of the Bible in English,** 3rd ed. New York: Oxford University Press, 1978. See pages 79–185.

Kubo, S. and Specht, W. **So Many Versions?** Grand Rapids: Zondervan, 1975. See pages 1–78.

MacGregor, G. **The Bible in the Making.** New York: Lippincott, 1959. See pages 216–34.

Moule, G. F. D. "English Versions Since 1611," Cambridge History of the Bible, 3 vols. ed. S. L. Greenslade. Cambridge: Cambridge University Press, 1963, Vol. 3, pp. 383–93.

Partridge, A. C. **English Biblical Translation.** London: Andre Deutsch, 1973. See pages 180–228.

Robertson, E. H. **The New Translations of the Bible.** Naperville: Allenson, 1959. See "Modern Versions Before Moffatt," pp. 39–72; "Moffatt," pp. 73–87; "An American Translations," pp. 88–101; "J. B. Phillips," pp. 102–18.

Chapter 18

English Versions
in the Fifties and Sixties

A discussion of all the English versions that were published around the middle of the twentieth century would take us beyond the limited confines of this book. We will mention several of these in passing and then concentrate on three versions of the Bible. In 1934 G. W. Wade had The Documents of the New Testament published. This was a fresh translation of the NT books, arranged in what the translator believed to be their chronological order. The Bible in Basic English was an attempt by Professor S. H. Hooke to render the Hebrew OT and the Greek NT into English, using only about 850 words, with some special "Bible" words added. The NT was published in 1940 and the whole Bible in 1949.[1] For those whose first language is not English this Bible is extremely useful.

Something similar was done by C. K. Williams, who in 1952 published The New Testament: A New Translation in Plain English. It limits itself to a list of 1,500 words common in English. As a missionary educator, first in India and then in Ghana, Williams had considerable experience in teaching people whose first language was not English. Like Wade, he had to resort to a number of "Bible" words, which are then explained in a glossary at the end.[2]

This version should not be confused with The New Testament in the Language of the People, published in America in 1937 by C. B. Williams. He tried to bring out some of the nuances of the Greek tenses—something not always easy to do, since English and Greek verbal uses are not alike.

Kenneth Wuest, of Moody Bible Institute, published a three-volume Expanded Translation of the New Testament (1956–59) in which he attempted not only to bring out the philological nuances of the Greek, but also the theological nuances. Such an expanded translation always runs the

[1]F. F. Bruce, *History of the Bible in English*, 3rd rev. ed. (New York: Oxford University Press, 1978), p. 175.

[2]Bruce, *History of Bible*, p. 177.

SPECIMENS OF THE ENGLISH TRANSLATION OF THE BIBLE
(Heb. 1:1-4)

Tyndale, 1525

1. God in tyme past diversly and many wayes: spake vnto the fathers by prophets: but in these last dayes he hath spoken vnto vs by hys sonne; whom he hath made heyre of all thynges: by whom also he made the worlde. Which sonne beynge the brightnes of his glory, and very ymage off his substaunce, bearynge vppe all thynges with the worde of his power, hath in his awne person pourged oure synnes, and is sytten on the right honde of the maiestie an hye, and is more excellent then the angels in as moche as he hath by inheritaunce obteyned an excellenter name then have they.

Coverdale, 1535

God in tyme past dyuersly and many wayes, spake vnto ye fathers by prophetes, but in these last dayes hath he spoken vnto vs by his sonne, whom he hath made heyre of all thinges, by whom also he made the worlde. Which (sonne) beynge the brightnes of his glory, and the very ymage of his substaunce, bearinge vp all thynges with the worde of his power, hath in his owne personne pourged oure synnes, and is set on the righte hande of the maiestie on hye: beynge even as moch more excellent then the angels, as he hath by inheritaunce obtayned a more excellent name then they.

Matthew, 1537

God in tyme past dyuersly and many wayes spake vnto the fathers by ye Prophetes but in these last dayes he hath spoken vnto vs by hys sonne, whom he hath made heyre of all thinges: by whom also he made ye worlde. Which sonne beynge the brightnes of his glory, and very ymage of hys substaunce, bearynge vp all thynges wyth the worde of hys power, hath in hys awne person purged oure synnes, and is sytten on hye, and is more excellent then the angels, in as moche as he hath by inheritaunce obteyned an excellenter name then haue they.

Great Bible (Cromwell's), 1539

God in tyme past diuersly and many wayes, spake vnto the fathers by Prophetes: but in these last dayes he hath spoken vnto vs by hys awne sonne, whom he hath made heyre of all thinges, by whom also he made the worlde. Whych (sonne) beinge the brightnes of his glory, and the very ymage of hys substaunce rulynge all thynges wyth the worde of hys power, hath by hys awne person pourged oure synnes, and sytteth on the righte hande of the maiestye on hye: beynge so moch more excellent then the angels, as he hath by inheritaunce obteyned a more excellent name then they.

The Geneva Bible, 1560

1. At sondrie times and in diuers maners God spake in ye olde time to our fathers by the Prophetes;
2. In these last dayes he hathe spoken vnto vs by his Sonne, whome he hathe made heir of all things, by whome also he made the worldes,
3. Who being the brightnes of his glorie, and the ingraued forme of his persone, and bearing vp all things by his mightie worde, hath by him self purged our sinnes, and sitteth at the right hand of the maiestie in the highest places,
4. And is made so muche more excellent then the Angels in as muche as he hathe obteined a more excellent name then thei.

The Bishops' Bible, 1568

1. God which in tyme past, at sundrie tymes, and in diuers maners, spake vnto the fathers in the prophetes:
2. Hath in these last dayes, spoken vnto vs in the sonne, whom he hath appointed heyre of all thynges, by whom also he made the worldes.
3. Who beyng the bryghtnesse of the glorie, and the very image of his substaunce, vpholdyng all thynges with the worde of his power, hauing by himselfe pourged our sinnes, hath syt on the ryght hande of the maiestie on hye:
4. Beyng so much more excellent then the Angels, as he hath by inheritaunce obtayned a more excellent name then they.

The Rheims New Testament, 1582

Diversely and many waies in times past God speaking to the fathers in the prophets: last of al in these daies hath spoken to vs in his Sonne, whome he hath appointed heire of al, by whome he made also the worldes. Who being the brightnesse of his glorie, and the figure of his substaunce, and carying al things by the word of his power, making purgation sinnes, sitteth on the right hand of the Maiestie in the high places: being made so much better then the Angels, as he hath inherited a more excellent name aboue them.

The Authorized Version, 1611

1 God who at sundry times, and in diuers manners, spake in time past vnto the Fathers by the Prophets,
2 Hath in these last dayes spoken vnto vs by his Sonne, whom he hath appointed heire of all things, by whom also he made the worlds,
3 Who being the brightnesse of his glory, and the expresse image of his person, and vpholding all things by the word of his power, when hee had by himselfe purged our sinnes, sate down on the right hand of the Maiestie on high,
4 Being made so much better then the Angels, as hee hath by inheritance obtained a more excellent Name then they.

The Revised Version, 1881

God, having of old time spoken unto the fathers in the prophets by divers portions and in divers manners, hath at the end of these days spoken unto us in his Son, whom he appointed heir of all things, through whom also he made the worlds; who being the effulgence of his glory, and the very image of his substance, and upholding all things by the word of his power, when he had made purification of sins, sat down on the right hand of the Majesty on high; having become by so much better than the angels, as he hath inherited a more excellent name than they.

Weymouth, 1902

God who in ancient days spoke to our forefathers in many distinct messages and by various methods through the Prophets, has at the end of these days spoken to us through a Son, who is the predestined Lord of the universe, and through whom He made the Ages. He brightly reflects God's glory and is the exact representation of His being, and upholds the universe by His all-powerful word. After securing man's purification from sin He took His seat at the right hand of the Majesty on high, having become as far superior to the angels as the Name He possesses by inheritance is more excellent than theirs.

Moffatt, 1913

Many were the forms and fashions in which God spoke of old to our fathers by the prophets, but in these days at the end he has spoken to us by a Son — a Son whom he has appointed heir of the universe, as it was by him that he created the world. He, reflecting God's bright glory and stamped with God's own character, sustains the universe with his word of power; when he had secured our purification from sins, he sat down at the right hand of the Majesty on high, and thus he is superior to the angels, as he has inherited a Name superior to theirs.

New American Standard Bible, 1971

1 God, after He spoke long ago to the fathers in the prophets in many portions and in many ways,

2 in these last days has spoken to us in His Son, whom He appointed heir of all things, through whom also He made the world.

3 And He is the radiance of His glory and the exact representation of His nature, and upholds all things by the word of His power. When He had made purification of sins, He sat down at the right hand of the Majesty on high;

4 having become as much better than the angels, as He has inherited a more excellent name than they.

Knox, 1945

In old days, God spoke to our fathers in many ways and by many means, through the prophets; now at last in these times he has spoken to us, with a Son to speak for him; a Son, whom he has appointed heir of all things, just as it was through him that he created this world of time; a Son, who is the radiance of his Father's splendour, and the full expression of his being; all creation depends, for its support, on his enabling word. Now, making atonement for our sins, he has taken his place on high, at the right hand of God's majesty, superior to the angels in that measure in which the name he has inherited is more excellent than theirs.

Revised Standard Version, 1946

In many and various ways God spoke of old to our fathers by the prophets; but in these last days he has spoken to us by a Son, whom he appointed the heir of all things, through whom also he created the world. He reflects the glory of God and bears the very stamp of his nature, upholding the universe by his word of power. When he had made purification for sins, he sat down at the right hand of the Majesty on high, having become as much superior to the angels as the name he has obtained is more excellent than theirs.

Jerusalem Bible, 1966

At various times in the past and in various different ways, God spoke to our ancestors through the prophets; but in our own time, the last days, he has spoken to us through his Son, the Son that he has appointed to inherit everything and through whom he made everything there is. He is the radiant light of God's glory and the perfect copy of his nature, sustaining the universe by his powerful command; and now that he has destroyed the defilement of sin, he has gone to take his place in heaven at the right hand of divine Majesty. So he is now as far above the angels as the title which he has inherited is higher than their own name.

Good News Bible (Today's English Version) 1966

In the past God spoke to our ancestors many times and in many ways through the prophets, but in these last days he has spoken to us through his Son. He is the one through whom God created the universe, the one whom God has chosen to possess all things at the end. He reflects the brightness of God's glory and is the exact likeness of God's own being, sustaining the universe with his powerful word. After achieving forgiveness for the sins of mankind, he sat down in heaven at the right side of God, the Supreme Power.

The Son was made greater than the angels, just as the name that God gave him is greater than theirs.

New English Bible 1970

When in former times God spoke to our forefathers, he spoke in fragmentary and varied fashion through the prophets. But in this final age he has spoken to us in the Son whom he has made heir to the whole universe, and through whom he created all orders of existence: the Son who is the effulgence of God's splendour and the stamp of God's very being, and sustains the universe by his word of power. When he had brought about the purgation of sins, he took his seat at the right hand of Majesty on high, raised as far above the angels, as the title he has inherited is superior to theirs.

Living Bible 1971

Long ago God spoke in many different ways to our fathers through the prophets [in visions, dreams, and even face to face], telling them little by little about his plans.

But now in these days he has spoken to us through his Son to whom he has given everything, and through whom he made the world and everything there is.

God's Son shines out with God's glory, and all that God's Son is and does marks him as God. He regulates the universe by the mighty power of his command. He is the one who died to cleanse us and clear our record of all sin, and then sat down in highest honor beside the great God of heaven.

New International Version, 1973

In the past God spoke to our forefathers through the prophets at many times and in various ways, but in these last days he has spoken to us by his Son, whom he appointed heir of all things, and through whom he made the universe. The Son is the radiance of God's glory and the exact representation of his being, sustaining all things by his powerful word. After he had provided purification for sins, he sat down at the right hand of the Majesty in heaven. So he became as much superior to angels as the name he has inherited is superior to theirs.

New King James Version, 1979

God, who at various times and in different ways spoke in time past to the fathers by the prophets, 2 has in these last days spoken to us by His Son, whom He has appointed heir of all things, by whom also He made the worlds; 3 who being the brightness of His glory and the express image of His person, and upholding all things by the word of His power, when He had by Himself purged our sins, sat down at the right hand of the Majesty on high, 4 having become so much better than the angels, as He has by inheritance obtained a more excellent name than they.

225

risk of reflecting the translator's theological biases, but for readers who do not know Greek, Wuest's expanded translations can be quite helpful.

The Amplified Bible, published between 1958 and 1965, was produced by a committee of twelve, on behalf of the Lockman Foundation in La Habra, California. With the use of curved and square brackets this version is partly translation and partly commentary.

The Watchtower Bible and Tract Society published the NT of the New World Translation in 1950, and the OT in 1953–60. This version reflects the doctrinal biases of the Jehovah's Witnesses. For example, John 1:1 reads, "The Word was a god."

William Barclay, who has the gift of making difficult things easy, and whose commentaries and studies of biblical themes are known the world over, had his New Testament published in two volumes: The Gospels and the Acts of the Apostles (1968) and The Letters and the Revelation (1969). His aim was to make the NT intelligible to the man who is not a technical scholar (the latter can make his own). Also, he wanted to provide a translation that did not need a commentary to explain it—something he admits is really quite impossible. It is a valiant attempt to make the NT speak for itself. Almost as valuable as his translation is the forty-five page Appendix to Volume I in which Barclay discusses the methods and problems of translating the Bible.[3]

All these independent efforts to render the Bible into English were eclipsed by the publication of the Revised Standard Version.

I. THE REVISED STANDARD VERSION

A. The Project

Two major efforts had been made to revise the AV of 1611; one was the ERV of 1881–85, and the other the ASV, done by American scholars in 1901. Both of these versions tried to preserve the language of the King James Version as much as possible, and in the light of the many modern speech versions that had been published since the beginning of the twentieth century, these versions seemed a bit archaic by now. Anyone who reads, for example, 2 Peter 2:3, "And in covetousness shall they with feigned words make merchandise of you," knows he is not reading modern English.

In order to protect the ASV of 1901 against unauthorized changes, it had been copyrighted. In 1928 this copyright, which had been held by Thomas Nelson and Sons, was transferred to the International Council of Religious Education—a council in which some forty major denominations of the United States and Canada are represented. This council appointed a committee of scholars to act as custodians of the text of the ASV.

In 1937 this committee's recommendation that a revision of the ASV should be made, was accepted by the council. This revision was to embody the best results of modern scholarship as to the meaning of the Scriptures, and express this meaning in English designed for both public and private use. At the same time it was to preserve what it could of the language of the King James Version.

---

[3]W. Barclay, "On Translating the New Testament," *The New Testament* (New York: Collins, 1968), pp. 308–52.

REVISIONS OF THE AUTHORIZED VERSION

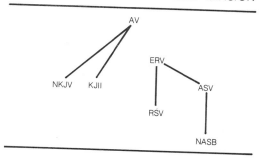

Thirty-two scholars, under the chairmanship of Dean Luther Weigle of Yale, were appointed to the revision committee. James Moffatt, whose version we have already discussed, served as secretary until his death in 1944. In addition to this committee, there was an advisory board of fifty representatives of the cooperating denominations. Among the denominations represented were American Baptists, Church of the Brethren, Church of God, Church of the Nazarene, Evangelical and Reformed, Mennonite Brethren in Christ, Methodists, Lutherans, Presbyterians, Southern Baptist, and others.

The committee was divided into an OT and NT section. Specific books of OT and NT were assigned to scholars in their respective sections who did their work privately. Then, for two weeks in summer and ten days at Christmas the two sections gathered and carefully went over the individual revisions.

The NT was published in 1946, and in 1952 the whole Bible appeared. Since the NT had already circulated for six years before the OT was ready, a number of changes were made in it before the complete Bible was published. A smaller committee was then appointed to prepare a revision of the Apocrypha as well. Since the ASV did not have these books, the revision was made of the Apocrypha published in the AV of 1611 and the ERV of 1895.

B. Principles and Policies

The modernization of English was one of the main purposes of the revision. This meant that "th" was replaced by "s" in endings of the third person singular: "saith" became "says," and "sendeth" became "sends." The long established idiom of Bible English, "and it came to pass," disappeared. The "thou," "thee," "thy," and "thine" were dropped, except where God is addressed. This created some problems in the Gospels where one doesn't always know, when Christ is addressed, whether the speaker thinks of him as divine or not. The revisers decided to use "you" whenever Christ is addressed prior to his ascension, and "thou" after his glorification. This gave critics the occasion to charge the translators with denying the deity of Christ. The matter gets complicated when Paul on the way to Damascus asks, "Who are you, Lord?" (Acts 9:5). Here "you" is retained even after Christ's ascension, since Paul did not know who it was that was speaking to him. One should, however, remember that most European languages do not make this kind of distinction in the second person pronoun when addressing the Deity. In French the familiar "tu" is used when addressing the Deity, and the formal "vous" for human dignitaries. Similarly in German God is addressed as "du" and the formal address is "Sie."

By eliminating the "ye" for the second person plural, English has no way of distinguishing between singular and plural "you," and that can be of significance in translating the Scriptures, but it is something that cannot be helped. When Jesus said, "Simon, Simon, Satan has asked to sift *you* as wheat. But I have prayed for *you*, Simon, that your faith may not fail ..." (Luke 22:31–32), the first two "you's" are plural, and the third is singular, but one cannot know this from the English translation.

Also, it was decided to put direct speech into quotation marks. This calls for interpretation in some passages. Where, for example, does Jesus' dialogue with Nicodemus, recorded in John 3:1ff. end? Should John 3:16 still have quotation marks?

The practice of printing poetical parts of the Bible as poetry has been carried further in the RSV than had been done in the ERV and ASV. In the rendering of the name Yahweh, the RSV discontinued using the word "Jehovah," as the ASV had it, and reverted back to the practice of the AV, giving it as "LORD."

Also, in contrast to the more rigid practice of the ERV of translating the same Hebrew and Greek word by the same English word, the RSV reverts to the practice of the AV in that it uses a variety of synonyms. For example, the Greek adjective *psychikos* is once translated "unspiritual" (1 Cor. 2:14), then as "physical" (1 Cor. 15:44), and as "worldly" (Jude 19). Such a variety of renderings is called for because the same word in different contexts has different meanings. However, it also calls for a measure of interpretation on the part of the translators.

In the OT the RSV is based on the traditional Masoretic Hebrew and Aramaic text. However, the revisers departed from this text on numerous occasions. Where they did, they usually had the support of the ancient versions. Where the Hebrew text was "emended" by the translators, they indicated this with the abbreviation "Cn" (correction) in the footnote. For these corrections they harvested considerable criticism. By 1952 the Isaiah Scroll of the Qumran texts was already available, and so the revisers incorporated thirteen readings from this manuscript in the RSV.

In the NT the revisers did not follow any one particular family of manuscripts and versions, but worked eclectically instead. This means that each variant reading was evaluated on its own merits. Almost all modern versions follow this policy now, but in 1946 this approach was still not accepted by all scholars.

The text of the prose passages was broken up into sense paragraphs as in the ASV, and not into separate verses as in the AV. The numbers of the verses, however, were printed for the sake of convenience.

C. Publication and Reception

Thomas Nelson and Sons agreed to bear the cost of printing and had the exclusive right to print the RSV for the first ten years. The initial edition of the complete version was printed in one million copies. One estimate has it that 1000 tons of paper, 2000 gallons of ink, 10 tons of type metal, and 140 tons of binder's board were needed for the first edition. It is not surprising, then, that the publishers made a survey of Bible reading in America before they undertook such an enormous project.

When the RSV was published in 1952, a United States postage stamp commemorated the five hundredth anniversary of the first Gutenberg Bible. The RSV made the newsreels and all major networks. NBC televised a Gutenberg Bible from its Washington studios.

The response of the readers to this major revision of the English Bible varied. Some praised it highly, others offered constructive criticism, and the revisers incorporated some of the suggested improvements in the 1962 edition.

Most of the criticism, however, was aimed more at the revisers than at the version itself. One minister burned the version with a blowtorch in his pulpit, remarking that like the devil it was hard to burn. He sent the ashes to the chairman of the RSV committee. That, of course, is better than burning the translators, which they did in the days of Tyndale.

Pamphlets entitled: "The Bible of the Antichrist," "The New Blasphemous Bible," and the like, were printed. An editor of a Sunday school publication wrote to Dean Weigle and asked: "Who is this Tom Nelson who has written a new Bible? I don't want Tom Nelson's Bible. I want the Bible the way the Apostle James wrote it." (Presumably he thought King James was the Bible's original author!) One woman began reading the RSV and frankly admitted that she loved it "almost as much as *the Bible*."[4]

Much of the criticism resembled the criticism the AV of 1611 was subjected to when it first appeared: the translators were accused of modernism, of unfaithfulness to the original text, of denying the deity of Christ, and the like. The revisers were charged with denying the "blood" of Jesus, since the phrase, "through his blood," was missing in Colossians 1:14. However, in Ephesians 1:7 the RSV does read, "In him we have redemption through his blood." The reason for the absence of the phrase in Colossians 1:14 is that few of the better manuscripts have it in Colossians 1:14. Since then the NASB and the NIV have been published, and neither of these has this phrase in Colossians 1:14 either. One critic wrote that, "any version of the Bible which omits Acts 8:37 . . . evidently has for its foundation a corrupted text." But NASB

---

[4]G. MacGregor, *The Bible in the Making* (New York: Lippincott, 1959), p. 238.

and NIV do not have this verse either, since the manuscript evidence for it is too weak.

The revisers were also accused of denying the virgin birth, since Isaiah 7:14 reads, "Behold, a young woman shall conceive and bear a son, and shall call his name Immanuel." ("Virgin" appeared in the margin.) It so happens that the Hebrew word *'almah*, used in Isaiah 7:14 may mean virgin, but does not say so explicitly. In Matthew 1:23, where this passage is quoted in Greek, and the word *parthenos* is used, the RSV does have "virgin." Since *'almah* means a young woman of marriageable age, normally in this culture a virgin, the Septuagint translators had rendered it as *parthenos* in Isaiah 7:14. The Jerusalem Bible may have struck upon a happy rendering; it translates *'almah* as "maiden." The doctrine of Christ's virgin birth is upheld in Matthew 1:23.

The charge that the translators had denied the virgin birth was based also on the RSV rendering of John 3:16, "For God so loved the world that he gave his *only* Son." "Only begotten" was the KJV rendering. The fact is that the Greek *monogenes* means "only," and the KJV was influenced more by the Latin of the Vulgate, which had *unigenitus*, than by the Greek. *Monogenēs* is the Greek equivalent of the Hebrew *yahid*, which means "only" or "beloved."

When a committee that is so broadly based and representing so many denominations publishes a revision of the Bible as is the case of the RSV, one would find it hard to fault the version for theological bias. That doesn't mean, however, that a version cannot be improved upon, and the 1962 edition has been improved at a number of places. One of these is Matthew 27:54 (and Mark 15:39), where the earlier, "Truly this (man) was a son of God," now reads "the son of God."

In 1962 Oxford University Press published an annotated RSV with introductions, essays, exegetical footnotes, maps, tables, and the like. Dr. and Mrs. Bruce Metzger of Princeton compiled a concordance to the RSV, also published by the Oxford Press. Costly though it is, every new English version calls for a new concordance.

The sales of the RSV have been phenomenal (twelve million the first ten years) and although it is a Protestant version, it has been officially approved by the Catholic Church as well. Without the publication of the Apocrypha in 1957 this would not have been possible. In 1965 a Catholic edition of the RSV NT, prepared by the Catholic Biblical Association of Great Britain, was published, and in 1966 the entire Bible appeared. At a number of places changes were made in the interests of Catholic doctrine.

Not only has it become the most widely used version in America, but it has also become very popular in England, in spite of the publication of the New English Bible and in spite of the lack of the intensive promotion it was given in North America. A number of commentaries that have appeared in the last few decades are based on the RSV. F. F. Bruce makes bold to say that "for the English-speaking world as a whole there is no modern version of the Bible which comes so near as the R.S.V. does to making the all purpose provision which the A.V. made for so many years."[5] And Robert Mounce

---

[5]Bruce, *History of Bible*, p. 203.

Members of the ʀsᴠ Bible Committee in June 1981 (with two doctoral students from Princeton Seminary who served as recording secretaries) on the steps of Speer Library, Princeton Theological Seminary. Front row from left: Lucetta Mowry; Walter J. Harrelson; William A. Beardslee; Bruce M. Metzger (chairperson); Charles D. Myers, Jr. (student); Robert C. Dentan. Middle row: Bruce Vawter, C.M.; Allen Wikgren; Reginald H. Fuller; George MacRae, S.J.; Harry M. Orlinsky; Delbert R. Hillers; Demetrios J. Constantelos. Back row: Paul S. Minear; James A. Sanders; William A. Holladay; Alfred von Rohr Sauer; J. J. McB. Roberts; Marvin H. Pope; Charles H. Cosgrove (student).

speaks of it as "the best translation in the English language for general use."[6]

The ʀsᴠ Bible Committee is not only a continuing committee, but it has been internationalized by members from Canada and Great Britain. In 1973 this committee published the ʀsᴠ Common Bible. This edition includes not only the Apocrypha accepted by the Roman Catholic Church, but several others included in the Greek Orthodox canon. In conversing with and witnessing to those in the Catholic or Orthodox tradition, such a Bible should prove very valuable.

II. THE MODERN LANGUAGE BIBLE

The Modern Language Bible (ᴍʟʙ) was earlier known as the Berkeley Version. The Berkeley Version was, to begin with, the work of Dr. Gerrit Verkuyl. He had translated the NT and it was published in 1945, after Verkuyl had moved to Berkeley, California.

Zondervan Publishing House then invited him to undertake the OT as well, and so with some twenty scholars working under his chairmanship the complete Bible was published in 1959. A revised Berkeley Version ap-

---

[6]R. Mounce, "Which Bible Is Best for You? *Eternity* Vol. 25 (April, 1974), p. 29.

peared in 1969, and the name was then changed to the Modern Language Bible.

The format of the 1959 version was so similar to that of the RSV, that it appeared to many readers as if it were a conservative counterpart to that version.

The Berkeley Version was not a revision but a new translation. It tended to stick closely to the Hebrew, Aramaic, and Greek, and its English suffered as a consequence. Some rather infelicitous renderings appeared in the 1959 edition. "My face-saver and my God" (Ps. 42:11); "men who sleep in Adamic dust" (Dan. 12:2). Robert Bratcher in his review of this version wrote:

> On the whole the English of this version lacks grace, style and that evident flavor of vernacularity. It is often rather wooden, stilted and stiff. The Berkeley Version is certainly nearer the language of today than the KJV; it is not, however, in this reviewer's opinion good modern vernacular English. Notwithstanding, it would still be useful were it not for the footnotes.[7]

Some of the footnotes are startling indeed. Conservative readers were now informed on the first page of the Bible: "Billions of light years are acceptable to devout Bible students." Genesis 3:12 has this moralism: "Passing the buck is as old as humanity; it shows lack of repentance." And a footnote to Genesis 3:8, where God walks in the cool of the day, reminds the reader that, "the hour of twilight remains a choice season for spiritual recreation—quiet communion." In 1 Samuel 16:23 the reader is advised to read Browning's "Saul," and to see

Rembrandt's "David Before Saul."

In all fairness, however, it should be said that much of this criticism was directed at the Berkeley Version of 1959. The Modern Language Bible of 1969 has removed many of these inadequacies, and is a monument to evangelical scholarship.[8] The Modern Language Bible had too many stiff competitors in the field, and so it has never become very popular.

III. THE NEW ENGLISH BIBLE

A. The Translation Project

The RSV (1952) stood in a long tradition of English Bibles that began with Tyndale (1524). Almost every English Bible is a revision of some existing English version. The New English Bible abandoned this four hundred and twenty-five year tradition. It is not a revision, but a completely new translation.

In 1946, the year in which the RSV of the NT was published in the United States, plans were laid in Britain to produce the New English Bible (NEB). The Church of Scotland took the initiative in approaching other churches, such as the Church of England, the Methodist, Baptist, and Congregational churches, to encourage this new translation. A Joint Committee was formed in 1947 and in 1948 this committee invited other churches as well as the British and Foreign Bible Society and the National Bible Society of Scotland to appoint representatives.

Three panels were assigned to translate respectively the OT, the Apocrypha, and the NT. A group of literary advisers went over the transla-

---

[7]R. Bratcher, *Bible Translator* Vol. 14 (July, 1963), p. 143.

[8]S. Kubo and W. Specht, *So Many Versions?* (Grand Rapids: Zondervan, 1975), p. 87.

tions to check them for English style. Each book, or part of a book, of the Bible was at first entrusted to an individual translator. His first draft was sent to all the members of the appropriate panel, who worked the translation over together with the translator when they met in committee. After thorough revision it went to the literary panel and finally it went to the joint committee, where the ultimate decisions were made.

The first edition of the NT was published in 1961. The complete Bible was ready in 1970 in two editions: a Library Edition in three volumes, and the Standard Edition in one volume, with or without the Apocrypha. Since this version was authorized by the Protestant Churches of the British Isles, it has a status that no private translation can have.

B. The Translation Principles

Professor C. H. Dodd, who was director of the whole project from 1949 until 1965, when Professor G. R. Driver became joint director with him, drew up a memorandum in which the principles that were to guide the translators were given. The English of this new version was to be "timeless," meaning that both archaisms and transient modernisms were to be avoided. There was no thought of preserving "hallowed associations" from former English versions of the Bible, for this was to be a completely new translation. The language was to be such that a reasonably intelligent person could understand it. Also, it was to have sufficient dignity to be read aloud.

At the same time the NEB was to be faithful to the original. To be faithful, it was understood, one had to translate by sense and not word for word. The concern of the translators must be to make the original Hebrew, Aramaic, and Greek intelligible to modern English readers. The hope of the translators was that the NEB not read like a translation at all, but rather like an original composition. The NEB, then, is a meaning-for-meaning translation.

One thing modern translators have to agree on before they begin to translate is the underlying Hebrew and Greek text. The translators of the AV did not worry much about that, for in 1611 it was generally held that there was only one standard text. The ERV of 1881–85 changed that, when the Westcott and Hort text was followed in the NT. Most new versions today are based on an eclectic text in which every major variant reading is weighed and the reading that seems best attested is chosen. The NEB was also based on an eclectic text and the Greek text of the NT was published by Professor R. V. G. Tasker.

In the case of the OT the Hebrew text is frequently emended where the translators thought it was in error. Where the Hebrew was obscure or corrupt in the eyes of the translators they indicated their correction by a footnote. There is considerably more conjectural emendation in the NEB than there was in the RSV.

A few illustrations will show the difference between the underlying text of the NEB and the RSV. In Mark 1:41, where the RSV has "moved with pity," the NEB reads "in warm indignation." The Greek verbs "to pity" or "be angry" look very much alike, and the translators of the NEB held that no scribe would change "pity" to read "anger," but a change in the other direction is likely, for no one wants to see Jesus angry. And so it was felt that "to be angry" was the original meaning. In Matthew 27:16 the NEB gives Bar Abbas the added name "Jesus," whereas the RSV does not. The manuscript evidence for the reading "Jesus Bar Abbas" is weak, but again it is argued that no scribe would give Bar Abbas that sacred name. It is, however, highly possible that a copyist would delete that name. Therefore, so the argument goes, "Jesus" stood in the original text.

Also, the NEB differs from the RSV in that it is a free translation of the meaning of the original; the RSV sticks much more closely to the original words and order of words. "Gird up your loins" becomes "brace yourselves" in the NEB; "Pray have me excused," now reads "please make my apologies"; "braided hair," forbidden by Paul, becomes "elaborate hair styles." Also, Semitisms are removed wherever possible by the NEB and replaced with English idioms. A "child of hell" reads "fit for hell"; "sons of the bridechamber" becomes "the bridegroom's friends"; "children of the kingdom" are "those born to the kingdom." There may be some question about rendering Genesis 1:2 as "a mighty wind" that swept over the surface of the waters, rather than "the Spirit of God" moving over the face of the waters. The Hebrew *ruach* can mean either "wind" or "spirit," and a "wind of God" is taken by the NEB translators to be superlative, hence "mighty wind."

In the OT the word "Lord" will be found frequently printed in capitals, but sometimes in normal type. The significance of this is to distinguish between the Hebrew word "Yahweh"

(LORD) and "Adonai" (Lord). Moffatt had tried to escape this dilemma by rendering "Yahweh" as "the Eternal," but that was based on the view that this Tetragrammaton means simply "He who is"—a view not generally accepted today.[9]

Like the RSV, the NEB uses quotation marks for direct discourse. Also, it preserves the "thou," when the Deity is addressed. It has only one column to the page and the text is divided into sense paragraphs, with the verse numbers in the margin.

As one might have expected, there are Britishisms here and there that American readers will find strange. What does "in spate" mean (Job 40:23)? "They shall beat their swords into mattocks" (Isa. 2:4) means "into plows," we suppose. It is to be expected, of course, that monetary terms should be those used in Britain. For example, "Are not sparrows five for twopence?" (Luke 12:6). Many words, such as sceptre, centre, theatre, have a different spelling than they have in American English.

It is considered good practice to translate the same Greek or Hebrew word by different English words, depending on the context. The NEB follows this practice. But why they would use "congregation" when referring to the *ekklesia* of Antioch (Acts 15:3), and "church" when the Jerusalem *ekklesia* is mentioned (v. 4) is hard to say.

C. The Reception

It cost more to publish the NEB than any other English Bible in England ever had before. Also, it took longer to prepare (twenty-four years). Moreover

---

[9]G. Hunt, *About the New English Bible* (Oxford and Cambridge University Presses, 1970), pp. 48f.

it was the first English Bible commissioned as a cooperative effort of all major Protestant churches; and it was the first major new translation of the Bible into English since Tyndale.

The NT, published in 1961, sold seven million copies before the whole Bible was ready. John Masefield, the Poet Laureate, acclaimed it as a work "greatly planned" and "manfully done," bringing to life that which slept. T. S. Eliot, on the other hand, thought it was a work of "dignified mediocrity." One wonders whether it would have been understood by the average person if T. S. Eliot had done the translating. As it is, many terms in the NEB will send the reader to his dictionary. Professor Henry Chadwick has called it "the Bible for the beat generation." If that is so, then Britain's beat generation is quite sophisticated.

In view of the many churches represented, this version could hardly be charged with denominational bias. However, some critics see in renderings such as "You are Peter, the Rock; and on this rock I will build my church" (Matt. 16:18), a Romanizing tendency. All the translators wanted to do was to bring out the assonance between the Greek words for "Peter" (petros) and "rock" (petra).

More criticism of the NEB has come from English stylists than from biblical scholars. On the whole, it is a brilliant piece of work. Kubo and Specht say:

> The translators have done a careful work on the basis of their theory of translation. The NEB breathes new life and vigor into the sacred text. It helps to clothe the Scriptures with words that are meaningful and colorful today. Even so, the American reader, at least, will find it necessary to refer occasionally to his dictionary of the English language.[10]

No version can make the Hebrew and Greek text of the Bible perfectly plain, but the NEB will take the reader a long way in grasping the message of the Bible. F. F. Bruce speaks of it as "a brilliant achievement, with some of the defects that accompany brilliance."[11] Gerald Hawthorne of Wheaton College describes it as "bold, imaginative, exciting. Based on most accurate up-to-date linguistic, textual, historical information."[12] The NEB is certainly a high water mark in Bible translation.

---

[10]Kubo and Specht, *So Many,* p. 162.
[11]F. F. Bruce, "Which Bible Is Best for You?" *Eternity* Vol. 25 (April, 1974), p. 29.
[12]G. Hawthorne, "Which Bible Is Best for You?" *Eternity* Vol. 25 (April, 1974), p. 29.

SUGGESTED READING

Bruce, F. F. **History of the Bible in English,** *3rd ed. New York: Oxford University Press, 1978. See pages 186–234.*

Kubo, S. and Specht, W. **So Many Versions?** *Grand Rapids: Zondervan, 1975. See pages 79–162.*

Lewis, J. P. **The English Bible/From KJV to NIV.** *Grand Rapids: Baker, 1982. See "The Revised Standard Version after Twenty-five Years," pp. 107–128; "The New English Bible," pp. 129–65.*

MacGregor, G. **The Bible in the Making.** *New York: Lippincott, 1959. See pages 235–73.*

Price, I. M. **The Ancestry of Our English Bible,** *3rd ed. revised by W. A. Irwin and Allen P. Wikgren. New York: Harper and Row, 1956. See "The Revised Standard Version," pp. 205–320.*

Chapter 19

Versions of the English Bible in the Seventies

So many versions of the English Bible were competing for readers at the beginning of the seventies that people were calling for a moratorium on new translations for at least a decade. Nevertheless, the seventies witnessed the publication of some outstanding English versions. Some of these were long in the making and actually had their beginnings in earlier decades. In this chapter we want to comment on several major versions that were published in the past decade.

So far we have said little about English versions produced by Roman Catholic scholars, and perhaps that is a good place to begin. The Douai-Rheims-Challoner version was the standard English Bible for Roman Catholics well into the twentieth century, although other versions produced by Catholic scholars appeared from time to time. Ronald Knox, in 1949, published a lively translation of the Latin Vulgate (NT in 1945). But when the Pope granted Catholic scholars permission to translate from the original Hebrew and Greek, enthusiasm for producing new and accurate versions sprang to life. We want to mention two major Catholic versions of the English Bible that were published as complete Bibles about the beginning of the seventies.

I. RECENT ROMAN CATHOLIC VERSIONS

A. Jerusalem Bible

This version (JB) has the distinction of being the first complete Catholic Bible translated into English from the original languages. Previously, all translations in the Catholic Church were made from the Latin Vulgate.

The JB owes its inception to the Dominican School of Bible and Archaeology in Jerusalem, which from 1948 onwards, under the leadership of Roland De Vaux, produced the French La Bible de Jérusalem in a series of volumes with textual notes. A one-volume edition of the whole work, with the notes abridged appeared in 1956. The Jerusalem Bible is the English counterpart of this French version, prepared by Catholic scholars under the leadership of Alexander Jones, of Christ's College, Liverpool. Among the notables working on this translation was J. R. Tolkien, author of *The Lord of the Rings.* The English version of the Jerusalem Bible was published in 1966.

The notes to the books of the Bible have been translated from the French version, but the JB is not simply a translation of the French JB. The translation of the English JB was done from the Hebrew and the Greek. The JB has much that will commend itself to both Catholics and Protestants, although some of the notes will probably offend Protestants. For example, the brothers of Jesus in Matthew 12:46, are said to be "not Mary's children, but near relations, cousins perhaps." A footnote on Matthew 1:24 states, "The text is not concerned with the period that followed and, taken by itself, does not assert Mary's perpetual virginity which, however, the gospels elsewhere suppose and which the Tradition of the Church affirms." A footnote to Matthew 16:18 reads, "The keys have become the traditional insignia of Peter." Because of the many notes, this Bible of 2,062 pages weighs just under five pounds. The Apocrypha, as they are called by Protestants, are found where they stand in the Septuagint and Vulgate. The text is printed in sense paragraphs and in one column per page.

A courageous break with tradition is seen in its use of "Yahweh" for the ineffable name, instead of the hybrid form "Jehovah," or the more common translation into English as "Lord." Also, the names of biblical characters are given in the form usually found in Protestant Bibles. In addition it has the "Sea of Reeds" for the Hebrew *Yam Suph*, instead of the "Red Sea."

The English of the JB is considerably freer than that of the RSV. The JB contains more poetry than any other English version. It is of such high quality that many Protestants use it with great profit. To give just a taste of this translation we give the JB's rendering of a familiar passage: "Do not model yourselves on the behavior of the world around you, but let your behavior change, modelled by your new mind. This is the only way to discover the will of God and know what is good, what it is that God wants, what is the perfect thing to do" (Rom. 12:2).

B. The New American Bible

If the English Protestant NEB was a sort of counterpart to the American RSV, the New American Bible (NAB) was the American Catholic counterpart to the English JB. Although the NAB was produced by the Catholic Church, several Protestant scholars were asked to assist in the project.

The NAB was in the making for several decades and was known originally as The Confraternity Version. The NT part was published in 1941, and in 1969 the OT was completed (including the Apocrypha). Since the NT had originally been done from the Vulgate (prior to the Pope's encyclical in 1943, permitting translation from the original languages), it now had to be retranslated from the Greek, and so the finished product of NAB was published in 1970.

This Bible has introductions to each book of the Bible. The text is set out in paragraph form with verse numbers in small type. At the end of the Bible is an article on divine revelation, a glossary of biblical terms, and a survey of biblical geography with some maps. The footnotes are fewer in number and less Catholic in nature than those of the JB. A footnote to John 21:15ff. has it that "The First Vatican Council cited this verse in defining that the risen Jesus gave Peter the jurisdiction of supreme shepherd and ruler over the whole flock." Unlike the JB the NAB prefers "Lord" to "Yahweh."

The English of the NAB is smooth, but not as colorful as that of the NEB. It is faithful to the original, but not in the word-for-word sense. Some renderings are striking: "In your prayers do not rattle on like the pagans" (Matt. 6:7); "The mouth speaks whatever fills the mind" (Matt. 12:34); "you ... leave the inside filled with loot and lust" (Matt. 23:25). Unfortunately it translates *agapē* by "charity." It translates the same Hebrew or Greek word in a variety of ways in different context. For example, the Greek *makarios* is given once as "blest," then as "happy," or "fortunate" or "pleased." The word *basileia* is given as "kingdom," "reign," "kingship," "dominion," and "nation."

The entire work is a remarkable achievement.[1]

II. THE NEW AMERICAN STANDARD BIBLE

The Lockman Foundation, a non-profit Christian corporation of La Habra, California, published the Gospel of John in 1960. This was followed by the four Gospels in 1962, the NT in 1963, and the entire Bible in 1971. This Bible is known as the New American Standard Bible (NASB)—also called the New American Standard Version (NASV).

The Lockman Foundation was concerned that the ASV of 1901, that "monumental product of applied scholarship, assiduous labor and thorough procedure," as the revisers speak of it, was fast disappearing from the scene. The Foundation felt called to rescue this noble version from inevitable demise.

A group of some sixteen men worked on each Testament. The twofold purpose of the editors was (1) to adhere to the original languages of the Bible, and (2) at the same time to obtain a fluent and readable style of current English.

For the NT the twenty-third edition of the Nestle Greek NT was followed in most cases, and this called for a number of changes in the ASV of 1901. For the OT, which was published in 1971, after about ten years of work, the revisers followed the latest edition of Kittel's Biblia Hebraica, correcting it only occasionally.

Instead of having sense paragraphs, as in the ASV and many other modern versions, the NASB reverts back to the pattern of AV in that each verse is printed as a separate unit. Like RSV it has dropped the "thou," "thee," and "thy," except when the Deity is addressed; and the pronouns when referring to the Deity are capitalized (an unnecessary innovation).

In the NT the NASB was concerned to bring out the difference between the Greek imperfect and aorist tenses. This often makes the English rather pedantic. Would a good English writer say: "And He was teaching them many things in parables, and was saying to them in His teaching ..." (Mark 4:2–3)?

---

[1] S. Kubo and W. Specht, *So Many Versions?* (Grand Rapids: Zondervan, 1975), p. 171.

Many imperfects are interpreted as "inceptive": "Now Jesus *started* on His way with them" (Luke 7:6). Where the "historical present" is used (i.e., the present tense for a past event), this is indicated by the use of asterisks. This is an attempt to convey the Greek but it is not really good English.

One point at which the NASB departed from the ASV is in the use of "LORD" instead of "Jehovah" for the Tetragrammaton YHWH. The Semitic idiom "and it came to pass," has been slightly modernized to read, "and it came about" or "and it happened."

A practice, begun by the Geneva Bible, is continued by the NASB, namely to put words that are not in the original, but that are necessary to make the sense clear in English, in italics. The NASB, however, has not been consistent in this practice.

The NASB represents a conservative and somewhat literal approach to translation. In its concern to be accurate, it has failed to be idiomatic and fluent. Kubo and Specht observe that, "Its stilted and nonidiomatic English will never give it a wide popular appeal. It does, however, have great value as a study Bible, and this is perhaps its significant place as a translation."[2] F. F. Bruce makes the interesting comment: "If the R.S.V. had never appeared, this revision of the A.S.V. would be a more valuable work than it is. As things are, there are few things done well by the N.A.S.B. which are not done better by the R.S.V."[3] Dr. Bratcher of the American Bible Society writes: "The NASV language is not really contemporary, the English is not idiomatic, and one wonders whether the revisors have reached their goals of making this Bible 'understandable to the masses'."[4]

It is, however, widely used among evangelical Christians in America.

III. THE LIVING BIBLE

Kenneth Taylor had for years felt the need of having a Bible in modern understandable English. He noticed when he conducted family worship that his children were often puzzled by the strange English of the KJV. He tried, therefore, to explain the passages in simple, everyday English that they could understand. This led to his first systematic attempt, in 1956, to produce a written paraphrase of an entire book of Scripture. He did this

Kenneth N. Taylor, President of Tyndale House Publishers. Dr. Taylor produced The Living Bible, a paraphrase of Scripture.

---

[2]Kubo and Specht, *So Many*, p. 179.

[3]F. F. Bruce, *History of the Bible in English,* 3rd rev. ed. (New York: Oxford University Press, 1978), p. 259.

[4]R. Bratcher, "Old Wine in New Wineskins," *Christianity Today* Vol. 23 (October 8, 1971), p. 16.

while riding the commuter train between his home in Wheaton and his office in Chicago, where he worked at Moody Press.

In 1959 Moody Press published his Romans for the Children's Hour. This was followed in 1962 with Living Letters. To begin with he couldn't get a publisher for these, so he printed 2000 copies on his own and took them to the Christian Booksellers Convention. Orders came slowly, but in 1963 Billy Graham, while confined to a hospital in Hawaii, read Living Letters, and ordered 50,000 for his television audience. The response was so overwhelming that Taylor eventually left Moody Press and launched his own Tyndale House publishing firm.

In 1965 Living Prophecies appeared, the Living Gospels, in 1966, and the Living New Testament, in 1967. The complete Living Bible (LB) came from the press in 1971. The translation of the entire Bible had taken him fifteen years (part-time)—seven on the NT and eight more on the OT.

Taylor's goal was to paraphrase, and the basic text for this paraphrase was the ASV of 1901. In one sense all translations are paraphrases. If one tries to restate the original author's thought in a different language, one has to paraphrase. For example, the French salutation, *Comment vous portez-vous*, if translated literally into English would be, "how do you carry yourself?" But the English equivalent is, "How do you do?" That is paraphrase, but it is also a reasonably exact translation. The question is, how far one takes the paraphrase. Moreover, if one paraphrases an already existing English version of the Bible, as Taylor did, one is paraphrasing a paraphrase, for the ASV is already, in one sense, a paraphrase of the Hebrew, Aramaic, and Greek of the original text. Taylor did, however, seek the assistance of Hebrew and Greek specialists, for he was concerned about accuracy also, and not just about the English.

In his preface, Taylor admits that there are dangers in paraphrasing, and where the Hebrew and Greek were not clear, the theology of the translator along with his sense of logic was his guide. "The theological lodestar in this book has been a rigid evangelical position." One cannot fault Taylor for this theological position, but a good translator keeps his theology out of the translation. To have a "rigid evangelical position" calls, above everything else, for faithfulness to the original text—something that Taylor does not always accomplish.

"This generation shall not pass away until all these things be accomplished" (Mark 13:30) may not be an easy text to explain, but Taylor's "Yes, these are the events that will signal the end of the age," bears hardly any similarity to the original wording (nor meaning, for that matter). In order to make OT passages apply to the modern state of Israel, he even uses the term "Israelis": "The Lord will have mercy on the Israelis; they are his special ones" (Isa. 14:1). He renders Zephaniah 3:8, "at that time I will change the speech of my returning people to pure Hebrew" (but the Hebrew text has simply "pure speech"). In Romans 4:9 circumcision is described as "keeping the Jewish rules." However, circumcision was commanded by God. John 1:17 is particularly infelicitous: "For Moses gave us only the law with its rigid demands and merciless justice, while Christ brought us loving forgiveness as well."

Is that really what the text says?

On occasion Taylor will use rather current euphemisms. For example, Eglon's servants thought "that perhaps he was using the bathroom" (Judg. 3:24). Then again, Taylor resorts to vulgar expressions (see 1 Sam. 20:30 in the first edition).

Perhaps Bruce is right when he speaks of the LB as a "simplified Bible for children,"[5] for to render the profound expression "the righteousness of God" simply as "a different way to heaven," may satisfy children, but is hardly adequate for adult Bible readers.

Some evangelical Christians react very negatively to a paraphrased Bible. In spite of its great popularity, an evangelist in North Carolina recently led students of a Christian high school in a Bible burning ceremony. The Living Bible, explained the evangelist, was a "perverted commentary on the King James Version," and so, together with rock-and-roll records, the Living Bible was publically burned.[6]

However, the LB is very popular today. Some twenty-five million copies have been sold by now. This is due largely to its English. Carl F. Henry writes, "Those who prefer to read the Bible in the language and style of the morning paper or of television newscasting will feel fully at home with the Living Bible."[7] Dr. La Sor of Fuller Seminary comments: "For just enjoying Bible reading this is great, but for serious Bible study it is insufficient."[3]

It is available today in many editions: hardback, red letter, self-help, indexed, reference, large print, leather, for children and young people, and special Catholic editions. For people who do not know "Bible English" the LB can bring home the message of Scripture in terms they can understand.

IV. THE GOOD NEWS BIBLE

A. The Publication

In 1966 the American Bible Society published a modern speech version of the NT, called Good News for Modern Man: The New Testament in Today's English Version (TEV). Its popularity was so great that a year later (1967) a second edition was published. This edition had already incorporated many changes in style and substance. Further improvements were made and in 1971 a third edition appeared. During the first six years of its existence some thirty-five million copies were sold worldwide,[9] and by the time the OT was ready, fifty million copies had been sold.

The OT part of the TEV has now also been completed, and together with the fourth edition of the NT the entire Bible was published in 1976 as the Good News Bible (GNB). Because of differences between British and American English, separate editions were prepared. Since then the GNB has appeared in several other languages.

Dr. Robert Bratcher, assisted by others, did the translation of the NT. For the OT the American Bible Society appointed a group of seven translators, all of whom had doctorates in

---

[5]F. F. Bruce, "Which Bible Is Best for You?" *Eternity* Vol. 25 (April 1974), p. 29.
[6]"Living Bible Burned," *Christian Century* Vol. 98 (July 1981), p. 696.
[7]C. F. Henry, "The Living Bible," *Christianity Today* Vol. 25 (Sept. 4, 1981), p. 98.
[8]W. La Sor, "Which Bible Is Best for You?" *Eternity* Vol. 25 (April 1974), p. 29.
[9]Kubo and Specht, *So Many*, p. 140.

They all ate and had enough. (9.17)

9 Herod said, "I had John's head cut off; but who is this man I hear these things about?" And he kept trying to see Jesus.

Jesus Feeds Five Thousand Men
(Matthew 14.13-21; Mark 6.30-44; John 6.1-14)

10 The apostles came back and told Jesus everything they had done. He took them with him, and they went off by themselves to a town named Bethsaida. 11 When the crowds heard about it, they followed him. He welcomed them, spoke to them about the Kingdom of God, and healed those who needed it.

12 When the sun was beginning to set, the twelve disciples came to him and said, "Send the people away so that they can go to the villages and farms around here and find food and lodging, because this is a lonely place."

13 But Jesus said to them, "You yourselves give them something to eat."

They answered, "All we have are five loaves and two fish. Do you want us to go and buy food for this whole crowd?" 14 (There were about five thousand men there.)

Jesus said to his disciples, "Make the people sit down in groups of about fifty each."

15 After the disciples had done so, 16 Jesus took the five loaves and two fish, looked up to heaven, thanked God for them, broke them, and gave them to the disciples to distribute to the people. 17 They all ate and had enough, and the disciples took up twelve baskets of what was left over.

Peter's Declaration about Jesus
(Matthew 16.13-19; Mark 8.27-29)

18 One day when Jesus was praying alone, the disciples came to him. "Who do the crowds say I am?" he asked them.

19 "Some say that you are John the Baptist," they answered. "Others say that you are Elijah, while others say that one of the prophets of long ago has come back to life."

20 "What about you?" he asked them. "Who do you say I am?"

Peter answered, "You are God's Messiah."

9.19 Mt 14.1-2; Mk 6.14-15; Lk 9.7-8. **9.20** Jn 6.68-69.

This page from the Good News Bible is typical of its contemporary design and art.

biblical studies and who had been (with one exception) missionaries in other lands. These worked under the chairmanship of Dr. Bratcher. A British consultant appointed by the British and Foreign Bible Society participated in this undertaking.

The preface to the GNB explains that this version is prepared both for those who speak English as their mother tongue as well as those who have acquired the English language. It is a distinctly new translation and does not conform to traditional vocabulary or style, but seeks to express the meaning of the original text in words and forms accepted by English-speaking people everywhere.

The version uses a limited vocabulary simple grammatical constructions, short sentences, and common language. Where possible it uses modern equivalents for such cultural items as Jewish instructions and customs, weights, measures, money, and hours of the day. That means it often uses terms not found in the original Greek. Since the English of the version was to be universal, the translators have avoided colloquialisms and, as much as possible, Americanisms. Idioms that are usually understood only in one language, are also avoided.

The NT was first marketed as a paperback, and illustrated by line drawings by Mlle. Annie Vallotton, a Swiss artist living in Paris. Now the entire Bible is available with line drawings. A word list at the end of the NT explains technical terms and rare words. It also has a fine set of maps.

Modern printing format is followed; verse numbers are placed in the text to enable readers to locate them. The text itself is divided not into verses but into relatively short paragraphs with headings to identify the content of each section.

From this description one can already gather some of the principles of translation that guided the translators.

B. The Policies

For the OT the translators used the third edition of Kittel's Biblia Hebraica as their basic text. In some cases emendations were made or the ancient versions were followed. Such departures from the Hebrew text are always indicated in the footnotes. In the case of the NT, the basic text was the third edition of The Greek New Testament, published by the United Bible Societies (1975).

The first aim of the translators was to provide an accurate rendering of the original Hebrew, Aramaic, and Greek into English. All aids available were used to establish the original meaning—something not always possible, of course. After establishing as carefully as possible the original meaning, the translators tried to express this in simple English. Obviously, then, this is not a word-for-word translation. Rather, the translation is based on the principle of "dynamic equivalence." The translator seeks to give the "sense" of the original in such a way that the present readers are stimulated to react to the message in the same way the biblical author hoped his first readers would respond. This is naturally a goal that can be achieved only approximately. "Dynamic equivalence" is the golden mean between a paraphrase and a translation in which we have simply a word correspondence. It is a meaning-for-meaning translation.

The translator wants to be true to

the message of the original text, but makes no attempt to translate the Hebrew and Greek words by English equivalents. The question is: "How would the original author have said this if he had spoken English?" In one sense this is not a novel view of translating, since Martin Luther followed a similar principle when he translated the Bible into his native German.

Besides being true to the sense of the original, the translators aimed at using commonly spoken English, avoiding both slang and elitist terms. A special concern of the translators was to use a language that non-Christians, who are unfamiliar with "Bible English," could understand. To show the difference in English between the RSV and GNB, let us note the following: "mad" is changed to "crazy" (1 Cor. 14:23); "pillars" of the church are "leaders" (Gal. 2:9); "to ask for alms" becomes "to ask for money" (Acts 3:8); "blasphemy" is "to talk against God" (Matt. 9:3); "redeemed" is "to set free" (Luke 1:68). In the OT, Noah's ark is a "boat" (Gen. 6:14); Moses' ark of bulrushes is a "basket made of reeds" (Exod. 2:3); the mercy-seat is "the lid on the Covenant Box" (Lev. 16:2); the Ethiopians of Psalm 68:31 become "the Sudanese." "Caesar" becomes "Emperor," "centurion" becomes "army officer," "publicans" are "tax-collectors," the "sanhedrin" is the "Council."

Technical religious terms are also recast. "Bishops" are "church leaders," "deacons" are "church helpers," "mammon" is "money." Where it was not feasible to give modern equivalents, the biblical words are explained in the glossary at the back.

People not used to theological lan-

guage will appreciate the fact that "repent" is translated at times as "turn away from your sins." To be "justified" is "to be put right with God." "Reconciliation" is "changing us from God's enemies into his friends." "Propitiation" is "the means by which our sins are forgiven." The word "destruction" is occasionally rendered as "hell," as in the case of Peter, who tells Simon Magus, "May you and your money go to hell" (Acts 8:20).

A special problem for translators is the handling of figures of speech and idioms. "The finger of God" now becomes "God's power" (Luke 11:20); "cut to the heart" is changed to "deeply troubled" (Acts 2:37); "He does not bear the sword in vain" becomes "his power to punish is real"; "a wide door" is a "real opportunity" (1 Cor. 16:9).

Semitisms are also erased: "Son of peace" is a "peace-loving man" (Luke 10:6); "daughter of Abraham" becomes a "descendant of Abraham" (Luke 13:16); "Father of glory" is "glorious Father" (Eph. 1:17); "children of the flesh" are "children born in the usual way" (Gal. 4:22–23). Amos's "for three transgressions of Damascus, and for four," becomes "the people of Damascus have sinned again and again" (Amos 1:3). The "Preacher" of Ecclesiastes becomes the "Philosopher" (Eccl. 1:1).

C. The Reception

Dr. Eugene Nida, who played a major role in the production of the Good News Bible, tells of a man in the southern states who was warned that he would be shot if he kept on distributing the GNB.[10] Fortunately, the re-

---

[10]E. A. Nida, *Good News for Everyone* (Waco: Word, 1977), p. 11.

sponse by and large has been overwhelmingly positive. A little girl, after reading the GNB, exclaimed, "Mommy, it must not be the Bible—I can understand it."[11]

For the first two weeks after the GNB appeared it was a celebrity in America. All three national TV networks carried stories on this version. More than a thousand newspapers in the country carried articles on it.

But attacks on the GNB were not slow in coming either. The translators were charged with denying the virgin birth because Luke 1:27 reads, "He had a message for a girl promised in marriage to a man named Joseph." However, in Luke 1:34 Mary says, "I am a virgin." So the charge is unfounded. The word "virgin" was often used in those days for unmarried girls, as in Matthew 25:1ff., where the kingdom of heaven is said to be like ten "virgins." Where virginity is in question, there the GNB has "virgin," but where the reference is to unmarried girls, it does not.

The charge was made also that the translators denied the "blood," for the GNB renders Ephesians 1:7, "For by the death of Christ we are set free." The "precious blood of Christ" by which we are redeemed is given in this form: "By the costly sacrifice of Christ, who was like a lamb without defect or spot" (1 Peter 1:19). "Blood" is understood as a metaphor for "death." One can illustrate this from a passage where the atonement is not in focus: "Whose blood Pilate had spilled" (Luke 13:1), is given as, "whom Pilate had killed." No one should object to that rendering, for to spill someone's blood is to kill

him. And to be redeemed by Christ's blood means to be rescued by his death.

Also, the translators were accused of denying the deity of Christ. Where the KJV reads: "Joseph and his mother knew not of it" (Luke 2:43), TEV has, "His parents did not know this." The objection to the word "parents," however, is without foundation, for the Greek in fact has "parents." It was an error on the part of the King James translators to substitute "Joseph and his mother" for "parents" (Greek: *goneis*).

Like other versions, the GNB has its weaknesses, but on the whole it is superbly done. It is both highly readable and accurate. One should not be fooled by its unpretentiousness, for it is, as Ramsey Michaels of Gordon-Conwell Seminary writes, "on balance the best and most accurate English translation of the NT" (he speaks only of the NT, since the OT was not yet published at the time).[12]

V. THE NEW INTERNATIONAL VERSION

A. Initiation and Publication

In the early 1950s some evangelical scholars, who were acutely aware of the archaic language of the KJV, began to envision a version of the Bible in modern English that would do for our day what the KJV did for its day. It was to be a version that could be used in public worship, for private study, and for memorization as well.

The Christian Reformed Church took the initiative by appointing a committee to find an existing version that would be acceptable to all the

---

[11]Nida, *Good News*, p. 10.

[12]R. Michaels, "Which Bible Is Best for You?" *Eternity* Vol. 25 (April 1974), p. 30.

churches of this denomination. When this failed, they appealed to the National Association of Evangelicals for help, and preliminary plans were made in 1961 to prepare a new translation. In 1965 representatives of a number of denominations met and agreed that there was still a need for a good Bible version in contemporary English. The project received new impetus when the New York Bible Society agreed to sponsor such a version financially.

The governing body of the project consisted of fifteen biblical scholars with Dr. Edwin Palmer as chairman. About one hundred scholars were invited to participate in the translation work. Originally the name was to be A Contemporary Translation, but since some of the translators lived in Canada, England, Australia, and New Zealand, the version came to be called the New International Version (NIV).

The initial translation of each book of the Bible was the work of a small team of scholars who met in places convenient to them, and then submitted their work to an Intermediate Editorial Committee. From here the translation was sent to the Editorial Committee, which again checked it carefully for accuracy. Then it went to stylists and other critics from all walks of life for review and suggestions. The executive Committee, a permanent body of fifteen members, made the final decisions before it was sent to the printer.

As for format, the NIV has the text in sense—rather than verse—paragraphs. The type is large and easily legible. The footnotes are mostly of an explanatory nature. Brackets are used occasionally for words not in the original but called for to make the sense

The late Edwin H. Palmer served as chairman of the committee that produced the New International Version.

plain. It no longer uses "thou," "thee," and "thine" in reference to the Deity.

For the OT the translators used the latest edition of Kittel's Biblia Hebraica, and where the reading of the Hebrew was doubtful the ancient versions were consulted. The Greek text for the NT was an eclectic one. Where the manuscripts differ, the translators had to come to a consensus on which reading to follow. Generally, they followed the text that now appears in the current Greek New Testament.

The project turned out to be very costly and at times it seemed as if the Bible Society, which changed its name to New York International Bible Society, would go bankrupt. Zondervan, who was to be the publisher, advanced some monies, and with the contribution of private donors the work was completed.

The NT of the NIV was ready in 1973, and in 1978 the OT together with the NT was printed as the New Interna-

THE GREEK TEXTS BEHIND MODERN TRANSLATIONS

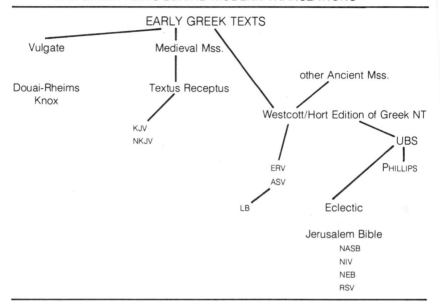

tional Version. Hodder and Stoughton printed the British edition of the NIV.

B. The Quality of the Version

A version is always judged on the basis of faithfulness to the original text and on its readability. The NIV has achieved both of these goals reasonably well. It is both accurate and clear. While the language may not be as colorful as that of Phillips or the NEB, it is more modern than that of the RSV. The RSV, of course, was a revision of the ASV, whereas the NIV is a completely new translation.

F. F. Bruce writes of this version: "An admirable version, combining fidelity to the NT text with sensitivity to modern usage. The avowedly conservative stance of the translators has not resulted in any bias in their work; it has rather enhanced the sense of responsibility with which they have undertaken their task."[13] Robert Mounce says it's "a sort of evangelical RSV . . . [which] may become the all-purpose translation for evangelical churches in spite of the plethora of recent modern speech versions."[14] When a student asked Dr. La Sor of Fuller Seminary why the NIV had been published, he answered somewhat facetiously, "So evangelicals won't have to use the RSV."[15] He goes on to say that the NIV does not have the freshness of the GNB or the high style of the NEB, nor the stilted style of the NAB.[16]

The NIV is undoubtedly a monument to evangelical scholarship and one of the best all-purpose Bibles available to English-speaking Christians.

---

[13]Bruce, "Which Bible," p. 28.

[14]Mounce, "Which Bible," p. 29.

[15]W. La Sor, "What Kind of Version Is the New International?" *Christianity Today* Vol. 23 (October 20, 1978), p. 18.

[16]La Sor, "What Kind of Version," p. 18.

SUGGESTED READING

Bruce, F. F. History of the Bible in English, *3rd ed. New York: Oxford University Press, 1978. See pages 235–68.*

Kubo, S. and Specht, W. So Many Versions? *Grand Rapids: Zondervan, 1975. See pages 163–99.*

Lewis, J. P. The English Bible/From KJV to NIV. *Grand Rapids: Baker, 1981. See "The Jerusalem Bible," pp. 199–214; "The New American Bible," pp. 215–28; "The New American Standard Bible," pp. 165–98; "The Living Bible Paraphrased," pp. 237–60; "The Good News Bible" pp. 261–92; "The New International Version," pp 293–328.*

TWENTIETH-CENTURY ENGLISH TRANSLATIONS

1900   Hayman's Epistles, London
1901   The American Standard Version, New York
1901   Modern American Bible, New York
1901   Moffatt's Historical New Testament, Edinburgh
1901   Way's Epistles, London
1901   Young People's Bible, Philadelphia
1902   Rotherham's Emphasized Bible, New York
1902   Twentieth Century New Testament, New York
1903   Fenton's Bible, London
1903   Weymouth's New Testament, London
1904   Worrell's New Testament, Louisville
1905   Lloyd's New Testament, London
1907   Moulton's Modern Reader's Bible, New York
1908   Rutherford's Epistles, London
1909   The Bible in Modern English, Perkiomen, Pennsylvania
1909   Weaver New Testament, Philadelphia
1912   Improved Bible Union Version, Philadelphia
1914   Numeric New Testament, New Haven
1914   Cunnington's New Testament, London
1917   The Holy Scriptures According to the Masoretic Text, Philadelphia
1918   Anderson New Testament, Cincinnati
1921   Shorter Bible, New York
1922   Plainer Bible, Jersey City
1923   Riverside New Testament, Boston
1924   Montgomery's Centenary Translation, Philadelphia
1925   People's New Covenant, Monrovia, California
1925   Children's Bible, New York
1926   Moffatt, New York, London (NT, 1913)
1927   Kent's Student's Old Testament, New York
1927   The Bible: An American Translation, Chicago
1928   Christian's Bible, Strasburg, Pennsylvania
1932   Chaplain Ballentine, Collegeville, Pennsylvania
1933   Torrey's Four Gospels, New York, London
1934   Royd's Epistles and Gospels, Oxford
1934   Old Testament in Colloquial English
1934   Wade, London
1935   Westminster Version
1937   Greber's New Testament, New York
1937   Martin's New Testament, Nashville
1937   Spencer's New Testament, New York
1937   Williams's New Testament, Chicago
1938   Book of Books, London
1938   Clementson's New Testament, Pittsburgh
1940   Dakes's Gospels, Chicago
1944   Wand's New Testament Letters, Brisbane, Australia
1945   Stringfellow's New Testament, Dubuque
1946   Lenski, Columbus
1946   Revised Standard Version: New Testament, New York, Toronto, Edinburgh
1947   Swann's New Testament, Louisville
1948   Letchworth New Testament, Letchworth, U.K.
1949   Basic Bible, Cambridge
1951   Authentic Version, Plattsburg, Missouri
1952   New Testament in Plain English, London
1952   Rieu's Penguin Bible, London
1952   Revised Standard Version: Old Testament, New York, Toronto, Edinburgh

1954	Kleist and Lilly's New Testament, Milwaukee
1954	Moore's New Testament, Chevy Chase, Maryland
1955	Knox, London
1955	Schonfield's Authentic New Testament, London
1956	Laubach's Inspired Letters, New York
1957	Concordant Version, Los Angeles
1957	Lamsa's, The Holy Bible, Philadelphia
1958	Hudson, London
1958	Meissner's Gospels, Portland
1958	Phillips's New Testament, New York
1958	Tomanek's New Testament, Pocatello, Idaho
1959	Modern Language Bible (Berkeley), Grand Rapids
1960	The Children's "King James," Evansville, Indiana
1961	New World Translation—Jehovah's Witnesses, Brooklyn
1961	Noli's Greek Orthodox New Testament, Boston
1961	One Way: The Jesus People New Testament, Pasadena
1961	Simplified New Testament, Grand Rapids
1961	Wuest's Expanded New Testament, Grand Rapids
1962	Children's Version, New York
1963	Beck's New Testament, St. Louis
1963	The Holy Name Bible, Irvington, New Jersey
1964	Anchor Bible, Garden City, New Jersey
1965	Amplified Bible, Grand Rapids
1965	Bruce's Expanded Paraphrase, Exeter
1966	The Bible in Simplified English, Collegeville, Minnesota
1966	Jerusalem Bible, London, New York
1966	Living Scriptures, New York
1967	Liverpool Vernacular Gospels, Liverpool
1968	Cotton Patch Version, New York
1969	Barclay's New Testament, London, Cleveland
1969	Children's New Testament, Waco, Texas
1970	King James II, Byron Center, Michigan
1970	The Mercier New Testament, Cork, U.K.
1970	New American Bible, New York
1970	New English Bible, Oxford and Cambridge
1971	Living Bible, Wheaton
1971	New American Standard Bible, Carol Stream, Illinois
1972	The Bible in Living English, New York
1973	The Common Bible, New York
1973	New International Version: New Testament, Grand Rapids
1973	The Translator's New Testament, London
1973	The Better Version of the New Testament, Muscle Shoals, Alabama
1975	The Word Made Fresh, Atlanta
1976	Good News Bible, New York (Today's English Version NT, 1966)
1976	Train Up a Child, Chicago
1977	The Gospels in Scouse, London
1977	Christian Counselor's New Testament, Grand Rapids
1978	The Holy Name Bible, Brandywine, Maryland
1978	The New International Version: Old Testament, Grand Rapids
1978	The New Jewish Version: The Prophets, Philadelphia
1979	The New King James Bible: New Testament, Nashville
1982	The New Jewish Version: The Kethubim, Philadelphia (Torah, 1962; Prophets, 1978)
1982	The New King James Bible, Old Testament, Nashville
1982	The Reader's Digest Bible, Pleasantville, New York

Chapter 20

God's Word in Human Language

When the Holy Spirit broke through all language barriers on the first Christian Pentecost, the church was born. Not only did several thousand visitors from all over the known world accept Christ when they heard the gospel in their own language, but the Holy Spirit gave the church a model for her missionary calling. Every nation and every tribe must be given the gospel in its mother tongue.

The church in the early centuries took this assignment seriously and translated the Scriptures into all the major languages that were spoken within the Roman Empire and, in some cases, beyond its borders. With the loss of spiritual vitality and missionary vision in the post-Constantinian period, Bible translation came to a halt. The medieval church did not encourage the translation of the Bible into the vernacular. For a thousand years prior to Wycliffe (1330–84), there was no English Bible.

The Reformation in the sixteenth century ushered in a new day. The Bible was now translated into all major European languages. With the birth of the modern missionary movement, the Scriptures have been translated into many hundreds of languages. And while there are still hundreds of language groups without the Word of God, English-speaking readers of the Bible are almost embarrassed by the plethora of versions available today. Indeed, there are so many English versions that some Bible readers find it hard to know which version to use. And since these versions differ from one another, people who are not familiar with the history of the Bible, as we have tried to sketch it in this volume, can become rather confused.

In this final chapter, then, we want to explore why there are so many translations and make some suggestions as to how to choose a version.

I. SO MANY VERSIONS

A. Discrepancies in the Manuscripts

If we ask why there are so many versions, one answer is that the translators do not always use the same Hebrew and Greek texts. As we have explained earlier, we have only the copies of the original manuscripts, and none of these copies is free from transcriptional errors. Every translator or reviser, therefore, has to decide which readings he is going to follow.

What, for example, shall a translator do with the "Longer Ending" of the Gospel of Mark? All major manuscripts end this Gospel at 16:8. The Gospel ends a bit abruptly in that case: "and they were afraid." This may explain why later copyists felt that it needed a longer ending. If we take the word "afraid" to mean "awe and wonder," then there is nothing inappropriate about ending the Gospel in this way. It could be that Mark had written a longer ending, but that it was lost. In any case, most modern versions give the longer ending, but put it in a footnote or in brackets with a footnote,

indicating that Mark 16:9–20 is not found in the better Greek manuscripts or ancient versions.

Something similar is done in modern versions with the story of the woman taken in adultery (John 7:53–8:11). This story is found in different places in the Greek manuscripts—after John 7:36 or 7:52, or after John 21:24, or even after Luke 21:38. It seems as if there was no certain place for it.[1] The language and style of this story is different from that of any of our Gospel writers. Perhaps it should be viewed as an authentic account, but not as part of John's Gospel. Translators, however, are faced with the problem of placing it. The AV has it as part of the text of John 8; the RSV puts it in the footnotes of John 8; the NIV sets it off from the text with a note, saying it is not found in most reliable manuscripts; NEB prints it as an appendix to John's

The wide variety of Bible translations available can help in understanding Scripture and in keeping its study fresh. It is important to understand the purpose of each translation in order to chose the best one for each need.

---

[1] F. C. Grant, *Translating the Bible* (Greenwich: Seabury, 1961), p. 118.

Gospel. However, even though the story may not have been part of John's Gospel originally, it has been held to be authentic throughout the history of the church.

Should a translator include the doxology in the Lord's Prayer or omit it, as the ancient Greek manuscripts do? The Latin Vulgate, the Bible of Western Christendom for a thousand years, did not have this doxology either. Modern versions omit it as a rule, but since the AV had it, and it has become a part of the church's liturgy, we may continue to include it when we pray the Lord's Prayer.

All of us are loath to give up Luke 23:34, "Father forgive them, for they know not what they do." But the manuscript evidence for its omission is impressive. The suggestion that some early scribe deliberately deleted the prayer, because he thought it had not been answered, hardly settles the question. Stephen apparently imitated this prayer of our Lord when he died a martyr's death. It is probably a genuine saying of Jesus, but out of place in our present manuscripts. In any case, the translator must decide whether he will include it or not.

Perhaps these four examples suffice to illustrate the point that every translator must face the question of variant readings in the Hebrew and Greek texts. This is one reason the versions differ.

B. The Character of the Biblical Languages

Hebrew and Aramaic are Semitic languages and have a different sentence structure from that of English, and even the Greek of the NT, although it is an Indo-European language, has syntactical features that are foreign to English. If we were to translate into English the order of the Greek words of Mark 13:1, we would shudder: "And going out he from the temple he says to him one of the disciples of him, Teacher . . ." The AV of 1611 and the ASV of 1901 translate Matthew 26:27, "Drink ye all of it," which, if strictly followed, means that the participants in the Lord's Supper are to empty the cup. RSV changes the word order to prevent such a misunderstanding and has, "Drink of it, all of you"—which is what the Greek means. Since the sentence structure of the original biblical language is different from ours, the translations of this language into English will vary.

Moreover, Hebrew and Greek have different verbal systems, and the tenses of the English verb have to be adapted to these. Greek, for example, has four past tenses (imperfect, aorist, perfect, and pluperfect). Besides, each of these tenses has nuances that are determined by their context. The imperfect of the verb "to throw," for example, can be "progressive" ("they were throwing"), or "customary" ("they used to throw"), or "iterative" ("from time to time they threw"), or "conative" ("they were about to throw") or "inceptive" ("they began to throw"). A translator, therefore, must study the context and determine for himself what kind of imperfect stands in the Greek text, and, obviously, he will not always agree with the next translator.

The Greek participle can be translated quite literally, but usually this produces bad English. Translators, therefore, have to interpret it either as temporal, causal, conditional, telic, or concessive. The context must guide translators in such an interpretation. The writer was brought up on Luther's version, in which Galatians 6:9 promises those who do good that they "will reap without ceasing" (*"ernten ohne aufhoeren"*) when God's time comes. The English versions usually take the participle as expressing a condition, and so we shall reap "if we do not cease" (from doing good). The Greek reads simply, "we shall reap, not ceasing" (i.e., ceasing because one has become weary). The English versions are very likely better here, but they do spoil a beautiful "interpretation" by Martin Luther.

The Greek NT has some inordinately long sentences of main and subordinate clauses. Ephesians 1:3–14, for example, is one long sentence in Greek. The AV has broken it into two sentences, but current translations break it up into five, six, or even fourteen sentences.

Moreover, there are rarely exact equivalents in English for Hebrew and Greek words. The French writer Renan once said, *"La vérité consisté dans les nuances"* (truth consists in the nuances). How, for example, shall we translate the Greek word *parakletos?* "Comforter," "Helper," "Advocate," "Encourager," "Consoler," "Counselor," or "Friend?" Besides having a list of options, a translator will not always translate the same word in the same way in every passage, because words have meaning only in context. What, for example, does the English word "bar" mean? We speak of a "bar of soap," "a candy bar," "he was admitted to the bar," "he put a bar across the window," "he hangs out in the bar," and so forth.[2] This explains, then, why

translations don't always render the same Greek or Hebrew word by the same English word.

Sometimes, translators are hesitant to give their interpretation, and choose to transliterate. The Greek *parakletos* may be given in English as "Paraclete," but that is not an English word. There are instances where transliteration is the best way out. For example, the verb *baptizō* is normally not translated at all, but simply transliterated as "baptize," but then one must ask one's denomination whether that means to "immerse," or "pour," or "sprinkle" (there have been "immersion" versions produced by Baptists, but such versions are usually discounted). One can, of course, put pictures which illustrate a particular form of baptism, into the baptism stories of the NT, but it is never safe to get one's theology from pictures.

A word may have two meanings, but the translator has to limit himself to one. Shall he say "born again" or "born from above" (John 3:3, 7)? The Greek word *anōthen* means both, but there is no English word that means both "again" and "from above."

At times a Greek word may appear to have an exact equivalent in English, but the cultural context gives it a different ring. When Jesus addresses his mother as "woman" (John 2:4) that sounds discourteous to us, but it wasn't at all in Jesus' day. What does the translator do? The RSV retains "woman," but softens it by adding an exclamatory "O" ("O woman"). The NEB has "mother," or avoids it altogether when Mary is addressed. Some suggest we should use "lady," or "my dear," or "madam," but since these are

---

[2]E. A. Nida, *Good News for Everyone* (Waco: Word, 1977), p. 79.

not really equivalents, it may be best to omit it altogether, as some versions do.[3] When Amos warns Israel that God gave them "cleanness of teeth" (4:6), he is not praising some method of cleaning teeth; he means he sent a "famine." Or, when the Lord says, "Upon Edom I cast my shoe," he doesn't mean that he despises Edom so much that he throws a sandal at Edom. Rather, it's a Hebrew idiom that means that God claims Edom for himself; Edom is his property.

C. English is Constantly Changing

Living languages constantly change; words take on new meanings, and new words are coined. Many words that were familiar to English readers in 1611, when the AV was published, are no longer common words or have changed their meaning. Recently I heard of a man with a heart disease who reported exuberantly to his wife that his heart was "fixed." "How's that?" she inquired. "Well, the Lord says so right here in the Psalm. 'My heart is fixed, O God, my heart is fixed.'" Whether God had in fact repaired his heart is not for us to decide, but the word "fixed" in the AV means to be "steadfast" or "settled," and not "fixed" in the modern mechanical sense of the word. Even the familiar sentence from the Shepherd Psalm, "the Lord is my shepherd, I shall not want," can be misconstrued to mean, "I have no desires." What it meant in 1611 is that the sheep has no need.

The word "Comforter" was first used in the English Bible of Wycliffe in 1386. But he translated from the Latin

Vulgate, and the Latin *fortis* means "brave" or "strong." It can be seen, from Ephesians 6:10, that Wycliffe used this meaning when he translated the Greek *endunamoo* ("be strong") by, "Be ye comforted." But that is not how we use the word "comforter" today. Quite aside from the fact that it is used for a cozy blanket or a baby's pacifier, it means to console the sorrowing. That explains why modern translators are hesitant to translate *parakletos* with "Comforter." English words change their meaning.

"In my Father's house are many mansions," is the promise of Jesus (John 14:2) according to the AV. "Mansions" to us today refers to grandiose dwellings about which we sing in some of our hymns. But, like the meaning of the original Greek *mone*, the Latin *mansio* meant originally "a remaining place." In the medieval period it was used for separate apartments representing heaven, earth, and hell. This is how the AV translators used it in 1611. William Tyndale earlier had rendered it as "halting places." The word "mansions," therefore, conveys a false meaning, for the word *mone* is probably best translated as "rooms."

The word "saints" is a literal translation of the Greek *hagioi*. But why then do new English versions, such as the NEB, give it as "God's people"? For the simple reason that by long usage the word "saint" is now used for people who are either paragons of virtue, or who, because of some great contribution they made in their day, have been "sainted" by the Catholic Church and on whom devout Catho-

---

[3]W. Barclay, "On Translating the New Testament," *The New Testament* Vol. 1, (New York: Collins, 1968), p. 338.

lics might call for help in their prayers.

The familiar words of the AV, "Now we see through a glass, darkly," sound like music to those whose ears have been attuned to them; but they are hardly contemporary English. How much better the Jerusalem Bible is: "Now we are seeing a dim reflection in a mirror" (which is about as close as one can come to the Greek text).

Our "conversation" is to be in heaven, says Paul, according to the AV (Phil. 3:20). But RSV has "Our commonwealth is in heaven," and JB has, "Our homeland is in heaven," and NEB reads, "we are citizens of heaven." Obviously, then, "conversation" did not mean only a "discussion" in 1611, as it does today.

To speak of the church as a "peculiar" people today does not mean what it meant in 1611, when, under the influence of the Latin, it referred to property (our "pecuniary"). How much better, then, the NEB, which has, "a people claimed by God for his own!"

Dr. Harold Fehderau, of the American Bible Society, classifies versions by language levels: (1) The archaic level, (2) the liturgical level, (3) the literary level, (4) and the common language level.[4] One might say that the KJV is a representative of the "archaic," the RSV of the "liturgical," the NEB of the "literary," and the GNB of the "common language" level. Other versions could be placed in these categories as well, but these examples will suffice. A less sophisticated way of classifying versions, as one wag put it, is to describe the LB as the Bible in pajamas, the GNB as the Bible in sports clothes, the NIV as the Scriptures in an office suit, the RSV as the Word of God in dinner dress, and the KJV as Bible in tails and top hat.

D. Different Ways of Translating

Every translator (or translation team) must agree on some basic principles according to which the translators are to work. First of all, it must be decided whether the new version is to be a revision of existing versions, or a fresh translation. If it is to be a revision (as was the case with the ERV, ASV, NASB, and RSV) then the reviewers must agree on whether it is only the English that is to be revised or whether the revision will reflect also a different textual base from that of the parent version. The ERV of the NT (1881) was a revision of the AV (1611), but it followed a text that was different from that of the AV in numerous places. The RSV was basically a revision of the ASV (1901), but strove to retain as much of the AV language as modern English would allow.

Versions such as LB, NEB, NIV, GNB are not revisions, but new translations; yet they differ greatly. The reason is that the translators followed different ground rules. The NEB is written in high-class modern English; the GNB is aimed at readers whose first language is not necessarily English. The NIV wanted to use "international" English. No one speaks "international" English, but the design was to use the kind of English that is understood by English-speaking people all over the world.

The LB began as an attempt to communicate God's Word to children; Phillips wanted to make Paul understandable to teenagers that had no

---

[4]H. Fehderau, "What Is Accuracy and Faithfulness in Bible Translation?" *Mennonite Brethren Herald* (March 3, 1979), p. 4.

church background. The target audience of the version determines its character to a considerable degree.

More importantly, translators must decide whether they are going to follow the word order of the Hebrew and Greek as much as English allows them to do, or whether they are going to do a sense translation. If the version is to have reasonably good English, then a "literal" translation is impossible. On the other hand, if one seeks to transfer the meaning of Hebrew and Greek sentences into English, then one opens the door a bit more widely to interpretation by the translator. However, there is no translation that is not at the same time an interpretation. This cannot be helped. For example, Hebrews 13:4 is found in two forms in the English versions: "Marriage *is* honorable in all ...," and "Let marriage be honorable in all...." Why the difference? Well, there is no verb in the Greek text, and so one translator supplies a verb in the indicative mood and makes it a statement, the other supplies a subjunctive, and makes it an exhortation.

Translators must decide on how paraphrastic their version is to be. Ronald Knox has said, "The translator ... must never be frightened by the word 'paraphrase'; it is a bogey of the half-educated."[5] Also, translators must decide on how colloquial their English is going to be. The LB uses colloquialisms that have been a great offense to some readers, Dr. Taylor, in his original rendering, has Saul in his fury call his son, Jonathan, "You son of a bitch!" (1 Sam. 20:30). The GNB has, "You bastard!" Such vulgar colloquialisms are not found in more sedate versions such as RSV, NASB, or NIV. Besides, there are colloquialisms that are ephemeral; they are used for a while and then disappear. Others are well established and will probably remain in English for a long time to come. The more colloquial a version is, the sooner it will be out of date.

Moreover, the translators have to agree on the cultural level of the English they are going to use. PHILLIPS is quite colloquial and yet has a rather sophisticated style. This is true also of the NEB. The GNB or the LB, however, deliberately move on lower levels of sophistication.

There are, then, many different ways of translating the biblical text into English, and that is why new versions are published again and again.

E. Special Translation Problems

One of the questions that has haunted translators is how to render the sacred name of God into English. If one gives it as Jehovah, one is using a nonexistent term, for Jehovah is a medieval form, composed by adding the vowels of the word "lord" (Adonai) to the consonants of the Tetragrammaton YHWH. Again, if one translates YHWH as "Lord," how shall it be distinguished in English from Adonai. The JB has dared to give it in what is believed to be the correct Hebrew form, namely Yahweh, but most versions shy away from using Yahweh.

Punctuation is another translation problem. Since the early manuscripts have few punctuation marks the translator has to supply them. The familiar passage in Psalm 121:1 in the AV reads, "I lift up mine eyes unto the hills, from

---

[5]R. Knox, *On Englishing the Bible* (London: Burns Oates, 1949), p. 317.

whence cometh my help." The NIV, however, puts that in question form: "I lift up my eyes to the hills—where does my help come from?" That changes the meaning appreciably.

In Ephesians 4:12 the presence or absence of a comma determines the meaning of the passage profoundly. It has been called the "fatal" comma. Without a comma after "saints," the meaning is that the pastors and teachers are there to equip the saints for their (i.e., the saints) ministry *(diakonia)*; if the comma is put in, the verse can mean that the pastors and teachers are to do the ministering, and the saints have thereby been absolved from their ministries. In John 18:37 we read: "Pilate said to him, 'So you are a king?'" (RSV). But the Greek manuscripts allow that phrase to be either a question or an affirmation. The context, however, would favor the question form. Professor Rieu's paraphrase reads: "So you are a king after all?"[6]

Also, there are still words in Hebrew and Greek whose meaning is not absolutely clear to this day. What does Behemoth mean? (Job. 40:15). The MLB has "hippopotamus"; the NEB has "crocodile"; NIV has "behemoth" in the text, with "hippopotamus" or "elephant" in the footnote; JB has left it untranslated, as "behemoth."

Sometimes a word in Hebrew and Greek is well-known to the translator but he doesn't necessarily know how the biblical writer uses it. When Paul said that the offender in the Corinthian church is to be given over to Satan "for the destruction of the flesh," he did not tell us what he meant by flesh. Nor did he give us a commentary on what he meant by the addition, "so that his spirit may be saved in the day of the Lord Jesus" (1 Cor. 5:5).

At times the translator knows the meaning of the original word but there is no English equivalent for it, because the word comes from a particular cultural context. Of the Coming One, John the Baptist says that he has his "fan" (AV) in his hand (Matt. 3:12). NEB changes that to "shovel," and RSV has "winnowing fork." Those who have witnessed this form of threshing in nontechnological societies know what is meant, but find it hard to describe such an instrument by one English word. Or, take the word *paidagogos* (from which our "pedagogy" is derived). The AV translates this word in Galatians 3:24 as "schoolmaster." The LB tells us that the law has been our "teacher and guide"; NIV "the law was put in charge"; JB has "guardian"; RSV "custodian." Why such differences? Not because of the poverty of English, but because there is no modern cultural equivalent to the *paidagōgos* of the ancient world. A *paidagōgos* was a kind of mixture of nurse, governess, chaperon, tutor, or a "nanny" under whose vigilant care children in earlier days grew up.

Another notorious difficulty for the translator is the translation of monetary terms. One way to go is simply to transliterate and use *denarius, drachma, talanton,* etc., and let the reader seek to discover their current values. Obviously, an American version will differ from a British version if one seeks to use current monetary terms (just as weights and measures differ). But if one uses dollars and cents, for example, then one still has to know the buying power of the origi-

---

[6]Grant, *Translating the Bible,* p. 155.

nal term in order to give the approximate current value. With rampant inflation a Bible version that uses such modern equivalents is quickly out of date. The unforgiving servant (Matt. 18:24) owed his lord "ten thousand talents" (RSV), "a half million pounds" (BARCLAY), "millions of dollars" (GNB), "three million pounds" (MOFFATT), "$10,000,000" (LB).

Numerous other problems that the translator must face could be mentioned, but this will suffice to illustrate the complexity of transferring the Hebrew and Greek texts into modern English. There can, therefore, never be anything final about any version of the English Bible. It will have to be revised again and again. The practical question that arises out of this situation is, how to choose a Bible.

II. CHOOSING A BIBLE

Some versions will appeal to some readers more than others. At times one hears it said: "I prefer the way this version gives it." If such a judgment is made on the basis of investigation, it is perfectly in order. However, one should not choose a Bible simply on the basis of personal appeal. What should guide us in choosing a version?

A. The Reader

People sometimes ask those who are familiar with the Hebrew and Greek: "Which is the best English version?" That question cannot be answered unless one asks, first of all, "For whom?" What is best for one reader may not be the best for another.[7] If, for example, one is looking for a Bible for

children, then LB may be a good choice. On the other hand, if one wants to have a version that has reasonably modern English, but sounds much like the KJV, then the RSV would be the choice. Someone with fine literary tastes may go for the NEB or PHILLIPS. Again, for the person who has acquired English as a second language, the GNB would probably be better. The GNB or PHILLIPS would also be good versions to recommend to non-Christians who are interested in reading the Bible for the first time, since these versions try not to use "Bible" English.

B. The Purpose

Another question one must ask in choosing a version is, what it is to be used for. If one is looking for a study Bible then ASV and NASB may be a good choice. If, however, one wants a Bible that is easier to memorize, and that is designed for public worship, then RSV or NIV would be good choices. For relaxed, devotional reading LB, GNB, or PHILLIPS will do. Should one be working with Catholics, then the NAB and JB should be used, although these can be used by Protestants with great profit as study Bibles as well. And now that the "Common Bible" is available, that too would be a good version to use with Catholics.

Perhaps it is not wise to limit oneself to one version, but to use several, if one wants to study the Bible seriously without a knowledge of Hebrew and Greek. (For memorization, of course, a person should stick with one.) If the Bible student uses only one version for Bible study there is always the danger

---

[7] R. G. Bratcher, "One Bible in Many Versions," *Interpretation* Vol. 32 (April 1978), p. 129.

of building too much on peculiar renderings found in this version. It may even be to our advantage to change versions occasionally just for our devotional reading, since we all get used to the language of a certain version so that the truths don't seem to grab us any more as they should. Sometimes a different version can bring God's Word home to us with new force.

C. S. Lewis, who had a great appreciation for Elizabethan English, and enjoyed the AV version of 1611, warns: "Early associations endear but they also confuse. Through that beautiful solemnity the transporting or horrifying realities of which the Book tells may come to us blunted and disarmed and we may only sigh with tranquil veneration when we ought to be burning with shame or struck dumb with terror or carried out of ourselves by ravishing hopes and adorations."[8]

C. The Format

Since the biblical books were like other books in format when they were originally written, there is no reason why a modern version should not look like other books. The division of the text into chapters and verses is very valuable for the location of passages but it does spoil the reading somewhat. Some modern editions, therefore, divide the text into sense paragraphs, with the verse numbers left in for the sake of convenience. Also, some prefer to have the text in one rather than two columns on the page. People with poor eyesight will want to choose an edition with large, bold print.

Some editions are richly supplied with footnotes, cross references, maps, tables, and the like. If the notes are of an explanatory nature they can be very valuable. Bibles with notes which seek to bend the reader to the theology of the author of the notes, such as the Scofield Reference Bible, by constant use tend to become almost as sacred as the text of the Bible itself. All such matters must be taken into consideration when one chooses a Bible. Most versions today, fortunately, are available in more than one format. If one is going to use a version daily, one may wish to get a Bible in hardcover; if, on the other hand, one wants to pass on NTs to non-Christians, one may wish to give Good News for Modern Man in paperback.

Almost every possible format of the Bible in English is ours for the asking today.

D. The Country

Those who live in the U.S.A. may find a version done in England too British in speech. Whereas KNOX, PHILLIPS, JB, and NEB may make fascinating reading, Americans will need to look up an occasional word in the dictionary. Readers in other lands, whose English is more British, may feel the same about some American translations. There are, however, several versions that should be acceptable to English readers all over the world. Since the RSV tried to retain much of the AV of 1611, which was used as widely in America as it was in Britain and her former colonies, this version has found universal acceptance. The GNB and NIV operate with the kind of English that is known the world over, and so these are equally accepted everywhere in

---

[8]Quoted in Dewey Beegle, *God's Word Into English* (Grand Rapids: Eerdmans, 1960), p. 82.

the world. On the whole, the differences in English spoken in different parts of the world today are not great enough to cause a serious problem in choosing an English version. Much more important is the question of accuracy.

E. The Accuracy

A version must, first of all, be based on the most accurate Hebrew and Greek texts. Secondly, these texts must be translated accurately. But how shall accuracy be defined? On the one hand, there are those who would object to an English Bible that has words that are not in the original Hebrew and Greek. But that is to ask for the impossible, since languages, as we have explained earlier, have different structures. There is, in fact, no English version that meets this criterion. If there were, it would probably be completely unintelligible.

On the other hand, there are those who hold that accuracy means a sense translation, a meaning-for-meaning rendering. In what is called "dynamic equivalence" the translator works on the principle of equal effect.[9] Wycliffe worked on the one extreme when he translated the Vulgate in a very literal fashion in his first edition of the English Bible. The second edition, published after his death, was freer. Tyndale's first version of the NT was also of that kind, but the second edition was more idiomatic. There is no doubt that sense translation yields a more accurate rendering of the original text than does the matching of words. However, there are limits to the freedom with which one handles the meaning of the original text. There is, for example, a vast difference between the NEB and the LB. Both strive to translate the meaning of the original text, but LB takes much greater liberties in the way it paraphrases the text. The freer a translation is, the greater is the potential for such a version to reflect the translator's theological biases.

Since translation cannot be done entirely without interpretation, a reader is always safer in choosing a version that has been done by a broadly based translation team, rather than by one individual. MOFFATT, GOODSPEED, KNOX, PHILLIPS, and the Living Bible, are representatives of the latter. In versions such as the NASB, RSV, NEB, NIV, and the GNB we can be quite sure that denominational or personal biases will not be reflected to the degree that this is possible in private translations. Sectarian versions, such as the New World Translation of the Jehovah's Witnesses, should be avoided. A South African version changes Song of Solomon 1:5, "I am black but comely, O ye daughters of Jerusalem" to "I am comely, and burnt brown by the sun." Alteration in the interests of *apartheid* must be rejected.[10] And feminists who advocate speaking of God as "it" or "they" violate not only the canons of language, but also of theology.

The Italian adage, *traduttore traditore* ("translators are traitors") has some point to it in the sense that no version perfectly represents all the nuances of the Hebrew and Greek texts. However, it is unfair to accuse translators (unless they are sectarian) of deliberately distorting the biblical

---

[9]S. Kubo and W. Specht, *So Many Versions?* (Grand Rapids: Zondervan, 1975), p. 143.

[10]Grant, *Translating the Bible*, p. 153.

text. Those who claim translators are guilty of modernism, of denying the deity of Christ, and other heresies, hardly recognize the complexity of translating from one language to another. Few translations are deliberate distortions of the biblical message, and so we can read most versions with considerable confidence. If, then, we will use several versions, so that one serves as a check on the other, we will not go wrong.

These several suggestions may be helpful in choosing a version. But once the choice has been made, we must make sure that this sacred book does not become simply a sacred symbol, and we must get into the habit of feeding our souls on the Word of God.

III. READING THE SCRIPTURES

"Reading Christians are growing Christians," said John Wesley. There is a wealth of Christian literature available today that can be very helpful to us on our Christian way, but it must never become a substitute for the reading of the Scriptures themselves. Those of us who are involved in the life of the church will hear the Scriptures read and expounded in public, but the question at the moment is the reading of the Bible in private. The following suggestions may be of help to the reader.[11]

A. Regularity of Habit

Although the individual believer has to work out his own pattern of reading, he should have a pattern. If we read the Bible only when we happen to think of it, the tendency will be to neglect it. It is simply not true that the things that we do habitually are of necessity meaningless. Good habits make life easier and freer.

Of course, if Bible reading is done routinely, without heart and without mind, it can be quite useless—as are all spiritual exercises when they become mere formalities. But it would be precarious if we were to read the Bible only when we were in a religious frame of mind. If we have no regular time, nine times out of ten something will come up that appears more important at the moment than Bible reading. Of course, one should not insist on reading the Bible just when the dishes need to be washed. In the long run those who make a habit of reading the Bible daily will be stronger and more mature in the faith.

B. Flexibility in Schedule

Having stressed the need for regularity, we should, however, not choose a pattern of Bible reading that allows for no changes or innovations or interruptions. There must be flexibility in the amount of reading one does. One cannot measure spirituality by the number of chapters one reads daily or by the number of times one has read through the Bible from cover to cover. One verse from a Gospel or an Epistle may at times give the reader sufficient food for thought. The matter may be quite different when one comes to Kings and Chronicles, where one will have to take longer passages in one sitting.

One must also be flexible in the matter of the time when the Bible is read. Some find it best to read the Scriptures

---

[11]D. Ewert, *How Our Bible Came to Us* (Winnipeg: Christian Press, 1975), pp. 61–63.

in the morning before their daily tasks begin. Others prefer another time of day. I was taught to observe a "morning watch," and it has become so much a part of my life that I feel guilty when for some reason or other I do not read the Scriptures before breakfast. But there may be those who have to be at work very early, or who work at night, for whom such a practice creates a hardship. Perhaps the busy mother must wait until later in the day or evening before she finds some quiet moments to read the Word. We must not let others force us into a straight jacket. All believers must find their own pattern. If because of some unusual circumstances we cannot adhere to an established pattern, we must be flexible enough to find a new one.

C. Variety in Method

To offset the danger of Bible reading's becoming routine, we must exercise our imagination a bit. Every now and then we ought to change the pattern of Bible reading (not necessarily the time). Some readers make it a practice of reading through the Bible from Genesis to Revelation. Others find that tedious, and may read through one OT book (perhaps a chapter a day) and then switch back to the NT. Or one may do a bit of reading from both Testaments daily. Some follow a course of readings outlined for them in some manual, perhaps related to weekly Sunday school lessons. In any case, there should be variety.

Reading habits of people vary. Some can't read with attention unless they use a marking pencil. If that is a help, they should use one. Others have a wide-margin Bible, so they can make notes. As I have suggested earlier, a person may change versions occasionally in order to see old truths in a fresh light. The rule of thumb is: anything that makes reading the Bible more meaningful ought to be encouraged.

D. Meditatively in Spirit

Simply to read the Bible is not enough. We must ponder its truths if we are to be built up. Johann Bengel's dictum is as applicable today as it was in the 1734 edition of his Greek NT: "Apply yourself wholly to the text; apply the text wholly to yourself." We must approach the Scriptures with a prayer for light, comfort, reproof, and instruction. It is really somewhat artificial to write about private Bible reading without writing on private prayer also, for the two are of one piece.

Some of us need helps to make Bible reading more meaningful. Occasionally I use a book of sermons on given biblical texts for my daily Bible reading. I have at times read through lighter commentaries on some biblical books. Books or calendars of "daily devotions" can also be used with great profit. I would suggest, however, that they should be used for variety only, and not all the time. There are also books of prayers available (such as the *Diary of Private Prayer* by John Baillie) that can stimulate our prayer life (and sometimes help us over dry periods).

All believers have days when nothing seems to leap at them from the pages of Holy Scripture. But that is no reason for despair. With some flexibility and imagination, with regularity and with prayer, we will be able to say with Jeremiah, "When your words came, I ate them; they were my joy and my heart's delight."

SUGGESTED READING

Barclay, W. "On Translating the New Testament," The New Testament. *New York: Collins,* *1968, Vol. 1, pp. 308–52.*

Bratcher, R. G. "Why We Need New Translations," in A Layman's Guide to Bible Versions *and Bible Enjoyment. Philadelphia:* Eternity Magazine *Vol. 25 (1974), pp. 22–26.*

Fee, G. D. and Stuart, D. How To Read the Bible for All Its Worth. *Grand Rapids: Zonder-* *van, 1982.*

Grant, F. C. Translating the Bible. *Greenwich: Seabury, 1971.*

Knox, R. On Englishing the Bible. *London: Burns Oates, 1949.*

Kubo, S. and Specht, W. So Many Versions? *Grand Rapids: Zondervan, 1975. See* *"Guidelines for Selecting a Version," pp. 200–207.*

MacGregor, G. A Literary History of the Bible. *Nashville: Abingdon, 1968. See "Is Trans-* *lation Possible?" p. 373–82.*

Mickelsen, A. B. and Mickelsen, A. M. Better Bible Study. *Glendale: Regal, 1977.*

Mounce, R. H. "How to Evaluate New Bible Versions," in A Layman's Guide to Bible *Versions and Bible Enjoyment. Philadelphia:* Eternity Magazine *Vol. 25 (1974), pp.* *27–28.*

Newport, J. P. and Cannon, W. Why Christians Fight Over the Bible. *Nashville: Nelson,* *1974.*

Nida, E. A. Good News for Everyone. *Waco: Word, 1977.*

Sproul, R. C. Knowing Scripture. *Downers Grove: InterVarsity, 1977.*

Sterrett, T. N. How to Understand Your Bible, *rev. ed. Downers Grove: InterVarsity, 1974.*

Stott, J. R. W. Understanding the Bible. *Glendale: Regal, 1972.*

GLOSSARY

- **Alexandrian Text Family**—Groups of manuscripts that display the same textual characteristics are called a "family." The Alexandrian family, represented by manuscripts such as Sinaiticus and Vaticanus, display the kind of text that was used in Alexandria in the early centuries of the Christian era.
- **Alexandrinus**—A fifth-century Greek manuscript of the Bible, brought to Constantinople from Alexandria. It came to England in 1627.
- **Apocalypse**—The Greek word for "revelation" (literally "unveiling"). The last book of the Bible is called "The Apocalypse."
- **Apocalyptic Literature**—Jewish literature from the second century B.C. to the first century A.D. that concerns itself with the end times. Some books of the Bible (for example, Daniel and Revelation) and some parts of biblical books (such as Mark 13) are also called "apocalyptic."
- **Apocrypha**—Jewish books not found in the Hebrew Bible but included in the Greek translation of the Old Testament and accepted as canonical by the Catholic Church.
- **Autographs and Autographa**—The original documents of the books prepared by the biblical writers.
- **Byzantine Text Family**—In the fourth century a certain type of Greek text established itself in and around Antioch. This was taken to Byzantium, the center of the Greek-speaking church, from where it spread widely. It is represented mostly by later manuscripts, versions, and church fathers.
- **Caesarean Text Family**—The type of manuscripts and versions that were at home in Caesarea and its environs about the third century, represented, for example, by the Codex Koridethi, several versions, and church fathers, such as Origen in his later years.

Canonicity—That divine quality of a book that legitimates its place in the collection of sacred books we know as the Bible.

Codex—In contrast to a scroll or roll, a codex is a book with pages.

Critical Text—A printed Greek New Testament in which variant readings and their manuscript support (called a "critical apparatus") are given in the margin or in footnotes.

Cursive Manuscript—A manuscript in which the letters of the words in a handwritten document are run together rather than printed singly.

Dead Sea Scrolls—Manuscripts of the Old Testament and other Jewish books found in caves near the Dead Sea since 1947.

Deuterocanonical—A word meaning "secondary" in terms of canonicity. Some contemporary Roman Catholic and Protestant scholars speak of the apocryphal books as "deuterocanonical."

Eclectic Text—Rather than simply following one family of manuscripts, an eclectic text is one in which each variant reading is evaluated on the basis of internal and external (i.e., manuscript) evidence.

Folio—A sheet folded in the middle so as to make two leaves (i.e., "folios") of a book.

Former Prophets—In the Hebrew Bible, Joshua, Judges, Samuel, and Kings are the four "former" prophets.

Hagiograph—The word means "holy writings" and was the Greek word used to designate the third division of the Old Testament books, called Ketubim in Hebrew.

Hexapla—Origen of Alexandria prepared an Old Testament in six columns including four Greek translations of Hebrew text, the Greek text in Hebrew letters, and a transliteration of the Hebrew words in Greek.

Ketubim—The Hebrew word for "that which is written" and designates the third division of the Hebrew Bible—The Writings.

Koine Greek—Koine means "common." It is Attic Greek spread over the entire Mediterranean world through the conquests of Alexander the Great. The New Testament was written in Koine.

Latter Prophets—The books of Isaiah, Jeremiah, Ezekiel, and the twelve Minor Prophets in the Hebrew canon were called the "latter" prophets.

Lectionaries—Prescribed Scripture lessons to be read in the churches during the church year.

Lower Criticism—The study of ancient manuscripts and versions of the Bible with the purpose of establishing the most trustworthy text of the Hebrew and Greek Testaments.

LXX—The number "seventy" designates the first translation of the Hebrew Bible into Greek. It was done in Alexandria, and one tradition has it that seventy translators participated in this effort.

Manuscript—Literally the word means a "handwritten" document, from the Latin *manus* and *scribo* (I write). Today we call even a typewritten document a manuscript.

Masoretes—Jewish scribes from A.D. 500–1000 who copied the Scriptures were called Masoretes—probably from the word *masar* "to hand down."

Megilloth—A word meaning "scroll." In the Hebrew Bible, Song of Songs, Ruth, Lamentations, Ecclesiastes, and Esther were designated as "Megilloth."

Minuscule Manuscript—A manuscript of the Bible written in small letters, usually with a flowing hand, in contrast to one with large letters, called "uncial" letters.

Mishnah—The collection of Jewish oral traditions published toward the end of the second century A.D. ("Mishnah" is derived from *shanah* "to repeat").

Nebiim—The Hebrew word for prophet is *nabi*. Nebiim is the plural and designates the second division in the Hebrew canon, called the "prophets."

Ostraca—Broken potsherds that were used at times by poor people to write notes on, including biblical sayings.

Palimpsest—A word derived from two Greek words meaning to erase and to write again. Some manuscripts of biblical books have been erased, and nonbiblical material written over the original text. In Latin a palimpsest is called *rescriptus*.

Papyrus—The papyrus plant was used to make writing material in ancient days. Our word "paper" is derived from the word "papyrus."

Parchment—Writing material prepared from the skins of animals was called parchment. Pergamum became famous for its production of writing material from leather.

Peshitta—The standard version of the Syriac church from the fifth century A.D. on was called "peshitta," meaning simple or clear.

Polyglot—A Bible in which not only original Hebrew and Greek texts are given but also various translations appear in parallel columns Polyglot means "many tongues."

Pseudepigrapha—Jewish literature, mainly from the intertestamental period in which the writers take pen names from the great heroes of Israel's history.

Received Text—The majority of New Testament manuscripts that have the kind of text that became popular in Antioch and that was brought to Byzantium. It was copied and re-copied until the days of printing. The printed Greek New Testament of the Elzevir brothers of Leyden, published in 1633, had the words "received text" in the preface.

Septuagint—The word derived from the numeral "seventy" and the name given to the first translation of the Hebrew Bible into Greek. The translation was made in Alexandria, beginning about 250 B.C.

Sinaiticus—A fourth-century manuscript of the Greek Bible discovered by Tischendorf in the monastery of St. Catherine near what is believed to be Mount Sinai.

Talmud—Commentaries and expansions of the Mishnah (a collection of Jewish oral traditions) were called Gemara. Mishnah together with Gemara form the Talmud (a word derived from *lamad* "to study"). During the period from A.D. 200–500 both a Palestinian and a Babylonian Talmud took shape.

Targums—Oral paraphrases and expansions of the Hebrew text in Aramaic for the benefit of those who attended the synagogue but could no longer understand Hebrew. These oral paraphrases were later written down.

Testament—The collection of biblical books written prior to the time of Christ are called "old" testament; the writings of the apostles in the first century of the Christian era, the "new" testament. "Testament" in these cases is used in the sense of "covenant."

Textual Criticism—The science that concerns itself with the establishment of the most trustworthy text from among the thousands of manuscripts and versions that have come down to us.

Textus Receptus—These Latin words occurred in the preface of the Greek New Testament published in Leyden in 1633 and mean "the received text" (i.e., the traditional text that goes back as far as the fourth century).

Torah—The Hebrew word for "law" is Torah. The word is used also for the five books of Moses, the Pentateuch.

Uncial Manuscript—A manuscript written in large letters, one might say "capital" letters.

United Bible Society Text—The American, the British and Foreign, the Scottish, the Dutch, and Württemberg Bible Societies have jointly published a Greek New Testament. The latest edition appeared in 1975.

Vaticanus—A fourth-century Greek manuscript of the Bible that lay hidden in the Vatican library since the fifteenth century but was not published until the nineteenth century.

Vellum—Manuscripts made of fine leather are called "vellum" manuscripts. The word comes from the Latin *velina*, meaning "calf" (our "veal").

Vulgate—The fourth-century Latin translation of the Bible by Jerome became so popular eventually that it was called "vulgate," in the sense of "common."

Westcott-Hort Text—The Cambridge scholars, Westcott and Hort, prepared a new Greek text in which the Received Text was disregarded and a text based on more ancient manuscripts, such as the Sinaiticus and Vaticanus, was printed. The first edition of the Westcott-Hort text was printed in 1881.

Western Text Family—A text type found generally in the western part of the empire supported, for example, by the Greek-Latin bilingual Codex Bezae, and by several ancient versions, such as the Old Latin.

BIBLIOGRAPHY

Aland, K. The Problem of the New Testament Canon. *London: Mowbray, 1962.*

Ackroyd, P. R. and Evans, C. F. eds. The Cambridge History of the Bible: From the Beginnings to Jerome. *Cambridge: Cambridge University Press, 1970.*

Barclay, W. The Making of the Bible. *New York: Abingdon, 1961.*

_____. "On Translating the New Testament," The New Testament. *New York: Collins, 1968, Vol. 1, pp. 308–52.*

_____. Introducing the Bible. *Nashville: Abingdon, 1972.*

Barrett, C. K. The New Testament Background: Selected Documents. *New York: Harper and Row, 1961.*

Beegle, D. M. God's Word Into English. *Grand Rapids: Eerdmans, 1960.*

Blackman, C. E. Marcion and His Influence. *London: SPCK, 1948.*

Bois, J. Translating for King James. *Translated and edited by Ward Allen. Nashville: Vanderbilt University Press, 1969.*

Bruce, F. F. History of the Bible in English. *3rd rev. ed. New York: Oxford University Press, 1978.*

_____. The New Testament Documents. *5th rev. ed. Grand Rapids: Eerdmans, 1970.*

_____. The Books and the Parchments. *3rd rev. ed. Old Tappan: Revell, 1963.*

_____. Tradition: Old and New, *Grand Rapids: Zondervan, 1970.*

Campenhausen, Hans von. The Formation of the Christian Bible. *Trans. J. A. Baker. Philadelphia: Fortress, 1972.*

Carson, D. A. The King James Version Debate. *Grand Rapids: Baker, 1979.*

Charles, R. H. ed. The Apocrypha and Pseudepigrapha of the Old Testament. *2 vols. Oxford: Clarendon, 1913.*

Cullmann, O. The Early Church. *Translated by A. J. B. Higgins. London: SCM, 1956.*

Danby, H. The Mishnah. *Oxford: Clarendon, 1933.*

Earle, R. How We Got Our Bible. *Kansas City: Beacon Hill, 1971.*

Ewert, D. How Our Bible Came to Us. *Winnipeg: The Christian Press, 1975.*

Filson, F. V. Which Books Belong in the Bible? *Philadelphia: Westminster, 1957.*

Finegan, J. Encountering New Testament Manuscripts. *Grand Rapids: Eerdmans, 1974.*

Geisler, N. L. and Nix, W. E. From God to Us. *Chicago: Moody, 1974.*

Goodspeed, E. J. **A History of Early Christian Literature.** *Revised and enlarged by R. M. Grant. Chicago: University of Chicago Press, 1966.*

_____.The Formation of the New Testament. *Chicago: University of Chicago Press, 1926.*

_____ . As I Remember. *New York: Harper and Brothers, 1953.*

Grant, F. C. **Translating the Bible.** *Greenwich: Seabury, 1961.*

Grant, R. M. **A Short History of the Interpretation of the Bible.** *New York: Macmillan, 1972.*

_____ . The Formation of the New Testament. *London: Harper and Row, 1965.*

Greenslade, S. L. **The Cambridge History of the Bible.** *Cambridge: Cambridge University Press, 1963.*

Harrison, R. K. **Introduction to the Old Testament.** *Grand Rapids: Eerdmans, 1969.*

Hennecke, E. and Schneemelcher, W. eds. **New Testament Apocrypha.** *2 vols. Translated by R. Mcl. Wilson. Philadelphia: Westminster, 1963.*

Herklots, H. G. G. **How Our Bible Came to Us.** *New York: Oxford University Press, 1954.*

Hunt, G. **About the New English Bible.** *Oxford and Cambridge University Presses, 1970.*

Hunter, A. M. **Jesus: Lord and Saviour.** *Grand Rapids: Eerdmans, 1976.*

_____ . Probing the New Testament. *Richmond: Knox, 1971.*

Jeremias, J. **Unknown Sayings of Jesus.** *Translated by Reginald Fuller. London: SPCK, 1958.*

Kenyon, F. G. **Our Bible and the Ancient Manuscripts.** *Revised by A. W. Adams. New York: Harper and Brothers, 1958.*

_____ . The Story of the Bible. *Revised by F. F. Bruce. Grand Rapids: Eerdmans, 1967.*

Knox, R. **On Englishing the Bible.** *London: Burns Oates, 1949.*

Kubo, S. and Specht, W. **So Many Versions?** *Grand Rapids: Zondervan, 1975.*

Lewis, J. P. **The English Bible/From KJV to NIV.** *Grand Rapids: Baker, 1981.*

Lightfoot, N. R. **How We Got the Bible.** *Grand Rapids: Baker, 1963.*

Longenecker, R. N. and Tenney, M. C. eds. **New Dimensions in New Testament Study.** *Grand Rapids: Zondervan, 1974.*

MacGregor, G. **The Bible in the Making.** *New York: Lippincott, 1959.*

McNamara, M. **Targum and Testament.** *Grand Rapids: Eerdmans, 1972.*

Metzger, B. M. **The Text of the New Testament.** *2nd ed. New York: Oxford University Press, 1968.*

_____ . The Early Versions of the New Testament. *Oxford: Clarendon, 1977.*

_____ . An Introduction to the Apocrypha. *New York: Oxford University Press, 1957.*

Mitton, C. L. **The Formation of the Pauline Corpus.** *London: Epworth, 1955.*

Nida, E. A. **Good News for Everyone.** *Waco: Word, 1977.*

Paine, G. S. **The Learned Men.** *New York: Crowell, 1959.*

Partridge, A. C. **English Biblical Translation.** *London: Andre Deutsch, 1973.*

Price, I. M. **The Ancestry of Our English Bible.** *Revised by W. A. Irwin and Allen P. Wikgren. New York: Harper and Row, 1956.*

Ramm, B. L. ed. **Hermeneutics.** *Grand Rapids: Baker, 1967.*

Reumann, J. H. P. **Four Centuries of the English Bible.** *Philadelphia: Muhlenberg, 1961.*

_____ . The Romance of Bible Scripts and Scholars. *Englewood Cliffs: Prentice-Hall, 1965.*

Richardson, C. C. ed. **Early Christian Fathers.** *New York: Macmillan, 1970.*

Robertson, E. H. **The New Translations of the Bible.** *Naperville: Allenson, 1959.*

Rowley, H. H. **The Unity of the Bible.** *Philadelphia: Westminster, 1955.*

Sanders, J. A. **Torah and Canon.** *Philadelphia: Fortress, 1972.*

Souter, A. **The Text and Canon of the New Testament.** *Revised by C. S. C. Williams. London: Duckworth, 1954.*

The Ecclesiastical History of Eusebius Pamphilus, *Translated by C. F. Cruse. Grand Rapids: Baker, 1973.*

Vööbus, A. Early Versions of the New Testament: Manuscript Studies. *Stockholm, 1954.*

Wegener, G. S. 6000 Years of the Bible. *Translated by M. Shenfield. London: Thames and Hudson, 1963.*

Wenger, J. C. God's Written Word. *Scottdale: Herald, 1966.*

Wenham, J. W. Christ and the Bible. *Downers Grove: InterVarsity, 1973.*

Wikgren, Allen. "The English Bible," Interpreter's Bible. *ed. G. Buttrick. Nashville: Abingdon, 1952. Vol. 1, pp. 84–105.*

Why So Many Bibles? *New York: American Bible Society, 1968.*

Wuerthwein, E. The Text of the Old Testament. *Translated by E. F. Rhodes. Grand Rapids: Eerdmans, 1979.*

INDEX

INDEX